EXPLORATIONS IN SOCIOLOGY

4

Sociology and Development

EXPLORATIONS IN SOCIOLOGY
A series under the auspices of
The British Sociological Association

I Race and Racialism
   edited by Sami Zubaida

II Knowledge, Education, and Cultural Change
   edited by Richard Brown

III Deviance and Social Control
   edited by Paul Rock and Mary McIntosh

Sociology and Development

edited by

EMANUEL DE KADT

and

GAVIN WILLIAMS

TAVISTOCK PUBLICATIONS

First published in 1974
by Tavistock Publications Limited
11 New Fetter Lane, London EC4
Printed in Great Britain
in 10 pt Plantin 2 pts leaded
by Cox and Wyman Ltd, London, Fakenham and Reading

ISBN 0 422 74330 5 (hardback)
ISBN 0 422 75740 3 (paperback)

Distributed in the USA by
HARPER & ROW PUBLISHERS, INC
BARNES & NOBLE IMPORT DIVISION

Contents

CONTRIBUTORS   vii

EMANUEL DE KADT
Introduction   1

PART ONE—Marxism and Development

DAVID LANE
Leninism as an Ideology of Soviet Development   23

JACK GRAY
Mao Tse-Tung's Strategy for the Collectivization of Chinese Agriculture: an Important Phase in the Development of Maoism   39

AIDAN FOSTER-CARTER
Neo-Marxist Approaches to Development and Under-development   67

PART TWO—Class

GAVIN WILLIAMS
Political Consciousness among the Ibadan Poor   109

ADRIAN PEACE
Industrial Protest in Nigeria   141

PART THREE—Marginality

SEBASTIAN BRETT
Low-income Urban Settlements in Latin America: The Turner Model   171

ALISON M. MACEWEN
Differentiation among the Urban Poor: an Argentine Study   197

PART FOUR—Dependence

PHILIP ELLIOTT AND PETER GOLDING
Mass Communication and Social Change: the Imagery of Development and the Development of Imagery   229

RONALD FRANKENBERG AND JOYCE LEESON
The Sociology of Health Dilemmas in the Post-colonial
World: Intermediate Technology and Medical Care in
Zambia, Zaire, and China   255

IAN CARTER
The Highlands of Scotland as an Underdeveloped Region   279

PART FIVE—Perspectives on the Future

W. F. WERTHEIM
The Rising Waves of Emancipation—from Counterpoint
towards Revolution   315

KRISHAN KUMAR
The Industrializing and the 'Post-industrial' Worlds: on
Development and Futurology   329

NAME INDEX   361

SUBJECT INDEX   365

Contributors

SEBASTIAN BRETT, born 1944, Oxfordshire. Studied at University of Oxford, BA(PPE), 1966. Lecturer in Sociology, University of York, 1969–72.

Awarded Foreign Area Fellowship, 1972, to study squatter settlement and economic marginality in Colombia.

IAN CARTER, born 1943, Luton. Studied at Universities of Bath and Essex. Assistant Lecturer and Lecturer in Sociology, University of Aberdeen, since 1968.

Author of articles on the historical sociology of Scotland and regional development in Scotland.

Currently engaged in research on farm servants in North East Scotland in the nineteenth century.

PHILIP ELLIOTT, born 1943, Ipswich. Studied at University of Oxford (PPE); University of Manchester, MA(Sociology), 1966. Research Fellow, Centre for Mass Communication Research, Leicester University, since 1967.

Author of *The Making of a Television Series*, 1972; *The Sociology of The Professions*, 1972; co-author with Halloran and Murdock of *Demonstrations and Communication: A Case Study*, 1970.

Currently engaged in research on news broadcasting.

AIDAN FOSTER-CARTER, born 1947, London. Studied at University of Oxford, BA(PPE), 1969; University of Hull (Sociology). Assistant Lecturer in Sociology, University of Hull, 1971–2; Lecturer in Sociology, University of Dar es Salaam, since 1972.

Currently completing a thesis on Marxism and underdevelopment.

RONALD FRANKENBERG, born 1929, London. Studied at Universities of Cambridge and Manchester, BA(Hons), MA(Econ) and PhD. Educational Officer, South Wales Area of the National Union of Mineworkers, 1957–60; Lecturer, Senior Lecturer and Reader in Sociology at

University of Manchester, 1960–68; Seconded Professor of Sociology and Dean of the School of Humanities and Social Science, University of Zambia, 1966–8; Joint Editor *African Social Research*, 1966–8; Acting Director of the Institute for Social Research; Joint Managing Editor *Sociological Review*, 1969; Professor and Head of Department of Sociology, University of Keele, since 1969.

Author of *Village on the Border*, 1957; *British Communities*, 1966; and various articles.

Currently interested in the Sociology of Medicine, Film, and Stratification in Africa.

PETER GOLDING, born 1947, Buckinghamshire. Studied at Manchester College of Commerce, BSc, 1969; University of Essex, MA (Sociology), 1970. Formerly Research Assistant at Centre for Mass Communication Research, University of Leicester; appointed Research Officer there, 1973.

JACK GRAY, born 1926, Glasgow. Studied at Universities of Glasgow and London. Reid Stewart Fellow of University of Glasgow, 1951–2; Scarborough Student, 1952–3; Assistant Lecturer in History, University of Hong Kong, 1953–6; Lecturer in Far East History, School of Oriental and African Studies, London, 1956–61; Lecturer in Politics (Modern China), SOAS, London, 1961–4; Senior Lecturer in Modern History (Far East) and Secretary of the Chinese Studies Committee, University of Glasgow, since 1964.

Author (with Patrick Cavendish) of *Chinese Communism in Crisis; Mao Tse Tung and the Cultural Revolution*, 1968; Editor of *Modern China's Search for a Political Form*, 1969.

Current research interests are in problems of social change and economic growth in communist China.

EMANUEL DE KADT, born 1933, Gent (Belgium). Came to England from The Netherlands, 1956. Studied at London School of Economics, BSc (Soc); Columbia University, MA; London School of Economics, PhD. Assistant Lecturer and Lecturer in Sociology at LSE, 1961–9; Research Specialist in Latin American Affairs at Chatham House, 1964–73; Fellow in Sociology, Institute of Development Studies at University of Sussex, since 1969; Deputy Director of Institute of Development Studies, since 1970.

Author of *British Defence Policy and Nuclear War*, 1964; *Catholic Radicals in Brazil*, 1970; Editor of *Patterns of Foreign Influence in the Caribbean*, 1972; Co-editor of *Employment and Unemployment in Less Developed Countries*, 1973.

Currently engaged in research on health, development, and dependence.

KRISHAN KUMAR, born 1942, Trinidad (West Indies). Studied at University of Cambridge (History) and London School of Economics (Sociology). Lecturer in Sociology at University of Kent at Canterbury, since 1967; Producer in Talks and Documentaries Department, BBC, 1972–3.

Editor of *Revolution: The Theory and Practice of a European Idea*, 1971.

Currently engaged in writing a book on futurology.

DAVID LANE, born 1933, Mynyddislwyn, Mon. Studied at University of Birmingham, B Soc Sc; University of Oxford, D. Phil. Lecturer at University of Birmingham, 1962–7; Lecturer at University of Essex, 1967–71; Reader in Department of Sociology, University of Essex, 1971–3.

Currently Fellow of Emmanuel College, Cambridge.

Author of *The Roots of Russian Communism*, 1969; *Politics and Society in the USSR*, 1970; *The End of Inequality?*, 1971; Co-editor (with G. Kolankiewicz) of *Social Groups in Polish Society*, 1973.

JOYCE LEESON, born 1930. Studied medicine at University of Manchester; returned some time later to study Public Health. Assistant Lecturer, Lecturer and now Senior Lecturer in Social and Preventive Medicine at University of Manchester; Fellow in University of Zambia working, with Ronald Frankenberg, on project entitled 'Health Behaviour in a Lusaka Suburb', 1967–8.

Author of several articles on social medicine and health and medical care in developing countries.

ALISON MACEWEN, born 1941, Australia. Studied at University of Edinburgh, MA(Social Anthropology and Sociology). Worked in research and community development in Argentina, 1964–6; Assistant Lecturer and Lecturer in Sociology, University of Ess ex, since 1967

Technical Assistant for Ministry of Overseas Development in Venezuela and Panama, 1970.

Currently engaged in research on occupational structures in Peru.

ADRIAN PEACE, born 1945, Huddersfield. Junior Research Fellow at
University of Sussex, 1969–72 (including eighteen months fieldwork in
Nigeria).

Currently Lecturer in Sociology at Manchester Polytechnic.

W. F. WERTHEIM, born 1907, St Petersburg (Russia) of Dutch parents.
Studied at Leiden University(law); in The Netherlands Indies as member of the judiciary and later as Professor at Batavia Law School, 1931–
46; Professor of Non-Western Sociology at University of Amsterdam,
1947–72.

Author of *Indonesian Society in Transition*, 1959; *East-West Parallels*,
1964; *Evolution and Revolution*, 1973.

GAVIN WILLIAMS, born Pretoria, South Africa. Studied at Univer-
sity of Stellenbosch (South Africa), BA; University of Oxford, B. Phil.
Lecturer in Sociology, University of Durham, 1967–70; Research
Fellow in Social Anthropology, University of Sussex, 1970–72;
Research Associate, N.I.S.E.R., Ibadan, Nigeria, 1970–71; Lecturer in
Sociology, University of Durham, since 1972.

Contributor to *African Perspectives* (edited by Allen and Johnson),
1970.

Currently engaged in writing a study entitled 'The Political Economy
of Ibadan' based on fieldwork undertaken in 1970–71.

EMANUEL DE KADT

Introduction

Problems of development have always looked quite different from the perspective of the economists' fraternity than from the sociologists'. There are many reasons for this; not least important is the fact that the real world's decision-makers have always turned to economists for diagnosis of their countries' ills and for advice on how to overcome them. 'Applied economics' is a good deal more respectable (and popular) than 'applied sociology', and outside the field of the social services and industrial relations not many professional sociologists are concerned with practical problems. While development economists have often incorporated their own 'do-it-yourself' sociology,[1] little attention has been paid to sociological models of development, and sociologists have been conspicuously absent from planning offices, certainly at the higher levels.

To some extent we have had ourselves to blame. For decades our gaze was fixed intently upon functionality and system maintenance, and social change was kept tucked away in a far corner of our consciousness and of our publications. When we did look at backward societies, as they were then called, we did so with the example of the west firmly on our mind, and we scrutinized the preconditions of 'modernization' – the path by which societies would somehow, probably through a neat succession of stages, arrive at the desirable state of being modernized, industrialized, and (implicitly) westernized. Our concept of change was intransitive, latterly integrated into a theory of neo-evolutionism, and certainly not much help to hard-pressed bureaucrats and politicians.[2]

Of course even in the heyday of functionalism there were those who maintained that its perspective was a distorting one, but they were a small minority (Bottomore 1972). It was to the great merit of C. Wright Mills that he kept this scepticism alive against overwhelming odds in the early fifties. The change of mood was heralded by the path-breaking articles of Lockwood (1956) and Dahrendorf (1958). The re-emergence of ideology in the United States after its end had been proclaimed by

Bell (1960), and of conflict generated mainly by the underprivileged Blacks, contributed to the final dethronement of the type of sociology then dominant in the industrialized societies.

But with regard to the underdeveloped countries the old perspectives lingered a while longer. It was not until the second half of the sixties, when André Gunder Frank stormed onto the scene in the guise of an academic Ché Guevara (Frank 1967; 1969), capturing the imagination of undergraduates everywhere with his provocative and startling (but also disturbingly oversimplified) model of metropolis–satellite relations, that much of modernization theory began to look jaded and that a new outlook really established itself. Frank's mentor was Paul Baran, who, more than any sociologist, should be regarded as the founding father of the neo-Marxist school, and who was the most distinguished representative on the Left of the tradition of work in 'political economy' (Baran 1957). It would of course be nonsense to suggest that the only important recent innovations in sociology have come from Marxist quarters. But in the field of development the contribution of the neo-Marxist school has been notable and especially significant because of the resulting 'dialectic' with non-Marxist approaches.

In the present volume the origins of the neo-Marxist school, as well as its distinctive characteristics, are examined in considerable detail by Aidan Foster-Carter. He argues that *mis*development ('something which is not even a progressive basis for something else, and, moreover, is not notably short-lived') is a more accurate concept than most available alternatives, and that the key to an understanding of that situation lies in the relationships of the less (or mis-) developed societies to the rich countries of the world. It is *that* relationship to which sociologists should devote their attention (and this 'bourgeois' sociology has failed to do), rather than worrying about structural differentiation or the preconditions for democratic political systems, about the need for entrepreneurship or for achievement-orientation. (But, as David Lane and Jack Gray so clearly show in their papers in this volume, Marxism both in its Leninist and in its Maoist forms *is* concerned with 'achievement-motivation', and with the need to instil it into the people if socialism is to be a success.)

The shift of focus implied by this new approach is monumental: it aims to displace our attention from the multiplicity of structural characteristics of the less developed countries themselves (and from the psychological characteristics of their inhabitants) to the international context, to the relationships between and across societies, and to the links of people in the poor countries with others in the industrialized nations. Foster-Carter shows how neo-Marxism stresses the need to understand the world as a 'totality', as a single integrated unit, and how it inquires into historical causes as well as into the processes that today help to perpetuate conditions whose origins lie in the distant past. It queries the mechanisms of transition, which modernization theorists have failed to specify explicitly, pointing out that the implicitly expected smooth, 'evolutionary' transformations of the typical social forms of (capitalist) underdevelopment are less likely to come about than much sharper, revolutionary breaks. Professor Wertheim's paper in this volume, a revision of his closing address to the Conference, focuses on this very problem: the force of his onslaught on modernization theory derives mainly from the criticism that it lacks a firm anchoring in class analysis. The exploited masses may be suppressed by governments wholly dissociated from popular forces, but they are essential ingredients in the development process. Attempts at 'stage-managing' their demands from above are bound to fail: without the *active* participation of the dominated majority, development is not possible. Wertheim argues that it is precisely because their needs are different from and opposed to those of the dominant classes, and their 'masters' overseas, that fundamental change cannot come in the form of gradual modernization. It must involve a dialectical process of emancipation that advances in waves. According to him, such waves (despite all appearances to the contrary) are still likely to occur in the form of peasant revolutions.

The change of emphasis brought about by neo-Marxism was necessary and overdue. This volume testifies to the profound impact it has had throughout the sociological community, certainly in the United Kingdom. It is true that this book is a collection of selected papers, chosen in part to make a reasonably coherent whole, and hence is not meant simply to be a fair reflection of the concerns of British development sociologists at the beginning of the seventies. But it is not wildly unrepresentative, and most authors in this volume have been influenced by the new outlook to some extent. What is perhaps more important about their papers is that they contribute to a better understanding of empirical reality in dependent, less developed societies, and hence modify some of the oversimplifications that certain of the new theorists of dependence have introduced with their sweeping vision. In a sense, there are 'lessons' in this volume for non-Marxists and neo-Marxists alike.

· · · ·

Let me begin with the lessons of neo-Marxism for the more 'conventional' sociologists. These are, it seems to me, mainly in two areas. Sociologists have been *shown* that it is of paramount importance to take account of the concrete ways in which the world economic and political system impinges upon the less developed societies, but more about that in a moment. They have also been *reminded* that in certain circumstances, and for certain problems, class analysis is crucial and fundamental. The issue of class relations comes up in quite a number of papers in this volume. That is no more than could be expected: after all, an interest in stratification *and* class is not new to British sociology. In one way or another these are touched upon by almost all contributors. But it is in Part II that the reader will find the papers that deal most directly with the empirical investigation of class relationships, those by Gavin Williams and Adrian Peace. They are related pieces, dealing with the same country (Nigeria) in the same period (1968–71).

In his paper Williams sets the tone early on, by stressing how important it is to analyse the way in which resources are distributed and appropriated by some groups (classes) at the expense of others. He is concerned not merely with the distribution of income and wealth, but with the expropriation of surplus. His research focuses on the way in which the different 'have not' groups have responded to the appropriative 'haves', and on the constraints inherent in the social structure that influence the chances of success of different types of response. It is this insistence on the need for examining the *relationships* between classes that differentiates the neo-Marxist approach from more conventional analyses of stratification.

This point has been made with much cogency by Pablo González Casanova (1969) in a recent essay, which is unfortunately not yet available in English. He contends that very little attention has been paid to the relationship of exploitation, the appropriation by some of the surplus produced by many. When we do look at this matter, we seldom go any further than making comparisons between the different strata that have emerged, at least in part, as a result of the process of exploitation: 'We tend to measure the *results* of exploitation – the inequalities between countries and men – rather than the *relations* of exploitation' (González Casanova, 1969: 114).

As with most aspects of neo-Marxist thought, this kind of sociological approach is heavily dependent upon economic concepts and formulations quite different from those elaborated in the neo-classical model. Who produces the surplus, what are the productive techniques used, and what is the social framework of the relations of production? Where spatially does the surplus arise and where does it end up? What gets done with it and who benefits? All these are technical questions to which clear answers need to be given, and it seems that Marxist economics still has a long way to go before it has achieved the necessary precision, even on so basic a matter as defining 'surplus'.[3] Jack Gray's paper in this volume does provide one way of approaching some of these questions. He shows how Maoist political strategies are concerned to mobilize surplus labour (Nurkse's 'Saving potential concealed in rural under-employment', 1958) in order to make up for deficits in subsistence production, as a substitute for capital inputs, and as a source of new capital assets.

But sociologists do not have to wait until these technical questions are entirely resolved in order to make a contribution to the clarification of related issues. Williams shows, for example, that some occupational groups in Nigeria (such as merchant traders) are *perceived* to be less 'exploited' or dependent than others (such as craftsmen or industrial workers), so that entry into the former type of occupation is sought by many. He compares the structure of aspirations with that of opportunities for the occupations of the urban poor and documents the existing disjunction in the field of trade. Small traders cannot break the stranglehold of large middlemen and yet lack the means to act collectively, as a 'class for themselves'.[4] Williams then looks at the situation of the peasantry, including their relationships with those who are their 'expropriators', and analyses the reasons for the emergence of a peasant consciousness as well as a capacity to act collectively. It is essential to understand that the Nigerian peasantry have become conscious that they are being exploited, that 'surplus' is being 'extracted' from them. Clearly this is an issue of prime significance even in the absence of a precise definition of surplus extraction.[5]

Adrian Peace takes the analysis of class relations in African towns a good deal beyond the hitherto prevailing view that such facts as tribalism and the existence of a labour elite have prevented African industrial workers from seeing themselves as a class and acting in class terms. He carefully examines the course of an industrial conflict in two enterprises and compares the workers' response in that context with their political reactions to the wider inequalities of Nigerian society. When confronting the government over the general issue of the cost-of-living allowance and the Adebo Commission's initially redistributive and later regressive recommendations, industrial workers tended (semi-consciously) to express their opposition to the social order and its inequalities and to identify broadly with 'the poor'. Although they did not develop a full-scale class consciousness, an incipient 'radical meaning system' (Parkin 1972) oriented their actions. But when issues related to their own place in the productive system dominated in the social situation, their response was, in Parkin's term, accommodative because, in contrast to the government, the managers of the expatriate enterprises were quite willing to give in to some of the workers' demands, those that did not really affect their fundamental interests. In examining the contradictions between the interests of the expatriate firms and the government (which represents the local elite and the locally rooted system of exploitation), and the effect of those contradictions on class relations in the country, Peace's work neatly makes the connection between class analysis and the analysis of dependence.

The other main focus of neo-Marxist sociology, that of the structures of dependence, will be encountered in Part IV of this volume. In an analysis which draws inspiration from Gunder Frank's work on Latin America, and from his suggestion that metropolis–satellite relations can also be found at the inter-regional level, Ian Carter examines the Highlands of Scotland as an underdeveloped area in a developed country. By means of a detailed examination of the historical evidence he shows how decisions taken outside that peripheral part of the British Isles have had a profound influence on the region's social and economic structure, not to mention on its culture and language. He claims that the underdevelopment of the Highlands resulted from the nature and terms of their *incorporation* into the cash economy, rather than their *exclusion* from it. Carter argues that the economy of the Highlands has always served the needs of the more developed areas, and his lament that in recent years the new investment in the area has created few jobs while the profits of the 'expatriate' enterprises have continued to be transferred to and spent in the south sounds remarkably familiar to anyone who has heard Latin Americans discussing their dependence on the United States.

In contrast to the simplified arguments Frank is wont to put forward, regional imbalances are not *only* the result of 'capitalist exploitation'. They often have their roots in differences of a geographic nature (resource base, climate, accessibility, etc.) which make investment in the 'growth pole' areas economically more rational (Perroux 1955; Nove forthcoming). But it *is* relevant to ask how the terms of trade between regions are determined, and how the benefits of economic activity in the less developed regions are distributed. If the profits leave the region, how much stays behind in wages? How do wages compare with those in the metropolitan area? What does income distribution look like in the peripheral region and how much poverty is there? What policies and institutions exist to deal with such questions? Carter's paper certainly gives empirical support to certain aspects of dependence theory and underlines the point made previously by economists such as Myrdal (1957), Hirschman (1958), or Friedmann (1966) that regional imbalances tend to grow rather than diminish if matters are left to the free play of the market, as they largely are in the political economy of capitalism.[6]

The international aspects of dependence are taken up in two papers. Philip Elliott and Peter Golding discuss the structure of dependence in the mass media, while Ronald Frankenberg and Joyce Leeson tackle the same issue in the field of health. Both papers bring out the importance for professionals in less developed countries of the models and procedures set in the industrialized world. The authors show that one is faced not merely with the ('inevitable') adoption of alien attitudes through the operation of reference group networks, but with *structural* domination by powerful interests, often of a material kind, which control (and market) the available technology with little regard for the needs of the inhabitants of the poorer countries of the world.

Elliott and Golding see news as a marketable commodity, and claim that the news media in the Third World – even when they are in the hands of the government – operate as part of international corporate capitalism. Communication networks continue to be neo-colonial, radiating from the metropolitan countries like the spokes from the hub of a wheel, and the content of those communications transmits to the dependent countries the image of the world as seen from London, Washington, Paris, and Moscow. Their case study of Nigeria demonstrates that images of social structures are simplified, conflicts of interest underplayed, established leaders given prominence, and that the hangover from the Cold War is everywhere still noticeable.

Frankenberg and Leeson provide a detailed analysis of the health system in Zambia, and in so doing also point to the patterns of technological and cultural dependence and their profound social effects. A growing number of people are now beginning to realize that the wholesale transplantation of western medical practices to countries such as

Zambia has been a disastrous mistake and that new solutions, which make use of cheaper and less sophisticated technology, as well as of personnel with more limited skills than those of full-blown physicians, are badly needed. And yet it has not been possible to break through the pattern of 'medical imperialism' in Zambia, mainly because the patterns of health care, which are inappropriate to the needs of the vast majority of the population, are forcefully demanded by the country's dominant class, who expect a standard of treatment and a type of care equivalent to that found in the industrialized world. The authors' brief comparison with mainland China is illuminating because it demonstrates that the success there of the new patterns of organization in the health field cannot be explained except by the fact that they are part and parcel of ('functionally related to') the overall conception of social order in that society, and hence any attempt at transplanting them elsewhere in isolation from those wider changes is likely to be difficult, if not impossible.[7]

Approaches that take their cue from the neo-Marxist model have made an unmistakable and seminal contribution to our understanding of problems of development. But it is surely nonsensical to move from such a statement to the contention that sociological work with different ideological or conceptual starting-points is simple 'mystification'. It is pernicious to argue that those who believe in the need for some kind of integration of the different sociological approaches – the 'liberals' – are 'only stupid reactionaries rather than ordinary ones', with whom discussions are 'a waste of time' (Frank 1969: xi, xvi). There is quite a range of internal problems in less developed societies that cannot be explained in terms of class; not all interests are class interests, nor is all 'authentic' consciousness class consciousness. It is even more unhelpful to maintain that work on less developed countries is worthless unless it deals (or worse, deals exclusively) with the problem of dependence, because *all* the ills of the underdeveloped nations result from 'the system', from international capitalism and its actors whose operations (transitively) 'underdevelop' the rest of the world. Perhaps 'the system' can, indeed, only change through revolution on a world scale. But this is not an eventuality on which sociologists can exercise a great deal of influence, nor one that lends itself particularly to the application of our professional skills.[8]

Meanwhile a lot of rather important problems need analysing.[9] A few examples will have to suffice. Take population. Some would have us believe that the world's population explosion is related to imperialism, others that the efforts to achieve population control are part of the rich world's schema to maintain control over the rest. Rather than get involved in arid arguments, we must surely ask where the demographic facts appear to be leading us; whether some countries need fast population growth (Singer 1970) while others desperately need to slow down the birth rate; or what (social) circumstances make for success or failure in family-planning campaigns.

Take education. Rather than show how school systems in Third World countries are inappropriate because they are copied from the capitalist west (which is largely true), or argue that only a radical solution such as 'de-schooling' can help to break the vicious circle (Illich 1971; Reimer 1971), it is necessary to ask some very serious questions about the social functions of schools in less developed countries, the allocative mechanisms for the occupational system, incentives and opportunities, teaching and testing.[10]

Finally, let us take agrarian reform. The *latifundia* in Latin America are brazen manifestations of what most readers of this book would agree to be iniquitous social systems, and they may well play a part in the international structure of exploitation and need to be eliminated through land reforms. But those reforms give rise to problems that demand some quite sophisticated sociological analysis – problems to which Marxist concepts (let alone ideology) give only very partial answers. Lehmann's work on Chile – before and after a socialist government took office – is a noteworthy example of such an analysis (Lehmann, 1971, 1972). It also touches on such matters (vexatious to some) as the operation of the bureaucracy or grass-roots participation, comparing ideological prescription with humdrum reality. Lane's paper in this volume also deals incisively with the latter type of question, and with the help of his brief but penetrating examination of the Soviet system, its achievements and shortcomings, we can understand the meaning and implications of Leninism as a development ideology. Perhaps it is instructive that Mao's economic strategy, as expounded in Gray's paper, seems to have been developed in the search for practical solutions to diverse and specific problems. While it is argued that such solutions are dependent on radical institutional changes, these changes may well create new problems – 'contradictions', as Mao would say. In contrast with the Soviet Union, such changes have been introduced in China at the grass roots and have been oriented to the specific problems of specific localities.

Gray's analysis emphasizes the central importance attached to such old-fashioned considerations as the provision of appropriate material incentives and the fostering of entrepreneurial initiative.

The two papers in Part III of this volume eloquently demonstrate the usefulness of concepts other than class or dependence and of the need continually to extend and deepen them. Sebastian Brett has brought together the ideas on squatter settlements of a sociologically minded architect and town-planner, John Turner. After presenting a synthesis and review of Turner's work, Brett does criticize him for neglect of the wider socio-political context in which the settlers' actions occur. Brett also stresses that land values, which influence settlers' security, respond to commercial operations by outsiders, who in most Third World towns are capitalist speculators uninterested in the well-being of the settlers. Even so he demonstrates the usefulness, from a sociological as well as from a policy-making point of view, of a careful analysis of the specific housing needs of low income groups (as opposed, say, to their work needs), and their variation over time in terms of life-cycle or migration history. As Brett argues, the individual 'bridge-headers' and 'consolidators' are not everywhere as distinct as Turner's typological scheme would suggest, nor can one always neatly distinguish one type of settlement from another. But to have shown that the shanty-town dwellers are no undifferentiated mass, and to have indicated what kinds of significant distinctions can be made, was an important advance.

Alison MacEwen in her paper also refers to the greater understanding of the shanty-town phenomenon that has emerged in the last few years. This is partly as a result of the length of time some of these originally illegal settlements have been established and of the ageing and differentiation that they have undergone. It is also the result of careful empirical research at the grass-roots level replacing argument based on superficial and tendentious assumptions. The focus of MacEwen's paper, based on research in Argentina, is on the internal differentiation in the shanty-town. In a sense shanty-town dwellers can be seen as a 'reserve army of labour' which helps keep wages low in unskilled sectors of the economy, and MacEwen documents how the life-chances of many are, indeed, very much worse than average. But while she recognizes the importance of class and class relations in Argentina, a competitive capitalist society into which the shanty-town is closely integrated, considerations of status and prestige are extremely important determinants of behaviour. And so among the *marginados* the apparently small differences in status (occupation, housing, education, style of life, material possessions) are given exaggerated importance and lead to a fragmentation of the area into neighbourhoods whose inhabitants keep their social distance and have little to do with each other.

Suppose someone were to do an investigation of the patterns of economic activity or of un- and underemployment in one of those shanty-towns discussed by MacEwen or Turner, with a view to planning a sensible programme of urban renewal. He would have to take account of quantifiable hypotheses, such as Turner's, relating to migration history, life-cycle, age of the shanty-town, and so forth. There really would be little point in stopping short, as some neo-Marxists would do, at the observation that those patterns are related to the operation of the international economic system, however much this may be true.

'Conventional' quantifiable hypotheses, then, *are* important, particularly if we are to collaborate with researchers from other disciplines, without which development studies are not going to make much headway. But we also need a broad perspective such as the one deriving from the neo-Marxist approach, which itself, with its focus on political economy, frames problems in an interdisciplinary way. For the unwary there are pitfalls in this area, and traps which some economists in particular seem to set for those willing to move towards interdisciplinary studies on *their* terms.

In the only serious discussion I have seen of the problems of interdisciplinary work in the field of development Michael Lipton produces a strongly worded statement of belief in the superiority of the economists' models and methods: 'We have to face the fact that economics, alone among the social sciences, has a number of clearly specified models, with gaps for real live data, tested in several less developed country (LDC) environments: benefit/cost and linear programming among optimizing models, and production functions and input-output among descriptive models, come to mind . . . To be brutal, economists are forced by the realities to seek to impose their own quantitative and testable hypotheses on [interdisciplinary] work in LDCs, so long as other [disciplines] do not put such hypotheses forward' (Lipton 1970: 12). I shall shortly return to the goods delivered by those very economists in less developed countries. But are their models, even in an academic sense, framed to produce the right answers, and is theirs perhaps a case of the methodological dog wagging the substantive tail?

Quantitative and incrementalist questions certainly need to be asked, and it is useful to be able to say that 'x' more of 'a' will produce 'y' more of 'b'. This sort of statement about housing, welfare, or the organization of health services, or about income distribution can perhaps help the planners reach decisions that make the life of the poor and dominated groups a bit more satisfactory, and so, in my opinion, should be applauded – unless one belongs to that group that gleefully watches things getting worse in the belief that only then will they get better (will they?). And yet, while such incrementalist questions are important, they do divert our attention away from the social relations that have brought about and perpetuate the inequalities (González Casanova, 1969), and from those aspects of the structure of interests and also of the institutions that govern the distribution of material or symbolic advantages, which in turn might explain why the incrementalist changes are not larger than they are. But on that area of reality the splendid models of Lipton's colleagues have little to say.

In so far as governments represent the powerful, or in so far as its bureaucrats partake in the privileges of the elite and benefit from exploitative class relations, questions about the structure of inequality, about class relations, elite privilege, or dominance of the key decision-making institutions are embarrassing and unwelcome. If attention is focused on those issues, policy recommendations emerge that have little chance of being implemented. Perhaps that is why, in the past, economists writing or advising on development problems have strayed little from their input-output tables or their linear programming models, which have been refined to a degree scarcely imaginable even a few years ago. But for all their sophisticated techniques and all their mathematical and computer models, the economists have not done all that well. In fact, in most respects their record has been pretty dismal. In international economic circles awareness of this situation is now beginning to emerge (the group of economists working in the UN Economic Commission for Latin America has, in this respect, been far ahead of its time). As disenchantment hardens with the results of the kind of economics that takes the structure of privilege and exploitation as given, attention seems indeed to be shifting to some of the underlying issues of inequality and class.

At the beginning of the United Nations' 'Second Development Decade', the Pearson Commission's Report (Pearson 1969), despite its heroic (or tragi-comic?) efforts at being optimistic, was a monument to the failure of development. There had been economic growth, as measured by the increase in *per capita* GNP, and in some countries not even that. Yet clearly this had neither been enough to make a dent in the situation of underdevelopment in most Third World countries, nor did it hold much promise for the future well-being of most of the globe's population. Thus, at the start of the seventies the dominant orientation prevailing among economists is beginning to change, and there are rather fewer than before who are willing to give the name 'development' to any process that fails to spread its benefits to large, and growing, sections of the population of a less developed country. Some, in fact, are now explicitly saying that the economic aspect of the process, *economic* development, is no more than (one of) the *means* towards a wider goal, and in doing so have come to accept a criticism long levelled at them by other social scientists, philosophers, and religious leaders. A growing number seem to agree that 'the realization of the potential of human personality' is indeed a 'universally acceptable aim' (Seers 1972a: 22), and that all development efforts should be directed at the search for the conditions necessary to achieve that aim. Clearly behind the impressive economic growth statistics of many countries there lies a reality that has made very little progress towards that wider goal.

Mesmerized by the goal of economic growth we have been left without the tools to measure the wider aspects of the development process. In spite of the long-standing efforts of the United Nations Department of Economic and Social Affairs to keep an interest alive in 'social' development, nobody took much notice of the *Reports on the World Social Situation* (UN Department of Economic and Social Affairs 1952–70). Nor was there much interest in the work on social indicators of development (United Nations Research Institute for Social Development, Statistical Unit 1969) or incorporation of them into the planning models so heavily dominated by indicators of economic performance. A recent special issue of the *Journal of Development Studies* (1972), devoted to 'Measuring Development', bears witness to this fact.

But there is growing consciousness that the very targets of development plans need reconsidering. It has been suggested that planners ought to start with the social and 'human' dimensions and work back to the necessary growth rate (ILO 1970), and the new concern, among development economists, is with the groups left behind by whatever economic growth has occurred. It started with the rediscovery of large-scale unemployment as a major unresolved, and growing, problem in less developed countries. The International Labour Office found a fresh *raison d'être* in the World Employment Programme (ILO 1969), and sponsored a number of policy-oriented investigations by international missions.[11] For political reasons, if for no others, their reports have not had much effect on the countries with whose problems they dealt. But they have helped to move thinking on development away from mere growth; first to the absence of adequate opportunities for work and hence for income of large numbers in the labour force (we are speaking of orders of magnitude of some 15 to 25 per cent), later to the distribution of income and welfare in a more general sense, and to the fate of those at the bottom of the heap in particular.[12] Robert McNamara's speeches, following the one that he made to the United Nations Conference in Trade and Development III (McNamara 1972), have suddenly focused on the needs of the neglected poor. The first step has therefore been taken, and income distribution has become a live issue.

If this is followed through, it might lead to proposals for new kinds of policies and even to the analysis of the effects of such policies on different social groups and their likely reactions to them, a task for which a certain amount of sociological sophistication would stand planners and politicians in good stead. So far, however, the new 'social' economists have not paid a great deal of attention to the structural obstacles that exist in many societies to the implementation of their progressive policies. As Charles Elliott has written: 'Even if one were able to identify, quantify and frame policies for the relief of the poverty of the urban and rural deprived, those policies would be ineffective unless they took account of the defensive reactions of competing classes and interest groups' (Elliott 1972: 47). The fashionable (but important) interest in employment, income distribution, and the like, can become a dangerous smokescreen unless attention comes to rest upon the socio-economic relations that underlie the unequal distribution of resources.

How will these be changed? For some the answer can only lie in revolution; Wertheim calls it the dialectic of emancipation. Others are more hopeful of the possibility that those representing the poor can out-manoeuvre those with entrenched interests in the perpetuation of the *status quo*. Hirschman (1971) is one of the latter, and he sees it as possible also in the field of rich country–poor country relations.

There are signs that the less developed countries can change the balance of advantage between themselves and the industrialized world some-what by mobilizing bargaining power through the creation of cartels for raw materials. The case of the oil-producing countries is perhaps too exceptional to be of widespread interest, but now the copper producers are moving in the same direction. The industrialized world still requires vast inputs of raw materials and consumes considerable amounts of tropical products, so that, in principle, more widespread moves towards 'collective bargaining' on the part of the less developed countries could well pay off.

But the chances of success of such efforts are hard to evaluate. They are dim in the fields of tropical foodstuffs: one only has to remember the shakiness of the international coffee agreement, the failure, so far, of progress in agreement on cocoa, and, in general, the effects of competition among producers for greater shares of hardly expanding markets.

The final paper casts serious doubts on the room for manoeuvre of less developed countries: Krishan Kumar's discussion of the potential implication for the less developed world of predicted trends in the rich countries. Futurologists and students of underdevelopment have worked in almost complete isolation from each other, and it is most useful to see their analyses brought together. The result is disquieting to say the least. All signs point to the increasing integration and inter-penetration of the 'post-industrial' countries, which are able to determine their own future, irrespective of the wishes or requirements of the Third World. The Russias, Britains, and Swedens of this world need the Ghanas, Indias, or even Brazils less and less, and in the long term they can probably even do without Zambia and its copper, or Kuwait and its oil. The developed countries may still benefit from the unequal relation-ship that exists, but they depend less and less on 'exploitation' of the Third World, whatever role that may have played in the past. Kumar documents this with reference to existing trends in the rich countries, and if things continue along the predicted lines, there is little doubt that the future of the less developed countries (or most of them) will be as gloomy as that spelled out for them by the futurologists.

But the crystal ball is a little clouded, and is *après tout* held in the hands of men who, as our venerable ancestor has said, make their own history. In the rich countries they are doing this by polluting the environment, and lately by reacting to the 'eco-threat'. According to some, this is a plot to prevent the poor countries from ever getting rich, and according to others (Foster-Carter among them) a chance for those not yet spoiled to lead the way towards a better world.

In their reading of the crystal ball sociologists will no doubt continue to differ profoundly. But those concerned with problems of development, whatever their *Weltanschauung*, will have to go on chipping away at the vast areas in which we do not have enough knowledge to understand even a little. The essays collected in this volume show that, despite all our differences, such an enterprise remains worth while.

Notes

1 Lewis, Hirschman, Rostow, Myint, and Hoselitz come to mind, to name only a few. Hoselitz, of course, ended up a Parsonian.

2 This point was first made by Ronald Dore (1965), who also introduced the distinction between modernization as an intransitive concept, something that somehow happened, and its use in a transitive sense, as related to the goals pursued purposefully by leaders of less developed countries.

3 See, for example, the discussion by Shigeto Tsuru of Marx's concern to analyse the way in which the economic system operated in terms of the relations between men (1954), the attempts of Baran and Sweezy (1968: 23) to define 'surplus', and González Casanova's quasi-mathematical model of exploitation which is, however, built on the slimmest operational foundations (1969).

4 The classic work on the subject of aspirations and opportunities is Eli Chinoy's *Automobile Workers and the American Dream* (1955), but others have also discovered this phenomenon in less developed societies. See for example Lopes (1971).

5 As Parkin has noted, social structures and economic systems differ in the extent to which they are 'transparent' – i.e. in the extent to which it is possible to *identify* the individuals or groups responsible for the allocation of rewards (or, obviously, for exploitation). The more opaque the situation, the more difficult it is to arrive at 'consciousness' (Parkin 1972: 160). Williams describes the quite transparent structure of exploitation in which the Nigerian peasantry was enmeshed.

6 See also the detailed and sophisticated analysis of regional inequalities with special reference to the position of the 'Celtic fringe' in Michael Hechter's recent paper (Hechter 1972).

7 This appears to be the case to some extent even in a country with an overall socialist policy such as Tanzania. See Segal (1972).

8 Those in doubt should go back to Weber's masterly 'Science as a Vocation' (Weber 1922).

9 This collection only touches upon a small fraction of those problems. The conference to which the papers, published here in revised form,

were originally read dealt with a somewhat wider range, but even there many issues were hardly broached.

10 An impressive and 'practical' sociological analysis of education and (under) development in one country can be found in the report of the International Labour Office Employment Mission to Ceylon (ILO 1971). For a closely argued critique of the school of de-schoolers see Dore (1972).

11 I have earlier referred to the reports of the Employment Missions (ILO 1970; 1971). A short and useful summary of some of the issues tackled in the first two Missions can be found in Seers (1972b).

12 John Weeks was an early critic of the new fashion of worrying about unemployment. See Weeks (1971); reprinted in Jolly *et al.* (1973).

References

BARAN, P. A. 1957. *The Political Economy of Growth*. New York: Monthly Review Press.

BARAN, P. A. and SWEEZY, P. M. 1968. *Monopoly Capital*. Harmondsworth: Penguin.

BELL, D. 1960. *The End of Ideology*. Glencoe, Ill.: The Free Press.

BOTTOMORE, T. 1972. Varieties of Political Expression in Sociology. *American Journal of Sociology* 78 (1: July).

CHINOY, E. 1955. *Automobile Workers and the American Dream*. Garden City, NY: Doubleday.

DAHRENDORF, R. 1958. Out of Utopia. *American Journal of Sociology* 64 (2: September).

DORE, R. 1965. On the Possibility and Desirability of a Theory of Modernization. In *Modernization in Asia*. Seoul: Asian Research Centre. (Reprinted in Institute of Development Studies Communications Series [old series] No. 38.)

—— 1972. False Prophets: The Cuernavaca Critique of School (mimeo). *IDS Discussion Paper* No. 12, October.

ELLIOTT, C. 1972. Income Distribution and Social Stratification: Some notes on Theory and Practice. *Journal of Development Studies*, 1972.

FRANK, A. G. 1967. *Capitalism and Underdevelopment in Latin America*. New York: Monthly Review Press.

—— 1969. *Latin America: Underdevelopment or Revolution*. New York: Monthly Review Press.

FRIEDMANN, J. 1966. *Regional Development Policy: A Case Study of Venezuela*. Cambridge, Mass.: MIT Press.

GERTH, H. H. and WRIGHT MILLS, C. (eds.). 1948. *From Max Weber*. London: Routledge.

GONZÁLEZ CASANOVA, P. 1969. *Sociologia de la Explotación.* Mexico: Siglo XXI.

HECHTER, M. 1972. Industrialization and National Development in the British Isles. *Journal of Development Studies* **8** (3: April): 155–82.

HIRSCHMAN, A. O. 1958. *The Strategy of Economic Development.* New Haven: Yale UP.

—— 1971. *A Bias for Hope: Essays on Development and Latin America.* New Haven: Yale UP.

HOROWITZ, D. (ed.) 1968. *Marx and Modern Economics.* London: McGibbon & Kee.

ILLICH, I. 1971. *De-schooling Society.* London: Calder & Boyars.

INTERNATIONAL LABOUR OFFICE (ILO) 1969. *The World Employment Programme.* Geneva: ILO.

—— 1970. *Towards Full Employment: A Programme for Colombia.* Geneva: ILO.

—— 1971. *Matching Employment Opportunities and Expectations: A Programme of Action for Ceylon.* Geneva: ILO.

JOLLY, R., DE KADT, E., SINGER, H. and WILSON, F. 1973. *Third World Employment, Problems and Strategy. Selected Readings.* Harmondsworth: Penguin.

JOURNAL OF DEVELOPMENT STUDIES. 1972. *Measuring Development: Special Issue on Development Indicators* (Guest editor: Nancy Baxter) **8** (3: April).

LEHMANN, D. 1971. Political Incorporation versus Political Stability: The Case of the Chilean Agrarian Reform, 1965–70. *Journal of Development Studies* **7** (4: July): 365–95.

—— 1972. *La Agricultura Chilena y el Periodo de Transicion.* Santiago and Brighton: ICIRA (Instituto de Capacitacion e Investigacion en Reforma Agraria) and IDS (mimeo).

LIPTON, M. 1970. Interdisciplinary Studies in Less Developed Countries. *Journal of Development Studies* **6** (1: October): 5–18.

LOCKWOOD, D. 1956. Some Remarks on the Social System. *British Journal of Sociology* **7** (2: June): 134–46.

LOPES, J. R. B. 1971. *Desenvolvimento e Mudança Social: Formaçáo da Sociedade Urbano-Industrial no Brasil* (second edition). São Paulo: Editora Nacional.

MCNAMARA, R. S. 1972. *Address to the UN Conference on Trade and Development.* Washington: International Bank for Reconstruction and Development.

MYRDAL, G. 1957. *Economic Theory and Underdeveloped Regions.* London: Methuen.

NOVE, A. (forthcoming). On Reading André Gunder Frank.

NURKSE, R. 1958. *The Problem of Capital Formation in Underdeveloped Countries.* London: Oxford University Press.

PARKIN, F. 1972. *Class Inequality and Political Order*. London: Paladin.

PEARSON, L. B. 1969. *Partners in Development*. London: Pall Mall.

PERROUX, F. 1955. Note sur la Notion de Pôle de Croissance. *Economie Appliquée* (Jan–June): 307–20.

REIMER, E. 1971. *School is Dead*. New York: Harpers.

SEERS, D. 1972a. What are We trying to Measure? *Journal of Development Studies* 8 (3: April): 21–36.

—— 1972b. Lessons of ILO Missions to Colombia and Ceylon. Brighton: IDS (Reprints No. 5).

SEGAL, M. 1972. The Politics of Health in Tanzania. *Development and Change* 4 (1): 39–50.

SINGER, P. 1970. *Dinâmica Populacional e Desenvolvimento*. São Paulo: CEBRAP (Centro Brasiliero de Analise et Planejamento).

TSURU, S. 1954. Keynes versus Marx: The Methodology of Aggregates. In Horowitz (ed.) 1968.

UNITED NATIONS DEPARTMENT OF ECONOMIC AND SOCIAL AFFAIRS. 1952–70. *Reports on the World Social Situation*. New York: UN (ref. E/CN5, 8 vols.).

UNITED NATIONS RESEARCH INSTITUTE FOR SOCIAL DEVELOPMENT, STATISTICAL UNIT. 1969. *Compilation of Development Indicators (for 1960)*. New York: UN (UNRISD/69/C. 31).

WEBER, M. 1922. Science as a Vocation. In Gerth and Mills (eds.) 1948.

WEEKS, J. 1971. Does Employment Matter. In Jolly *et al.* (1973).

PART ONE

Marxism and Development

DAVID LANE

Leninism as an Ideology of Soviet Development

Most analysis of Soviet society concentrates on its peculiar political features, either its totalitarian or its socialist character, and surprisingly few writers have tried to interpret the USSR as a developing society.[1] One exception is Marcuse's classic study *Soviet Marxism* which in many places recognizes that the Soviet regime ensures 'total mobilization of the individuals for the requirements of competitive total industrialization' (1958: 259). This relative lack of emphasis in the west in considering the Soviet Union as a model of development stems from two sources. First there is the west European Marxist tradition of regarding 'socialism' as a qualitatively superior social and moral system to capitalism, and this is also the primary concern of Marcuse. But Marxism as interpreted by Lenin, and particularly by his followers in the USSR who have articulated the ideology of Leninism, is very much concerned with the role of development in societies that are economically at the pre-capitalist stage. Second, and perhaps more important, is the view that Russia in 1917 was far ahead of societies that are now regarded as underdeveloped or undeveloped. As Rostow (1960: 95) has put it, 'the Russian take-off was under way by the 1890s . . .'. Also, Russia has a long and deep European tradition, which distinguishes it from many other countries of the Third World. While these objections must be given a prominent place when evaluating Soviet experience they do not detract from the fact that Russia in 1917 was one of the most backward countries in Europe, having a predominantly rural, agricultural, and illiterate peasant population. Since the Revolution, one of the most significant features of the evolution of the USSR has been planned economic and social development.

An analogy may perhaps be made with Lipset's emphasis on 'America's key values' originating in its revolution: 'The United States was the first major colony successfully to revolt against colonial rule. In this sense, it was the first "new nation"' (1964: 2). In a similar way, the

Soviet Union's key values may be said to lie in its revolutionary origins and in the goals of the leaders of the revolution. The Soviet Union might be called the First Planned Society. While the American ideology of 'equality and opportunity' has been of some appeal as a mobilizing force to developing countries outside the United States, the Soviet variant of Marxism–Leninism is one of the major ideologies of modern times.

In this paper I shall attempt first to identify the major components of Lenin's views about social change in backward areas. These provide a set of ideas from which was derived the ideology of Leninism propagated in the USSR after Lenin's death. Second, I shall highlight some of the ways in which the ideology of Soviet social change followed or departed from Lenin's declared intentions. It should be made clear that it is not possible to demarcate clearly between Lenin's theories of change and the utilization of these ideas as social levers (the sense in which I am using the word ideology), because Lenin was actively aware of the potency of ideas as instruments of social change. Nevertheless, 'Leninism' in this paper refers to the set of values, beliefs, and policies derived from Lenin's works which may be said to have guided the actions of the leaders of the Soviet Union during the 1930s. *Leninism*, therefore, is the doctrine coined by Stalin in the USSR after Lenin's death.

The thesis of this paper is that Leninism provided an ideological stimulus for and legitimation to the formation of a large-scale industrial system; whereas Lenin's views also contained idealistic socialist values concerning the organization of an industrial society, many of which have not been taken up in the USSR. Hence Lenin's own theories and the official doctrine of Leninism do not always coincide. But in many ways they do, for Lenin was a passionate advocate of what was once fashionably called 'modernization' as a goal for underdeveloped countries. In terms of contemporary theories of modernization, Lenin advocated public participation in the polity, the diffusion of secular-rational norms, and the 'transformation of the modal personality' towards a type characterized by achievement (Lerner 1968: 386). In contrast to anarchism, which involves the immediate gratification of needs, Lenin called for the deferment of such gratification and he added to Marxism a Weberian ethic of work. Unlike modern development theorists, Lenin also centred his analysis on class and class conflict. Under Stalin these ideas were transformed into the ideology of Leninism, which provided a value system contributing to a community of beliefs and sentiments that justified the three main components of building socialism in one country: rapid industrialization, collectivization, and the cultural revolution. The value content of Leninism as an ideology is what Parsons has called a value pattern of 'instrumental activism' (1971; 124). In emphasizing the importance of industrialism in societies that are pre-capitalist, Lenin stressed the importance of Marxists adopting a positive attitude to economic development and Leninism goes further by adding a doctrine of planned economic growth to Marxism.

Lenin's thought about social change in backward societies may be analysed under four major headings. First, flowing directly from Marxism, is the advocacy of the benefits of advanced forms of industrial organization, even as embodied under capitalism. Second, a theory of imperialism is clearly articulated which condemns the political forms of western capitalism as they affect underdeveloped countries and shifts the locus of the class struggle to the working class in the latter. Third, there is an organizational theory of centralized decision-making. Fourth, Lenin postulates a participatory role in public affairs for the masses. These four elements, it may be noted, contain two pairs of apparently contradictory propositions: the first, grounded in Marxism itself, is hostility to capitalism and acceptance of its cardinal industrial character, and the second is an emphasis on obedience to centralized authority and involvement in decision-making by the individual. His theories channel emotional sentiments against a common external enemy (the imperialist states) and they release and direct the energy of the masses towards industrial development and growth. The importance of Lenin's ideas in the USSR lies not in the analysis of advanced forms of industrial capitalist society but in the provision of an ideology under Stalin. These ideas were formalized into a doctrine (Leninism) that justifies the opposition to capitalism of peoples living under different forms of colonialism and that defines an unequivocal policy of industrialization.

Paradoxically, Marxism, which provided an indictment of bourgeois society in the capitalist states of western Europe, played an important role in justifying the industrial form of capitalism in pre-revolutionary Russia against democratic and peasant socialist idealists. Liberal Russian writers such as Pestel, Tolstoy, and Herzen emphasized values of individual freedom and the liberation of the peasant. Their ideology was democratic rather than bourgeois. They deplored the development of industrial capitalism and advocated the retention of traditional social-istic elements in Russian life, particularly the peasant commune. Russia's indigenous business class, while growing in numbers and importance in the late nineteenth and early twentieth centuries, was nowhere comparable to its counterpart in western Europe, and while Russia had many creative writers advocating democratic ideals, the business class did not produce a theorist such as Adam Smith, Ricardo, or Marshall to rationalize and legitimate their activity. Russian Marxist and Soviet social thought to some extent fills this gap by providing an ideology of economic, political, and social development. Two major Marxist works of nineteenth-century Russia, Plekhanov's *Our Differences* and Lenin's *The Development of Capitalism in Russia*, sought to show the inevitability of, and benefits that would flow from, industrial progress. In *The Development of Capitalism in Russia*, Lenin emphasized that the 'progressive' role of capitalism was particularly apparent in 'the increase in the productive forces of social labour and in the socialization of that labour' (*P.S.S.* 3: 597; *C.W.* 3: 595).[2] The increase in productive forces not only provides a higher level of material production, but also liberates labour itself: 'Compared with the labour of the dependent or bonded peasant, the labour of the hired worker is a progressive phenomenon in all the branches of the economy' (*P.S.S.* 3: 600; *S.W.* 3: 598). Russia in the late nineteenth century, Lenin argued, was suffering not only from the oppression to which capitalism gave rise but also from the effects of retarded development, from the 'abundant survival of ancient institutions that are incompatible with capitalism ... [and which] immeasurably worsen the condition of the producers, who [to quote Marx] "suffer not only from capitalist production, but also from the incompleteness of its development"'.[3] Lenin's prognosis was that even under the Tsars the process of the development of capitalism had to be speeded up and political strategy was related to that aim. At that time (these words of Lenin were published in 1899) the possibility of industrialization taking place under a socialist political order was not seriously considered in Russia. The revolutionary upheavals in 1905, however, posed the question of whether a society emerging from feudalism could pass straight to the socialist stage. In 1906, Trotsky and Parvus, in their theory of combined development, and also Lenin, with his ideas about 'continuous' revolution, argued that this was possible, although they were then concerned with political strategy rather than with the economic structure of a socialist order. They assumed that gaining the help of the proletariat, following a socialist revolution in western Europe, was an important condition for the success of such a revolution.

Further justification for a socialist revolution in societies undergoing capitalist industrialization was provided in Lenin's work on imperialism published in 1916. Here Lenin gives to backward nations a leading role in the movement forward to socialism. He points out that the spread of capitalism, involving the export of capital, destroys the traditional pattern of class relations and culture and, at the same time, places such societies at the forefront of the class struggle. The working-class in the advanced societies of the west may be bribed with the tribute exacted from the developing nations abroad, leaving the masses in those countries to overthrow capitalism.[4] In Lenin's view, the advanced form of economic progress of the imperialist states is paralleled by a high degree of anti-capitalist political consciousness in the developing world, which is characterized by a three-sided class struggle between autocracy (or other forms of traditional rule), the bourgeoisie, and the proletariat.

During the course of the First World War, Lenin now came to regard the 'bourgeois revolution' to be only an intermediary and short-lived stage in the political emancipation of these nations. For Russia, national emancipation would have required breaking the links with imperialism through the seizure of power by the proletariat, although Lenin continued to believe that assistance would be necessary from the west. Here then is the basis and justification of what present-day Soviet Marxist–Leninists term the 'non-capitalist mode of development' led by the working-class, and the western experience of industrialization is considered unique and irrelevant as a process to the needs of countries now in an underdeveloped state. Hence the call for political revolution led by the working class is echoed in the works of such contemporary western writers as Paul Baran and André Gunder Frank as the first necessary step for the industrial development of underdeveloped countries.[5]

In addition to the justification of a socialist revolution in an underdeveloped nation, Lenin also formulated a policy of industrialization under socialism. This followed quite logically from Lenin's early thought, for if industrialization was desirable under the autocracy, it was doubly so when the deleterious effects of bourgeois ownership relations were no longer present. As capitalist industrialization could develop under the autocracy without a strong indigenous capitalist class, then Lenin and his supporters were quite right in saying that industrialization could proceed just as well under the Bolshevik party. In 1923, Lenin regarded the view that the USSR did not have the objective economic conditions for socialism as pedantic, and he dubbed as 'timorous reformists' social democrats who put forward such views (*P.S.S.* 45: 378; *C.W.* 33: 476). In the context of Soviet Russia and of other countries developing today, 'socialism' has come to have a quite different meaning from that which it has in the advanced industrial countries of western Europe. In the former, 'socialism' means political power wielded by previously under-privileged strata (often manual and non-manual workers and peasants), utilized for the *industrial development* of the economy, and socialist construction is almost synonymous with industrialization. It cannot be emphasized too strongly that, in Lenin's thought, the evils ensuing from large-scale industrial production (the enslavement of labour by the machine, the oppression of the working-class, the prostitution of marriage, the ruination of the handicraftsman, and the degradation of the small-scale peasant) were attributed to *capitalism*, whereas under socialism, the benefits of large-scale industrial production would accrue to the people as a whole. In this way one of the most important roles of Lenin as a Marxist theorist and of Leninism as an ideology was to rationalize and to legitimate the power of the Bolshevik party to create an industrial society.

This was stated clearly by Lenin in 1920 when he defined communism as 'Soviet power plus the electrification of all the country' (*P.S.S.* 42a: 30; *C.W.* 31a: 392. See also *P.S.S.* 42b: 159; *C.W.* 31b: 516). In this slogan Lenin sums up the political and the industrial components of his policy. The emphasis in western studies of the Soviet Union is often on the political side of the equation, stressing the link between communism and 'Soviet power'; but the economic goals are also important and especially so for developing countries. Without a priority being given to heavy industry, illustrated in the above slogan by the widespread distribution of electric power, 'socialist construction [as Lenin pointed out] would remain only a sum of decrees' (*P.S.S.* 42a: 30). The distribution of electricity to the countryside would also have the effect of changing the mode of production in agriculture and would provide a technical basis for its industrialization.

Lenin also recognized that industrialization could not be achieved without an ethic of work. In 1918 in *The Immediate Tasks of Soviet Power* he acknowledged that 'the Russian is a bad worker compared to the workers of the advanced nations'. Therefore a major task of the government was 'to teach the people how to work' (*P.S.S.* 36:189; *C.W.* 27: 259). Love for one's work is one of the highest principles of Leninist morality, given its best-known form in the slogan 'he who does not work, neither shall he eat'. Lenin also linked this ethic to the organization of work. The abolition of classes, he argued, would 'for the first time open up the way for competition on a really mass scale' (*P.S.S.* 36: 190; *C.W.* 27: 259). To reach this goal, the most advanced managerial techniques of capitalism had to be adopted. Even the practices of Taylorism, which Lenin described as 'the last word of capitalism', had to be utilized. For 'its greatest scientific achievements [lie] in the field of analysing mechanical motions during work, in the elimination of superfluous and awkward motions, in the working out of correct methods of work, and in the introduction of the best system of accounting and control etc' (*P.S.S.* 36: 189–90; *C.W.* 27: 259). Lenin called for combining Soviet rule with the 'latest progressive measures of capitalism' and the Soviet government, he said, 'must introduce in Russia the study and teaching of the Taylor system and its systematic trial and adoption'. Lenin stressed the importance of work and absolutely condemned idleness. He put in one category 'the rich, the swindlers, the idlers and the rowdies' whom he dubbed as the 'dregs of humanity . . . [like] an ulcer inherited from capitalism' (*P.S.S.* 35: 200; *S.W.* 2: 515), and he strongly condemned 'slovenliness, carelessness, untidiness, unpunctuality, nervous haste, the inclination to substitute discussion for action and talk for work . . .'. The Bolshevik leadership also deplored immediate and unrestrained sexual fulfilment,[6] which is another aspect of the desired psychological predisposition of deferred gratification necessary for development. These quotations from Lenin are sufficient to make the point that the nature of the industrial order which the Bolsheviks wanted to build had many of the features of advanced capitalism existing in the west; the ideology is quite hostile to anarchist and populist thought, which is anti-industrial and has developed as a protest against industrialism as much as against capitalism. Its emphasis in favour of industrial development also sets it aside from social democracy of the British Labour Party type which, in theory, emphasizes more humane concerns and social equality.

The third element I described as being part of Lenin's theory of social change was his views on organization. In his first major work on political strategy, *What is to be done?*, Lenin had formulated his concepts of democratic centralism. Party organization represented for Lenin rational decision-making, which ensured that decisions would be correct and arrived at in an efficient and business-like manner. This was not unlike the ways in which he later conceived of how other organizations should be run. Hence he strongly opposed decentralized and localized forms of power. In *State and Revolution* he makes clear that 'Revolution consists in the proletariat destroying the "administrative apparatus" and the *whole* state machine . . .', but he emphasized that, during the 'dictatorship of the proletariat', the state itself would continue, and the old state machine would be replaced 'by a new one, made up of the armed workers'. Revolution consists of the new class 'commanding and governing with the aid of a *new* machine'. When discussing large-scale industry, Lenin points out that 'The technics of all these enterprises makes absolutely imperative the strictest discipline, the utmost precision on the part of everyone in carrying out his allotted task, for otherwise the whole enterprise may come to a stop, or machinery or the finished product may be damaged' (*P.S.S.* 33:109; *S.W.* 2: 351). A parallel may be drawn between Lenin's views on capitalism and bureaucracy on the one hand and industrialism and management on the other. While Lenin opposed bureaucracy because of its oppressive class character, management he regarded as necessary in an industrial system, and capitalism, he believed, had devised advanced forms of organization. He likens a socialist economic system to the postal service: 'once we have overthrown the capitalists . . . and smashed the bureaucratic machine of the modern state . . . we shall have a splendidly equipped mechanism which can very well be set going by the united workers themselves . . . Our immediate aim is to organise the whole economy on the lines of the postal service so that the technicians, foremen and accountants, as well as all officials, shall receive salaries no higher than "a working-man's wages", and under the control and leadership of the armed proletariat' (*P.S.S.* 33: 50; *S.W.* 2: 304). In other words, with the abolition of class interests (presided over by the working class) the regular organization of things would begin to replace coercion and manipulation of people.

Centralized direction and control were not, in Lenin's view, authoritarian and dictatorial. He strongly advocated direct participation by the masses in administration. He saw socialism as an economic and moral form of society superior to capitalism and he also subscribed to idealistic, participatory, and egalitarian values.[7] The revolution would eliminate antagonism between classes and the state would begin to 'wither away'.

'Under socialism much of "primitive" democracy will inevitably be revived, since, for the first time in the history of civilised society, the *mass* of the population will rise to taking an *independent* part, not only in voting and elections, but *also in the everyday administration of the state*. Under socialism *all* will govern in turn and will soon become accustomed to no one governing' (*P.S.S.* 33: 116; *S.W.* 2: 357).[8]

To prevent the rise of a bureaucratic class he also advocated that the pay of officials should not 'exceed that of a workman' (*P.S.S.* 33: 109; *S.W.* 2: 351) and such views have played an important role in giving the early Soviet system an image of equalitarianism.

Adam Ulam has emphasized this anarchistic component in Leninism and has argued that the appeal of Marxism in countries at a low level of development is due to 'the essentially anarchist character' of its protest against capitalism (1955: 28). Lenin, however, at all points very carefully modifies his utopian goals for practical policy purposes. Early after the Revolution, the Party Programme of 1919 pointed out that 'while aspiring to equality of remuneration for all kinds of labour and to total communism, the Soviet government cannot consider as its task the immediate realization of this equality at the present moment when only the first steps are being made towards the transition from capitalism to communism' (*K.P.S.S.* 1953: 423). Also, in practice, the withering away of the state would be a protracted process of unknown length (*P.S.S.* 33: 96; *S.W.* 2: 340), and during the period following the revolution the need for 'subordination and control' (*P.S.S.* 33: 49; *S.W.* 2: 303) would continue. Indeed, in contradistinction to the anarchists, Lenin had always emphasized participation in a framework of central control and subordination of lower bodies to higher ones. The contradiction in Lenin's thought was between what was practical and necessary, given various forms of political and social constraints, and what was desirable and possible under ideal conditions.

To discuss the way in which the stock of Lenin's ideas was turned into an ideology of normative power designed to legitimate the Soviet form of industrialization and industrialism that occurred under Stalin would require a very detailed analysis. In general terms, the evolution of Leninism as an ideology may well be illustrated by reference to Weber's principle of 'elective affinity' (1948: 62–3), which helps to show why many of Lenin's ideas became wedded to the developmental interests of Soviet Russia's political elite; for there can be no doubt that Leninism provided a set of goals, beliefs, and institutional practices which legitimated the Soviet development process and those who directed it. In short, Leninism is the developmental ethic of Marxism. It harnessed the revolutionary potential of Marxism for planned industrial growth as well as for revolutionary change, and, in doing so, it sanctified the rise of a political elite that was able to channel economic surplus from workers and peasants to large-scale industrial development. Stalin defined Leninism as 'Marxism in the epoch of imperialism and of the proletarian revolution . . . Leninism is the theory and tactics of the dictatorship of the proletariat in particular' (1934a: 10). The Soviet Union has not followed a capitalist[9] path of growth in an economic sense and has been successful in sponsoring all-round economic development and rapid urbanization. Let me now illustrate how some of Lenin's ideas have been routinized into the doctrine of Leninism.

First, the theory of imperialism helped to legitimate the building of socialism in one country, but the form the Soviet industrial and political system has taken has departed considerably from Lenin's original views. While Lenin emphasized that one country should *begin* to build socialism, and he heartily supported attempts to create the conditions for building socialism in backward countries (*P.S.S.* 45: 378–80; *C.W.* 33: 477), he did not envisage, as does the doctrine of Leninism, that socialism could be *completed* in one country. While the component of imperialism has undoubtedly acted as a rallying cry for colonialist and ex-colonialist countries, Lenin did not envisage a situation in which the Soviet form of the dictatorship of the proletariat would be regarded as the 'international doctrine of the proletarians of all lands [which) is suitable and obligatory for all countries without exception, including those where capitalism is developed' (Stalin 1934b: 104). While Lenin identified an important cleavage between developed and underdeveloped countries, he also pointed to the world proletariat as the prime revolutionary force, as epitomized in the slogan: 'Workers of the world unite!'. In both Stalin's *Foundations of Leninism* and *Problems of Leninism* very little attention is given to this task and the emphasis is shifted to the importance of completing the construction of socialism in one country. With the passage of time, emphasis has moved from the world proletariat to the national liberation movements. These changes in stress are clearly linked to the changing international status and policy interests of the Soviet government.

A second proposition I made was that Lenin's thought combined both centralization of authority and direct participation in making decisions. The centralized forms of state and party administration have played an important part in reallocating resources and thereby reducing regional inequalities: the secession of national minorities has been prevented and economic growth has been widely distributed over the USSR to the benefit of the more backward regions. But democratic centralism has been utilized to mobilize people into an industrial society rather than being used as a mechanism to ensure rationality in the sense of the expression of class consciousness. Voting at elections, for instance, instead of being a method of popular recall and control has become both a kind of audience participation and an expressive mechanism indicating loyalty to the Soviet order. Participation in the economic planning procedure through various forms of meetings and discussions, although often ritualistic, is important from a mobilizing and symbolic point of view. Such activities communicate and identify the masses with specific goals. They are not, however, 'socialist' in the way desired by Lenin, and the USSR has failed to produce any really advanced forms of direct administration by the masses.

A similar change has taken place in the sphere of the division of material rewards. Lenin had a genuine belief that, with time, and under a system of central planning, people would work for altruistic reasons, and monetary incentives and material inequality would, like the state, wither away. During the Soviet process of rapid industrialization, however, income differentials were introduced, not merely as a matter of expediency, but as something necessary to promote efficient industrial production and egalitarianism was opposed *in principle* by Stalin. Hence Marxism–Leninism, as developed in the Soviet Union after Lenin's death, has been an ideology in which the construction of socialism is almost synonymous with industrialization. In the *Fundamentals of Marxism–Leninism* it is pointed out that

'Socialist industrialisation is the development of large-scale industry, and primarily heavy industry, to a level where it becomes the key to the reorganisation of the entire national economy on the basis of an advanced machine technology, it ensures the victory of socialism and strengthens the country's technical and economic independence and defence capacity in face of the capitalist world' (Kuusinen 1961:688).

Soviet Marxism–Leninism, therefore, provides an ideology that justifies industrialization on a large scale. Centralization, nationalization, state control, and an adamant belief in the virtues of modern technology are fundamental characteristics of the model that has been devised.

The challenge to other developing countries, which have rejected the capitalist form of industrialization, is whether they can combine forms of state ownership and control, facilitating rapid economic growth, with Lenin's concern for more direct forms of political participation and for greater social equality. Both Lenin and Stalin used as a point of reference the organizational model of what they believed was the most advanced form of capitalism in the west; and the value pattern of 'instrumental activism' is also similar to that of advanced capitalist countries. Hence it is not surprising that, as the Soviet Union has matured as an industrial state, it has appeared to 'converge' in many respects with industrial practices under capitalism. This paper has shown that this may originate in the values of the Soviet system, which became wedded to the interests of her rulers in a way unintended by, but derived from, Lenin. From a comparative sociological point of view, the experience of other socialist societies may help to show whether a policy of industrialization without capitalism may be combined with greater direct participation and equality than has been the case in the USSR, or whether the efficient organization of an industrial system, as such, requires symbolic ritualistic forms of political mobilization, a hierarchy of status, and unequal material rewards.[10]

Notes

1 Daniel Bell (1958), for instance, in his survey of theories of Soviet society does not mention any developmental theory, although Alex Inkeles (1966: 3–17), Alec Nove (1961: 29–38), and W. Donald Bowles (1962: 483–504) have written introductory articles on the subject. Irving L. Horowitz attempts to cast Soviet experience in a comparative developmental mould. While he identifies many salient features of Soviet industrialization, his emphasis is heavily political and he does not, in fact, describe the underlying assumptions of the Soviet leaders' strategy:

> 'The Soviet assertion and insistence on the monolithic appearance of socialist politics, particularly as this developed under Stalin, was a response to the absence of genuine theory, and inability to make useful generalizations concerning strategies for social development.' (1966: 135)

He sees the Soviet industrialization process as a choice between 'two types of Marxism, one humanistic but without power, the other authoritarian and with great power'. Also of note is a book by John Kautsky (1962: 70) who has tried to fit the 'Russian revolution into the broad historical pattern of the nationalist revolutions in underdeveloped countries'. In addition, there are a number of studies of economic aspects of Soviet growth: Wilber (1969), Nove and Newth (1967), and Dobb (1963).

2 *Polnoe sobranie sochinenii (P.S.S.)* (1958–70), translated into English in *Collected Works (C.W.)* (1960–70), and *Selected Works (S.W.)* (1963–4). References are to volume number and page number.

3 Marx (1958: 9) cited in Lenin (*P.S.S.* 3: 601; *S.W.* 3: 599).

4 Lenin did not explicitly write this because of the restraints of the censorship. But the political implications are clear. See the Preface to the 1917 edition of *Imperialism, the Highest Stage of Capitalism (P.S.S.*

vol. 27 *S.W.* vol. 1), where Lenin refers to the Tsarist censorship and the need to make the book theoretical and economic. In 1923 Lenin explicitly justified revolution in the 'countries of the East' even when 'the conditions were not quite the usual ones' (*P.S.S.* 45: 379–80; *C. W.* 33: 477–8).

5 Soviet writers are ambiguous on this point. They see the world socialist system as the chief gain of the international revolutionary movement. While they advocate the setting-up of states on this model, they also support the national liberation movements by which a greater degree of national independence from the imperialist powers may be achieved. A *national* bourgeoisie, the peasantry, and the army, may play a decisive role. See C.P.S.U. (n.d.: 31–35); T. A. Yakimova (1968: 56–74).

6 As a writer in *Izvestiya* put it in 1925, 'Drown your sexual energy in public work. . . . If you want to solve your sexual problem, be a public worker, be a comrade, not a stallion or a brood mare' (cited in Carr, 1958: 33–4).

7 Lenin's ideals and his faith in the masses are often ignored in western writings on Lenin. See Barfield (1971: 45–56).

8 *In the Immediate Tasks of Soviet Power* (28 April, 1918) Lenin defines one of the principal characteristics of proletarian democracy as 'the people themselves determine the order and time of elections and are completely free to recall any elected person' (*P.S.S.* 36: 203; *C.W.* 27: 272).

9 'Capitalist' in the sense of private ownership of the means of production, profit maximization, and a market determining prices and the allocation of resources.

10 I am grateful to John Barber of Jesus College, Cambridge, Michael Mann, and Colin Bell for helpful suggestions.

References

BARFIELD, R. 1971. Lenin's Utopianism: State and Revolution. *Slavic Review* **30** (1).

BELL, D. 1958. Ten Theories in Search of Reality. *World Politics* **10** (2).

BOWLES, W. D. 1962. Soviet Russia as a Model for Underdeveloped Areas. *World Politics* **14** (3).

CARR, E. H. 1958. *A History of Soviet Russia.* Vol. 5. *Socialism in One Country.* (Part One) London: Macmillan.

C.P.S.U., n.d. *The Programme of the Communist Party of the Soviet Union.* London: Soviet Booklet No. 83.

DOBB, M. 1963. *Economic Growth and Underdeveloped Countries*. London: Lawrence and Wishart.

HOROWITZ, L. 1966. *Three Worlds of Development*. New York: Oxford University Press.

INKELES, A. 1966. Models in the Analysis of Soviet Society. *Survey* No. 60.

KAUTSKY, J. 1962. *Political Change in Underdeveloped Countries: Nationalism and Communism*. New York: John Wiley.

K.P.S.S. 1953. *KPSS v rezolyutsiyakh i resheniyakh s'ezdov konferentsiy i plenumov TsK*. Moscow: Gospolitizdat.

KUUSINEN (ed.) 1961. *Fundamentals of Marxism*. Moscow: Foreign Languages Publishing House.

LENIN, V. I. P.S.S./C.W. *Polnoe sobranie sochinenii* (Russian Fifth Edition. Moscow, 1958–1970)/*Collected Works* (English Edition. Moscow: Progress, 1960–70).

—— P.S.S. Vol. 3/C.W. Vol. 3.: Razvitie kapitalizma v Rossi (The Development of Capitalism in Russia).

—— P.S.S. Vol. 36/C.W. Vol. 27: Ocherednye zadachi Sovetskoy vlasti (The Immediate Tasks of Soviet Power).

—— P.S.S. Vol. 42a/C.W. Vol. 31a.: Nashe vneshnee i vnutrennee polozhenie i zadachi partii (Our Foreign and Domestic Position and the Tasks of the Party).

—— P.S.S. Vol. 42b/C.W. Vol. 31b.: Doklad vserossiyskogo tsentral'nogo ispolnitel'nogo komiteta i soveta narodnykh kommisarov o vneshey i vnutrenney politikc 22 Dek. (Report on the Work of the Council of People's Commissars December 1922).

—— P.S.S. Vol. 45/C.W. vol. 33.: O nashey revolyutsii (Our Revolution).

LENIN, V. I. P.S.S./S.W. *Polnoe sobranie sochinenii* (1958–70)/*Selected Works*. (Moscow: Progress 1963–4).

—— P.S.S. Vol. 27/S.W. Vol. 1.: 'Imperializm, kak vysshaya stadiya kapitalizma' (Imperialism, the Highest Stage of Capitalism).

—— P.S.S. Vol. 35/S.W. Vol. 2.: Kak organizovat' sorevnovanie? (How to Organise Competition?).

—— P.S.S. Vol. 33/S.W. Vol. 2.: Gosudarstvo i revolyutsia (The State and Revolution).

LERNER, D. 1968. Modernisation. *International Encyclopedia of Social Sciences*. Vol. 10. New York: Macmillan and Free Press.

LIPSET, S. M. 1964. *The First New Nation*. London: Heinemann.

MARCUSE, H. 1958. *Soviet Marxism*. London: Routledge & Kegan Paul.

MARX, K. 1958. *Capital*. Moscow: Foreign Languages Publishing House.

NOVE, A. 1961. The Soviet Model and Underdeveloped Countries. *International Affairs* **37** (1).

NOVE, A. and NEWTH, J. A. 1967. *The Soviet Middle East: A Communist Model of Development*. London: George Allen and Unwin.

PARSONS, T. 1971. *The System of Modern Societies*. Englewood Cliffs, New Jersey: Prentice Hall.

ROSTOW, W. W. 1960. *The Stages of Economic Growth: A Non-communist Manifesto*. London: Cambridge University Press.

STALIN, J. V. 1934a. *Foundations of Leninism*. Moscow: Cooperative Publishing Society of Foreign Workers in the USSR.

—— 1934b, *Problems of Leninism*. Moscow: Cooperative Publishing Society of Foreign Workers in the USSR.

ULAM, A. 1955. The Historical Role of Marxism and the Soviet System. *World Politics* 8 (1).

WEBER, M. 1948. *From Max Weber: Essays in Sociology* (Edited by H. H. Gerth and C. Wright Mills). London: Routledge and Kegan Paul.

WILBER, C. K. 1969. *The Soviet Model and Underdevelopment*. Chapel Hill: University of North Carolina Press.

YAKIMOVA, T. A. 1968. *Nekapitalisticheski put' razvitiya ranee otstalykh stran*. Moscow.

JACK GRAY

Mao Tse-Tung's Strategy for the Collectivization of Chinese Agriculture: an Important Phase in the Development of Maoism

INTRODUCTION

In a previous essay (Gray 1969) I have suggested that Mao's ideas concerning economic growth included the following cardinal points:

1. Economic growth is, to Mao, an important end in itself; much of his social and political theory, which appears at first sight to militate against rapid economic growth, is, in fact, designed to secure it.

2. In seeking growth, Mao stresses:

(a) that production must take priority over procurement;

(b) that material incentives are of decisive importance in the successful inducement of economic and social change;

(c) that rapid economic growth must depend to a considerable extent on the fostering of entrepreneurial abilities, albeit in a context of collectivized communities, such as, the ability to innovate, foresight, and willingness to take risks. Growth cannot wholly depend upon bureaucratic decision-makers at the higher levels.

3. Adverse social and psychological attitudes are the major obstacles to rapid economic growth, rather than are the scarcity of resources or capital. The primary problem is to make the community aware of the possibilities of modern technology and social organization and to provide them with an education, through participation, in these possibilities.

4. Finally, and more specifically, Mao sees China's vast and underemployed population as China's 'greatest resource' – the chief source of capital. Labour-intensive development, especially in the rural areas, is the keystone of his economic policies.

In a further analysis (Gray 1972) I have suggested that Mao does not accept that economic scarcities are the only, or the decisive factor in economic growth; but rather that the problems are largely social and psychological and that solutions must, therefore, be sociological as well as economic, sought through a process of radicalizing economic ideas, parallel to the processes of political radicalization.

At the beginning of 1956, in the course of the last stage of the co-operativization of agriculture in China, a three-volume collection of descriptive and analytical accounts of existing agricultural co-operatives was published, with a preface and editorial comments by Mao Tse-Tung himself, under the title of *The High Tide of Socialism in the Chinese Countryside*.[1] Most of the accounts were articles reprinted from the rural press, or reports by cadres engaged in the movement at *hsien*[2] level and below (usually below), written mainly in 1955, but containing a few items of earlier date from 1954. This collection was Mao's answer to those members of the Chinese Communist Party who opposed the rapid co-operativization of agriculture.

The collection is therefore propaganda. But it is more than this because the criterion of choice of the items included is quite clearly not that of the co-operative described being an outstanding success, although it is obvious that the selection represents a level of achievement higher than the average at that time. The basis of choice was that this co-opera-tive had solved one problem involved in the establishment and consolida-tion of the Agricultural Producers' Co-operatives (APC),[3] with the implication that a problem that could be solved in one village in China was capable of solution everywhere. The solutions are by no means standardized. In one thousand, three hundred and twenty pages packed with facts, it provides an incomparable view of the problems, practical and ideological, of the organization of agriculture, as interpreted by Mao Tse-Tung; and therefore also provides an insight into Mao's economic ideas at that time, as applied to the countryside.

At the same time, the material is too unsystematically presented to permit any statistical treatment. The function of the *High Tide* was to spur to action; not to explain, but to inspire. Functionally, it attempts the creation of a myth. Such a myth may be based fully upon reality, or it could be made up out of whole cloth; but even in the latter case, if the myth became a datum of decision-making in China, then it cannot be ignored. If it became a part of the furniture of the minds of Mao Tse-Tung and his supporters, then its spiritual force (as Mao might say) became a material force, for good or ill. This paper, however, will seek to show that the myth is at least a plausible one, certainly a fascinating one, and possibly one of those myths that, although it may not represent the whole truth about social change and economic growth in China, may express some vital half-truths.

The situation in 1955 was critical, both economically and politically. Economically the position was dominated by the sharp increase in the spring in the amount of grain that had to be marketed in the rural areas and thus, having been returned to grain-deficient peasants and grain-deficient villages, represented a net loss to the stock of grain available to feed the urban population and the armed forces. The attempt to deal with this situation by administrative means fell foul of the ambivalent attitudes of the village cadres – party members on the one hand, village farmers on the other (Bernstein 1969).

The speed-up of the co-operativization of agriculture was almost certainly, in part, a response to this situation. The essential nature of that response, as we shall see, was an insistence that the grain-deficient villages could increase their production to become self-sufficient in grain. This, rather than the increase of procurement demands generally, or a politically dangerous and administratively difficult inquisition into the actual needs of a hundred-million peasant families, was Mao's solution. The framework for the drive to self-sufficiency was the APC. Although the village that increased production, and was, therefore, able to sell more to the state, *is* highly praised, the warmest tributes in the *High Tide* go to the deficient villages that reached self-sufficiency.

There were, of course, other factors involved in the speed-up of collectivization. It was a widely (although not in China a universally) held assumption that the first attempt at a planned economy would demand the fullest possible control of production, in agriculture as well as in industry. There were also fears of a re-polarization of the Chinese village, in the wake of land reform, which had left a system of peasant proprietorship still involving substantial, although much reduced, inequalities. The most urgent problem, however, was that of the grain-deficient village.

Experience of the collectivized agriculture of the Soviet Union leads us, in looking at any other collectivist agricultural system, to ask whether the primary purpose of the organization of agriculture was to make possible the exaction of a greater surplus from existing production (or the exaction of the surplus at cheaper rates), or to make possible increases of production and only then to increase the absolute quantities exacted. In no case can there be a clear answer; even in the Soviet Union, efforts to increase production were made. In China, on the other hand, the direct dependence of the health of industry upon the vagaries of the harvest in a precarious climate might lead to frequent, and perhaps sometimes counterproductive, procurement pressures in one region or another.

The *High Tide* formula, however, is very clear: the purpose of the organization of agriculture is to increase production. The evidence of this is so ample as to make it unnecessary to give detailed references. In virtually every one of these descriptions of co-operatives, involving discussion of organization, distribution, techniques, accounting, and problems of incentives, the practical aim is the increase of production.

Politically, throughout the communist world, collective agriculture had been discredited, and its supporters were on the defensive. It had been dismantled in Yugoslavia, it was disintegrating in Poland, and in most of the rest of eastern Europe it had stalled far short of full implementation. The controversy in China must be seen against this background. By early 1955, only about 14 per cent of China's rural population were in co-operatives. There was still time to stop the movement before widespread implementation committed the Party to a *fait accompli*. However, in China there was a strong argument against quick collectivization which was absent elsewhere; in China's poor and under-employed rural society, the mechanization of agriculture, which was a principal argument for the creation of large-scale farms elsewhere, was largely irrelevant; and at China's existing level of industrialization, rapid mechanization was impossible even if it had been desirable.

Formally, the controversy in China was over the speed of collectivization and not over the principle; but against this background it is likely that, had collectivization been slowed up at this stage, it would never have taken place at all; and both sides in China must have been well aware that this was what was at stake.

Mao's insistence on the rapid completion of the organization of agriculture in China was, therefore, not only in opposition to important elements in his own party, but went against the current tendencies in the rest of the communist bloc. His orthodox belief in collectivization was by then, in fact, a sort of heresy.

There was nothing orthodox in the economic implications of Mao's form of collectivization. This was collectivization *before* mechanization. What arguments justified this? The lines of argument will emerge from a study of the *High Tide* materials. At this point, we will merely draw attention to the basic assumption, which was that the initial stages of increased production, increased incomes, and capital accumulation in agriculture, could be achieved by the rational use of existing labour, organized co-operatively on the village scale, partly in more intensive cultivation, but also for labour-intensive construction and the diversification of the rural economy. Mao's collectives were, from the beginning, community development projects rather than merely being enlarged farms; and the Great Leap Forward and the Communes were, one might say, implicit in them from the beginning.

Nurkse's classical statement of 'The Saving Potential Concealed in Rural Underemployment' was published in 1958 – the year of the Communes. But Mao Tse-tung had already begun to act on assumptions similar to those of Nurkse in 1955. Nurkse's argument may be summarized as follows:

> 'The "unproductive" surplus labourers on the land are sustained by the "productive" labourers . . . The productive labourers are performing "virtual" saving . . . But . . . it is offset by the unproductive consumption of the people who could be dispensed with . . . If the productive peasants were to send their useless dependents . . . to work on capital projects and if they continued to feed them there, their virtual saving would become effective saving . . .
>
> All that happens is a re-allocation of labour in favour of capital construction. There is in principle no necessity for either group of people to tighten their belts . . . Mobilization of the concealed saving potential . . . will be incomplete if the remaining peasants cannot be stopped from eating more than before . . . A food deficit may also arise if the investment workers . . . have to eat a little more than before . . . or because they need to be given an inducement to leave the farms . . . Moreover a leakage arises through the cost of transporting food from the farms to the places where capital projects are established. This particular leakage can be reduced by scattering the projects in rural areas . . . In these circumstances the formation of capital through the use of surplus labour is self-financing only if the mobilization of the concealed saving potential is 100 per cent successful . . . It seems to be a question of all or nothing . . . On reflection, however, it will be seen that the surplus labour can still be employed for capital formation if some complementary saving can be secured from outside the system.'

Nurkse then comments on the multiplier effect of inputs of such supplementary capital from outside. In his notional example, which is, however, a reasonable one, the overall saving ratio could be increased by this means from 4 per cent to 17 per cent of national income.

'In practice, however, it may be extremely difficult to get the necessary complementary saving from domestic sources . . . All this points to the need for preventing the leakages or holding them down to an absolute minimum . . .

The peasants are not likely to save the surplus voluntarily . . . and peasants are notoriously hard to tax . . . Taxation in kind may be attempted, or some form of requisitioning and controlled deliveries . . . Whatever the machinery employed may be, some form of saving enforced by the state may prove to be indispensable for the mobilization of the saving potential . . .

In the analytical scheme we have used so far in this chapter, there is theoretically no need for anyone to cut down his consumption below the original level. Yet it is a harsh and austere programme . . .

It is well to bear in mind that by far the greater part of a country's real capital structure consists of objects that require local labour and local materials . . .

A tremendous need for capital investment in agriculture . . . exists and must sooner or later be met; but this does not exclude the possibility of there being some immediate scope for organisational reforms that would release a certain quantity of simple tools which the investment workers could take with them and use . . .'

Nurkse anticipates the main objections to his theory:

'Some economists maintain that disguised unemployment on the land is only a seasonal phenomenon . . . This is undoubtedly true in some countries . . . (Even so) the question of making productive use of it still arises.'

In the light of this statement of the theoretical case for using the rural underemployed as a substitute for capital, let us look at the evolution of Mao's economic ideas, and in particular at the economic ideas underlying the speed-up of collectivization in 1955–6.

First, however, although it is no part of the purpose of this article to examine precisely and in detail the possibilities that Chinese rural society offered for the exploitation of surplus labour, it is at least necessary to establish generally the fact that some such possibilities existed. The obvious source is Buck's *Land Utilisation in China* (1964).

'The amount of man labour in China is almost unlimited and one of the great problems is the discovery of enough productive work to keep this vast human army profitably employed . . . Farm work occupies the full time of only a little over two thirds of the farm population . . . The availability of subsidiary work is an important consideration in a country like China where farms are so small and supplementary income to farming is necessary . . . The proportion of able-bodied men, over 15 and under 60 years of age, engaged in full time work was only 35% . . . Idleness averaged 1·7 months per able-bodied man . . . The winter months . . . are responsible for 80% of the idle time.'

As Buck's sample under-represents the poorer end of the Chinese rural economic spectrum, this can be taken as, if anything, an underestimate of underemployment. More important, the existence of surplus labour in a system in which the family was the economic unit does not encourage a high rate of labour utilization; Buck's figures in fact do not reveal the major part of the surplus, which is concealed by the sharing-out of existing jobs, familiar to anyone who has lived in a Chinese society. The months of full idleness are only the tip of the iceberg; the rest is impossible to measure. Finally, in the winter months, farmers in China, even more than farmers elsewhere, have to invent jobs to fill their time. Buck's figure of an average of about 1·7 months of idleness in the four winter months is thus misleading, at least for north China, and probably even for the south. Most winter labour in these conditions is unproductive labour, or nearly so.

In fact, the only real measurement of underemployment in China is the measure of what that labour has performed when fully utilized. Mao's labour-intensive construction cannot be pre-judged on the pre-1949 figures. Even these inadequate figures, however, show that a very considerable potential existed in China.

The three volumes of the *High Tide* collection are introduced by a preface by Mao himself. The preface reveals that the origins of the collection lay in the documents put before the Enlarged Plenum of the 6th meeting of the 7th Central Committee, actually before a Central Committee swamped by enthusiasts from the grassroots. (This was Mao's first use of 'public opinion' to disarm his opponents in the Party leadership.) In the intervening months (his preface is dated 27 December, 1955) the proportion of peasants in APCs had risen to over 60 per cent of the farming population. Mao looked forward to complete organization at the lower APC level by the end of 1956, and

complete collectivization by 1959 or 1960. His strategy for collectivization was largely economic. It was based upon his belief that the best
pre-war yields could be doubled 'or even trebled' *in the course of* the
collectivization process.

In a note concerning the employment of women in a cotton-growing
APC in Chekiang (cotton being the most labour-intensive of all China's
major crops), Mao takes up the central question of whether or not the
collectivization of agriculture would merely exacerbate the labour
surplus. His argument was, in brief, as follows:

'Before the organisation of agriculture, many parts of the country
had a surplus of labour; since the development of the co-operatives,
many of them are now conscious of an acute shortage of labour, so
that (as in the case of this particular Chekiang APC) it has become
necessary to use the labour of women members fully. This is contrary
to what many people anticipated. In the past it was widely believed that
the APCs would intensify the problem of surplus labour. Actual conditions have disproved this. If some APCs still have a surplus, this is
because they have not yet broadened the scale and content of their
production or used their labour in a sufficiently intensive way. This
process is only in its infancy, and will go on indefinitely; agricultural
productivity will be multiplied, beyond what at present can be
imagined. Industrial development will be even further beyond our
power to imagine; and science, culture, education, public health, etc.
will have a comparable development.'

This may be taken as his fundamental argument.

The first APC described, Wang Kuo-fan's APC in Hopei Zunhua
hsien, was clearly meant to stand as the symbol of the possibilities of the
APC, not because it was typical – indeed it was the extreme case of
poverty, lack of capital, and lack of resources – but for that very reason,
because it provides an *a fortiori* argument for the possibilities of
organized labour. If Wang Kuo-fan's APC could make so much of
so little, how much more could be done in places better endowed
with resources and capital. This is collectivized labour at its most
heroic.

Wang's village was one of 154 households deep in the forests, so poor
that the state had to provide over 50,000 *catties*[4] of relief grain. It, therefore, represented the most urgent problem that the rapid organization of
agriculture was meant to solve – that of the grain-deficient village. When
the collectivization movement began in 1952, Wang, a member of the

village Party branch, persuaded twenty-two other households to form a co-operative, with 230 *mou*[5] of land, three starving donkeys, and not a single cart in which to transport manure; the middle-peasant members of the pre-existing Mutual-aid Team refused to join the new APC. The problem was how to find and feed animals and buy tools. Wang insisted that the society was too poor to incur debts, even from the state. He proposed that the members should raise capital by cutting fuel on the hillsides and selling it. The wives remained to spread the winter manure, while seventeen men trekked to the next *hsien* to cut fuel. In three weeks they earned $430[6] with which they bought an ox, a cart, a few sheep, and some small tools. But they still had to get through the spring dearth.

They went back to the mountains again, and raised another $210 which provided food for the two poorest families and some fodder for the animals; and with this supplementation, and by sharing their grain, they lasted out the spring. They gathered together all the sweet-potato seed available, dug a forcing pit, and raised seedlings, getting an early crop and raising $500 by selling their surplus. Meanwhile, by more intensive cultivation they succeeded in getting a harvest 60 per cent greater than they had as a group achieved before. Out of this, they were able to buy further beasts and tools, giving them common property worth $2 400. As a result of this success, more families, including more prosperous families, joined the APC, increasing its acreage to 500 *mou*. The beasts and equipment of the more prosperous members were, at Wang's insistence, hired but not bought, again in order to save the cost of loans, and Wang showed that hire charges would be profitable to the owners if the beasts and tools were fully used, not just in normal production, but in soil improvement and agricultural construction. Wang also insisted on continuing to use surplus labour to collect fuel, as a means of increasing savings without investing capital. The APC members collected enough firewood to buy three more oxen. In the event, out of the subsequent year's production, they were also able to buy two donkeys and two rubber-tyred carts, fodder, and fertilizers.

By the end of three years, the APC had grown to 140 households with twelve oxen, of which seven were bred on the farm, five carts, a flock of 100 sheep, altogether $6 000 of common property, 600 *mou* of orchard, 1 000 *mou* of new timber planting, and over a quarter of a million willow trees on the river bank, all representing newly-created wealth.

For the purpose of the present argument, it does not matter too much if the achievements of Wang Kuo-fan's APC may have been somewhat exaggerated; the account of these achievements is not given in a form that would permit a critical analysis of its operations. Our present interest in it is that it dramatically expresses Mao's ideas of the possibilities of organized farming. In this respect, the following points should be noted: first, the group of poor peasants concerned had no savings whatever; they were in heavy deficit, dependent on relief. Second, they were grossly underemployed. Third, they therefore used their surplus labour to accumulate savings through work which required no capital whatsoever, other than available sickles and carrying poles; and by this means were able to get through the dearth and buy some simple capital equipment for the improvement of their farming. Fourth, their new resources, along with their surplus labour, were invested immediately in soil improvement and agricultural construction, and in the diversification of their economy into forestry, fruit-growing, sheep-raising, and the growing of willows to provide raw materials for handicraft occupation. Fifth, the originator of this successful co-operation was an individual of foresight, who persuaded his fellows to forego present consumption and short-term casual economic opportunities, in order to invest in co-operative enterprise, and provided a suitable means – the collection of fuel – to raise the necessary capital. Wang Kuo-fan was, in short, an entrepreneuer. Sixth, the Wang Kuo-fan APC not only increased production, ceased to be a deficit village, and accumulated capital at a very rapid rate, but also raised the incomes of its members substantially in so doing. Seventh, the ability of the original group to enlarge itself by the adherence of other households of the village, until it embraced 90 per cent of the population, is represented as the consequence of the APC's proved ability to provide better incomes than individual farming could in local circumstances. The implied argument is not concerned with ideology, but with the offer and demonstration of material incentives.

The rest of the *High Tide* is largely an elaboration of these points. Although its chief concern is with methods of securing the collectivization of agriculture, its content is very largely economic. Of forty-six headings in its subject index, twenty-six are explicitly concerned with economic matters; not only this, but the prescriptions for political leadership with which the other twenty headings are concerned are for the most part related to the best means of maximizing the communication of these economic ideas and of the economic organization – down to every detail – in order to make them good.

THE PRODUCTION PLANS OF THE APCS

The planning of production was an essential feature of the development of an APC, and the *High Tide* contains much material on such planning, including both the content of the plans and the methods of planning. Three relatively long-term plans for APCs in different provinces may serve as an introduction to the details of Mao's economic strategy in relation to co-operative agriculture at this time.

(1) Huang Ning hsien, Kwangtung, the Red Star APC

This is a convenient first example because it is explicitly based upon a stated surplus of labour. In this APC of 120 households in a semi-mountain area, there was only 0·7 *mou* of arable land per head, the total number of labour units (including part-time women's labour) was 233·5. Each of the 325 *mou* of land required forty labour days, a total of 13 000. Work in the 650 *mou* bamboo plantation took a further 3 000, and 2 200 were required for the accumulation of manure: total, 18 200. Assuming that the labour force worked for eight months in the year, however, there would be 49 440 labour days available. The problem was how to use this surplus of labour, in the first place to overcome the regular dearth in spring and summer suffered by almost 100 of the 120 families.

The first means of productively absorbing labour was its more intensive use on the existing arable land. This is a real possibility, which many observers of China ignore.

Probably the most valuable of such uses is the collection of greater quantities of organic material suitable for fertilizers; supplies of rotting or rottable organic material, which can add humus and plant nutrients, are usually available or creatable and their total cost is often only the cost of their transport to the fields.

Also important is increased frequency of tillage with hoe and rake, or their mechanized equivalents. Full aeration of the soil can in itself release existing nutrients as well as improving root action, and perhaps (although this is controversial) improve the soil's capacity to retain water. Tillage is manure, Jethro Tull said, and modern experiments have proved him correct.

Increased labour in the removal of weeds can by itself raise crop yields substantially, and the constant turning in of small weeds provides a significant quantity of assimilable nutrients.

Closer planting is possible, up to the limit where the crowding of plants would deprive them of water at the root, and air and light at the foliage. This had already been advocated in China since the 1930s. The main determinant of planting distances in capital-intensive farming is often the convenience of the machine; but if labour is very plentiful for hand cultivation, many kinds of plants can be placed much closer together; and in so far as the increased demand for water and manure can also be met by more intensive labour, there is a real possibility of substantially increased yields by closer planting. All these methods were used in this APC.

The second method was the diversification of field crops, to include spring wheat and beans, oil-bearing plants, and melons for spring harvesting. This increased labour input, both by diversifying crops and by lengthening the growing season, and it increased gross income by $5.5 per head. The bamboo groves were exploited as the basis of handicrafts, a water-powered mill was built and a bean mill, and limestone was burned to provide lime for sale. It was estimated that by the end of the year these activities would increase gross income by a further $17 per head. The total capital outlay for these ventures and for the purchase of pigs and fish-fry, four deep ploughs, two animals, and seed and fertilizers, was $8.1 per head. On this basis, the APC provided, out of its side-occupation profits alone, their capital cost, $1 215 given in relief to the poorest families, and $1 000 of common savings deposited in the credit co-operative.

The third method is the extension of irrigation. It is important to appreciate that, while the final solution to Chinese problems of water control demanded, and were seen to demand, large-scale modern works controlling whole river systems, much could be done locally to improve irrigation and extend it to land not previously watered. The possibilities in China were especially large because of the destruction of existing irrigation facilities in the course of prolonged war. Much of this renovation and expansion could be done by labour-intensive methods.

Another line of development involving little or no capital, but usually demanding higher labour inputs, was the replacement of low-yielding by high-yielding crops – the replacement of millet, maize, and wheat by paddy rice, sweet potatoes, or peanuts.

Such labour-intensive means of raising production occupy a prominent place in the APC plans described in the *High Tide*.

The savings from the first new operation were the foundation of the APC's further production plans, based on the development of forestry, diversified agriculture, and side-occupations. In the forests, the existing bamboo groves were to be renovated by weeding; pine plantations were to be freed of bamboos, thinned (selling the thinnings as fuel), and lopped to encourage upright growth. Further plantings of bamboos and pines and a mixed plantation was to be made, in all about 100 *mou* of new planting. Unirrigated land was to be planted with a variety of vegetables, or with melons, and flax, using inter-planting and catchcropping. Embankments were to be used to raise fodder and peanuts. Side-occupations included the further development of lines already experimentally introduced; little further capital investment was needed. All this was based upon a mass conference in which members of the APC are said to have put forward over a hundred suggestions; the APC management chose from those the lines that would bring the quickest returns for the least risk. In all, it was calculated that income would be increased by $41 per head, and 31 000 additional days of labour would be provided. On calculation, labour expended on these occupations would give a gross return of 60c. per day. This is a lower rate of return than the minimum subsistence wage, quoted in the article itself, as 80c. per day.

This particular plan represents, although in a more elaborate form, the same stage of development as that described in the case of the Wang Kuo-fan APC – a use of labour which, in any other circumstances, would be regarded as hopelessly unprofitable, in order to supplement an existing deficit on subsistence, and provide the first small savings for investment. In the Red Star APC, these aims were achieved. What makes it economic is that first, the labour has little or no opportunity cost, and second, the co-operative organization ensures that a proportion of the returns is saved and invested.

(2) A large APC in Hopei, Hojian hsien

The second example differs in many respects from the first. A northern village, with about three *mou* per head but a much shorter growing season, it too was poor, but is not said to have been in deficit on subsistence. It is much nearer the average Chinese village, if there is such a thing. Its production plans were worked out with the help of the local agricultural extension team, not worked out by the villagers on the initiative of a village Party member, as in the Kwangtung example. They are described in terms of probable yields per acre. The APC had access to a tractor station, but in spite of this, much of its planning is in terms of the use of surplus labour.

Plans were based on the potential of unutilized or underutilized, low-lying marshy land and sandy and gravelly land. The APC was a very large one, made up by the merger (probably as a part of this comprehensive plan) of existing societies. It had 507 households, 6 998 *mou* of land, 570 labour units, excluding women who could provide a further 250. The first point in the plan is the increase of yields on the existing arable by deep ploughing, better seed-strains, and increased inputs of manure. The second is increasing diversity of crops – more cotton, more oil-bearing crops. In addition, however, the gravelly land, then unused, was to be planted with red thorn and mulberries, given a productive shelter belt of willow trees, interplanted meanwhile with vegetables. Flax and melons would be grown on banks. Bottoms subject to seasonal floods would be used for a quick annual crop of fodder. Dry rice would replace kaoliang on the more cultivable patches of gravel soil, along with spring wheat and flax. Orchards were to be under-planted. Water-holes were to be planted with reeds and stocked with fish. In addition, better management of fruit trees (a very necessary matter in China, and an easy one in co-operative conditions) would much increase yields. Pigs, poultry, sheep, and bees were to be kept on a large scale, the APC owning the breeding stock.

This is clearly a different case from the first. With three and a half *mou* per head, even in northern conditions there would be a lesser, although still significant, labour surplus. Much more could be done by more normal investment, as the plans show; nevertheless, surplus labour is still important, although not used here so largely as it was in the Kwangtung example, as a means of earning savings directly for future investment. Instead, it was used directly as a form of investment – in the improvement of orchards, the diversification of crops, the planting of permanent crops (mulberries, etc.), the improvement of soil, the planting of shelter belts, and in inter-planting and catch-cropping.

(3) Heilungehiang

Our third example is an area of extensive agriculture not usually associated with a surplus of labour. Here, the point is that, with the cooperative use of ample means of production (in terms of existing techniques), both human and animal labour were underutilized. There was, therefore, even here a labour surplus of 30 per cent, and a surplus of animal power of 10 per cent. Savings were about $10 per head.

Characteristically, the first recommendation of the *ch'u* Party in drawing up a plan for the consideration of the APC members was immediately to improve horse-drawn tools in order to release even more labour power. This was then to be used in the reclamation of 1 800 *hsiang*[7] of land, the planting of anti-erosion belts, the development of a new irrigation system around an existing canal, and the creation of fish-ponds in association with this. The plan was to be carried out in stages over three years. Here, capital (in the improvement of tools) was used to release labour, which would then be used as a form of capital.

These three examples explicitly described long-term planning. But planning is a constant theme. Such planning was fundamental to the successful creation and development of collective farms whose purpose was precisely to pool resources in order to create a margin of capital, and especially to pool resources of surpus labour.

The three examples given above are worth comparing. They may be said to represent three phases of the exploitation of surplus labour in the course of economic development from the poorest level in China:

first, the use of labour in order to make up a deficit on subsistence and to provide the first investable savings;
second, the use of labour directly invested as a substitute for capital in the strengthening and diversifying of the collective economy by labour-intensive construction;
third, when the stage of partial mechanization releases further labour, the investment of this new source of labour for the creation (still by largely labour-intensive means) of new capital assets.

Throughout, it must be remembered, is the possibility of contributing to income by considerably increased intensity of the use of labour in existing arable farming.

Given that the land is being worked with maximum intensity, the marginal productivity of labour unused in this way is near zero. Thus the returns to any use made of this labour in other ways can be economic, even if they are less than the average return to labour on the farm. Anything which this labour produces is a net gain, for its subsistence is already provided for in the family, and this labour has little or no oppor-tunity cost, in the absence of alternative employment either in country or in town.

Nurkse's model suggested that the transfer of underemployed labour to construction (unpaid because supported out of existing production) must be attended by leakages, and these must reduce the standard of living of the group concerned. These leakages must be supplemented, and should if possible be minimized, if the standard of living is not to fall. In Nurkse's model, it was assumed that this supplementation must come from outside; and any capital for equipment, which cannot be found out of the surplus simple equipment available through its duplication on fragmented farms, must also come from outside.

China's collectivized effort towards the investment of surplus labour was also subject to leakages, but not to the extent that Nurkse envisaged. The Chinese effort at this time was primarily within the village. The construction labourer ate at home or carried his family rations; so the consumption of the other members of the family could not rise because a member was absent. By the same token, no inducement to move to a distant construction site was necessary. However, participation in heavy construction work, usually in winter conditions, demanded substantially more calories than poor peasants normally have to eat in the idle season; and where a substantial part of the able-bodied male villagers were participants, this form of leakage might be significant. Moreover, Nurkse's (admittedly theoretical) assertion that, if necessary, the surplus workers can make their own tools, is not in practice completely applicable. Some means of transport is necessary for any agricultural construction; some materials must be bought even for the simplest structure in which to keep animals, and so on. A certain amount of capital in the form of tools, beasts, and carts must be necessary in almost all cases; and for processing crops – a convenient form of diversification – simple mills or presses are needed.

The collective organization provided means of offsetting these leakages. Collective management resources could check any tendency to increase consumption beyond an agreed limit, while at the same time permitting a distribution of profits, which would attempt to maximize incentives in relation to the total available for distribution. Collectivism could bring the small surplus of the more prosperous villagers, represented by their savings, beasts, and tools, into the equation. Their savings could cover leakages, their tools and beasts could provide the necessary capital goods, both to be repaid out of the increased production resulting from construction.

Those in possession of savings and equipment, however, are those who have the maximum opportunities for profitable individual enterprise. The chief political problem of the collectivization movement was to persuade them, or a sufficient number of them, that investment in the APC would, at least in the long term, provide a greater income. Their participation is vital; it is their capital that can set off the multiplier through putting surplus labour to work. If, indeed, this surplus labour was China's greatest source of investment, then the capital of the middle-peasants was the chief key to the whole economic development of rural China.

THE PROBLEM OF INCENTIVES

This brings us to the problem of material incentives. It is impossible to read the *High Tide* descriptions of co-operatives (remembering that these accounts have prescriptive force) without being aware that the problem of incentives looms very large in Mao's mind. For example, the question of just and effective remuneration for labour within the co-operatives occupies more space in the collection than any other single issue; and questions of remuneration for tools and beasts handed over for use by the co-operative is almost as constant a theme. Moreover, the whole 'educational' effort involved in Mao's collectivization movement was concerned with the possibility of rapidly increased production and, out of this, of increased personal incomes. The campaign was almost entirely an appeal to enlightened self-interest.

For the poorer peasants and the poorer co-operatives, the incentive is simple and overwhelming – to escape from extreme poverty by the rational use of their labour. For the more prosperous, the collective had to be represented as a better investment of the middle-peasant's resources, in the long run, than any available to him as an individual farmer. The basic argument was that these resources, in the hands of small individual farmers, were inevitably underutilized; and if the poor could look forward to full employment on the basis of their collective use, the richer could look forward to the full utilization of their resources, in the hands of the formerly underemployed poor, and share in the increased production that would accrue from the combination of under-employed labour and underemployed capital.

The increased production, however, was not seen as a single increment resulting from the full use of equipment on existing arable under-existing crops, but as a continuing improvement as a result of its use in construction, diversification of crops, and (in particular) the extension of irrigation. It was, in theory, a plausible case for greater long-term profits for all the farmers.

It is desirable, however, that as far as possible, the middle-peasant

participants should gain from the APCs operations right from the beginning. There is much stress in the *High Tide* on this point, although no
case is given where *all* individual middle-peasants gain.

The rich peasants, of course, were excluded from the co-operative
farms at this time. Their position is, therefore, not relevant.

To explore the possibilities, let us create an APC and examine its
working. The figures are based on examples in the *High Tide*; but as
statistical analysis is not possible on such a sample, they are impressionistic only.

Let us invent a village of 100 households, of which twenty are middle-
peasants, and eighty are poor peasants. This is not typical: it is an APC
with an unusual proportion of poor peasants dependent on the resources
of a small minority.

It is necessary for the reader to be patient with this rather elaborate
little exercise; it is the only way in which to demonstrate the process by
which Mao Tse-tung hoped that, with feasible increases in production,
virtually the whole village could be made to see the possibilities – the
eventually unlimited possibilities – of his community-development
approach to social change and economic growth.

Let us postulate that the middle-peasants have each fifteen *mou* of
land, and the poor peasants ten *mou*, a fairly typical distribution of land.
We also assume that income is in proportion to land worked; this
assumption is reasonable according to Buck's findings.

The total land is 1 100 *mou*. Average net income is $50 per *mou* (i.e.
each middle-peasant earns $750 p.a. and each poor peasant $500 p.a.).
On the formation of the APC, charges are incurred:

(a) Administrative expenses, recommended to be 1 % of
    gross income, say 2 % of net income $1 100
(b) Middle-peasants' hire to the APC tools and beasts
    worth $200 per household, at a hire charge of 20 % of
    value. One instalment due in the first year $ 800
(c) Loans of $100 per middle-peasant household, at
    17 % interest as prescribed $ 340
                                                            ─────────
    Total charges $2 240[8]

Each middle-peasant household receives an income of $40
in hire fees, and $17 in interest.[9]

Reduced by the amount of these charges, total net
income is now $52 760

Dividend paid to land might be 40 per cent, 50 per cent, or 60 per cent.
In a village with land distribution of this kind, it would almost certainly have been set at 60 per cent to land.

Each middle-peasant family will receive dividend on land of	$ 432
Each poor peasant	$ 288

Middle-peasants would gain in labour from their greater skill. With wage differentials running from eight through standard ten to twelve, let us assume that the middle-peasants average eleven, and the poor peasants nine points per day.
Their remuneration for labour will then be

Middle-peasants per year	$ 247
Poor peasants	$ 202
Total middle-peasant income will be: 432+247+57 =	$ 736
Total poor-peasant income will be: 288+202 =	$ 490

To the formation of this APC, therefore, the poor peasants would sacrifice about $10 per year of income and the middle-peasants about $15. This is the cost of bringing the land, capital equipment, and savings of the middle-peasants into relation with the surplus labour of the poor. This of course assumes no increase of production and, therefore, of incomes. A 1 per cent increase in production would make up the deficit in middle- and poor-peasant incomes of $1 100, incurred to meet administrative expenses.

Let us assume that there is a labour surplus of 30 per cent – a very moderate figure for poorer Chinese villages. With 100 households and 300 working days in the year, and (to take the simplest case) one able-bodied adult male per household, the available labour is 30 000 labour days of which 10 000 are surplus. Let us see how this labour might be used. We have seen that, in the poorest case described (the Red Star APC), the returns to labour in the variety of uses to which surplus labour was put were about 60c. per labour day. This is below subsistence, and well below the rate for hired labour.[10] It is, however (once the capital charges are met, and we have met them as above) *all net gain* to the community as a group.

Assuming this minimum rate of return, 10 000 labour days could produce an income of $6 000, or an increase in total net income of 11 per cent.

However, if this labour is used for capital construction, which does not pay off in the short term, if it produces no additional income before the next distribution of APC income, while increasing by 30 per cent the labour days upon which payment is due, it will depress the value of the labour day. On our assumption that all members of the APC will work equally, this does not matter among APC members: the same proportion of the same total wage fund would still go to every family. In fact, however, this equal participation by all families in construction labour, or in the replacement of labour for construction is unlikely, especially when members of the APC retain an interest in a private sector, and enjoy unequal opportunities of profiting from it at rates that give an immediate economic return to their labour. Also, future gain may not be a strong inducement to work in a population habituated to under-employment. Nor will the richer peasants be inclined to carry on investing in what, without increases in production, is a losing investment to them.

One of the major novelties of Mao's strategy in agricultural construction is precisely in avoiding, as far as possible, a gestation period. Agricultural construction at this time and since, was staged so as to ensure that this winter's work paid off by the next autumn harvest. This was explicitly ruled in one case, and there is ample illustration of the principle. It represents, indeed, the traditional way in which clan and community development was phased in imperial China.[11]

However, the reclamation of land or the extension of the irrigated area meant an increase in the labour necessary for annual farming operations, and so would gradually reduce the surplus available for further construction. Hence Mao's apparently paradoxical interest in labour-saving mechanization as the second stage of rural development.

Let us assume that our APC has used its 10 000 man days of surplus labour as follows:

(a) To increase the intensity of farming on the existing
    arable land by 2 000 man days, or 10% of man days
    with a net gain in production of 5% $2 750

(b) To develop auxiliary occupations: assume the net
   return to labour is the minimum, 60c. per day,
   5 000 man days $3 000
(c) To reclaim land for irrigated cultivation, 100 *mou*,
   using remaining 3 000 man days, and giving an
   income of $50 per *mou* $5 000

   Total increased income $10 750

We have assumed that loans from middle-peasants and
hire of tools are the only capital expenses; that existing
production represents the land-tax norm, so that no taxes
are paid on the increased production. We postulate that
20 per cent of the increase is deposited as common savings,
20 per cent used as next year's additional production
expenses, and the other 60 per cent is distributed on the
existing pattern,

   i.e. of $6 450, 60% goes to land and 40% to labour.
   i.e. to land $3 870
         to labour $2 580

If this is distributed in the same way, land and labour
payments will rise by approximately 12 per cent.

   Middle-peasant income rises from $736 by $83 to $ 819
   Poor peasant income rises from $490 by $60 to $ 550
   Common savings out of the increase $2 150

Returning to the problem of incentives in the light of this model, it
can be seen that according to the model, a very slight increase in
production (2 per cent) will prevent incomes from falling.

As far as the middle-peasant group is concerned, they have received
an increase of income in the first year of $73, for an investment of
$100.

When we turn to the second year of collective operation it is obvious
that the surplus labour force available for construction has now been cut
down; of the 3 000 man days used on reclamation nearly 2 000 will be
required to work this additional arable, leaving only 1 000 for construction.

One possible step is to encourage the village women to replace the
men as far as possible, releasing them for capital construction. Another
is to use the savings of the first year to buy carts and animals in order to

eliminate the use of human labour for transport. These were normal steps at this stage in the APCs. If female labour released 5 000 man days in the first year it was used, and if the use of animals for transport released a further 1 000, the construction force could be increased to 7 000.

The second year of operation might be as follows:[12]

1. The reclamation of a further 100 *mou* (3 000 labour days) $5 250
2. Building a small reservoir to irrigate 200 *mou*, stocked with carp. New irrigated land yields 40% more, or $77 per *mou* (4 000 labour days) $4 200
                                                                    ―――――
                                                                    $9 450

Additional distributed income will be $5 670
Middle-peasant family gets on average, additional income of $ 73
Poor peasant family gets on average, additional income of $ 53

The new reclamation, and the increased need for labour on the newly-irrigated land will decrease the surplus labour force to 3 500,[13] but it should be possible to double the contribution of female labour to 10 000 labour days; this would be about the limit. It would bring available labour up to 13 500 labour days. Used in similar ways in the third year, it might bring in further income of about $12 000

Additional distributed income will be $ 7 200
Middle-peasant gets on average an extra $ 92
Poor peasant gets $ 67

Consequent new commitments reduce the labour force available for construction by 7 000 labour days to 6 500. With female labour fully employed, and with sufficient savings to begin to develop multiple-cropping, processing of crops, and handicrafts on a larger scale, as well as the development of animal husbandry, the APC is likely to have from now on a growing shortage of labour.

It must now use the savings accumulated through the use of surplus labour to begin the process of mechanization in order to save labour for the continuation of agricultural construction. Its total capital accumulation (allowing for 60 per cent distributed each year, and 20 per cent set

aside for increased production expenses the following year) has amounted
to $14 010.

Having followed this fictitious enterprise thus far, we must now ask
if it has more than illustrative significance. It is based (impressionistic-
ally but reasonably) on the reported achievements of the examples
recorded in the *High Tide* collection. These were the growing points of
the new system, and do not indicate the average performance of the
APCs in 1955. It indicates, however, what Mao Tse-Tung believed was
in principle possible. From a technical point of view, such achievements
were perfectly possible; they represented in every way developments
well known and advocated since the 'thirties. From the point of view of
natural resources, they are equally reasonable; and economically (i.e.
from the point of view of the availability of labour and capital), they
are unexceptionable. As the APCs concerned were so often widely
opened to inspection, and were often the centres of local co-operative
networks, their achievements (told with details of time, place, and persons) could not have been too much exaggerated in descriptions that
were first published locally.

In the event, the process of collectivization was rushed; insufficient
time was given for the operation of the ideas here exemplified. Yet
experiment on these lines seems to have laid a basis sufficiently strong
enough for Chinese agriculture to be completely socialized without
drastic disruption, although certainly not without trouble.

It was in its further development, however, that Mao's idea of a spiral
process of rural economic growth and social change was important.
Beginning from the investment of labour in construction, proceeding
through increasing labour scarcities as new opportunities were developed, creating *both* the demand *and* the savings for gradual mechanization
and diversification of the village economy, it could spiral out to reach in
the end the full modernization of village life.

By 1958, changing views of China's future development made these
ideas much more relevant. The Chinese Communist Party had begun in
1949 (in common with many other underdeveloped countries) with the
assumption that the key to economic growth was the building of an
enclave of heavy industry planned by the state. If this was provided
the rest would follow through inevitable spread effects. This did not
happen in China. It did not happen in India either. In both countries,
there was a parallel reaction towards the idea of giving priority to *local*,
rural development, both agricultural and industrial. The social and
political implications of this were profound. An enclave of heavy

industry could be built up, and indeed would naturally be built up, by a technocratic elite. Local, rural development, however, faced all the social and psychological inhibitions and all the vestigial but still influential inequalities of village life. Policies for such local, self-help development must be policies dealing with all aspects of life, demanding a new political leadership, new policies in education and health, and the promotion in effect of a 'cultural revolution'. It would also require the re-tooling of existing heavy and modern industry to the requirements of local development. Above all, it could only be an exercise in education through participation.

The ideas carried out in the *High Tide* provided the beginnings of appropriate attitudes and policies. When the change of emphasis was made, these ideas became the basis of the Great Leap Forward.

The Great Leap was an attempt to induce the local communities, from the *hsien* level down to the APCs (later merged into communes), to build up their own economies, using labour as far as possible as a substitute for capital, employing simple intermediate technologies, and aiming at diversification as well as growth of production. The Great Leap aimed at simultaneous development rather than selective, specialized forms of production, based on the assumption (a reasonable one for pre-modern rural conditions) that, for any one venture to be successful, the complementarities of a diversified system must be built up at the same time – even if control and balance had, for a time, to be jeopardized. The redress of imbalances and the elimination of bottlenecks was the duty of the higher level of organization – the *hsien* in relation to the APC, the province in relation to the *hsien*. Planning was now seen in terms of a response by the higher level to the conditions created by an all-out effort at diversified development based on local initiative.

A vast new effort of central investment in modern industry, however, was regarded as a pre-condition of local intermediate technology development. Much of this investment took the form of an attempt to create, or to complete the creation of a centre of heavy industry in each provincial capital. This centre would serve as the main source of iron and steel, machine tools, design skills, and trained personnel, as well as of modern agricultural machinery such as pumps and insecticide sprays, for the local communities. The central ministries, and those key factories which remained under their direct control, assumed the same responsibilities towards the province as the province undertook on behalf of the *hsien*. The higher levels were no longer to *dictate* what was to be produced, but to *respond* to what was being attempted lower down, and to the impulses from below.

At the base of the pyramid was the APC, the village collectively organized. It was the self-help efforts of half a million of these villages that were to provide the markets for production at higher levels, and these self-help efforts were based on the *High-Tide* 'spiral'. The Great Leap was, in fact, an attempt to induce this growth spiral at an accelerated and accelerating speed; this was the rationale behind the ever-increasing local production targets which – in theory, and sometimes in practice – represented the rapid widening of a sense of new possibilities in the minds of China's peasants. These ever-increasing targets also represented, in theory at least, an accelerating dialectic between increasing labour scarcities as new forms of production were attempted, and increasing savings for capital investment as the new production paid off. Accompanying the process also was a further dialectic, in which rapidly improving means of production were reflected in new forms of production relations represented finally by the Commune.

Behind this rationale was the belief that, in Chinese rural society ignorance, fear, continuing social inequalities, and what one could call (although the Chinese did not) the whole 'survival mentality' of the poorer peasants, were more important obstacles to economic growth than economic scarcities themselves. The Great Leap was, one might say, a sociologist's rather than an economist's solution to the problem of poverty; and to judge it in purely economic terms and on the basis of its immediate economic results, is to misunderstand the nature of the solution. This solution involved an essentially educational process – the radicalization, by mass-line methods and mass participation in decision-making, of popular social and economic attitudes and expectations.

The process was at first wasteful and chaotic; the right wing of the party brought it to an end. By 1961, centralized, bureaucratic methods were re-imposed, and the Great Leap concept had lost many of its supporters, notably Liu Shao-ch'i, who became President of the Chinese People's Republic in place of Mao in 1959.

From late 1962, however, the Maoists began to attempt to re-assert their influence and their policies. By 1965 they had been successful in some respects and in some places, but found themselves faced with opposition which had by then hardened out into a systematic Liebermanist alternative favoured by Liu Shao-ch'i. This was the main reason why Mao Tse-Tung, with the support of the young, the poor, and the peasant levies of the PLA launched the Cultural Revolution; and since the Cultural Revolution, the policies represented by the Great Leap have been re-applied, although with less haste and less radicalism than in 1958.

These present policies can be seen as the culmination of a long history of elaboration of a few basic ideas concerning the nature of social change and economic growth. These ideas originated in the special conditions of the Border Regions; but the critical phase of their development as an alternative to the western/Soviet centralized capital-intensive model came in the collectivization campaigns and is represented by the strategy adopted in the *High Tide*.

Notes

1 *Chung-kuo nung-ts'un ti she-hui-chu-i kao-ch'ao*, Pekin, 1956. *The Socialist Upsurge in the Chinese Countryside* (Mao, 1957) is a brief, partial translation.

2 *Hsien* populations average 350,000, but can vary from 100,000 to 500,000.

3 Agriculture Producer Co-operatives (APCs) were relatively small in 1955–6. Their size varied enormously according to the intensity of local agriculture, but they tended to have no more than 200 or 300 families. By the end of 1956 they were increased in most cases to three or four times this size, but were somewhat reduced by the end of the year. They were essentially farming institutions, unlike the later communes, which had formal administrative and political as well as economic responsibilities.

4 One *catty* equals approximately $1\frac{1}{3}$ pounds.

5 One *mou* equals approximately one-sixth of an acre.

6 As of 1955–6, the official exchange rate between the Chinese dollar and the US dollar was 2·36:1.

7 One *hsiang* equals 7 *mou*, or between an acre and an acre and a quarter.

8 This is reasonable on the basis of *High Tide* prescriptions, and it is also close to Nurkse's 4 per cent saving, which was to provide the multiplier via the utilization of surplus labour.

9 If, alternatively, the tools and beasts are sold outright on instalments over five years at 17 per cent interest, his income will be $34 on this account instead of $40 hire charges – little difference.

10 The *average* return to labour in our model is just over $1 per labour day.

11 I am indebted to Professor Denis Twitchett for reminding me of this significant fact.

12 More intensive tillage adds 5 per cent net to the value of net agricultural production.

13 About 2 500 are required for the reclaimed land and 1 000 for the newly irrigated land.

References

BERNSTEIN, T. P. 1969. Cadres and Peasant Behaviour under Conditions of Insecurity and Deprivation: the Grain Supply Crises of the Spring of 1955. In A. Doak Barnett (ed.) 1969.

BERNSTEIN, H. (ed.) 1973. *Development and Underdevelopment.* Harmondsworth: Penguin.

BUCK, J. L. 1964. *Land Utilization in China.* New York: Paragon.

DOAK BARNETT, A. (ed.) 1969. *Chinese Communist Politics in Action.* Seattle: University of Washington Press.

GRAY, J. 1969. The Economics of Maoism. *Bulletin of the Atomic Scientists* 25 (2): 42–51. (Reprinted in Bernstein, H. (ed.) 1973.)

GRAY, J. 1972. The Chinese Model: some Characteristics of Maoist Policies for Social Change and Economic Growth. In Nove, A. and Nuti, M. (eds.) 1972.

MAO TSE-TUNG. 1957. *The Socialist Upsurge in China.* Peking: Foreign Languages Press (a selection from the Chinese original).

NOVE, A. and NUTI, M. (eds.) 1972. *Socialist Economics.* Harmondsworth: Penguin.

NURKSE, R. 1958. The Saving Potential concealed in Rural Employment. In *Problems of Capital Formation in Underdeveloped Countries.* Oxford: Oxford University Press.

AIDAN FOSTER-CARTER

Neo-Marxist Approaches to
Development and Underdevelopment[1]

'. . . But (the Western European Capitalist countries) are not completing this development (towards socialism) as we previously expected they would. They are completing it not through a steady "maturing" of socialism, but through the exploitation of some states by others . . .' (Lenin, *Better Fewer, But Better* (his last article), 1923)
'. . . There are two types of capitalism – capitalism of the imperialist countries and colonial capitalism . . . In the colonies capitalism is not a product of local conditions and development, but is fostered by the penetration of foreign capital.' (Trotsky, speech at the third anniversary of the Communist University of the Toilers of the East 1924)
'. . . For a long time now, history has been made without the Left in Europe.' (Fanon)

I. INTRODUCTION

This is a large topic, so what follows will inevitably be discursive. The wording of the title conveniently sets the scene in some respects:

(a) 'Neo-Marxist'

This is not a term beloved by Marxists, who tend to argue that if something is Marxist then it is Marxist *tout court*, and that if it is not Marxist it must be revisionist or otherwise heretical. This Marxist, however, regards 'neo-Marxist' as a useful and necessary term for distinguishing a sub-set of Marxist thought: namely, that which has attempted, mainly since 1945, to come to terms with the now notorious paradox of Marxism's practical successes in underdeveloped countries and its comparative failures in more developed ones. The division is by no means purely chronological, which would be of little analytical value; on the

Aidan Foster-Carter

contrary, there still survive what might by opposition be called 'palaeo-Marxist' schools of thought, meaning those who do not regard the world as having changed sufficiently to warrant modifying fundamental Marxist positions.[2]

(b) Approaches'

The dual grouping just made reflects Marxism's double existence as theory and history, a feature shared for obvious reasons by few if any other sociological schools – although bourgeois development theory also, of course, has its roots and its 'praxis' in the real world, in Indochina and elsewhere, as we shall see below – and is a simultaneous source of both strengths and problems. To differentiate as I have done between theorists and activitists is not to ignore that most people are both, or that at any rate there is a constant interaction between the two spheres (Fanon and Guevara are particularly hard to place, embodying as they do that much vaunted but rarely achieved unity of theory and practice). Thus neo-Marxism as an academic phenomenon is largely a response to the way in which people like Mao and Ho have changed the world, and also to the concomitant failure of other people, such as Rostow, to do the same.

Since development *is* about changing the world, on any view, the practical achievements of such Marxists are of intrinsic importance. But problems arise precisely in the connexion between what they say and what they do. Marxism's claim to be *the* science of social life has too often been taken as conferring on the utterances of (especially successful) Marxist leaders a certain sanctity. By contrast, one argument of this paper is precisely the reverse: that the problematic in neo-Marxism consists in the failure of even the most seemingly radical of revisionists to come to terms with the drastic implications of the very success of Marxism-as-practice for the coherence of Marxism-as-theory. Minimally, so far from taking participants' theories at face value, one must distinguish (i) what people *say* they are doing (ideology); (ii) what they *think* they are doing (consciousness); (iii) what they are *really* doing (social science). I am not blind to the philosophical difficulties of such a stark formulation, especially that of (iii); but I would argue that, in general, social science is not feasible without such an analytical schema, and that, in the particular case of neo-Marxism, I hope that the need for a value of such distinctions will be illustrated in the course of the discussion.

(c) 'Development and Underdevelopment'

Terminological considerations are unavoidable, since an important part of the neo-Marxist position has been to criticize not just bourgeois theories but the very words in which the subject-matter is characterized. Thus Jalée (1963) attacks the idea of a 'Third World' even while using it, Rhodes (1968) criticizes the traditional/modern dichotomy, and Bettelheim (1967) points out the misleadingness of the notion 'underdeveloped', while Frank polemically suborns and transitivizes it like a captured weapon: 'I underdevelop you', actively. Here we may note a paradox. The idea of 'development' in social science, meaning the progressive alteration and succession of different types of socio-economic formation over time, is firmly Marxian in origin. In a sense, then, Marxism is the prototype of development theory as such (as Rostow's sub-title obliquely acknowledges). '*Under*development', by contrast, is essentially a non-Marxist term in its initial conception; so that the rise of a neo-Marxist school centred on the problem of underdevelopment (albeit conceived very differently from its original bourgeois meaning) and must be seen against a backcloth of the perceived inadequacy, not only of bourgeois descriptions and prescriptions, but also of traditional Marxist ideas about 'backward' countries.

This dual ancestry of neo-Marxism structures the remainder of the paper. We shall trace its background in both Marxism and bourgeois thought (and in the changing worlds of both); we shall then offer a critical account of its distinctive and novel features, again as compared with both traditional Marxist and non-Marxist approaches. Finally we suggest some prospects and tasks, and venture some predictions.

2. THE BACKGROUND

(a) In Marxism

(i) *Karl Marx*

Recent works by Avineri, Carrere D'Encausse and Schram, and Hobsbawm (1964: 83), among others, have collated and commented upon Marx's own views on the non-European world; here there is space only for a very compressed account. Marx was hostile to what he termed the 'Asiatic Mode of Production', chiefly on the ground of its unchangingness; and while he was equally hostile to the hypocrisy and brutality of colonial conquest and rule, he undoubtedly saw the latter as in some sense historically necessary. But in what sense? On the one hand, a country like India (a) could not change autonomously, and (b) was so weak that someone was bound to conquer it. On the other hand, (c) young European capitalism had its own expansionary dynamic, which affected and made use of the non-capitalist rest of the world in a number of ways. Thus at least three conceptually distinct 'necessities' tend to be conflated into a single grand Necessity, with unfortunate consequences. Marx is also ambiguous on the nature of the capitalist impact. At first it seems to have been an entirely one-way process of depredation, very useful – perhaps crucial – for the accumulation necessary to transform commercial into industrial capitalism. Thus transformed, however, European capitalism acquires an interest in actually 'developing' its colonies: Marx (Marx and Engels 1968a: 83–7) waxes eloquent as a technological determinist, convinced that railways above all will put India on the road of capitalist development. Evidently he does not regard as ultimately significant the question of whether capitalism arises endogenously within a particular country and social structure, such as the case of European feudalism, or whether it is introduced from outside. In fact, the whole question of the relationship of capitalism as a system to its concrete manifestations – rival, *national* and colonial capitalism – hardly seems to arise. Capitalism is seen as a *process*, or even a thing, which, irrespective of its origins, once implanted in a society, will develop in a certain direction, albeit not necessarily in any fixed order of mechanical stages. Marx was of course well aware that capitalism's fundamental tendency was to generate both wealth and poverty; but he seems to have envisaged this occurring *within* successive national societies (Britain, France, Germany, America), rather than taking the form of international polarization. In particular, the vision of capitalism as inherently progressive was never clouded by any notion that colonial capitalism might be a different phenomenon; that capitalism as a whole should be viewed, not as a process or pattern of processes, but as a *relation* of unequal partners of whom one developed at the expense of the other. Such notions are almost totally foreign to Marx.

Almost, but not quite. Marx was of course living before the late nineteenth-century imperialist expansion that brought such issues into sharper focus. However, he had before him the spectacle of three centuries of Latin American 'development' (and several decades of political independence), on which he is almost completely silent, and would have done better to say nothing at all, since 'ephemeral' is too kind a word for his naïve, ignorant, and indeed racist comments (cf. Aguilar 1968:

64, 67). But there was Ireland, on which Marx's (and Engels's) observations were consistently more profound. Whereas in India:

'(England will) fulfil a double mission: one destructive, the other regenerating – the annihilation of the old Asiatic society, and the laying of the foundations of Western society in Asia . . . What they will not fail to do is to lay down the material premises for (development) . . . Has the bourgeoisie ever done more?' (Marx and Engels 1968a: 85)

Ireland by contrast:
'has been stunted in its development by the English invasion and thrown centuries back . . . By consistent oppression (the Irish) have been artificially converted into an utterly impoverished nation.' (Marx and Engels 1968a: 319)

This idea of 'stunting' is very close to some neo-Marxist conceptions of underdevelopment, especially Frank's. Importantly, it does not sound like the sort of thing that could be said to 'lay the foundations' or 'material premises' for further development, except in some entirely negative and vacuous sense. Yet despite such comments on Ireland there is in Marx no conception that underdevelopment is anything more or less than *un*development, nor any idea of the supreme irony of one stagnant historical cul-de-sac being forced into the stream of world history in such a way as to condemn it to another, different, yet no less negative, blind-alley.

(ii) *Marxism becomes history*

Two important aspects of Marxist thought have been left until now for discussion, on the ground that their significance becomes more apparent in the events of the half-century since Marx's death than in their theoretical treatment by Marx. One is the national question, the other the peasantry.

Marx, as is well known, was not fond of peasants, regarding them as a usually reactionary force that was in any case doomed to disappearance from the historical stage. His followers, however, in Europe at any rate, if anything outdid the master in their rigorous refusal to have anything to do with the class that, in many of their countries, formed the majority of the population: Mitrany, in a largely forgotten study, has shown how options and alliances which might have changed the course of European history in this century were consistently spurned and ignored. In Russia, where admittedly Marxists had to struggle against Narodnik idealization of the peasantry, Plekhanov described them as 'non-existent, historically speaking' and Gorky was still more scathing. None the less, it is obvious that in a country 80 per cent rural, the 1917 Revolution was in itself merely an urban, industrial phenomenon; it was the (quite different) peasant revolution, and also the ensuing civil war that made the revolution nationwide. But if the Bolsheviks thought they should simply 'use' the peasants for their own ends, then they very soon learned otherwise. Bettelheim (1970b) offered an original and important analysis on this point, showing how all participants in the so-called 'debate', however they might differ about the speed and timing of industrialization, shared the same baneful view of the task in hand: namely, to advance the historical process and strengthen the USSR by building up a minority sector (heavy industry) at the expense of majority. The peasantry, in other words, were seen not as the subject of development (that role, of course, was the proletariat's), but as the object of development, which was to come from them without in the slightest being for them.

What this means is well illustrated by Preobrazhensky's 'pseudo-theory' (as Bettelheim (1970b: 200) calls it) of 'primitive socialist accumulation'. On this view, the new socialist state is faced with a problem analogous to that of early capitalism: the accumulation of capital, which once the system is established will be internally generated, must in the first instance be derived from elsewhere. Capitalism could solve this by plundering all sorts of non-capitalist sectors: petty production, colonial trade and robbery, taxation of peasants, and the like. Socialists have less freedom of manoeuvre, at any rate as regards colonial plunder: 'A socialist state . . . repudiates on principle all the forcible methods of Capital in this sphere.' ('Principle', we may note in passing, is rather weak ground for an historical materialist.) Happily, though, the taxation of 'pre-socialist' economic formations is 'quite different'; indeed, it 'must inevitably play a very great, a directly decisive role in peasant countries such as the Soviet Union' (Preobrazhensky in Shanin 1971a: 223). Just how these two are 'quite different' is as unclear to the outsider as it must have been to the victims.

Let us now examine the 'national question'. As Davis has indicated, Marx and Engels had no consistent theory here, except the maverick criterion of generally opposing whatever might aid Tsarist Russia. Their followers have tended to hold a dual view. While the nation was outmoded in the most advanced capitalist nations, as the 1914–18 war indicated, it might still be on the agenda in more backward areas, especially colonies, where nationalism could be a potent force that might be harnessed for socialist purposes. And yet, on the one hand, to consistently ignore national issues in the name of internationalism (as did Rosa Luxemburg, most notably) seemed hopelessly utopian and self-denying in political practice: while on the other hand, once the Pandora's box of nationalism was opened, there was no shutting it. The chequered history of the term 'proletarian nation' can illustrate some of the contradictions: attributed variously to pre-1914 Italian extreme right-wingers or syndicalists (themselves not always distinct, as Mussolini's career indicates), it was utilized by Fascism; yet as early as 1930 Chinese communists were thus characterizing their country's position in the world; and lately it has been applied by Moussa to the 'Third World' as a whole.

It may be that the fascist 'solution' is no longer feasible for less developed countries today. Yet nationalism has its problems, even in the service of a Marxist party. However much Lenin, and especially Trotsky, might insist on the need for world revolution and an internationalist perspective, the reality of 'socialism in one country' inevitably formed the basis for quite other policies; and importantly, even the later advent of a communist bloc meant, as Emmanuel (1970: 17) expressed it, not socialism in several countries, but 'several socialism-in-one-countrys'. Once again, as with the peasantry, we shall see below how neo-Marxists have been compelled to give greater autonomous weight to the nation and nationalism, especially in the colonial context.

But what of the dynamics of capitalism as a whole? Theoretically, the most important innovation after Marx was the characterization of the epoch of 'Imperialism' by Hobson, Hilferding, Kautsky, Luxemburg (1951), and of course Lenin (n.d.). The connotation of this term has shifted in the last half-century (this again is an important aspect of neo-Marxism), and that shift makes it easy to forget a very important fact: that the classical discussion of imperialism was basically as concerned as Marxism always was with the problems of the advanced capitalist countries, and that the less developed countries were brought into the model, if at all, chiefly as a sort of *deus ex machina* to explain the failure of events in the advanced countries to turn out as anticipated. Thus the quietism of western workers required the theory of the 'labour aristocracy', which in turn required the colonies. The new world was brought in to redress the balance of the old, and for no other purpose. More narrowly even than this, the principal image conjured up by 'imperialism' was of inter-imperialist rivalry, as shown by the Great War, rather than of the effects of imperial rule on the victims.

It is not our task to go into the different specific theories here.[3] The
vital point is that none of them go in essence beyond Marx in attributing
an independent weight, role, or nature to the Third World. One partial
exception might appear to be Trotsky's theory of permanent revolution,
or more especially – since 'permanent revolution' is an idea found in
Marx – his 'law of uneven and combined development'. Certainly
Trotskyists have been prominent among contemporary Marxists who
have given a greater weight to the Third World. And yet, from our perspective, Trotsky is a disappointment. He characterizes 'unevenness'
as 'the most general law of the historical process (which) reveals itself
most sharply and complexly in the destiny of the backward countries.
Under the whip of external necessity their backward culture is compelled
to make leaps . . .' (1964: 85). Similarly, he talks of 'the privilege of
historic backwardness'. Now this is an obvious advance on a mechanical,
attentiste, 'stages' theory (which was not Marx's by any means, although
some of his followers were this way inclined). It suggests that the world
is one, that all are caught up in the great rush forward, and even that the
more backward countries may, because of their backwardness, be 'weak
links' where the revolution is triggered off. But this still leaves the Third
World as essentially an extra in someone else's movie, although it has
its moment of glory; the basic revolutionary honours belong, as ever, to
the workers of Europe. And despite all the imagery of 'skipping',
'leaping', 'telescoping', and the like, the *direction* of progress is un-
changed. One might have expected the interesting and far-reaching idea
of 'an amalgam of archaic with more contemporary forms', which gives
the backward countries' development 'a planless, complex, combined
character' (Trotsky 1964: 85), to have provoked a deeper study of the
possible implications of the co-existence in space and time of what were
originally postulated as *successive* stages, related but never contemporaries. Such a train of thought could perhaps have led to an idea of
'blocked' development. Yet on this count Trotsky is as blithely optimistic as Marx. He talks of 'the capitalist awakening of the colonies', and
even asserts that 'the colonies are beginning to lose their colonial
character' (Trotsky 1964: 79). At best, the theory of permanent revolution allows for capitalism in underdeveloped countries, raising problems
which only socialism can solve, and hence cutting short its own existence.
The idea of 'misdevelopment' – something which is not even a progressive basis for something else, and moreover is not notably short lived –
arises no more in Trotsky than in Marx. And of course, Trotsky had
notoriously little faith in peasants: 'The Chinese peasantry is even less

capable of playing a *leading* role than the Russian', he wrote in 1928 (1946: 244).

Lenin is in much the same case. He no more understood the full import of the remark which prefaces this paper than Trotsky did of his. As the context makes clear, Lenin's focus was the survival of the Soviet Union: the staying power of capitalism was obviously worrying to him, and it is as a determinant of this, and no more, that he brings in the Third World. A few lines later, it is true, he is thankful to note that the Third World also weighs on his side of the scales, with the famous remark: 'Ultimately, the outcome of the struggle will be settled by the fact that Russia, India, China, etc., constitute the vast majority of the world's population' (1923, cited in D'Encausse and Schram 1969). Yet still this 'vast majority' is for him only a tactical consideration. Perhaps he did not have time to reflect on the implications of this unexpected, non-maturational pattern of development for all those involved, especially the exploited. Certainly he seems, perhaps even more than Marx or Trotsky, to have taken a naïve view which anticipates Harrod-Domar, as when he wrote: 'The export of capital greatly affects and accelerates the development of capitalism in those countries to which it is exported' (cited in Galeano 1970: 32).

One of Lenin's ideas did, however, prefigure the later revolution of Marxism, namely the famous notion of a 'labour aristocracy'. Commenting on the Stuttgart Congress of 1907, which had witnessed vehement argument over the idea of a 'socialist colonial policy' supported by some delegates, Lenin noted that, thanks to colonialism, 'the European proletariat has *partly* reached a situation where it is *not* its work that maintains the whole of society but that of practically enslaved natives of the colonies' (cited in D'Encausse and Schram 1969). More generally, the 'labour aristocracy' idea, already postulated by Engels in order to help explain the quietism of British workers, and made possible strictly by colonial super-profits, was triply characterized as temporary, partial, and opportunistic. Yet it has proved to be the thin end of a sizeable wedge on all counts. Emmanuel in particular, who has generalized the theory to a national level ('From "aristocracy of labour" to aristocractic nations'), remarks that a century is something more than 'temporary', and that 'it is vain, and contrary to historical materialism, to blame the bureaucrats of the working-class parties and the masses' lack of awareness . . . awareness also forms part of reality . . . By inserting the word opportunist between a primary cause and an ultimate effect, nothing of what it is aimed to save is in fact saved' (1970: 14). In sum, this is one more instance of Marxism making what was intended simply as a tactical, conjunctural shift that, as time goes by, has come to look increasingly strategic and structural.

Few of the other figures of this period can find extended treatment here. Stalin, despite the enormous negative importance of all that he represented for later trends in Marxism, wrote nothing that can be taken seriously except, perhaps, *Marxism and The National Question* (1935). Meanwhile Gramsci, isolated in prison, was developing analyses of the specific features of Italy that (as befitted his Sardinian background) gave due weight to the peasantry, and even suggested that southern Italy and the Islands were 'exploited colonies' of the 'capitalistic metropolis' of northern industry. But Gramsci was not part of the ongoing practical development of Marxism at that time.

Colonial affiliates of the Comintern did question the secondary role which Marxist theory and Comintern practice appeared to give them. Nguyen Ai Quoc (later to be known as Ho Chi Minh) accused the Fifth Comintern Congress (1924) of neglecting the colonies; while the Indian M. N. Roy at the Third Congress (1922) opposed Lenin's optimistic assessment of the 'Jacobin' potential of the Asian bourgeoisie, and of the ability of colonial peoples to rely on the fraternal commitment of the metropolitan proletariat. Roy's scepticism on the latter count was aptly witnessed by settler delegates from Sidi-Bel-Abbes to the Comintern, stressing the inability of the Arab 'natives' to achieve the 'economic, social, intellectual and moral evolution' necessary for communism (cited in D'Encausse and Schram 1969: 197).

In 1923, Sultan Galiev, who immediately after the October revolution had been Assistant Commissar for Nationalities, was attacked and expelled from the party. Thereafter he developed some interesting ideas, known only through quotations from his enemies. Declaring that 'The Muslim peoples are proletarian nations' and that 'the national movement in the Muslim countries has the character of a socialist revolution', by 1928 he was advocating a new colonial international to exercise, ultimately, 'the dictatorship of the proletarian nations of the East over the former colonial powers of the West' (cited in D'Encausse and Schram 1969: 36). Fanon never went half so far.

(b) The Bourgeois Background

Neo-Marxism, as an academic phenomenon, is by no means descended in an unbroken line from traditional Marxism. The changing world situation, and more specifically, the increasingly perceived inadequacies of conventional western analyses and responses thereto, have, as it were, autonomously contributed to the flowering of neo-Marxism.

Some aspects of the development idea, such as the paternalist notion of trusteeship and leading people onward and upward to civilization, already have a long history within colonialism. But specifically *economic* development – and *a fortiori* political and social – as a theoretical concern does not seem to pre-date the Second World War. This is perhaps not surprising, since it was only a very few years earlier that the advanced capitalist countries had stumbled onto the principles of their own survival, with the acceptance of Keynes's ideas; prior to this they could hardly be expected to entertain or even comprehend any notion of development (with its implicit assumption of planning) even for their own economies, let alone those of their subjects. But then came the war, which was characterized by large-scale economic and social planning on the part of all participants (it could hardly have been otherwise). It was followed by what one might dub 'the UNRRA (United Nations Reconstruction and Refugee Administration) era', which probably played a very great part in forming the development idea.

Those post-war years, in which Europe itself experienced mass starvation and displacement of millions of persons, and was faced with the task of rebuilding its shattered economies, formed the crucible for many current notions. An obvious example is 'aid'. Marshall Aid, wherewith the USA successfully rebuilt the capitalist economies of western Europe, was dually influential thereafter as theory and ideology. Both were equally misleading. The theory, which might be called the 'yeast fallacy', assumed that capital injections were sufficient to make an economy grow; thus ignoring the specific situation of post-war Europe, where, although physical capital stock was destroyed, there was still plenty of educated and skilled human capital plus appropriate institutions. Such *re*-construction was hardly comparable with the simple construction, from scratch, required in poor countries; still less, on the neo-Marxist analysis, with the *de*struction of irrelevant 'growth' and breaking of links with the world economy that genuine development might require.

Still, the comparison was made; so also was a moral judgement. Although Marshall freely acknowledged that his programme served American interests (and successive politicians of 'donor' countries have never scrupled to make the same admission), and although loans from private and public sources to foreign governments were by no means a novel phenomenon requiring a new name, none the less the value-laden terminology of 'aid' was introduced and has stuck. Hence another consequence of the UNRRA era was the generalization of the perspective of want requiring relief from Europe to the world, as mediated by Boyd Orr and others. (It was he who at about this time discovered that two-thirds of the world's population were starving.) As with Marshall Aid, it did not sink in that the needs of the Third World might be somewhat different from 'relief and rehabilitation', or rather that if this was so, then the west might be the disease rather than the self-appointed doctor. From this epoch, evoked in de Castro's forgotten book, dates the familiar image of 'world hunger', which is still probably the chief lens through which most people in developed countries view the problems of underdevelopment. Nor was it long before the related theme of 'Malthusiasm' – as it was nicely dubbed – screaming the horrors of over-population, was firmly established.

The effect of the Cold War on development scholarship was deep and lasting. It was recognized, with the Chinese revolution and the spread of Soviet power into the largely agricultural economies of eastern Europe (which had themselves been the subject of some early, and now curiously dated, UNRRA-type speculations as to how they might be industrialized), that communism obviously had, as Watnick noted, a certain 'appeal'. But this perception, so far from leading to scientific investigation of what connexion might underlie this appeal, served merely to strengthen the determination to *exclude* communism, both physically from the 'Free World' (as in the Korean War) and analytically from development analysis. Thus, on the one hand, communist systems were characterized largely in terms of totalitarianism, political in-fighting, forced labour, oppression, and general misery; while, on the other hand, with a contradiction that seems to have gone unnoticed, the task of development was defined as being to find an *alternative* path – as opposed to this awful system, which surely nobody could possibly have wanted. It was assumed, in fact, that western capitalism could, would, and should develop the 'Free World'.

The rest of the story is well known: it has formed our world-view. During the last two decades, it is said, the colonial powers (with one or two recalcitrant exceptions to be sure) have voluntarily and peacefully led their former subjects to independence, and both before and after this have maintained an interest in assisting their development – and also in warding off the big bad wolves.

In time, however, the activities of Marxist revolutionaries led some academics to reconsider the received view. First there was Mao's China. For those who did have ears to hear – which of course included much of the Third World, even while 'world opinion' (i.e. western) was deaf to China – it became clear, with the Great Leap Forward, the Sino-Soviet split, and latterly the Cultural Revolution, that China was following an original path of development, to which even her own self-description hardly did justice.

Cuba was another turning-point, especially for the United States. The entirely unexpected direction in which Castro's revolution evolved, exposed – even, one suspects, to their authors – the analytical bankruptcy of the official social science 'explanations' of communism (Schlesinger, Draper, *et al.*), forced as they were into absurd speculations as to whether Castro had 'really' been a communist all along, or had been 'infiltrated' of late by agitators like Guevara. The patent fatuity of such psychological approaches in terms of *personality* provoked a sociologically fruitful interest in the logic of *situations*; so that, quite unawares, a good many people adopted the quintessentially Trotskyist idea that only a socialist revolution could solve even the bourgeois-democratic aspects of development. By the late 1960s, the crisis of non-development in the Free World (especially India) was visibly so acute that attention was forced upon alternative models. And the whole development scenario by the 1970s – with United Nations Conference on Trade and Development (UNCTAD), the first and second 'Development Decades', Pearson's and Myrdal's (1969) gloomy one – was seen as almost entirely negative.

Above all, there was – and is – Vietnam. What began supposedly as a typical defence of a friendly democracy against external communist aggression, *à la* Korea, turned into a seemingly endless morass for the USA, which in turn provoked reflections that should have been made years before on the nature and origins of the conflict, of the respective regimes of North and South, and of guerrilla warfare. It became increasingly clear that successive Saigon regimes were, in fact, 'puppets': that they could probably not even survive without US support, let alone promote development. Comparisons with other US client states elsewhere in the world were inevitable where, if there was no war (or not much) there did not seem to be much development either. By contrast, the characters of both the Northern regime and the National Liberation Front have tended to be viewed not as external and oppressive but as essentially indigenous and expressive of the real development problems

of Vietnam. Again, the picture has arisen of the USA *preventing*
development – and preventing it, this time, with a will, not hesitating to
use genocidal and ecocidal methods graphically summarized in General
Le May's notorious aphorism: 'Blow 'em back to the Stone Age.'
As we shall see, the spectacle of the most advanced technology being
unable to contain peasant guerrillas has also prompted some re-
evaluations of the nature of development as such, which form an interesting part of neo-Marxism.

Let us now look at three strands in western academic response to
these trends, which all played a part in creating neo-Marxism. First, one
must not forget the so-called 'revisionist' school of historians of the
Cold War.[4] Second, the 1950s saw the beginnings of what might be
called the 'rehabilitation of Africa'. Hodgkin and Davidson, in particular,
by drawing attention to forgotten aspects of African history (for example,
that there *was* such a thing), provided an important cultural impetus for
and understanding of the struggle for independence and against
colonialism. In francophone Africa, Sartre's *Black Orpheus*, the idea of
'negritude', the journal *Présence Africaine*, and the work of Cheikh
Anta Diop were similarly important.

And third, of course, is development itself. Here the key figure is the
late Paul Baran, whose *Political Economy of Growth* (1957) was to be
enormously influential in later years. Such diverse figures as André
Gunder Frank and Ché Guevara, have fulsomely acknowledged their
debt to him. Baran's was perhaps the first book by a Marxist author to
focus largely on the problems of underdevelopment (we have already
seen how the classic literature on 'imperialism' is not really about
underdevelopment as such). Well-versed in bourgeois economics, Baran
was able to expose the inadequacies and above all the ideological nature
of the conventional development theory, insisting that development was
inevitably a revolutionary and not an evolutionary process, and that
despite all illusions of 'partnership' there were, and had always been,
deep conflicts of interest between western capitalism and the progress of
underdeveloped countries. More than this, he insisted that western
development had taken place at the *expense* of (in a deep and lasting
sense) the underdeveloped countries, and that the only solution for the
latter was to 'break out' of the imperialist system into socialism. All
these were ideas later to be built upon by neo-Marxism, of which
Baran can truly be called the founding father. Baran and *Monthly
Review*, founded by his close associate Paul Sweezy, have encouraged the
development of the implications of his analysis of underdevelopment.

Gundar Frank's analysis of underdevelopment as a *process* and, at the same time, as the source of metropolitan development, provided a systematic exposition of neo-Marxist analysis. Other writers[5] have attempted to rehabilitate the peasantry into an active role in the Marxist system. Meanwhile, the very rhetoric of aid has led liberals as well as socialists to question its premises.[6] Also there have sprung up recently, on both sides of the Atlantic, radical 'study groups', usually on an area basis, some of which have been producing a prolific 'counter-scholarship',[7] Above all, far removed from western academic discourse, revolutionaries in the hundred countries of the Third World are working out their own specific theory and practice, which (if past experience is anything to go by) we shall only hear of *post-festum*, after they have come to power.

3. DISTINCTIVE FEATURES OF NEO-MARXISM

(a) As Against Bourgeois Theory

(i) *Ideology*

A basic aspect of neo-Marxist development theory has been its critique of its bourgeois rivals and their application to specific problems. Bourgeois development theory, which purports to be value-free science, is exposed as ideology, deliberately or otherwise serving western foreign policy and economic interests or reflecting western prejudices.

Bourgeois theorists tend to assume that development is a process of evolution from a 'traditional', undeveloped state to that 'modern', 'developed' state that is assumed to pertain in industrial capitalist societies, notably the USA. Development becomes a question of how '*we*' (the bearers of 'modernity') can make *them* more like *us*. This approach excludes any recognition of the historic importance of violence to the development of England and other 'developed' countries (cf. Moore). It also fails to recognize that today's underdeveloped countries have been underdeveloped in order to develop industrial capitalism in the metropolitan counties, and that their position is in no way comparable with that of pre-industrial Europe (or even Meiji Japan).

The evasion of the role of the developed countries in causing and perpetuating underdevelopment enables bourgeois development theorists to blame the people of the underdeveloped countries for their own plight. Much development theory is simply a variation of the theme 'the poor

are poor because they are lazy'. Specific theories have been attacked in
Frank's (1972) and Hilal's seminal papers and elsewhere, as have certain
recurrent themes, e.g. 'nation-building' with its faith in the developmental capacity of 'national bourgeoisies', and 'entrepreneurialism'
treated as a panacea and taken out of its historical and structural context. Both represent the wishful thinking characteristic of much
bourgeois development theory. Finally, neo-Marxists have stressed the
class nature of underdeveloped countries – class formation being the
inevitable consequence of capitalism.

As against neo-Marxism's negative critical role, its positive and distinctive features naturally mirror what it regards as the sins of omission
and commission of development theory. These might be grouped as
follows:

(ii) *Totality*

Neo-Marxists insist that the world must be understood as basically
a single, integrated unit; perhaps following Lukacs's dictum that the
essence of Marxism is not any idea of economic base, but the method of
totality. A prime example is Frank's schema of a chain of metropolis–
satellite relationships, ranging down from 'the world metropolis which is
no one's satellite' via nations, capital cities, regional and local centres,
large landowners and merchants, small peasants and tenants, to the
landless labourer (the last being a simple satellite who is no one's metropolis; all intermediate units function simultaneously as both). Surplus is
continuously extracted outwards and upwards as it is created, developing
some at the expense of others.

(iii) *History*

By contrast with the historical, residual category of 'traditionalism',
neo-Marxism has focused on the specific historical experiences of those
societies that are today underdeveloped – thus *inter alia* proving its point
about the creation of underdevelopment by developed societies, since
this is largely of what the conveniently forgotten past consists. Frank
(1969a: 148) again has shown how the most 'ultra-underdeveloped'
parts of the world today, such as the Brazilian *Nordeste*, were charac-
rized at one time by 'super-satellite development' until, for various reasons, the world metropolis lost interest. They are not and were not, that
is, *tabulae rasae* simply *lacking* in development, but if anything the
reverse; 'development occurred where there was poverty, and underdevelopment occurred where there was wealth'.

(iv) *Revolution*

Perhaps the chief lesson of this rediscovery of the past is that 'history tells us that changes of this magnitude are rarely accomplished peacefully' (Lichtheim 1971: 169). The peaceful and evolutionary nature of many development theories, and the concomitant failure to specify a mechanism of change between 'stages', is a major bone of contention with neo-Marxism, which argues that not only is there no *a priori* reason to see development as evolutionary (hopes for peace and quiet aside), but there is massive empirical evidence for the reverse view. And, of course, this is not just a question of the past. Those revolutionary movements, especially communist, against which bourgeois development theory defines itself as a 'non-communist manifesto', are correspondingly seen by neo-Marxists as pre-eminently *the* way forward to development; and the major obstacle to development is not the 'traditional' psychological or social patterns of poor countries, but the interests of the west and their *compradores*.

(v) *Class*

Revolutions, for Marxism, are struggles between classes. This particular tool of sociological analysis has undergone a similar blurring into 'stratification' in development studies, as in other areas of sociology, and Marxists therefore have been as concerned to rehabilitate it. On the one hand, activist Marxists such as Lenin, Mao, and Cabral have analysed their actions primarily in class terms, while, on the other hand, theorists have insisted that classes *exist* against the politically motivated denials of this, and are analytically a far more fruitful concept than blurred rivals like 'elite', 'mass', and 'status'. Moore, again, has provided a powerful picture of classes as historical actors in development. In particular, many neo-Marxists have investigated four classes – the bourgeoisie (national, *compradore*, and petty), proletariat, 'non-working-class' (or lumpen proletariat), and peasantry – and compared and contrasted their origins, characteristics, roles, and potential with those of their equivalents in developed countries. So far, however, there have been few examples of specific analyses of whole class structures: an outstanding exception is Arrighi's (1970) rigorous work on Rhodesia.

(vi) *Economy*

Since class is derived from economic function, clearly – *pace* Lukacs – Marxism has something basic to say about the economic sphere. In contrast to other areas of sociology, where Marxism is often alone in championing the importance of economic factors, development is characterized by something of a consensus on this score: development *is*, pre-eminently, economic. Neo-Marxism, however, has quite distinctive economic perspectives. Structural surplus-sucking is a markedly different model of the international system from altruistic aid-awarding. More specifically, the Harrod-Domar growth model has been confounded by Griffin's work on Latin America, which suggests that foreign capital actually diminishes domestic saving and capital formation.

The monopolistic tendencies of capitalism are seen to come to full fruition in the multi-national corporations, whose concentration of resources and ability to operate across national boundaries enable them to determine the fate of countries whose budgets are a fraction of their own, to treat international financial transactions as internal accounting problems for the firm, and to shift investments and sources of supplies across the world to suit their own interests. Amin and others have distinguished 'growth' from 'development', notably in the enclave and import substituting economies of tropical Africa. On the subject of socialist (eastern European) economies, there has been no unanimity. By some they are excoriated as state capitalist or little better; for others they offer an escape from underdevelopment.

(b) As Against Traditional Marxism

One of the most striking features of many neo-Marxist writers – Frank is a prime example – is how little they quote from, or otherwise attempt to articulate themselves to the classical canon of Marxism. One might even make this a defining characteristic of neo- as against palaeo-Marxism; the former open-minded, viewing the world inductively and bringing in Marxian elements by way of explanation (though possibly also establishing its own orthodoxies); the latter clinging dogmatically to a Marxist *Weltanschauung* and deducing scholastically from this what the world 'must be' like. But empirical strength may be theoretical weakness.

(i) *Imperialism*

As previously noted, the connotation of this term within Marxism has moved somewhat over the past half-century. It is still used to characterize modern capitalism as a whole in the age of monopoly and, within this, attention has lately returned to the classical theme of inter-imperialist rivalry (Mandel). But neo-Marxism is particularly interested in the specific nature of imperialism as it presents itself to its victims: how it alters them, and how it can be defeated. This shift of emphasis of course parallels the emergence of the Third World as an actor in its own right. The more traditional concerns survive, however, and produce some interesting disputes. On one side, such various writers as Magdoff, Jalee, and Emmanuel agree that the underdeveloped countries are crucially important to the west, whether (in the traditional trinity) as sources of raw materials, as outlets for investment, or as markets for finished products. The raw material argument has implications for the currently fashionable concern with ecology, which requires separate consideration. As for investment outlets, on which Lenin placed great emphasis, the classic Marxist argument that saw capitalism's central problem as the generation of ever more surplus than the system could absorb, is *prima facie* hard to reconcile with the increasing evidence that there is a net capital *out*flow from poor countries to rich, i.e., 'aid in reverse'. Similarly, the Third World as a market seems to have been down-graded by the increasing extent to which developed countries trade with each other.

Emmanuel (1972), in a major study, enlists a mixture of economic and social arguments in support of his view that impoverishment has now shifted 'to the planetary level', which 'profoundly alters the nature and make-up of the revolutionary battlefronts'. Because of international differences between developed and underdeveloped countries in relative productivity and wage rates, the western proletariat not only shares in the exploitation of the Third World but actually gains more from this than do western capitalists (because super-wages become normal, while super-profits can only be temporary) – a conclusion that has naturally infuriated the orthodox, as a paper by Ayrton testifies.

On the other hand, writers such as Miller *et al.*, Barratt Brown, and Kidron maintain what might be called a 'redundantist' position. Without doubting that the west underdevelops the Third World, they deny that this process is particularly crucial any longer to the torturer even while it maims his victim. For Kidron, arms-spending is now the necessary waste-absorber of modern capitalism, which, in addition, is increasingly inward looking in terms of trade and investment, and has a technology based on skills rather than raw materials. Hence, rather like a certain school of thought concerning the place of black Americans in US society, the Third World is held to be by no means super exploited but simply irrelevant: its poverty is residual rather than structural.

(ii) *Nationalism*

The preceding discussion has at several points suggested that nation-alism has played a part not adequately recognized by such terms as 'superstructural'. In societies where capitalism was not the natural growth from preceding conditions, which it was in Europe, it was inevitably viewed primarily as an alien intrusion rather than an imman-ent socio-economic trend, which irrevocably disrupted endogenous social processes without offering any immediate or evident recompense. Just how different the response provoked by this assault was from the assumptions of classical Marxism can be illustrated with many examples. Meisner has described the basic nationalism of Li Ta Chao, founder of Chinese Marxism. The national character of the Vietnamese revolution is well known, and documents from Laos and Cambodia show the same emphasis on driving out foreigners as a basic aspect of social change. On the psychological level, Fanon has described how every object – western medicine, radios, the veil – takes on a significance in the cultural battle with colonialism.

The late Amilcar Cabral, former leader of the PAIGC (African Party for the Independence of Guiné and Cape Verde Islands) of 'Portuguese' Guiné, may be taken as an example of this trend. So far from accepting the view that colonialism marks the beginning of history for peoples like his, he insists rather that 'it made us leave history – our history' (1969: 56). Imperialism confuses pre-existing class struggles by uniting the whole people against it: 'As a dominated people, we only present an ensemble *vis-à-vis* the oppressor.' The colonial period is a kind of hiatus, 'the negation of the historical process of the dominated people by means of violent usurpation of the freedom of development of the national productive forces'; against which 'the national liberation of a people is the regaining of the historical personality of that people, its return to history'. Cabral is constantly pre-occupied with the seemingly abstract theme of the 'right of peoples to make their own history'; indeed, in some general theoretical remarks he goes so far as to postulate the level of productive forces rather than class struggles as the motive force of history, so that pre-class societies in Africa may avoid 'the sad position of being peoples without any history'. (Hegal characterized Africa as 'no historical part of the world' and Marx doubtless would have followed him.)

This goes beyond 'nationalism' as narrowly conceived, but it raises a central point about the role of neo-Marxism. Not only as regards development, but in other spheres too, Marxism has become a world-view whereby hitherto inchoate or subdued groups take hold of their reality and, in Mao's simple but graphic phrase, 'stand up' to assert themselves. From this angle, such apparently diverse phenomena as Black Power, student power, women's liberation, gay liberation ('out of the toilets and into the streets'), *and* peasant revolutionary nationalism in colonial countries, are all part of a single trend. This concept of Marxism as a tool of self-crystallization and self-transformation for all manner of oppressed groups is very different from the strict Marxist model, in which the proletariat occupies the central position, as a kind of incarnation of *all* oppression, and, by virtue of its specific role within mature capitalism, makes a revolution that is a sufficient but also a necessary condition for general emancipation. We need a theoretical perspective that will provide a general account of the processes whereby individuals and groups come to define their larger selves in terms of certain characteristics, and not others, in different situations (for instance, class, race, nation).

(iii) *Classes*

This problematic leads on to the central and complex question of class analysis in neo-Marxism. Classes are not simple heuristic categories but are themselves agents of change. It is as such that Marxists are interested in them. Furthermore, classes exist in and through their (dynamic) relations with one another. It is characteristic of colonial and neo-colonial situations that different modes of production, in various relations to one another, exist side by side, each generating contradictions within itself, and generating contradictions among one another. Thus ultimately, any class can only be analysed in terms of the historically specific constellation of class relations.[8] For reasons of brevity, we shall nevertheless have to deal with classes schematically, and assume that certain typical constellations recur over different underdeveloped countries.

(a) *'feudal' groups and 'feudalism'*. Neo-Marxism, as against traditional Marxism, uses this term sparingly; many would agree with Thorner that 'the time has come to treat European experience in categories derived from world history, rather than to squeeze world history into western European categories'. Suret-Canale has applied it in Africa; but most neo-Marxists would in any case probably agree with Frank that capitalism has now so transformed the entire world that 'feudal' or any kind of pre-capitalist sectors are virtually extinct.[9]

D

(b) *the 'national bourgeoisie'*. Traditional Marxism tended somewhat to champion this group, variously against reactionary 'feudal' elements and puppet *'compradores'* in league with imperialism. Lenin, in his 1922 debate with M. N. Roy, characterized the (Asian) national bourgeoisie as 'capable of representing sincere, militant, consistent, democracy, a worthy companion of the great preachers and worthy public men of the end of the eighteenth century in France' (quoted Williams 1970: 234). By contrast, neo-Marxism would characterize them as a 'lumpen bourgeoisie' and as such 'the immediate enemy', in Frank's words: both product and victim of imperialism, too weak by far to be the spearhead of change. They are incapable (as Fanon has insisted) of carrying out the classic progressive role of the European bourgeoisie. Herein lies a vicious paradox: the incapacity of *indigenous* capitalism is rooted in the effects of *foreign* capitalism's (imperialism's) concomitant inability to promote development.

(c) *the 'petty bourgeoisie'*. This category has often had a residual flavour in Marxism, but its importance for neo-Marxism is considerable. A figure like Cabral, admitting that the bourgeoisie and working class are either non-existent or not obviously militant, while the peasant masses are not spontaneously revolutionary, places great stress on the role of petty bourgeois intellectuals as originators of revolutionary ideas by virtue of their *relative* deprivation in the colonial social structure. As a service class, however, this group does not possess the economic base to take power itself; hence, says Cabral, it must, if it is not to betray the revolution 'be capable of committing suicide as a class in order to be reborn as revolutionary workers' (1969: 89). Post distinguishes the petty bourgeoisie (self-employed, small businessmen) from the lower middle class (a service class of non-manual employees). Each of these models itself on the capitalist and middle-class bureaucrats respectively (groups which tend to fuse at the upper levels). These groups dominate the opportunities in the commercial and administrative sectors of the economy in which the petty bourgeoisie and lower middle-class respectively to them are occupied, and the less well-placed look for patronage in order to secure their advancement. At the same time, the petty bourgeoisie find that the national bourgeoisie monopolize the resources and opportunities necessary for the development of their productive activities. Thus, the demand for free access to competitive markets has radical implications in a monopolistic economy, typical of underdeveloped countries. But since they compete among themselves, and aspire individually to entry into the 'charmed circle' of monopolistic advantages, they cannot enforce such a demand. As for the lower middle-class, they too are excluded from advancement by the hold of their (more educated) bureaucratic superiors in higher office, which may become a significant source of conflict. (Sékou Touré exemplifies the radical potential of this stratum in a colonial situation.) But they too tend to seek to enter the 'charmed circle' rather than to abolish bureaucratic privilege (Williams *infra.* 114–22, and 1972).

(d) *The proletariat.* The 'lynchpin' (in Wright Mills's term) of the Marxian system, its role in the Third World, seems ambiguous. In the context of the underdeveloped economy, industrial workers are both few – because colonial capitalism creates little industry – and relatively privileged.[10] The latter does not necessarily exclude them from revolutionism: Fanon's 'wretched of the earth', it must be remembered, is a substantial deviation from Marxism, inasmuch as Marx never implied that *absolute* poverty was a stimulus to revolution – often the reverse. But, while few neo-Marxists go so far as Fanon in rejecting the proletariat, it is still true that spontaneously it appears no more revolutionary in underdeveloped than in developed societies. (But *cf.* Peace, *infra.*)

(e) *the 'lumpen proletariat'.* This term is more an insult than a concept, as Worsley (1969: 39–40) has remarked. By contrast with the interstitial flotsam against whom Marx and Engels (1968b: 44) vented the harshest of even their considerable vocabulary of abuse ('. . . dangerous class . . . social scum . . . that passively rotting mass'), the substantial group thus denoted in underdeveloped countries seems to play a role as a 'reserve army of labour' and to have, by virtue of this 'marginality' between rural and urban societies, a revolutionary potential. Fanon certainly thought so and Cabral also in part concurs. It must be said, however, that, as yet, such potential remains largely unrealized. And here too there are problems of definition: it is not altogether clear who exactly the lumpen proletariat are, or whether they can be defined other than residually. (In particular, the frontier between them and some sections of the 'petty bourgeoisie' seems tenuous.) Moreover, the theory of a 'reserve army of labour' is quite compatible with full employment (as long as wage labour pays better than alternative forms of employment).[11]

(f) *the peasantry.* Most of the crucial innovations of neo-Marxism concern the peasantry. They are not an easy subject for Marxist or indeed any sociological analysis, although important analytical and historical contributions have been made by Alavi (1965) and Wolf. Shanin, who dubs them 'The Awkward Class', has commented on their low and even multiple 'classness', whereby the observer is faced with a hopeless melange of kin, economic, and social relations changing seasonally and over time. We have already seen how traditional Marxism downgrades them. Marx's concern was with industrial capitalism, which he saw as irrupting into a world hitherto entirely rural in its economic base, and ultimately transforming it into an entirely industrial state in which, at most, rural workers would be a very minor sub-category of workers as such.

That the world has *not* evolved thus has been a central theme of this paper. In a situation characterized by uneven development and negative underdevelopment – as well as by much planned intervention by all sorts of social forces affecting the 'secular' evolution of capitalism, a point to whose implications we shall return – some of the specific qualities and vices claimed for worker and peasant respectively seem less fixed. Such a situation generates a multiplicity of contradictions and hence sources of conflict, the coincidence of which may, as in Russia in 1917, provide an explosive revolutionary potential. Thus Lenin argued (1963: 103) that in such a context, a revolutionary party should speak for *all* oppressed classes. Mao showed in practice how a peasantry could fulfil the revolutionary task which the urban based proletariat was unable to carry through.

Lenin's notion of 'trade-union consciousness' as the limit of spontaneous proletarian political development has been generalized by Cabral's distinction between a 'physical' and a 'revolutionary' force: the former will not of itself explode, but can be ignited by the latter. This elementary distinction would seem to eliminate a great deal of misplaced controversy. These days it is not a question (if indeed it ever was) of a class developing 'naturally', because of its position in production relations, a certain consciousness. Rather, an unevenly developed world presents a market of images, separating the roles of catalyst and reagent but at the same time thereby allowing that no group need, in principle, be excluded by an isolated mode of production from taking a central place in the revolutionary process. And since, in fact, most revolutions in this century have been peasant ones, the reflexes of orthodoxy on the part of both friends who call them 'proletarian' and foes who call them 'un-Marxist' are equally misplaced.

(iv) *Revolution*

Much of the preceding class discussion has also been about the nature of revolution as a process. Debray turned revolutionary theory on its head, by substituting the guerrilla *foco* as the spark that ignites class consciousness, instead of seeing class consciousness as arising out of the organized struggle of the classes themselves. (But then Luxemburg (1961) accused Lenin of adopting a similarly, if less extremely 'vanguardist' perspective.) Hobsbawm (1970) has detected a methological error in the approach of Debray and others, suggesting that they regard class consciousness as a relatively constant potential, which can be unleashed by finding the right key; whereas, in reality, it is a dynamic and changing phenomenon, responding to perceived events and circumstances.

(v) *Communism*

Nowhere is this weakness more apparent than in neo-Marxism's efforts to grapple with something that Marxism originally, for obvious reasons, did not have to face: namely, the consequences over one-third of the globe of attempts to realize Marxism in political practice. From Lenin's and Trotsky's original perspectives of the Russian Revolution as triggering an almost immediate European and world upheaval, there has supervened a half-century of increasing and finally bewildering national idiosyncrasies. Perhaps the major fault of Marxist (and bourgeois) accounts has been to persist in regarding all these as epiphenomena of a single underlying trend, 'communism'; only now is the variety being fully acknowledged. One wonders at the temerity of those who, like Dunayevskaya and the Trotskyists, have attempted to reduce such diversity to a single essence: 'state capitalist', 'degenerated worker's state', and the like. Official designations of 'socialism' are equally opaque: the Russian announcement a few years ago that they were now on the path to 'full communism' recalls nothing so much as the claim of Jehovah's Witnesses that the world ended in 1918 – unnoticed, of course, save by the elect. Neo-Marxism's major failure from our perspective lies in not analysing communism as a system of relations, whether on its own or as a sub-system of the world economy. One needs to know just how, if at all, the various levels of dependency of Albania, Mongolia, Cuba or eastern Europe, differ from (say) Frank's metropolis – satellite schema: as it stands, the latter brings in communism simply as a *deus ex machina*, achieved by 'breaking out' of imperialism. But in a world of uneven and combined development, where different stages co-exist in space and time, communism requires to be linked in more structurally with the overall system: no land is an island, however professedly autarkic. We need further development of Sweezy's notion of transition as ambiguous – it may go either way, forwards or backwards

– or Lange's rather mechanistic theory that socialism still has particular 'laws of motion', but that unlike capitalism it is 'in rhythm' with them. Also promising is Ota Sik's attempt, cited by Barratt Brown (1972: 47), to provide the economic dimension to Soviet imperialism by exploring how highly centralized planning requires a degree of prescience and control over supplies and markets that may not take account of national boundaries; there must be scope for such analyses, especially in eastern Europe.

(vi) *Morals and Action*

A notable feature of neo-Marxism in practice rather than theory has been its stress on the necessity and possibility for self-transformation. One sees this on the individual level with Malcolm X, George Jackson, or Cleaver, and on the social plane variously in the Cuban and Chinese emphasis on 'socialist man' and moral incentives, and Cabral's and Kim Il Sung's notion of ideologically proletarianizing those who are not industrial workers (petty bourgeoisie or peasants) so as to make of them reliable cadres. But a theoretical account of this angle is lacking: it would be a project different from the efforts of an earlier, Kantian school of Marxists, such as Max Adler, who, as Marek recalls, tried to supply what they regarded as a missing moral categorical imperative to Marxism. The direction of advance will have to be more methodological than ethical or even psychological: for the 'gap' between Marxism-as-history and as-action, which Sartre detected, still remains, as illustrated in the notion of 'voluntarism' as a Leninist sin: thou shalt not give the forces of history a push. In this sense Marxism needs its own phenomenology, just as bourgeois sociology is moving the same way. As Hilal notes, Fanon is the single major example of this approach to date.

(vii) *Town and Country*

What Marx characterized as one of the most basic social antagonisms has been little studied in its own right by Marxists ancient or modern, except tangentially in discussions of worker and peasant consciousness and the like. Frank, however, has stressed the exploitative role of the Latin American city as an important link in his metropolis-satellite chain; McGee has noted the parasitical and non-indigenous character of the typical Third World City; and, most notoriously, Lin Piao has taken up Marx's likening of the relationship between backward and advanced countries to that between country and town, with his image of the 'world-village' encircling and overcoming the 'world-city'.

It seems imperative in our day to purge Marxism's traditional contempt for the 'idiocy of rural life'. As argued above, advances in communication make it simply inept to regard any area as too 'backward' for socialist ideas. Even if peasant society is due to perish ultimately under socialism, a political practice based on expediting this process is bound to be elitist, terroristic, and self-defeating.

(viii) *Ecology*

Recent developments, however, cast some doubt on whether such a scenario is feasible at all. As Barratt Brown (1972) and others are beginning to notice, capitalism is proving to be destructive in a manner and on a scale hitherto beyond the conception of even its fiercest enemies. The rate at which modern imperialism is ever more rapidly using up irreplaceable fossil fuels and other mineral resources suggests that these will largely be extinct by the end of the century. Synthetic alternatives may to some extent be available, but it is hard to see this as 'built-in' in the manner assumed by the dwindling band of optimists. If the peasant revolutions of our time represent the cast of extras taking over the drama then the ecological perspective means that the very *stage* is suddenly transformed into the plot. Most ecologists have ethnocentrically concentrated on the developed world, and insisted that it will have to experience 'de-growth'. The corollary for underdeveloped countries is that they will never attain the living standards of the presently 'over-developed' world, for two reasons: there are not enough mineral resources to maintain the whole world at such a level, and, even if there were, the necessary energy-consumption would cause a climatic catastrophe (melting of the polar ice-caps, and the like).

For Marxists, abundance is out: arguably it was always an ultimately meaningless notion, but henceforth 'scarcity' will have to be accepted as more than just a bugbear of bourgeois economics defending unequal social relations. Industry is out too, in some sense; certainly centralized heavy industrialization as a socialist strategy is no longer feasible, which may be no bad thing; and palaeo-Marxists will have to learn to love the peasants after all.

Malcolm Caldwell (1971a) is perhaps the sole Marxist who has, to date, thought all this through. He argues that not just capitalist underdevelopment, but industrial society as such, must now be seen as an historical cul-de-sac, and that further social development will come from a stage 'further back'. Such a formulation, heretical as it sounds, surely represents a genuine and necessary creative development of the idea of

unevenness and combination of stages. For those who are not cata-
strophically affected by the crisis are, of course, the peasants, and, more
particularly, those peasant societies that conceive of their development
in terms of the peasantry, such as China (whose avid conservationism is
grudgingly admired by ecologists). Caldwell cites the example of the
Pathet Lao, with not a proletarian in sight; and certainly the struggle of
the Indo-Chinese peasantries against the American machine (literally)
takes on a new light in this perspective.

It would be mistaken to view this prospect as a regression: the world-
historical experience of urban industrialism will have been a massive
cultural fact, and the social forms that follow it will not be remotely
comparable to the universal ruralism that, for most of human history,
preceded it. (In any case, there is no reason to suppose that particular
technologies, which are mainly skills rather than resource based, will not
survive and indeed flourish.) But there is no denying the paradox and
the challenge: Marxism, which like sociology itself represents above all a
response to the unprecedented social changes of rising nineteenth-
century industrialism, is being asked in the twentieth century to preside
over the de-industrialization of part of the globe and the rural-based
ecologically evolutionary (although initially, of course, politically
revolutionary) development of the rest. Those who insist that such a
process has nothing to do with Marxism merely ensure that what they
choose to call Marxism will have nothing to do with what happens in the
world. For this Marxist, at least, a model of Marxism that treats with
compassion and respect not only the natural world on which human life
depends, but also that preponderant rural portion of humanity that
Marxists have all too often assimilated to nature (and thereby felt justified in exploiting as a mere object in the name of historical progress) is
neither heretical nor regressive; on the contrary, it shows, as Marxism
has always tried to do, the only possible way forward.

Notes

1 For reasons of space, this published version has been reduced in
   length by about one-third from the original paper presented at York.
   In particular, section 2(b), 'The Bourgeois Background' has been more
   than halved. The author is currently working on this topic in a separate
   paper – 'The development of development: a study in ideology'.
   I should like to thank Gavin Williams for the sympathetic skill of his
   editorial surgery, which rendered this major operation almost entirely

painless. He also made a number of valuable suggestions, which I have incorporated, especially in the discussion of class (Section 3(b)(iii)).

I should also like to acknowledge the constant stimulus of colleagues in the self-defined 'Hull School', especially Ivor Oxaal and David Booth, and their tolerance of the unequal exchange whereby I continually borrow their books and their ideas.

As most bibliographical references are to a writer's *ouvre* rather than a specific title, references in the text are made only to the names of the authors, unless it is essential to distinguish particular items.

2 Examples of palaeo-Marxism might include Perlo, Dutt, and, in some respects, Harris. Ostensively defined, the neo-Marxists would include (in alphabetic order, and implying nothing about their widely differing qualities): Alavi, Amin, Ar righi, Baran, Bettelheim, Buchanan, Caldwell, Debray, Emmanuel, Frank, Gerassi, Greene, Hensman, Horowitz, Jalee, Jenkins, Magdoff, Shanin, Sweezy, and possibly Moore, on the one hand; and on the other hand Cabral, Castro, Fanon, Guevara, Ho, Kim Il Sung, and Mao.

3 See the surveys by Barratt Brown (1972) and Kemp, also Sutcliffe and Owen's collection.

4 viz. Fleming, Morray, Alperowitz, Kolko, Horowitz, *et al.*

5 viz. Alavi, Caldwell, Shanin, and Wolf.

6 e.g. Hayter, Hensman, and the group which produced the Haslemere Declaration.

7 Some are listed at the end of the bibliography.

8 On the use of 'class' and 'contradiction' in the analysis of an underdeveloped society (Jamaica), see Post.

9 But see Laclau's critique of Frank.

10 See for example, Arrighi and Saul (1968); Arrighi (1970).

11 On the 'employment' debate, cf. Weeks (1972).

*References**

*   In addition to works cited in the text, this bibliography also includes other works which in the author's opinion have contributed to or are symptomatic of the phenomenon under consideration.

ABDELL-MALEK A. (ed.) Forthcoming. *Armée et Nation dans les trois Continents.*

AGUILAR, L. A. 1968. *Marxism in Latin America.* New York: Knopf.

ALAVI, H. 1962. The Burden of US Aid. *New University Thought 2.*

—— 1964. Imperialism Old and New. *Socialist Register.*

—— 1965. Peasantry and Revolution. *Socialist Register.*

ALLEN, C. and JOHNSON, R. W. (eds.) 1970. *African Perspectives*. Cambridge: Cambridge University Press.

ALPEROWITZ, G. 1965. *Atomic Diplomacy: Hiroshima and Potsdam*. New York; Simon & Schuster.

AMIN, S. 1965. *Trois Expériences Africaines de Développement: le Mali, la Guinée, et le Ghana*. Paris: Presses Universitaires de France.

—— 1966. *L'Économie du Maghreb*. Paris: Editions de Minuit.

—— 1967. *Le Développement du Capitalisme en Côte d'Ivoire*. Paris: Editions de Minuit.

—— 1969. *Le Monde des Affaires Sénégalais*. Paris: Editions de Minuit.

—— 1970. *L'Accumulation a l'Échelle Mondiale Critique de la Théorie du Sous-développement*. Paris: IFAN-Anthropos.

—— 1971a. *L'Afrique de l'Ouest bloquée: l'Économie Politique de la Colonisation 1880–1970*. Paris: Editions de Minuit.

—— 1971b. *The Maghreb in the Modern World*. Harmondsworth: Penguin.

AMIN, S. and COQUERY-VIDROVICH, C. 1969. *Histoire Économique du Congo, 1880–1968*. Paris: IFAN-Anthropos.

ARRIGHI, G. 1970a. *The Political Economy in Rhodesia*. The Hague: Mouton.

—— 1970b. International Corporations, Labour Aristocracies, and Economic Development in Tropical Africa. In R. I. Rhodes, 1970.

ARRIGHI, G. and SAUL, J. S. 1968. Socialism and Economic Development in Tropical Africa. *Journal of Modern African Studies* 6.

—— 1969. Nationalism and Revolution in Sub-Saharian Africa. *Socialist Register*.

The above refs. for Arrighi and Arrighi and Saul can be found in ARRIGHI and SAUL (1973) *Essays on the Political Economy of Africa*. New York: Monthly Review Press.

AVINERI, S. 1969. *Karl Marx on Colonialism and Modernisation*. New York: Doubleday.

AYRTON, R. 1971. Some Aspects of Contemporary Imperialism. Paper presented at conference on 'Racism in the Political Economy of Britain' (December) London.

BAIROCH, P. 1963. *Révolution Industrielle et Sous-développement*. Paris: SEDES.

—— 1967. *Diagnostique de l'Évolution Économique du Tier-monde, 1900–1966*. Paris: Gauthier-Villars.

BARAN, P. 1957. *The Political Economy of Growth*. New York: Monthly Review Press.

BARRATT BROWN, M. 1970. *After Imperialism* (2nd ed.). London: Heinemann.

—— 1972. *Essays on Imperialism*. Nottingham: Spokesman.

BECKFORD, G. 1972. *Persistent Poverty: Underdevelopment in Plantation Economies of the Third World*. New York: Oxford University Press.

BETTELHEIM, C. 1959. *Studies in the Theory of Planning*. London: Asia.

—— (*et al.*) 1965. *La Construction du Socialisme en Chine*. Paris: Maspero.

—— 1967. *Planification et Croissance Accélérée*. Paris: Maspero.

—— 1968a. *La Transition vers l'Économie Socialiste*. Paris: Maspero.

—— 1968b. *India Independent*. London: MacGibbon & Kee.

—— 1970a. *Calcul Économique et Formes de Proprieté*. Paris: Maspero.

—— 1970b. Chine et URSS: Deux Modeles Industrialisation. *Temps modernes*: 289–90.

BUCHANAN, K. 1963. The Third World: It's Emergence and Contours. *New Left Review* **18**.

—— 1972. *The Geography of Empire*. Nottingham: Spokesman.

CABRAL, A. 1969. *Revolution in Guinea: An African People's Struggle*. London: Stage One.

CALDWELL, M. 1970. The Revolutionary Role of the Peasantry. *International Socialism* (41).

—— 1970. The Role of the Peasantry in Revolution. *Journal of Contemporary Asia* **1** (1: Autumn).

—— 1971a. *The Imperialism of Energy and the Energy of Imperialism*. (pamphlet) London.

—— 1971b. Oil Imperialism in South-East Asia. *Journal of Contemporary Asia* **1** (3).

CALDWELL, M. and HENDERSON, J. T. 1968. *The Chainless Mind: A Study of Resistance and Liberation*. London: Hamish Hamilton.

CAMMETT, J. M. 1967. *Antonio Gramsci and the Origins of Italian Communism*. Stanford: Stanford University Press.

CARRERE D'ENCAUSSE, H. and SCHRAM, S. 1969. *Marxism and Asia: An Introduction with Readings*. London: Allen Lane.

CASTRO, F. 1968. *History will Absolve Me*. London: Cape Editions.

CASTRO, F. (Edited by KENNER, M. and PETRAS, J.) 1972. *Fidel Castro speaks*. Harmondsworth: Penguin.

CHALIAND, G. 1969. *Armed Struggle in Africa: with the Guerillas in 'Portuguese' Guinea*. New York: Monthly Review.

—— 1970. *The Peasants of North Vietnam*. Harmondsworth: Penguin.

CLAIRMONTE, F. 1960. *Economic Liberalism and Underdevelopment: Studies in the Disintegration of an Idea*. London: Asia Publishing House.

CLEAVER, E. 1968. *Soul on Ice*. London: Cape.

—— 1971. *Revolution in the Congo*. London: Stage One.

DAVIDSON, B. 1959. *Old Africa Rediscovered*. London: Gollancz.

—— 1961. *Black Mother*. London: Gollancz.

—— 1964a. *The African Past*. London: Longmans.

—— 1965. *The African Awakening*. London: Cape.

—— 1964b. *The Liberation of Guiné*. Harmondsworth: Penguin.

—— 1971. *Which Way Africa?* (rev. ed.) Harmondsworth: Penguin.

DAVIS, H. B. 1967. *Nationalism and Socialism: Marxist and Labor Theories of Nationalism to 1917*. New York: Monthly Review Press.

DEBRAY, R. 1967. *Revolution in the Revolution?* Harmondsworth: Penguin.

—— 1970. *Strategy for Revolution*. London: Cape.

DEBRAY, R., HUBERMAN, L. and SWEEZY, P. (eds.) 1968. *Regis Debray and the Latin American Revolution*. New York: Monthly Review Press.

DE CASTRO, J. 1952. *The Geography of Hunger*. London: Gollancz.

DIOP, C. A. 1955. *Nations Nègres et Culture*. Paris: Éditions Africaines.

DOS SANTOS, T. 1970. The Structure of Dependence. *American Economic Review* **60** (May).

—— 1969. La Crise de la Théorie de Développement et les Rélations de Dépendence en Amérique Latine. *L'Homme et la société* **12** (avr-juin).

DRAPER, T. 1965. *Castroism: Theory and Practice*. New York: Praeger.

DUMONT, R. 1965. *Lands Alive*. London: Merlin.

—— 1966. *False Start in Africa*. London: André Deutsch.

—— 1970a. *Cuba: Socialism and Development*. New York: Grove.

—— 1970b. *Cuba est-il Socialiste?* Paris: Éditions du Seuil.

DUMONT, R. and ROSIER, B. 1969. *The Hungry Future*. London: Methuen.

DUMONT, R. and MASOYER, M. 1971. *Development and Socialism*. New York: Praeger.

DUNAYEVSKAYA, R. 1964. *Marxism and Freedom* (second edition). New York: Twayne.

DUTT, R. Palme. 1957. *The Crisis of Britain and the British Empire*. London: Lawrence & Wishart.

EHRENSAFT, P. 1972. Semi-industrial Capitalism in the Third World: Implications for Social Research in Africa. *Reader in East African Society and Environment* **5** (Dar es Salaam). Also *Africa Today* January, 1971.

EL-KODSKY, A. 1970. *Nationalism and Class Struggles in the Arab World*. Monthly Review.

EMMANUEL, A. 1970. The Delusions of Internationalism. *Monthly Review* 22–2 June.

—— 1972a. *Unequal Exchange: A Study in the Imperialism of Free Trade*. London: New Left Books.

—— 1972b. White Settler Colonialism and the Myth of Investment Imperialism. *New Left Review* **73**.

FANN, K. T. and HODGES, D. 1971. *Readings in US Imperialism*. Boston: Porter Sargent.

FANON, F. 1967. *The Wretched of the Earth*. Harmondsworth: Penguin.

—— 1968. *Black Skin, White Marks*. London: MacGibbon & Kee.

—— 1970a. *A Dying Colonialism*. Harmondsworth: Penguin.

—— 1970b. *Towards the African Revolution*. Harmondsworth: Penguin.

FITCH, R. and OPPENHEIMER, M. 1966. *Ghana: End of an Illusion*. New York: Monthly Review Press.

FLEMING, D. F. 1961. *The Cold War and its Origins* (2 vols). New York: Doubleday.

FRANK, A. G. 1969a. *Capitalism and Underdevelopment in Latin America* (revised edition). New York: Monthly Review Press.

—— 1969b. *Latin America: Underdevelopment or Revolution.* New York: Monthly Review Press.

—— 1969c. The Development of Underdevelopment. *Monthly Review* **18** (4: September).

—— 1970a. The Wealth and Poverty of Nations. *Economic and Political Weekly.* July (Bombay).

—— 1970b. *Lumpen Bourgeois et Lumpendeveloppement.* Paris: Maspero. English edition (1972) New York: Monthly Review Press.

—— 1972. *Sociology of Underdevelopment and Underdevelopment of Sociology.* London: Pluto Press.

FREIRE, P. 1970. *Pedagogy of the Oppressed.* New York: Herder & Herder.

FURTADO, C. 1971. *Obstacles to Development in Latin America.* New York: Doubleday.

GALTUNG, J. 1971/2. A Structural Theory of Imperialism. *Journal of Peace Research.*

GALEANO, E. 1970. Latin America and the Theory of Imperialism. *Monthly Review* **21** (1: April).

—— 1969. *Guatemala: Occupied Country.* N.Y.: Monthly Review Press.

GERASSI, J. 1965. *The Great Fear in Latin America.* New York: Collier-MacMillan.

GERASSI, J. (ed.) 1971. *Towards Revolution* (2 vols). London: Weidenfeld & Nicholson.

GERASSI, J. Forthcoming. *The Coming of the New International.*

GORKY, M. 1971. *On the Russian Peasantry.* Ladyzhnikov, 1922. (In SHANIN 1971: 367–71.

GOTT, R. 1970. *Guerilla movements in Latin America.* London: Nelson.

GOUGH, K. and SHARMA, H. (eds.) Forthcoming. *Imperialism and Revolution in South Asia.* New York: Monthly Review Press.

GRAMSCI, A. 1957. *The Modern Prince, and Other Writings.* London: Lawrence & Wishart.

GREENE, F. 1968. *A Curtain of Ignorance: How America is deceived about China.* London: Cape.

—— 1970. *The Enemy: Some Notes on the Nature of Contemporary Imperialism.* London: Cape.

GRIFFIN, K. B. 1969. *Underdevelopment in Spanish America: An Interpretation.* London: Allen & Unwin.

GRUNDFEST, H. 1951. Malthusianism. *Monthly Review* September.

GUEVARA, E. 1969a. *Guerilla War.* Harmondsworth: Penguin.

—— 1969b. *Reminiscences of the Cuban Revolutionary War*. Harmondsworth: Penguin.

—— 1969c. *Venceremos! (Collected Speeches and Writings)*. London: Panther.

HALPER, S. A. and STERLING, J. (eds.) 1972. *Latin America: the Dynamics of Social Change*. London: Alison & Busby.

HARRIS, N. 1968. *Beliefs in Society: the Problem of Ideology*. London: Watts.

—— 1970. The Revolutionary Role of the Peasantry. *International Socialism* 41.

—— 1971. Imperialism Today. In Harris, N. and Palmer, J. 1971.

HARRIS, N. and PALMER, J. 1971. *World Crisis: Essays in Revolutionary Socialism*. London: Hutchinson.

HASLEMERE GROUP. 1971 & 1968. *Poverty is Violence: Exploitation of the Third World*. London: Haslemere Declaration, first edition 1968, second edition, 1971.

HAYTER, T. 1971. *Aid as Imperialism*. Harmondsworth: Penguin.

HEIMANN, E. 1952. Marxism and Underdeveloped Countries. *Social Research* September.

HENSMAN, C. R. (ed.) 1969. *From Gandhi to Guevara: The Polemics of Revolt*. London: Allen Lane.

HENSMAN, C. R. 1971. *Rich Against Poor: The Reality of Aid*. London: Allen Lane.

HILAL, J. 1970. *Sociology of Development* (mimeo.). Durham.

HILFERDING, R. 1923. *Das Finanzkapital*. Vienna.

HOBSBAWM, E. 1964. *Introduction to Karl Marx: Precapitalist Economic Formations*. London: Lawrence & Wishart.

—— 1970. Guerillas in Latin America. *Socialist Register*.

HOBSON, J. A. 1938. *Imperialism: A Study* (third edition). London: Allen & Unwin.

HO CHI MINH. 1967. *On Revolution: Selected Writings 1920–67*. London: Pall Mall.

HODGKIN, T. L. 1956. *Nationalism in Colonial Africa*. London: Muller.

HODGKIN, T. L. (ed.) 1967. *Nigerian Perspectives: An Historical Anthology*. London: Oxford University Press.

HOROWITZ, D. (ed.) 1967. *Containment and Revolution*. London: Blond.

HOROWITZ, D. 1969a. *From Yalta to Vietnam*. Harmondsworth: Penguin.

HOROWITZ, D. (ed.) 1969b. *Corporations and the Cold War*. New York: Monthly Review Press.

HOROWITZ, D. 1971. *Imperialism and Revolution*. Harmondsworth: Penguin.

JACKSON, G. 1971. *Soledad Brother: Prison Letters*. Harmondsworth: Penguin.

—— 1972. *Blood In My Eye*. London: Cape.

JALEE, P. 1963. Le Tiers Monde? Que Tiers Monde? *Revolution* 1 (7: November).

—— 1968. *The Pillage of the Third World*. New York: Monthly Review Press.

—— 1969. *The Third World in World Economy*. New York: Monthly Review Press.

—— 1972. *Imperialism in the Seventies*. New York: Monthly Review Press.

—— 1971. *Le Tiers-Monde en Chiffres*. Paris: Maspero.

—— 1965/66. Des Revisionnismes. *Partisans* December/January.

JENKINS, R. 1971. *Exploitation: The World Power Structure and the Inequality of Nations*. London: MacGibbon & Kee.

KALECKI, M. 1971. Theories of Growth in Different Social Systems. *Monthly Review* 23 (5: October).

KAUTSKY, K. 1901/2. Krisen Theorien. *Neue Zeit* 2.

KEMP, T. 1967. *Theories of Imperialism*. London: Dobson.

KIDRON, M. 1962. Imperialism – Highest Stage but One. *International Socialism* 9.

—— 1965. *Foreign Investments in India*. London: Oxford University Press.

—— 1968. *Western Capitalism since the War*. Harmondsworth: Penguin.

KIM IL SUNG. 1970. *Selected Works* (4 vols). Pyingyang.

—— 1971. *Revolution and Socialist Construction in Korea: Selected Writings*. New York: International Publishers.

KOLKO, G. 1969. *The Politics of War*. London: Weidenfeld & Nicolson.

LACLAU, E. 1971. Capitalism and Feudalism in Latin America. *New Left Review* 67 (May–June).

LANGE, O. 1962. *Problems of the Political Economy of Socialism*. New Delhi: People's Publishing House.

—— 1963. *Political Economy* 1. New York: MacMillan.

—— 1970. *Collected Papers in Economics and Sociology*. Oxford: Pergamon Press.

LENIN, V. I. n.d. *Imperialism, the Highest Stage of Capitalism*. Moscow: Foreign Language Publishing House.

—— 1963. *What is to be done?* Oxford: Clarendon Press.

—— 1964. *The Development of Capitalism in Russia*. Moscow: Foreign Language Publishing House.

—— 1947. *The State and Revolution*. Moscow: Foreign Language Publishing House.

—— 1965. *Alliance of the Working Class and Peasantry*. Moscow: Progress Publishers.

—— 1969. Better Fewer but Better (1923) (cited in D'Encausse and Schram 1969).

LENTIN, A. P. 1965. *La Lutte Tricontinentale*. Paris: Maspero.

LICHTHEIM, G. 1971. *Imperialism*. London: Allen Lane.

LIN PIAO. 1965. *The International Significance of Comrade Mao Tse-Tung's Theory of People's War*. Peking: Foreign Language Press.

LUKACS, F. 1971. *History and Class Consciousness*. London: Merlin Press.

LUXEMBURG, R. 1951. *The Accumulation of Capital*. London: Routledge & Kegan Paul.

—— 1961. *The Russian Revolution and Leninism or Marxism?* Ann Arbor: University of Michigan Press.

MAGDOFF, H. 1969. *The Age of Imperialism*. New York: Monthly Review Press.

—— 1970. Is Imperialism Really Necessary? *Monthly Review* 22 (586: October/November).

—— 1971. Economic Myths and Imperialism. *Monthly Review* 23 (7: December).

MCGEE, T. G. 1967. *The Southeast Asian City*. London: G. Bell.

MALCOLM, S. 1965. *Autobiography*. London: Hutchinson.

MANDEL, E. 1964. L'Apogée du Néo-capitalisme et ses Lendemeins. *Temps Moderns* (August/September).

—— 1970a. *Europe versus America?* London: New Left Books.

—— 1970b. The Laws of Uneven Development. *New Left Review* 59 (January/February).

MANDLE, J. 1972. The Plantation Economy: An Essay in Definition. *Science and Society* 36 (2: spring).

MAO TSE-TUNG. 1961. *Selected Works* (4 vols.) Peking: Foreign Language Press.

MAREK, F. 1969. *Philosophy of World Revolution*. London: Lawrence & Wishart.

MARINI, R. M. 1971. *Sous-développement et Révolution en Amerique Latine*. Paris: Maspero.

MARX, K. 1961. *Capital* (3 vols.) Moscow: Foreign Language Publishing House.

—— 1964. *The Eighteenth Brumaire of Louis Bonaparte*. New York: International Publishers.

—— 1964. *Precapitalist Economic Formations*. London: Lawrence & Wishart. (See also Avineri (1964) *op. cit*. Shanin (1971) *op. cit*. pp. 229–371.)

—— 1965. *The Class Struggle in France 1848–50*. Moscow: Progress Publishers.

MARX, K. and ENGELS, F. n.d. *On Colonialism*. Moscow: Foreign Language Publishing House.

—— 1968a. *On Ireland*. London: Lawrence and Wishart.

—— 1968b. *Selected Works*. London: Lawrence and Wishart.

MEISNER, M. 1967. *Li Ta-Chao and the Origins of Chinese Marxism.* Cambridge, Mass.: Harvard University Press.

MILLER, S. M. *et al.* 1970. Does the US Economy require Imperialism? *Social Policy* (September/October).

MILLS, C. W. 1969. *The Marxists.* Harmondsworth: Penguin.

MITRANY, D. 1961. *Marx against the Peasant.* New York: Collier-Mac-Millan.

MOORE, B. 1967. *Social Origins of Dictatorship and Democracy: Lord and Peasant in the Making of the Modern World.* London: Allen Lane.

MORRAY, J. P. 1961. *From Yalta to Disarmament.* New York: Monthly Review Press.

——1962. *The Second Revolution in Cuba.* New York: Monthly Review Press.

MOUSSA, P. 1963. *Les Nations Prolétaires.* Paris: Presses Universitaires de France.

MURRAY, R. 1971. Internationalization of Capital and the Nation State. *New Left Review* **67** (May/June).

MYRDAL, G. 1969. *Asian Drama: An Enquiry into the Poverty of Nations.* London: Allen Lane.

—— 1970. *The Challenge of World Poverty.* London: Allen Lane.

NIRUMAND, B. 1969. *Iran: The New Imperialism in Action.* New York: Random House.

O'CONNOR, J. 1970. International Corporations and Underdevelopment. *Science and Society* **34** (1: spring).

PALLOIX, C. 1972. *L'Économie Mondiale Capitaliste* (2 vols). Paris: Maspero.

PEARSON, L. B. (ed.) 1970. *Partners in Development: Report of the Committee on International Development.* London: Pall Mall.

PERLO, V. 1957. *The Empire of High Finance.* New York: International Publishers.

PETRAS, J. 1971. *Politics and Social Structure in Latin America.* New York: Monthly Review Press.

PLEKHANOV, G. (Quoted by SHANIN, 1971: 239.)

POMEROY, W. (ed.) 1968. *Guerrilla Warfare and Marxism.* New York: International Publishers.

POMEROY, W. 1970. *American Neo-colonialism: Its Emergence in the Philippines and Asia.* New York: International Publishers.

POST, K. Unpublished manuscript on Jamaica.

PREOBRAZHENSKY, E. 1965. *The New Economics.* London: Oxford University Press (Excerpts in Shanin, 1971: 219–26).

RHODES, R. I. 1968. The Disguised Conservatism in Evolutionary Development. *Science and Society* **32** (4: fall).

RHODES, R. I. (ed.) 1970. *Imperialism and Underdevelopment: A Reader.* New York: Monthly Review Press.

RODNEY, W. 1972. *How Europe underdeveloped Africa.* London: Bogle L'ouverture.

ROSTOW, W. W. 1971. *The Stages of Economic Growth: A Non-communist Manifesto* (second edition). Cambridge: Cambridge University Press.

SACHS, I. 1966. On Growth Potential, Proportional Growth and Perverse Growth. Czechoslovak Economic Papers 7, Prague.

SARTRE, J. P. 1960. *Critique de la Raison Dialectique.* Paris: Gallimard.

—— 1963. *Black Orpheus.* Paris: Presume africaine.

—— 1967. Preface. In FANON 1967.

SCHLESINGER, A. 1961. *Cuba.* US Department of State Publications, 7171. Inter-American Series 66 (April).

SHANIN, T. 1966. The Peasantry as a Political Force. *Sociological Review* 14 (1). (Also in SHANIN (ed.) 1971: 238–63.)

—— 1970. Class and Revolution. *Journal of Contemporary Asia* 1 (2: winter).

SHANIN, T. (ed.) 1971. *Peasants and Peasant Societies.* Harmondsworth: Penguin.

SHANIN, T. 1972. *The Awkward Class.* London: Oxford University Press.

STALEY, E. 1954. *The Future of Underdeveloped Countries: Political Implications of Economic Development.* New York: Harper.

STALIN, J. 1935. *Marxism and the National Question.* London: Lawrence & Wishart.

STEIN, S. J. and STEIN, B. H. 1970. *The Colonial Heritage of Latin America: Essays on Economic Dependence in Perspective.* New York: Oxford University Press.

SULTAN GALIEV (cited in Carrere D'Encausse and Schram (eds.), 1969.

SURET-CANALE, J. 1971. *French Colonialism in Tropical Africa.* New York: Universe.

SUTCLIFFE, R. B. 1970. The Third World and Social History. Oxford, mimeo.

—— 1972. *Industry and Underdevelopment.* Reading, Mass.: Addison-Wesley.

SUTCLIFFE, R. B. and OWEN, R. 1972. *Studies in the Theory of Imperialism.* London: Longmans.

SWEEZY, P. 1968. The Proletariat in Today's World. *Tricontinental* 9.

SWEEZY, P. and BETTELHEIM, C. 1971. *On the Transition to Socialism.* New York: Monthly Review Press.

TERRAY, E. 1972. *Marxism and 'Primitive' Societies: Two Studies.* New York: Monthly Review Press.

THORNER, D. Peasant Economy as a Category in Economic History. In SHANIN 1971: 202–18.

TROTSKY, L. 1962. *Permanent Revolution.* New York: Pioneer.

—— 1964. (Ed. I. Deutscher) *The Age of Permanent Revolution: A Trotsky Anthology*. New York: Dell.

—— 1966. *Problems of the Chinese Revolution*. New York: Paragon Reprints.

—— 1970. *History of the Russian Revolution* (3 vols). London: Sphere.

WATNICK, M. 1952. The Appeal of Communism to the Peoples of Under-developed Areas. *Economic Development and Cultural Change* 1 (1).

WEEKS, J. 1971. The Political Economy of Labor Transfer. *Science and Society* 35 (4: winter).

—— 1972. Employment, Growth and Foreign Domination. *Review of Radical Political Economics* 4 (1: spring).

WERTHEIM, W. Forthcoming. *Evolution and Revolution*. Harmondsworth: Penguin.

WILLIAMS, G. 1970. Social Stratification of a Neo-colonial Economy. In ALLEN C. and JOHNSON R. W. (eds.) 1970.

—— 1972. The Political Economy of Colonialism and Neo-colonialism in Nigeria. Unpublished paper.

WODDIS, J. 1972. *New Theories of Revolution*. London: Lawrence & Wishart.

WOLF, E. R. 1969. On Peasant Rebellions. *International Social Science Journal* 21.

—— 1970. *Peasant Wars of the Twentieth Century*. London: Faber & Faber.

WORSLEY, P. 1967. *The Third World*. London: Weidenfeld & Nicolson.

—— 1969. Frantz Fanon – Revolutionary Theorist. *Monthly Review* 21 1: May).

Organizations

Africa Research Group (ARG): P.O. Box 213, Cambridge, Massachussets 02138, U.S.A.

North America Congress on Latin America (NACLA): P.O. Box 27, Cathedral Park Station, New York, NY 10025.

Committee of Concerned Asia Scholars (CCAS): 9 Sutter Street, Room 300, San Francisco, California 94104.

Pacific Studies Center: 1963 University Avenue, East Palo Alto, California.

Association for Radical East Asian Studies (AREAS): c/o School of Oriental and African Studies, London University.

PART TWO

Class

GAVIN WILLIAMS

Political Consciousness among the Ibadan Poor[1]

COLONIAL CAPITALISM AND SOCIAL DIFFERENTIATION

Colonial capitalism has transformed significant social relationships into commodity relationships. It has thereby differentiated the colonized society along new lines, so that people's life-chances are determined by their access to and exclusion from resources introduced by the colonial political economy. At the very simplest level of analysis, Ibadan, like other societies, divides into two, those who have, and those who have not. The distinction is given expression in the Yoruba word *mẹkunnu*, best rendered in English as 'an ordinary person', or in the plural as 'the common people'.[2] Depending on the context, the *mẹkunnu* may be distinguished from the *olowo* (wealthy), who constitute the most obvious antithesis, but also from the *ọmọwe* (educated), *ọlọla* (noble, in Ibadan, implying chiefs), or *alagbara* (powerful).

The *mẹkunnu* are a diverse, and vaguely demarcated category including people with such different 'class situations' (Weber 1948: 181) as traders, farmers, and industrial workers. This paper will accordingly examine the differences among these groups with respect to their specific class situation, the demands they make, and the resources that they can use to realize these demands. But we must not lose sight of what they share with each other: a common awareness of being excluded from the significant opportunities for gaining rewards in society, and aspirations and values derived from interaction with one another in the compound, the town, and the market. We shall concern ourselves particularly with the ways in which different groups of people among the *mẹkunnu* – the wage-employed, the self-employed, and the farmers – seek to advance their own interests and 'end their suffering'.

The basis of the colonial economy of Ibadan was, and still is, the cultivation of cocoa, which spread rapidly in the years 1892 to 1912. This entailed a migration of people from the city to the rural areas and the emergence of a peasantry (Post 1972) which, in recent years, has come to develop a distinct rural consciousness. The cultivation of cocoa created lucrative opportunities in the export-import trade for mercantile firms, and on a smaller scale, for the intermediaries whom they needed to buy the cocoa from the farmers and to sell the imports financed from cocoa to the farmers and others. The development of the produce trade and the expansion of feeder roads in the twenties opened up opportunities in road transport for those, notably produce buyers, best placed to take advantage of them. Further, the multiplier effects of the cash derived from cocoa provided a market for foodstuffs, for a variety of crafts, with pre-colonial crafts being eclipsed by those using imported tools and materials, and for a host of petty traders. The increasingly complex needs of administration and the educational efforts of the missionaries created a new stratum of clerks, particularly significant with the increasing administrative importance of Ibadan from 1939 onwards. Colonial rule also required the emergence of a small wage-labour force in construction, on the docks, in the ports, and on the railways.

Those who made best use of the new opportunities in trade and education found their opportunities for further advancement blocked by the administrative, educational, and commercial policies of the colonial administration and the mercantile firms. It was these groups who led the opposition to colonial rule and who, during the nineteen-fifties, negotiated the terms of the relationship between Nigeria and the colonial interests in such a way as to give themselves access to a large part of the surplus value exacted from the peasantry and from the exploitation of mineral resources. This labour laid the foundations for a neo-colonial economy, characterized by the rapid growth of the capital-intensive, technologically advanced, import substitution sector, of direct state involvement in the economy, and thus by the expansion of opportunities for wage employment, government employment, and for indigenous entrepreneurs as well as for foreign capital (Williams 1970; Osoba 1967).

Thus in contemporary Nigeria, the significant levers of economic power continue to be in foreign hands. But the activities of the state administration, now controlled by businessmen, bureaucrats, professionals, and army officers in their own interests, ensure their association with foreign interests in the expropriation of the surplus and enable them to carve out areas of economic activity where the rewards are reserved to them. These groups constitute the 'haves', many of whom are, however, of humble origin and retain links with their lineages and townsmen. Our concern here is with the response of the 'have nots' to the expropriation of resources, rewards, and opportunities at their expense by the 'haves'.

VALUES AND ASPIRATION IN CONTEMPORARY IBADAN

Ibadan was established as a warcamp. It was a town where rewards went to the brave and enterprising. A man wishing to establish himself politically would gather a following that would follow him both in war and in the affairs of the town and be compensated by grants of land and the exercise of influence with the powerful. Thus both leaders and followers valued initiative, independence, and generosity very highly (P. C. Lloyd 1970). These are the same values that one would expect to arise from the opportunity and reward system of colonial western Nigeria. Thus the successful men were precisely those who best exemplified these values;[3] these values in turn legitimated their rewards. Examples of men from humble origins who became successful traders lent credence to a picture of a society with open mobility. These men were thus an 'elite' in Nadel's (1956) sense, an imitable reference group that provided a model for the aspirations of others.

Education provided an important channel of mobility in southern Nigeria, initially very often for those from the humblest homes. People thus look to the expansion of educational opportunities to provide their children with a chance to make good. Education is closely associated with the techniques and products of modern technology with which the accepted goals of 'progress' and 'development' are associated. The indispensability of the educated for the achievement of a 'modern' and 'civilized' society legitimates their rewards and prevents the control of power by the educated from being questioned as such, however much their exercise of that power may be disliked.

Increasingly social status is associated with sheer wealth and with the status symbols of modern capitalism (expensive cars, large houses) as well as lavish expenditure on customary ceremonies (funerals, naming ceremonies). Recognition of wealth as the criterion for social status is, however, often grudgingly given. Ibadans (but not in my experience elite Yoruba) tend to distinguish sharply between the *olowo* (the rich man, pure and simple), and the *ọlọla* (man of honour), defined by one respondent as 'those who had been installed as chiefs, had plenty of farm and town land, and had given it to their people', and, by implication, whose honour cannot be bought – even though people are well aware that chieftaincy titles usually go to the man with the longest purse. The distinction between sheer cash and pure honour (Weber 1948: 192) here, as elsewhere, reflects concern at the fact of wealth alone deciding a man's status (and even the allocation of titles). As a watch-repairer of an honourable lineage (*ile ọla*) regretfully explained, 'The *olowo* is more respected than the *ọlọla* because he can back it up with money'.

We have seen that the values and goals in terms of which the success of the rich is defined are to a large extent shared by the poor and define their aspirations, thereby legitimating the rewards of the rich. But competitive individualism as a universal value has its own contradictions – it creates aspirations which, by their very nature, can only be realized by the few. As long as the rate of expansion of opportunities can be maintained, its contradictions need not become apparent. But in time the 'haves' come to be seen as monopolizing opportunities. The 'haves' own struggle for themselves and their offspring to survive and prosper in a competitive world leads them to regulate their relations with the predatory relatives by whom they regard themselves as being surrounded. The poor in turn find the door shut in their faces when they seek the help of a potential patron. As many people told me, 'Everyone has his own responsibilities now'.

The gulf between the 'haves' and the 'have nots' becomes even more marked as the 'haves' develop a distinct style of life and circle of interaction (P. C. Lloyd 1966, 1970; B. Lloyd 1966), based on the mutual esteem of their peers and, all too often, a scarcely disguised contempt for the poor and illiterate. Education is here the key ingredient. In many respects the poorly paid clerk's life-style may be more sharply distinct from that of his illiterate contemporaries than is the life-style of a wealthy but illiterate trader. But the wealthy, literate, or illiterate, are busy ensuring their own children the best possible education, while the highly-educated are well placed to provide the standard of living to which they believe themselves entitled. The ensuing 'convergence of elites' means an increasing divergence between the life-styles of the 'haves' and the 'have nots'.

Thus we find that attitudes towards the rich are ambiguous. They are admired for their success, but berated for their selfishness. The government are often accused of looking after the interests of the 'haves'.

'The government looks after the interests of the privileged few. They help their people, and if it is not their people, it is the people of their people' (middle-aged woman, primary school teacher).

'The government are looking after the progress of the rich people; they want people on top to remain there and the poor people to remain poor' (mechanic, age 29, primary six education).

'The rich get richer and the poor get poorer. The rich wanted it that way, because if the poor were better off they would have the power to oppose the rich' (labourer, middle-aged, illiterate).

On the other hand, the ambiguities in attitudes towards the rich were clearly expressed in a discussion with two petty contractors during which the first, when asked whom he respected most in Nigerian society replied: 'Those who are rich people and who help the poor.' His friend later commented:

'When there are politicians, we don't want politicians and we ask for the military government. But the military government do worse than the politicians. What we must do is love (*fẹ*) one another. What I mean is that we must try to help all. If one is in a big position, then one must not think of oneself and just one's own people, but of all the other people who are poor.'

While the poor put their hopes in the education of their children, they complain variously that the expansion of education has meant a decline in its quality so that free primary education is of little value, while the elite (and the politicians who introduced free primary education) send their children to better, fee-paying schools; that scholarships established for the benefit of the poor were being given to the sons of rich men; that the dull children of rich parents could bribe their way into secondary school at the expense of poor but brilliant students; that secondary school fees were beyond the means of many poor parents; and that even if their children do graduate from secondary school after much hardship for their parents, it is the children of the rich who get the jobs, irrespective of qualification.

The palpable corruption of political life, which extended beyond the politicians to the elite generally and beyond the period of 'political' rule to the present, brought the legitimacy of the elite's earnings, so often based on extortion sustained by violent repression, into question. Wasteful consumption by men who spend another man's annual and even life-time income in a few hours intensifies resentments by the 'have nots'. The ambiguity of status recognition according to wealth and power was cynically exemplified by one respondent: 'We respect politicians – like we respect murderers.'

In an uncertain and competitive world where fortunes are seen to be made and lost and one's own fortune often appears to be beyond one's control (but is at the mercy of the international cocoa market, or other more immediate contingencies), God, fate, and luck are common (and not unwarranted) categories for the explanation of success or the lack of it. And where there is sharp rivalry over the allocation of scarce resources within the lineage, between lineages, and between ethnic groups, accusations of witchcraft, poisoning, and ethnic favouritism are rife. Thus the disparities between the rich and poor can be explained in terms of personal effort, magic, or good fortune. But although God may decide whether a man will become rich, or win a contract or title, He comes in very secular guises, such as political patrons or ministry officials, for contracts, or the Olubadan and his senior chiefs, for titles. People are very well aware of the secular steps to be taken to achieve their goals. Thus fatalistic explanations, often of a theological sort, are complemented by secular ones, which often point to the illegitimacy of a man's means of advancement, and, as we have already seen, refer increasingly to structured discrimination against the poor.

IBADAN TOWNSMEN – CRAFTSMEN AND TRADERS

Ibadan is a city of some eight hundred thousand people. It divides roughly into the indigenous quarters, the homes of the descendants of the nineteenth-century settlers of Ibadan, and the stranger and elite quarters, occupied largely by migrants attracted to Ibadan by commerce, administration, or professional employment. Our concern here is with the indigenous Ibadans. They occupy distinct areas of the city, and live mainly in the compounds of their patrimonial lineages. They tend to interact largely with one another, and most particularly, with those resident in their own compound, and with people of a similar age and status or of a similar occupation. Chieftaincy titles are competed for among all the Ibadan lineages. Quarters are not clearly defined. The authority of lineage heads and of chiefs in their own quarters has long been largely displaced by that of courts and bureaucrats, and local influence is often exercised by men of wealth rather than by men of noble lineage.

Although cocoa production continues to be the base of Ibadan's economy, even its oldest quarters are distinctly urban in character. Unlike Lagos and Kano, the city has had little industrial development. It remains a centre of administration and commerce rather than manufacture. The majority of its population are self-employed traders and craftsmen, with a minority of clerks and labourers employed by the government and various business houses and contractors.

In this paper we shall examine the position of the craftsmen and petty traders in the urban economy of Ibadan and the cocoa farmers of the rural areas, with respect to their class situation, their aspirations and demands, and the resources at their disposal, with a view to explaining their respective abilities to undertake collective action to enforce their interests.[4]

Numerous craftsmen practise their trades in Ibadan. They include motor mechanics, tailors, watch-repairers, carpenters, bricklayers, iron-benders, plumbers, radio technicians, goldsmiths, electricians, barbers, shoemakers, and photographers. Craftsmen take on apprentices for a fee (often between five and ten pounds) and the use of some years of the apprentices' labour time (anything from two to seven years). Although some youngsters do become apprenticed to traders, success in trade often requires more capital and more experience than any youngster can manage. Thus trading is an aspiration (and an almost universal one) to be financed out of savings.

The market situation of the craftsman is dependent on his ability to expand his clientele in the face of competition from the surplus of producers that exists in relation to the available demand.[5] All craftsmen depend on the overall level of demand for their products, which in Ibadan is closely bound up ultimately with the level of the cocoa price and with government expenditure and the multiplier effects thereof. The demand for their particular products is also dependent on the price of the tools and materials that they require for their work. Tailors want cheap, imported cloth, and mechanics cheaper, imported cars to be available, thus creating more opportunities for themselves. But lacking control over the levels of demand or government policies of import restrictions, craftsmen can do nothing but compete as best they can with one another, and agree collectively to restrict cut-throat competition lest they undercut each other's standards of living. Competition from manufactured products (often highly subsidized, cf. Weeks 1972a, 1972b) restricts the market for the output of craft production.

Yoruba crafts have usually been organized into guilds (*egbe*). Guild heads are formally recognized by the ruler of the town, and in the older crafts especially, a guild's officers will hold titles ranked and named according to the common Yoruba political titles. They are responsible for regulating their trade in their town, which includes settling disputes

among craftsmen, and between craftsmen and customers, determining
who is allowed to practise the trade (which includes regulating apprenticeships and the entry of strangers to practise in the town), representing
their members to the town's authorities, and maintaining prices. During
the nineteen-thirties the Ibadan guilds were incorporated into the
system of tax collection and assessment, which consolidated the position
of their officers who were recognized by the authorities. Today, however, the craft guilds appear to be in disarray. Allegations of embezzle-
ment of funds are common; attendance at meetings and payment of
subscriptions is irregular; disputes over office and the establishment of
rival guilds occur; and there is little evidence of guilds being able to
enforce their own regulations, particularly among the stranger community, but also among Ibadan sons. On the other hand, even their most
disgruntled members are not happy to go it alone, recognizing the
importance of combining with one another, and new guilds are formed
almost as rapidly as the old ones fall apart.

Craft organizations have suffered from the replacement of the colonial
system of native administration, in which they had a recognized place
supported ultimately by the colonial administrations, by the system of
elected councils and subsequently of appointed administrations in which
even recognition of guild officers by the Olubadan could not ensure their
effective authority over their members. Ibadan's attractions as the
administrative capital and commercial centre of western Nigeria have
drawn to it large numbers of non-Ibadan craftsmen who cannot easily
be brought under the authority of the local guilds. Most crucially, the
guilds have been unable to control entry to their crafts. The apprenticeship system is designed to slow down the rate of entry into the craft and
lengthen the period of free service to the master. But as apprentices
provide labour for their masters and are thus crucial to the success and
expansion of their businesses, each master has an interest in taking on as
many apprentices as he can handle, therefore, in the long term, accentuating the oversupply of entrants to his trade. Thus we have conditions
which dictate the need for collective organization to restrict competition, but which undermine effective collective action at the same time.
Again, prices can often be maintained – but only by virtue of an inflationary situation, or by the price being sufficiently near to what the
equilibrium price would be under free-market conditions to limit any
temptation to undercut. As we shall see in the case of traders, restrictions
on trade can be effected by the stronger against the weaker. But in the
case of numerous individual producers who compete against one

another, collective action is unlikely to provide an effective weapon for the weak against the strong.

This being the case, craftsmen must look to their own individual resources for advancement. This means finding the money to purchase the necessary equipment, which may require a generous sponsor, expanding one's clientele, which depends ultimately on satisfied customers spreading the word, and which can be assisted by a wide circle of friends, and, through these successes, attracting sufficient apprentices to increase turnover. The expansion of any craft business faces severe problems. The competition among craftsmen limits their rate of return on labour and capital and thus the resources available for reinvestment. Demand tends to be seasonal in many crafts, and is uncertain in nearly all. Although a man may save rapidly in order to pay the initial fees and equipment costs necessary to establish him in trade, once established, a variety of demands (for school fees, ceremonial expenses, house building) all limit his capacity to save. But even when he can save, his expansion is limited by his own labour time and if he can employ several apprentices, his ability to organize and supervise them. Since his prices are calculated on the basis of low labour costs, both of his own and that of his unpaid apprentices, he is not in a position to reorganize his business on capitalist lines. There are some opportunities to be gained from various sorts of co-operative arrangements. These usually involve the sharing of certain minimal resources (e.g. a shop site, expensive equipment, bulk buying of materials), informal arrangements for mutual assistance (including credits), and sharing of customers (e.g. between craftsmen in related trades – welders, battery chargers, and mechanics, for example (Koll 1969: 41–4), so that if A cannot take on work immediately, B will be available to do so in order to prevent the customer being lost to outsiders). But such arrangements do not enable craftsmen to overcome the barriers to expansion: they only allow them to improve their competitive position and perhaps to extend the barriers a little.[6]

Consequently craftsmen aspire to reinvest their profits in trading concerns where the same limitations do not apply and where opportunities for expansion are indefinite, at least in principle. Further, they recognize that much higher profit margins (and far higher returns to labour time) are enjoyed by the traders who sell them materials than by themselves. Thus we find that tailors aspire to become cloth traders, mechanics to trade in motor parts, drivers to own their own taxis. In each case, their craft experience should enable them to build up a circle of potential clients and to learn many of the ways of the trade they seek to enter. The crucial barrier is usually capital, so that advancement lies in the hands of potential sponsors in whose eventual generosity crafts-men must put their fate, however disappointing their current experience might be.

An illustration of the weak position of craftsmen was provided by an officer of the Ibadan Bricklayers' Association. One of their aims is to regulate relationships with their clients, so that the association will intervene when houseowners complain about shoddy or incomplete work, and when bricklayers complain about debts being unpaid. But, he said, 'if the houseowner is a lawyer or a big man (*enia pataki*), then there is nothing we can do. . . . The law has died completely in Nigeria'. He complained that the high price of (hoarded) cement was cutting the demand for houses, that the Price Control Board officials 'have friends who are (distributive) agents', and that the bricklayers themselves could do nothing about this 'because we have no power and no money'. Non-bricklayers use their influence to get (government) contracts, which they then farm out to bricklayers, taking huge profits for themselves. The bricklayers (and other craftsmen in the building trade) 'can do nothing about this either, because the people who have the contracts have more power'. Why do the bricklayers not refuse to carry out the work? 'It is a case of hunger. If they do so, they will not have any food. Those without a penny will not have a chance and they will take the work when offered it.'

For most clerks and craftsmen, hopes for the future lie in trading (and in contracting). Traders and contractors are involved in a series of hierarchial distributive networks, which include the buying and bulking of produce for export, supplying goods to public institutions (such as the army, schools), and the sale of imported and locally manufactured goods. As might be expected, profits are highest and competition least at the top end of the selling/purchasing hierarchies, where monopolistic profits may be made by privileged suppliers/buyers (e.g. distributive agents for imported or manufactured goods, licensed produce buyers, 'army con-tractors' and 'army wives'). Throughout the trading hierarchy, advance-ment is seen to require privileged access to clients or suppliers (e.g. contracts with the government, army, and schools, where prices can be artificially inflated and profits guaranteed; produce-buying licences, and quotas to distribute tariff-protected goods in short supply, such as beer, textiles, cement) and/or assistance to provide the capital in order to start at a higher point in the distributive hierarchy (and, of course, privileged access can be bought at a price). During the colonial period, most suc-

cessful produce buyers and traders started their careers as clerks to or
agents with mercantile companies, thereby overcoming the initial
hurdles of capital and clientele. Men who entered the distributive
hierarchy lower down have rarely prospered to any great extent. Since
then, of course, political influence, and lately influence with (and marriage to) senior army officers has become the most effective way of
overcoming initial hurdles.

Consequently, entrepreneurial skills are aimed at securing a corner
on the market rather than at innovations or at increases in efficiency, and
this requires the influence or financial assistance of a better placed sponsor. In addition to this, traders at the wrong end of the bulking or
distributive network are dependent on those who are better placed for
supplies and credit. Thus the economics of the distributive trades dictate the dependence of the poorer on better placed patrons.

There is considerable resentment of the richer by the poorer in such a
set-up. Several respondents bitterly regretted the passing of the
expatriate companies who provided the credit with which they financed
their operations. They argued that the Europeans had been chased away
by those who 'want to take the European's money for themselves', and
berated the selfishness of those who had replaced the European companies. These men operate through a much smaller number of middlemen, taking many of the middlemen's functions over for themselves or
have secured a place as privileged agents to foreign importers or manufacturers, thus closing off opportunities for those further down the
distribution hierarchy.

On the other hand, the petty traders aspired to gain entry to the closed
circle of privileged distributers, and they had to look to the established
traders to provide the help that might enable them to do so, while, more
immediately, relying on these same traders for supplies and credit. One
produce buyer complained to me bitterly that the licensed buyers (to
whom he now sold, having previously sold to an expatriate firm) did not
help buyers like himself to get licences, nor did they provide them with
adequate credit. But when I suggested that the system of Marketing
Board licenses should be abolished (as in any case, buyers like himself
often delivered their produce straight to the Board's store with only a
chit from the licensed buyer to enable them to do so), he opposed this, as
that would 'spoil the trade'!

While at the top, traders are primarily concerned to gain privileged
access to monopolistic advantage, at the bottom they seek to regulate the
trade in order to prevent ruination by cut-throat competition. Thus

attempts to eliminate one of the stages in the bulking process (e.g. farmers selling directly to urban retailers; wholesalers buying from farmers instead of through farm-gate middlemen; Hausa ram sellers or Ijebu palm-oil sellers selling directly to customers rather than through Ibadan middlemen) will be fiercely opposed as depriving someone else of his rightful living. But where capital requirements for entry are low, traders' ẹgbẹ are in the same position as the craftsmen and can do no more than try to recruit new entrants to the trade and to their association. As with craftsmen, price maintenance is only likely to be successful in an inflationary situation or when the price is set near to what the equilibrium price would be under free market conditions. Cooperation is important to enable groups of traders to share certain costs (e.g. through bulk-buying arrangements, joint chartering of transport) and arrangements for mutual assistance, but not enable them to manipulate prices to their own advantage in the long term or to form a united front against the wealthier traders.

The introduction of the price control regulations revealed the weakness of the petty trader and the strength of the monopolist wholesaler only too well. First, it led to immediate restriction of output by producers and to immediate hoarding by wholesalers, who were able to sell at massively inflated prices (cement prices went up to twenty-five shillings per cwt., as against a control price of twelve shillings and sixpence) and by conditional sales. Enforcement of price control regulations, which included bans on hoarding, would be difficult in any case in a country with as many small retail outlets as Nigeria has. Many traders reported that price control inspectors simply took their 'dash' and left. Most prosecutions were of petty traders who were buying their supplies at more than the retail control price. The one 'big' wholesaler in Ibadan to be prosecuted was fined £150, a derisory sum to him, while other flagrant hoarders went ahead untouched.

Petty traders in controlled commodities such as beer, cement, and tinned milk were unable to get many supplies and charged extortionate prices for them. Unlike the wholesale distributors, they could not increase profit margins sufficiently to compensate for their reduced turnover. Hence they demanded that they be allowed to buy directly from the factories instead of through the recognized agents. Ibadan beer retailers held a series of public meetings at which they formed an association with the help of the United Labour Congress (ULC), Nigeria's largest trade-union centre, and demanded that half the supply for Ibadan be sold to them through the association, allowing the agents the other half (it was, it appears, felt to be unfair to deprive the agents of their means of livelihood entirely). Despite the optimism of the traders, nothing ever came of the negotiations, the breweries reputedly answering that they could only supply the association when their established customers' needs were met (!).[7] This leaves the beer sellers' only hope lying in the increase of supply as a result of the ending of import restrictions on beer.

Why were the beer sellers, a substantial number of traders, with the sympathy of the (large) drinking public unable to force the employers (and/or the government) to accede to their demands? After the first meeting, one middle-aged woman expressed scepticism at the association's chances of success. There had been meetings before, but it was always the 'big men' (and women) who came to lead the association. They could always get others to follow them by offering to supply them beer at a cheaper price. It was difficult to get any clear evidence of profiteering on the part of the officers of this particular association. What is clear was that they failed, and never thought of using the one weapon that *prima facie* was available, viz. a boycott of the distributors, and thus of sales, until prices were reduced. This was because the distributors themselves owned large retail outlets and could break the boycott and induce others to do so. Undoubtedly the expatriate brewing company would have been sensitive to any pressure put on it by the government, but one could hardly expect anything from the government when its leading figures, or their wives, were themselves agents, or else friendly with them. Here, as in so many other instances, the dependence of the small man on the favour of the big man prevents any action (short of firing the hoarders' shops perhaps) to stop his being exploited along with the consumer, even though he is perfectly well aware of being exploited, and of who the exploiters are.

The ability of a trade association to represent and enforce its members' interests effectively depends on the resources that it can command. Most craftsmen and petty traders have few resources. What is more, they are only marginally involved in the crucial relations of exploitation (the exaction of Marketing Board surpluses and the allocation and theft of state funds) characteristic of neo-colonial Nigeria. So they do little more than appeal hopelessly for the favour of the authorities. By contrast, organizations such as the Motor Transport Union can and do exercise influence with leading government and political figures and exercise sanctions as they see fit. 'To them that hath, it shall be given'; those who are able to organize effectively in defence of their interests prove to be those whose individual resources are considerable.

Any individual craftsman's or petty trader's chances of success depend upon his personal skills and contacts and his ability to take advantage of new opportunities, especially of possibilities for innovation. But as a class, the situation of craftsmen and petty traders is determined, on the one hand, by the rate of exploitation of agricultural production and the (real) world price of agricultural exports and, on the other, by the expropriation of resources and opportunities essential to their livelihood by merchant traders and manufacturers, foreign and local.

Undoubtedly, a certain populist consciousness exists among them. It is exemplified in the very use of the term *mẹkunnu*. It has its economic roots in common dependence on the proceeds of cocoa cultivation and common exclusion from significant opportunities, and its social framework is embedded in the networks of mutual interaction and communication that link the *mẹkunnu* into coherent communities. But the social relations of production and distribution in which Ibadan craftsmen and petty traders are involved, and the forms of social organization to which these relations give rise, do not bring them into solidaristic relations with one another in opposition to their exploiters. Their relations with the merchant traders and the 'haves' generally are mediated through relations of patronage and clientage rather than through impersonal market relations, or corporate forms of social organization.

In the nineteen-fifties in Ibadan, craftsmen, and most particularly, petty traders and contractors, were the key supporters of the late Adegoke Adelabu (see Post & Jenkins 1973), the populist leader of the Ibadan *mẹkunnu*. They looked to him to secure for the small man the favours that were monopolized by the (predominantly educated) 'big men' who dominated Ibadan affairs in the post-war period, and continued to dominate regional politics throughout the 'fifties and right up to the present period. Today, in the absence of conditions enabling such a leadership to emerge, the urban *mẹkunnu* tend to adopt individualist stratagems (e.g. the search for patronage) in order to advance their interests. They lack the means to act collectively, of their own accord, on their own behalf, and in their own interests. They cannot act as a 'class for themselves'. In Marx's (1969: 378) words: 'They cannot represent themselves. They must be represented. Their representative must at the same time appear as their master.'

IBADAN FARMERS AND THE AGBEKOYA REBELLION

The spread of the money economy under colonial auspices, the attractions of cocoa as a profitable crop, and the existence of demobilized warriors seeking a new source of income at the end of the Yoruba wars in 1893, led fairly rapidly to the occupation of uncultivated land to the south, east, and north of the city beyond the existing farmlands, and, in turn, to the planting of cocoa trees (Berry 1967). The commitment of farmers' scarce resources to cocoa (however profitable) subordinated them to the changing requirements of the world market, over which they could exercise no control, and to the exactions of the intermediaries on whom the farmers relied for the marketing of their crop. Colonial administration subjugated them to the power of the state and thus to those who wielded state power at their expense, and, in addition, to manipulation by the possessors of a literate and 'greater' culture. In short, colonialism created a peasantry (Post 1972) in the rural areas of Ibadan.

Ibadan, unlike other Yoruba towns of importance, had no *ọba* (king) and thus no conception of all lands being held by the *ọba* for allocation to the town's lineages. As the demand for cocoa land gave it a monetary value, hunter-warriors who had camped beyond the outlying farmlands, and chieftaincy families who claimed farmlands nearer to the city, claimed the right to allocate these lands and establish tenants on them. Despite conflicts over these rights between the chiefs and the hunter families, and resistance by the farmers to the claims of the 'landlords' (also known as 'overlords'), these rights were recognized by the colonial authorities whose main concern was to stabilize claims to land and to establish some kind of intermediate authority in the rural areas.

As Galetti *et al.* (1956) showed, landholdings, particularly of cocoa land, are very unequal. However, a wealthy cocoa farmer is likely to invest his profits in education for his sons rather than in expanding his sons' landholdings, or to seek more lucrative returns than are offered by farming from produce-buying and from other trading activities (cf. Essang 1971a, 1971b). This does not mean that there is no market in land (money has been passing hands in exchange for land since the early years of the century). But it does mean that there is a drift of people and resources from rural to more urban occupations, which inhibits the development of a '*kulak*' stratum (Alavi 1965) capable of rationalizing agricultural production and dominating rural society through their *economic* superiority over other farmers. The close relationship between country and town (where all Ibadan farmers will have claims to residence and citizenship through their urban based lineages) means too that unsuccessful farmers with insufficient land to make a living will seek urban employment, or ensure that their sons do so, returning to the farm only at weekends, if at all, to meet a part of their needs.

Consequently the backbone of rural society in Ibadan is the independent smallholding peasant. He is permanently resident in a rural hamlet (or perhaps a village). He may owe nominal allegiance to an 'overlord' from whom his own family gained their land, and will, if he can, employ some labour (usually Igbirra or Hausa migrants) on a seasonable basis. In the terms used by Mao (1965) and sociologically established by Alavi (1965), he is a 'middle peasant'. His land will have been sufficient for him to make a living, but as he and his trees have aged together, his cocoa acreage and his labour power (and the family and other labour at his disposal) will have declined. Today he is middle-aged or elderly. Few youngsters do not seek a more promising future in the towns.[8]

This is not to suggest an absence of stratification in the rural areas, but rather that the most significant basis of stratification sociologically lies in people's occupations (e.g. produce buying against farming) and in their relation to urban sources of significant political and economic power. This is particularly true of the relation between 'landlord' or 'overlord' families and their tributary tenants. The amount of tribute is small (£2 to £3 *per annum* per village today).[9] But under colonial rule the 'overlords' were the essential intermediaries between rulers and ruled. They often had access to urban sources of patronage. The tenant's claim to land depended to some extent on his overlord's prior claim, as well as on his recognition of the tenant's claim. The dependence of the tenant on his overlords facilitated the exploitation of the tenants through customarily sanctioned practices, such as *iṣakole* (tribute in cash and kind), and *owe* (communal labour, here used as a tributary service), and through irregular exactions to meet the cost of the 'overlord's' litigation, the celebration of his festivals or, in some cases, the mere lining of his pockets. But with the end of colonial rule and the beginning of the system of native administration, the 'overlords'' fortunes depended increasingly on their electoral fortunes and the favour of the regional government, while the passing of time confirmed their erstwhile tenants in their rights to land.

One economic factor stratifying rural society is access to labour, where only a limited supply is available at a price equivalent to its marginal product, and the value of which is in turn fixed for the farmer by the Marketing Board. Wealthy farmers, village *bale* and their close kin and associates are able to arrange the migration of sufficient seasonal labour to meet their own needs; these labourers are only available to the poorer men when the needs of the wealthier have been met. This factor tends to overlap with the distinction between 'tenant' lineages and the 'over-lord' lineages.

Agitations against the exploitative and oppressive practices of mercantile firms, middlemen, and government officials have long been a feature of political life in Ibadan.[10] However, leadership usually came from urban produce-buyers (as in the opposition to the 'cocoa pool' in the thirties cf. Nowell 1938), educated farmers (such as Akinpelu Obisesan, once a mercantile clerk and for thirty years president of the Ibadan Co-operative Produce Marketing Society), and populist politicians. The most successful of these was the late Adegoke Adelabu, to whom the farmers gave their support in the fifties. The *mekunnu* looked to him to wrest favours for them away from the educated elite who had come to dominate both civic and regional affairs. He opposed the rationalizing reforms of the last colonial administration and the new Action Group Government. These reforms included the replacement of the chiefs by literate customary court presidents; the reform of tax, so that assessment was in the hands of local committees and collection in the hands of tax clerks and *akoda* (native administration officials) instead of the chiefs and family heads; the introduction of a town-planning authority, and the capitation taxes required to finance the introduction of free primary education. Each found its echo in the *Agbekoya*[11] rebellion and in the attacks in the rural areas on Action Group supporters (often *bale* and their kin and associates) that followed Adelabu's death (Post & Jenkins 1973). But NCNC[12] leadership, down to the nomination of councillors for rural areas, remained firmly in urban hands, while the leading NCNC councillors and committee members in the Akanran area (Ibadan South East) were invariably men with a secondary occupation (crafts, or petty trading) in addition to farming.

The introduction of the marketing-board system meant that the farmer could be exploited much more effectively by the government and the (urban) beneficiaries of its policies. It also made the process of exploitation direct and clear and was effected through a specifically political decision about the price rather than mediated through the incomprehensible fluctuations of market prices.

Nigerian governments have sought to exploit the cocoa-marketing surpluses for development purposes, including infrastructural investment, public utilities and amenities (roads, education, medical services, water and electricity schemes), and for direct contributions to the progress of industrial investment. These amounted to a massive, and disproportionate, fiscal contribution by the farmers (Kriesel 1969: 54–7; National Issues Society 1969: 169–70)[13] who have never, in return, been compensated by a producer price for cocoa in excess of the world price. In addition, the government has sought additional revenue by increasing direct taxation and various levies, promising the farmers various benefits and forms of assistance in return. The taxes certainly materialized, rising from the 'colonial' figure of 7s. *per capita, per annum* to a *minimum* tax liability of £5. 10s. in 1968; but the benefits did not. Government investments in agriculture were concentrated on expensive and wasteful government directed programmes such as the farm settlements. Direct assistance to peasant farmers was small, was usually publicized for electoral advantage, and given to the urban hangers-on of political leaders and the politically manipulated and urban-led Farmers' Union. Utilities and amenities in the rural areas were rare and their allocation determined by the electoral interests of particular politicians.

With taxes came tax collectors and a variety of petty council officials, such as town-planning officials, clerks, and sanitary inspectors, who embezzled money, exacted bribes from the farmers for the non-implementation of incomprehensible regulations, or just demanded the bribes. Accounts of the oppression of politicians and officials in the rural areas up to the *Agbẹkọya* rebellion make them sound more like the activities of an army of occupation than an indigenous administration.

The *Agbẹkọya* rebellion began in September 1968. It arose in the wake of political, and consequently economic disruption, a cocoa price consistently lower than had obtained in the halcyon years of the fifties, cut-backs in government expenditure, increases in prices, and in a series of taxes consequent upon the Nigerian Civil War (Ayooea 1969: 8.9.15; National Issues Society 1969). In Egba and Ibadan and other divisions, specifically those where unrest was concentrated in 1968–9, cocoa production has long been in decline. Farmers have lacked the resources and/or incentives to cut out old trees and replant, so that the old trees have been leaching away the soil fertility and their output has been declining steadily. Swollen shoot too, has killed many trees in Ibadan Division. The rebellion took place at a time of continued political bitterness among the Yoruba elite, and also among supporters of the

NNDP[14] who, having been ousted by the military coup of 1966, regarded themselves as under-represented in the State Government, and thus put their hopes behind the agitation for an Oyo state (which would include Ibadan), which they could expect to dominate.

Thus in 1968 the farmers saw themselves as exploited and oppressed by a government that refused to pay fair prices for their cocoa, sent corrupt officials to persecute them, denied them the benefits and amenities that they had been promised, demanded higher and higher taxes, and now added a series of further tax demands when the farmers simply did not earn enough to meet their existing obligations.

Agitation[15] began in September 1968 in Oyo against the wrongful use of community educational rates. New increases in the water rate and increased tax assessments fueled resentments and agitation spread rapidly to Ibadan, Egba, Remǫ, Ijebu, and the Ǫsun Divisions. The arrest of tax defaulters was the main spark for attacks on the authorities. In several cases, *ǫba's* palaces were attacked and burnt down because they had allegedly called for the soldiers to assist tax collections, and in some cases, they had embezzled public funds. Attempts at intercession by the Governor and the Olubadan proved fruitless; Ibadan farmers shouted them down as *ole* (thieves).

Relative calm reigned between January and June 1969 during which time the Ayoola Commission conducted an inquiry into the rioting. This produced some concessions, but did not meet the farmers' central demands, viz. a reduction of taxes to 30s. *per annum* and the withdrawal of all council officials from the rural areas. In late June, farmers' representatives in Ibadan agreed to pay 65s. tax, but clearly did not carry the farmers with them. On 25 June, Folarin Idowu, a farmers' leader, declared at a public meeting at Akanran that the farmers would pay only 30s. tax. When the government finally began its long delayed tax raids on 1 July, the police were ambushed at Olorunda corner, near Akanran; agitation spread throughout Ibadan division and to Ogbomoso, where the Soun was mercilessly hacked to pieces. In the villages, heads bore much of the brunt of the farmers' anger and in Ibadan Division the *balę* of virtually every town and village of any size fled hurriedly to Ibadan.

Mass arrests could not force the farmers to acquiesce to the government's demands. After reports of the deaths of prisoners in jail, farmers invaded Ibadan on 16 September and released 464 prisoners from Agodi jail (opposite the State House and garrison). The police and army pursued the farmers again into their rural strongholds. After six days of fighting, the government forces took Egbeda and sacked Fada, the headquarters of *Agbẹkọya* leader Tafa Adeoye, while elsewhere coping with co-ordinated attacks from farmers on the Akanran road and in Egba Division. Despite brave words from the Governor, peace proposals were in the air. A secret meeting with Chief Awolowo, former Action Group leader and Federal Finance Commissioner, forestalled the farmers' final plan, allegedly the firing of Ibadan City itself by setting the petrol pumps ablaze. Tax raids were halted and most of the farmers' demands were accepted in an announcement on 15 October.

The announcement of 15 October, 1969 (*Daily Times*) made the following concessions: tax was reduced to £2 *per capita, per annum*; there was an amnesty for all farmers arrested except for those charged with murder; all local government staff would be withdrawn from the villages and the rural district councils would be administered from Ibadan; motor park and market fees would be suspended and could only be introduced if councils showed evidence of capital expenditure on them; no special rates would be levied without the express permission of the people concerned; the jurisdiction of the town-planning authorities would be restricted to modern lay-outs; non-farmers would be excluded from the farmers union; the government would appoint representative advisory committees; the assets of local government staff would be investigated, and there would be an end to tax raids and to army and police patrols. Two significant demands were not met. The first was the demand for a Yoruba Central State, put to loud cheers at the meeting at the Olubadan's palace on 9 October by two farmers' representatives, but elsewhere denounced by Tafa Adeoye at his meeting with Awolowo as being the concern of politicians and not of farmers against whom the demands for such a state were being raised (*Daily Times*, 10 and 14 October, 1969). The second was the demand for an increase in the cocoa price to £250 per ton. Tafa had declared to Awolowo on 5 October (*Daily Times*, 14 October, 1969) that if this was not met the farmers would organize a hold-up of cocoa. For the moment, however, the government replied that an increase in mid-season would only benefit the middlemen and not the farmers.

Immediately after the settlement, Tafa Adeoye was installed in the offices of the Farmers' Union in Ibadan. It was widely rumoured that he had been bribed by the government, and by Chief Awolowo. Without its driving objective, the *Agbẹkọya* was riven by factionalism. In an attempt to revive his waning fortunes Tafa Adeoye demanded a cocoa price of £250 per ton (which was then below the prevailing world price). There were unconfirmed rumours of plans to hold up cocoa and to burn it in the stores and of the rapid spread of *Agbękǫya* activities into the prosperous cocoa-growing area of Ondo Division, whose farmers were far more concerned with the issue of the cocoa price than with the level of taxes. After the announcement that the cocoa price would be £150 per ton, rumours of impending unrest and reports of farmers' meetings led Governor Adebayo to issue a scarcely veiled warning against 'saboteurs'. On 16 September, 1970, Tafa Adeoye was arrested, and subsequently imprisoned in Jos in Northern Nigeria, and about forty farmers were arrested on charges of breach of the peace and membership of the banned *Agbękǫya*. The unrest which the government feared never materialized, and Tafa Adeoye was released after six months. But in 1972, the government sought to re-establish their officials in the villages, which lead to armed resistance and attacks on police posts (*West Africa* 25 February, 1972).

An assessment of the *Agbękǫya* rebellion must start by asking who were the *Agbękǫya*, who led them, and for whose issues were they fighting. In the rural areas of Ibadan and Egba Division, where the most bitter fighting took place in 1969, there is no doubt that it was farmers resident in the rural areas who carried out the fighting. Elsewhere too, most reports refer to farmers, and most court charges were preferred against farmers, though in these cases the conflicts took place in the towns (Oyo, Ogbomoso, Isara, Ijebu-Igbo, all of which have many farmers resident). Throughout 1968–9 the conflicts took place in areas of declining cocoa production, most particularly in Ibadan and Egba Divisions and in Southern Osun Division, from where hunters were recruited to fight in Ibadan in Spetember, 1969. Beer (1971) has shown the parallels between the areas where disturbances took place during the cutting out of swollen shoot and during the *Agbękǫya* rebellion.

The ambushes themselves were carried out largely by hunters, who had the necessary skills and equipment (juju charms and dane guns), supported by farmers armed with matchets. Military units were organized separately in each area, with messengers linking farmers with one another in a ring in each of the Ibadan districts. Co-ordination between Egba and Ibadan farmers was obvious in the aftermath of the Agodi prison break in September. Farmers from Southern Osun Division supported the resistance at Egbeda. During the final stage of the rebellion, at least, resistance appears to have been directed from Tafa Adeoye's own village, which lies within the arc formed by the Ibadan–Ife road (which passes Egbeda) and the road from Ibadan through

Akanran. From here units were deployed with apparent sophistication
to various parts of Ibadan Division, and contact was maintained with
Agbẹkọya elsewhere.

Hunters are themselves farmers and unlikely to be wealthy farmers.
With individual exceptions, it was the tenants who took part in the
rebellion of June to September, and the 'overlords' (among whom are,
of course, the village heads, the *balẹ*) and their families who did not.
Although Akanran, for example, was regarded as the centre of the
rebellion, few of its residents (mainly Obisesan and their close followers,
supported the rebellion, while support was almost universal in the surrounding hamlets. A prominent opponent of the rebellion from Ibadan
North declared to me that 'they are not the sons of the owners of the
land. Their fathers have no farm land. But they gather themselves
together to destroy a man's property . . . and chased away the sons of
those people who had given their fathers land.' The *balẹ* and their
families were opposed for supporting the government on whom their
local authority ultimately depended. Many farmers also reported that
their oppressive 'landlords' had been put in their place and would no
longer attempt to exploit their tenants.

I have already suggested that the backbone of rural society in Ibadan
Division is independent smallholders, or 'middle peasants'. The limited
information I have on participants tends to confirm that they formed
the basis of the *Agbẹkọya*. One issue which the farmers raised to explain
their plight, their inability to recruit labour, tends to confirm this. For
'poor peasants' by definition are liable to be employed as seasonal
labourers rather than be employers themselves. The wealthiest farmers,
while concerned about the supply of labour, are still able to outbid the
others for the available supply. The few wealthy farmers in the Akanran
area, and those whose local influence is derived from their association
with the urban sources of authority, either fled the area or were chased out
when the fighting took place – at least as far as I could judge. Finally,
the ideas expressed by the participants are those typical of an independent (middle) peasantry. They emphasize that those who took part
were the 'real farmers' (*agbẹ gidi*), a concept which implies rural residence and farming as one's primary occupation, but also a reasonable
holding of land and cocoa. A man without enough land to support himself is despised by such farmers as 'riff-raff'.

Thus the rebellion grew out of the crisis faced by the 'middle peasants'
in areas of declining cocoa production, who were caught between low
prices for their produce, increased prices for the goods they need to

purchase in the towns, and a sharp rise in direct taxation already at a disproportionate level in relation to their incomes.

The rebellion partly arose out of, and was partly encouraged by, the development of a specifically rural or peasant consciousness. The basis of this consciousness is expressed in the concept of *agbẹ gidi*, which we have already mentioned. Together with this concept goes an emphasis on the ultimate dependence of the whole society, indeed of all societies, on the farmer who provides people with their food. The sharp drift of population from the rural areas to the towns and the post-war inflation of food prices (accentuated by two seasons of inadequate rains) give a particular sharpness to this point in Nigeria today. Farmers emphasize the virtues of hard work and back-breaking labour, especially their own, and refer contemptuously to the 'semi-literates who roam about the town doing nothing' (when they could be providing the farmers with much-needed labour).

This peasant consciousness includes, too, an awareness that resources are being expropriated from the peasantry through taxes, through the exactions of corrupt officials, through 'cheating by produce buyers', and, most particularly, through the marketing board surpluses, and that they are being used to benefit the people, and especially the wealthy people, of the urban areas. Little of this money is used to provide them with the modest amenities that they need. As Akufo (Ibadan West) villagers declared to a *Nigerian Tribune* reporter on 6 July, 1969 at the height of the conflict: 'We do not know the reason why we should pay tax because we do not know how the money collected in the past was spent. We pay our taxes but we have no good road to transport our farm products to the city for sale.'

The resources that are allocated to the farmers by the government are seen to be appropriated by corrupt officials, politicians, and the so-called representatives of the farmers. It is to distinguish themselves from the recipients of this assistance, 'who claim to be farmers but are not', that the farmers emphasize that *they* are the *real* farmers as can be seen by the fact that they *live on the farms* (*l'oko ngbe*) and *not* in the town.

As we have seen, tax was the central issue in the conflict, amidst a large number of other issues. Several farmers in fact told me that it was not so much the tax that had led the farmers to go to fighting, but the tax collectors, town-planning officials, and sanitary inspectors. But tax had to be central because, as Kanmi Isola Osobu wrote (*Nigerian Tribune* 27 September, 1969), tax collection 'is the occasion when the all-powerful government has for once to "come down" to the people and ask for funds'.[16] Thus, just as the interim Adebo award provided the issue, and the ability to strike provided the means for the wage earners to give vent to a more general dissatisfaction with the existing social order and the deprivation of their 'rights',[17] so tax provided the farmers with the necessary issue and sanction with which to confront the authorities.

Prior to the *Agbękǫya* rebellion, peasants had always been represented politically by others: produce buyers, chiefs, and politicians.[18] They provided the crucial link between the peasants and their rulers. At the beginning of the anti-tax agitation, men with political experience (and ambitions) seem to have played a leading role in many instances. In Akanran, the farmers who got together to discuss what they could do about extortionate tax demands first went to the leading figures in the village for advice, who included a wealthy farmer and a trader in kola nuts. These men, with Tafa Adeoye, were among those who negotiated with the civic authorities in December, 1968, for the return of the officials to the rural areas.

Tafa Adeoye had come to prominence when Govenor Adebayo addressed the farmers on 15 November, when he reportedly declared that they would have to kill him before he paid his tax. Unlike any previous farmers' leaders, he had no education whatsoever (not even Koranic education), had never had any occupation but farming, and no record of previous political activity. He came from a tenant family (although not tenants to the Obisesan), whose urban lineage had never aspired to a title. He had a reasonable holding of cocoa but would never have been described as prosperous. He was a typical 'middle peasant' who articulated the farmers' determination to resist further exactions and displayed the courage necessary for such resistance.

The other initial leaders of the Akanran farmers are alleged to have tried to bargain with their position in order to gain government recognition on local courts and councils. They were the sort of men who saw themselves as negotiating a reasonable compromise with the government to the benefit of their members. It was they who first negotiated an abortive agreement that the council officials should be allowed to return, after they had presented the farmers' grievances to the authorities in December, 1968, and it was they who accepted the government's compromise of a £3. 10s. tax in May, 1969. They reckoned without the new determination on the part of the farmers and the uncompromising leadership which the crisis had thrown up. Consequently they were discarded and fled to the town in July. It was from this point that the 'middle peasants' in the persons of Tafa and his associates took over their own leadership.

The 'natural rulers' (*ǫba* and chiefs) became as central an object of the farmers' hostility as the crisis developed as were the council officials. Caught in the classic predicament of the colonial African chief, the *ǫba, balę,* and chiefs appealed for conciliation, but asked the farmers to pay their taxes and desist from violence. The farmers saw 'their fathers' as betraying 'their sons'. One *ǫba* and several chiefs were murdered; several *ǫba* and numerous *balǫ* had to flee for their lives. Six senior Ibadan chiefs were coupled with two commissioners (Mr Adisa and Prince Lamuye) and Alhaji Busari Obisesan (chairman of several government bodies) as those whom Tafa Adeoye blamed for the conflict when he met Governor Adebayo on 6 November (Nigerian Tribune, 7 November, 1969). The links between the peasantry and their rulers, which Moore (1967) and Wolf (1969) regard as a crucial constraint on peasant rebellion had snapped.

The farmers are also reported to have approached prominent Ibadan politicians in October. They were told that the politicians could do nothing (Chief Agbaje[19] was the prominent exception here) as they were now in opposition. Only if they, Ibadan people, had a state of their own would they be able to look after the farmers' interests. From this arose the farmers' demand for a Yoruba Central State, which even in early October, 1969, was seen as so important that both General Gowon himself and Chief Awolowo made concilatory noises on the subject (*Daily Times* 2 October, 1969; *Daily Service,* 8 October, 1969; *Sunday Times,* 12 October, 1969). As we have seen, this was a demand which the farmers sacrificed in order to reach a settlement. Tafa Adeoye himself declared to the *Daily Times* on 5 November, 1969: 'State or no state, we are not interested. All we want is better prices for our cocoa. It is politicians who are crying for the creation of states and that has nothing to do with us.'

The rebellion went beyond the selective allocation of resources at the disposal of urban politicians. Consequently, the farmers were unable to manipulate the rebellion to their own ends (at least on this key issue). Political violence did not, on this occasion, involve arranging to employ thugs to attack others, but demanded leaders who would risk their own lives to resist oppression and exploitation. The politicians, whatever encouragement they might have given to the farmers in the hope of political reward, stayed on the sidelines. And that is where the farmers want to keep them. Quoting Tafa's *Daily Times* interview again:

'They caused all the trouble but when the police and army attacked us, none of them, except Chief Awolowo, intervened for us.'

'From now on there shall be no more elections as far as we are concerned. We have all decided not to support any political party any more and we shall not vote for anyone any longer. We have had enough.'

Like the industrial workers described by Adrian Peace and unlike the self-employed craftsmen and traders, the farmers have organized themselves, under their own leadership, to enforce their interests collectively. Their common dependence on the cocoa price and common experience of deprivation and oppression as rural-dwellers have led to a recognition of a common fate. They have shown that they have the consciousness and determination to resist oppressive and forcible exactions.

But at the same time, they remain dependent on the educated, urban elite for the provision of amenities. They know that the educated have failed them, and have indeed used farmers' organizations and money to cheat the farmers. But even Tafa Adeoye himself looks to the educated to turn the government away from its evil ways and save the farmers from their suffering.[20] And on the key issue, the cocoa price, the farmers remain at the mercy of their rulers (and the foreign consumers and manufacturers of chocolate). They lack the means to intervene effectively in the routine process of resource allocation. They are unable to withdraw from the colonial political economy to which eighty years of cocoa cultivation have subordinated them. They lack the resources and the education (or the outside leadership) necessary to take over the economy and see that it is organized in their interests.

Notes

1 The research on which this paper was based was financed by a grant made by the Social Science Research Council to Dr. P. C. Lloyd, University of Sussex, for the study of social stratification among urban Yoruba.

2 The best definition of the *mẹkunnu* that I was given was 'those without money in the bank, those without money in hand, those who have to work before they can eat'.

3 See Peace's paper in this volume. Cf. P. C. Lloyd 1970, whose paper forms the background to the project of which this and Peace's paper are products.

4 For a comparable study of industrial workers see Peace's paper in this volume. Brevity prevents due consideration being given here to other significant groups among the *mẹkunnu,* viz. women, labourers, clerks, soldiers. Nor do I consider here the pre-emption of opportunities from Nigerian businessmen by expatriate firms. On this see Williams 1970: 230–35; Akeredolu-Ale 1971, 1972.

5 As Koll (1969: 22) explains, 'In the craft sector . . . the only entry restriction is success; and since success can only be measured after some time, more shops are opened than can be kept running'.

6 Craftsmen are discriminated against by the massive subsidization of capital-intensive and often foreign enterprises (Weeks 1972b), by the operation of bureaucratic controls (e.g. import licences), and by the criteria for government assistance which require them to meet bureaucratic regulations and associated costs that are beyond their means or cut into their narrow profit margins (Koll 1969: 93–95).

7 On the advantages of 'agency' arrangements to the manufacturers, see Olakanpo, n.d.

8 The decline of labour-power in the rural areas is a product of the consistent expropriation of the agricultural surplus by urban-based classes, and thus the concentration of resources and opportunities in the urban areas at the expense of the rural areas.

9 On Ibadan land-tenure, see Ward Price 1939; Obisesan, Diaries and Correspondence: N.A.I.; Oyoprof 3/1881. The position in the neighbouring Ife division is sharply different. There tenants (often migrants from other parts of Yorubaland) pay tribute of one to three cwt. of cocoa per *farmer,* which at present prices, could amount to £7. 10s. (one cwt.) per acre. Despite this, tenants in Ife are reported to hold a favourable view of their landlords who have established them on the farmland, and on whom their very place in the community is dependent (Famoriyo 1969; cf. Adegboye 1966a, 1966b; Berry forthcoming). Akanran (Ibadan Division) farmers, established on their land for more than a generation, treasure no such appreciation of the generosity of the 'overlords'.

10 On this, see Beer, 1971: 144–93; 394, n. 1.

11 *Agbẹkọya* (Yor.: the farmers renounce suffering), one of *several* names expressing similar sentiments used by farmers' associations during the rebellion of 1968–9 which is discussed below.

12 National Council of Nigeria and the Cameroons (later National Convention of Nigerian Citizens): governing party in the Eastern Region, 1951–66; member of Federal coalition governments 1954–66; main opposition party in Western Region, 1951–62. Banned, with all other political parties, since 1966.

13 On the uses to which at least part of these surpluses were put, cf. Coker 1962.

14 Nigerian National Democratic Party. Formed 1964 from dissident Action Groupers of the United Peoples Party and western members of the NCNC who had made up a coalition government in 1963 in the wake of a split in the Action Group, and which ruled the west from 1951 to 1962. The blatant rigging of the 1965 elections led to widespread rioting which was ended only by the military coup of 1966. Although ideological conflicts were important, the conflict was also interpreted in ethnic terms, the Action Group being labelled an 'Ijebu' party (especially in Ibadan) while the NNDP was particularly associated with the people of the old Oyo province (including Ibadan). See Post & Vickers 1973, especially Ch. 10; Dudley 1970.

15 This account is based on Ayoola, 1969 and *Daily Times, Nigerian Tribune*, and *Daily Service* for 1969, and on interviews conducted in Ibadan Division in 1971. For a fuller account, see Beer 1971: 388–98, 437–506, 585–600.

16 Tax rebellions have been common in Southern Nigeria since taxes were introduced. They were especially widespread in various parts of the old Oyo province which opposed the tax increases by the Action Group Government in the mid-fifties.

17 See Peace's paper in this volume.

18 This is less true of the *Maiyegun* than of other farmers' associations. It emerged in 1947 in opposition to the cutting out of cocoa trees affected by 'swollen shoot' disease. It split, and its peasant core was incorporated into Adelabu's NCNC.

19 On Chief Agbaje's significance for the *Agbekoya* movement, see Beer 1971, p. 145.

20 Interview with Tafa Adeoye, October, 1971.

References

ADEGBOYE, R. 1966a. An Analysis of Land Tenure Structure in some selected Areas in Nigeria. *Nigerian Journal of Economic and Social Studies* 8: 259–68.

—— 1966b. Farm tenancy in Nigeria. *Nigerian Journal of Economic and Social Studies* 8: 441–54.

AKEREDOLU-ALE, E. O. 1971. Nigerian Entrepreneurs in the Lagos State. Unpublished Ph.D. dissertation. University of London.

—— 1972. Values, Motivations and History in the Development of Private Indigenous Entrepreneurship: Lessons from Nigeria's Experience, 1946–66. *Nigerian Journal of Economic and Social Studies* 13: 195–219.

ALAVI, HAMSA 1965. Peasants and Revolution. *The Socialist Register*: 241–77.

ALLEN, C. H. and JOHNSON, R. W. (eds.) 1970. *African Perspectives.* Cambridge: Cambridge University Press.

AYOLA REPORT. *Report of the Commission of Enquiry into the Civil Disturbances which occurred in certain parts of the Western State of Nigeria in the month of December 1968.* Ibadan: Government of the Western State of Nigeria.

BEER, C. H. 1971. The Farmer and the State in Western Nigeria. Ph.D. thesis. University of Ibadan. (To be published by Ibadan University Press.)

BERRY, S. S. 1967. Cocoa in Western Nigeria, 1890–1940. Unpublished Ph.D. dissertation. University of Michigan.

—— Forthcoming. *Cocoa and Socio-economic Change in Rural Western Nigeria.*

COKER REPORT. 1962. *Report of the Commission of Inquiry into the Affairs of certain Statutory Corporations in Western Nigeria.* Lagos: Government of Federation of Nigeria.

DUDLEY, B. J. 1970. Western Nigeria and the Nigerian Crisis. In Panter-Brick, S. K. (ed.) 1970.

ESSANG, S. M. 1971a. The Impact of (the) Marketing Board on the Distribution of Cocoa Earnings in Western Nigeria. Unpublished paper. Ibadan: Nigerian Institute for Social and Economic Research.

—— 1971b. Institutional Arrangements and Income Distribution in a Primary Export Economy (Western Nigeria). Unpublished paper.

FAMORIYO, O. A. An Appraisal of Farm Tenancy Problems in Ife Division. Unpublished MA dissertation, University of Ibadan.

FEUER, L. (ed.) 1969. *Marx and Engels: Basic Writings on Politics and Philosophy.* New York: Fontana.

GALETTI, R., *Nigerian Cocoa Farmers.* London: Oxford University Press.

GALETTI, R., BALDWIN, K. and DINA, I. 1956. *Nigerian Cocoa Farmers.* London: Oxford University Press.

GERTH, H. H. and WRIGHT MILLS, C. (eds.) 1967. *From Max Weber: Essays in Sociology.* London: Routledge.

KOLL, M. 1969. *Crafts and Co-operation in Western Nigeria.* Freiburg i. Br.: Bertelsmann Universitatsverlag.

KRIESEL, H. C. 1969. *Cocoa Marketing in Nigeria.* CSNRD–21. East Lansing: 204 Agricultural Hall, Michigan State University.

LLOYD, B. B. 1966. Education and Family Life in the Development of Class Identification among the Yoruba. In P. C. Lloyd (ed.) 1966.

LLOYD, P. C. 1966. Class Consciousness among the Yoruba. In P. C. Lloyd (ed.) 1966. *The New Elites of Tropical Africa.* London: Oxford University Press.

—— 1970. Social Stratification in Western Nigeria. Unpublished seminar paper. University of Sussex.

MAO TSE-TUNG. 1965. Analysis of Classes in Chinese Society. In *Selected Works 1*: 13–21. Peking: Foreign Languages Press.

MARKETING BOARD. 1969. *Statistical Information on Western Nigeria controlled Produce No. 5.* Unpublished mimeograph. Ibadan: Statistics Division, Western Nigeria Marketing Board.

MARX, K. 1969. The Eighteenth Brumaire of Louis Bonarparte. In L. Feuer (ed.) 1969.

MOORE, B. JR. 1967. *The Social Origins of Dictatorship and Democracy.* London: Allen Lane.

NADEL, S. F. 1956. The Concept of Social Elites. *International Social Science Bulletin* 8: 413–24.

NATIONAL ISSUES SOCIETY. 1969. Tax Policy in Western Nigeria. In Ayoola Report, 1969: 167–82.

NAI. Nigerian Archives, Ibadan.

NOWELL REPORT. 1938. *Report of the Commission on the Marketing of West African Cocoa.* Cmnd. 5845. London: HMSO.

OBISESAN PAPERS. Diaries and Papers of the late Chief Akinpelu Obisesan. Used with the kind permission of Mogaji Oyewo Obisesan.

OLAKANPO. n.d. (c. 1967). A Preliminary Report on Indigenous Enterprise in Distributive Trades in Nigeria. NISER mimeo.

OSOBA, O. 1967. The Colonial Antecedents and Contemporary Development of Nigerian Foreign Policy. Unpublished Ph.D. dissertation. Moscow State University.

PANTER-BRICK, S. K. (ed.) 1970. *Nigerian Politics and Military Rule: Prelude to the Civil War.* London: Athlone Press.

PEACE, A. 1972. Industrial Protest in Ikeja. Paper read to BSA Conference (infra.).

POST, K. W. J. 1972. Peasantization and Rural Political Movements in Western Africa. *European Journal of Sociology.*

POST, K. W. J. and JENKINS, G. 1973. *The Price of Liberty* (a biography of the late Alhaji Adegoke Adelabu). London: Cambridge University Press.

POST, K. W. J. and VICKERS, M. 1973. *Structure and Conflict in Nigeria.* London: Heinemann.

WARD PRICE, H. 1939. *Land Tenure among the Yorubas.* Lagos: Government Printer.

WEBER, M. 1948. Class, Status and Party. In Gerth, H. H. and Mills, C. Wright (eds.) 1967.

WEEKS, J. F. 1972a. Employment, Growth and Foreign Domination in Underdeveloped Countries. *Review of Radical Political Economics* 4 (1).

—— 1972b. Factors determining the Growth of Output and Employment in the Labour Intensive Sector in Poor Countries. Unpublished paper.

WILLIAMS, G. P. 1970. The Social Stratification of a Neo-colonial Economy. In Allen, C. H. and Johnson, R. W. (eds.) 1970.

WOLF, E. R. 1969. On Peasant Rebellions. *International Social Science Journal* **21**: 286–93.

Acknowledgements

The author wishes to thank the Social Science Research Council (U.K.) for the grant which enabled him to undertake fieldwork in Ibadan, Nigeria under the direction of Dr. P. C. Lloyd, and N.I.S.E.R. for the use of its facilities. I wish to thank Adrian Peace and Gillian Williams for valuable comments, and the people of Ibadan City and Ibadan South East Division for all that I have learnt from them, for their hospitality and generosity. For this paper, special thanks must go to Raufa Yesufu, Latifu Yesufu and 'Femi Durosaro, my research assistants and interpreters and to Ayo' Otunla to whom I owe some of my data, and whose help and friendship has facilitated my research in so many ways.

ADRIAN PEACE

Industrial Protest in Nigeria[1]

INTRODUCTION

Despite the lack of detailed empirical studies of industrial workers in sub-Saharan Africa, commentaries on new forms of social stratification have attempted to place the industrial labour force in its appropriate position *vis-à-vis* other socio-economic groups. Such commentaries have tended to be impressionistic, but together they testify to the economic, social, and political significance of this highly strategic population of wage-earners in predominantly agrarian societies.[2]

Several accounts have rightly noted that African industrial workers have failed to develop a sustained organizational base and concerted strategies with which to increase their share of scarce resources, although they are far better placed to do so than other groups.[3]

Industrial plants are generally concentrated in a few urban centres, facilitating recognition of, and co-operation in support of, shared economic interests. Industrial employment creams off the educated and ambitious rural youth who provide potential leaders and cadres for the labour movement. Under colonial rule, a national system of wage negotiation was developed, and this came to be applied to both the public and the private sectors, thus linking the welfare of all wage-earners to the *modus operandi* of the political class (Weeks 1971b). Furthermore, feelings of relative deprivation are heightened in the urban areas since the ruling elites are urban dwellers *par excellence* and flagrantly display their material wealth (Lloyd 1966a, 1966b).

The most important factors of all in promoting a political consciousness among workers are the clear division of labour in the industrial system and the workers' distinctive relationship to the mode of production. The division between those who own the means of production and those who merely sell their labour power is unparalleled in other areas of African economic life. In Marxist terms, the Nigerian industrial worker is a proletarian. As a member of a propertyless, contractual labour force his class situation is, in this respect, essentially the same as that of his British or American counterpart. His situation contrasts sharply with those of farmers and entrepreneurs, the two largest occupational categories in Nigeria today.

The central problem is not then the existence (or otherwise) of these new economic class relationships, but the extent to which they form the basis for expressions of class consciousness – social action that acknowledges common economic interests among those who share the same relationship to the mode of production, and takes account of the behaviour of other social classes to whose interests their own are fundamentally opposed.

Many reasons have been given for the failure of wage-earners in developing countries like Nigeria to organize themselves into powerful labour movements. During the colonial period, industrial workers were alleged to be 'target workers' whose lack of 'commitment' to industrial employment was held to stand in the way of the articulation of class interests. Today the virtual opposite is being promoted. Wage-earners are held to constitute a 'labour aristocracy' enjoying the inheritance of colonial rule and with vested interests in the *status quo* (Arrighi and Saul 1968; Arrighi 1970). On the structural level, tribal organization not only serves as the basis of urban social relationships, but is said to carry over into class institutions and proves divisive within the trade-union movement (Scott 1966; Yesufu 1962).[4] On the cultural level, elements of the value-systems of the open mobility-system characteristic of certain traditional African societies, are said to continue to operate in the new urban-industrial context, preventing the emergence of a distinct lower-class consciousness (Lloyd 1967).

The cumulative effect of these and other distinctive factors is held to make gradual and sustained mobilization of class consciousness exceptionally difficult. Industrial action is likely to take the form of spontaneous disorganized protests directed against particular injustices and deprivations, which can be broken by a show of force or slight political manoeuvre.[5]

Such interpretations are numerous and cannot be fully considered here. Suffice it to say that their applicability to workers and unions at Ikeja, the subject of this paper, is marginal. What these interpretations share is a common failure to ask what workers actually *do* and what interpretations they put on their actions. Here I will examine the development of a particular conflict situation in order to examine the structure of class relationships, and to show how the workers' actions can be interpreted as expressions of class consciousness.

THE IKJEJA INDUSTRIAL ESTATE AND THE DEVELOPMENT OF INDUSTRIAL RELATIONS

The Ikeja Industrial Estate is situated some ten miles north of Lagos. On the estate some fifty factories provide employment for roughly 20,000 workers, predominantly Yoruba from the Western State, but with some from the Mid-West and the Eastern States. Expatriate influence is much in evidence and the casual observer notes immediately the names of well-known European companies. The range of goods is wide: building materials, textiles, paints, rubber products, beer, cocoa, pharmaceuticals, enamelware, and footwear, to mention the most important.

The Estate was developed in the late 1950s and early 1960s by the Regional Government at Ibadan when Ikeja fell within the Western Region. Since indigenous businessmen at that time lacked the finances to establish capital-intensive plant on the scale anticipated by the Western Region Government, expatriate capital and technology have dominated the Estate from the very beginning. On the eve of Independence, such major colonialist firms as the United Africa Company were undergoing substantial restructuring, including the change from imperialist traffic, based on the export of primary produce and consumption goods, to manufacturing and industrial enterprise. The heaviest capital investment thus comes from companies based in the advanced industrial societies of the western world (Kilby 1969).

The government's role has been essentially promotional of the intensive utilization of capital, plant, and technical expertise, attempting to minimize difficulties and costs of an internal politico-economic nature, especially those relating to cheap wage labour.

The Federal Government has also done little to regulate industrial relations procedure. The major determinant of formally constituted bargaining procedures between managements and workers has been the capital-intensive technology imported from advanced industrial societies. The costs of building new factory shells and developing, importing, and installing modern machinery were exceptionally high and, as in the case of the first United Africa Company firms, involved the transfer of substantial capital resources from long-established areas of profit accumulation. Factories operating immediately after Independence were test cases for the new imperialism, and future investment would be greatly inhibited by low profit returns due to loss of production through perpetual labour disputes. Expatriate managers have therefore had considerable incentive to promote house unions within their factories and to formalize their relationships with workers.

On the other side, encouraged by relatively high wages and good conditions of service, employees from precisely those sectors of the wage-earning economy in which colonial rulers had promoted industrial relations on the British model (such as the Railway Corporation or the Ports Authority) were the first to organize their less experienced co-workers. An added feature was the established tradition of paternalism among expatriate managers reared in the major companies of the colonial era, a paternalism that today contrasts all the more strongly with non-paternalistic exploitation by Lebanese, Indian, and Syrian companies. The latter are small-scale plants, with a low technological base, for the assembly of electrical equipment and the like. Workers can be trained within the space of a few days to maximum output levels. Those who attempt to form unions are often replaced at will by docile 'applicants' ever available in Lagos, and prepared to accept the lowest wages and worst working conditions without protest.

Ultimately, however, the strength of unionism depends on the nature of the labour force. Migration to the metropolitan area from Yorubaland and beyond is a highly selective process drawing on the young educated population of the towns and villages. Factories generally recruit workers in their late teens and twenties with primary six or modern school education. At this stage their education is complete but limited. The shopfloor worker, with little chance of promotion to highly skilled or supervisory work on high wages, sees such employment as a means to accumulating sufficient capital for the critical transition to the role of entrepreneur.

We can briefly conceptualize the cognitive map of the young factory worker in the following terms. On the one hand, the factory situation provides regular employment and steady income, part of which he can save. But, essentially, it is a *closed* mobility-system. Well-paid white collar and supervisory posts are out of his reach, for these are the preserve of those with qualifications and training gained before entering industrial employment. Improvements in economic standing are achieved by negotiated wage increases, or by moving to a new firm offering slightly higher wages. The worker needs the union to act as a bargaining force in order to shorten his time as a wage earner, to stave off rampant inflation in the urban centre, and thus keep his rate of saving steady.

On the other hand, a combination of his experience in the established Yoruba township and the new environment of the Lagos suburb, Ikeja or Agege townships, points to the *open* mobility of the entrepreneur, the independent man. The low economic return from farming leads to an increased awareness in the established towns of the economic rewards and high status accruing to the trader, transporter, or businessman. And in the new urban situation too, such impressions are reinforced by his day-to-day experience in such a centre as Agege township adjacent to the Ikeja Estate, where wealth, prestige, and local political influence are the preserve of the uneducated and semi-literate transporter, trader, garage, and general provisions store owner. It is the successful independent man, not the industrial manager or civil servant, alongside whom the wage-earner lives and establishes interpersonal relationships, who is the key reference point in the cognitive map of the industrial employee, and is the one with whom he can most clearly identify.

The most important consequence of this instrumental approach to industrial employment is high attachment to trade unions where they exist. The success or otherwise of the union determines the individual's chances of achieving the virtually universal goal of entrepreneurship beyond the confines of the factory. This is increasingly marked where low wages and the rocketing cost of living force workers to stay in wage-earning employment considerably longer than they initially anticipate on first migrating to the new urban-industrial context. Notwithstanding the almost universal desire to leave the factory, voluntary resignation rates are very low and the labour force at Ikeja is becoming increasingly stabilized.

Thus, where unions do exist in the large factories at Ikeja, even though they are limited to individual companies, workers are vitally concerned about the success of negotiations with management and firm in supporting their leaders. Workers have arrived at an accommodation with the existing productive relationships and the structured inequalities arising therefrom (Parkin 1971: 91).

Strike action and lockouts are employed infrequently, although they are regarded as legitimate tactics when other channels have broken down. But where the formal negotiating procedure is broken on one or both sides, then the value-system, which legitimates those procedures, is itself under attack and may be in danger of rejection. Implicitly, if not

explicitly, such a rejection of established procedures illustrates dissatisfaction with the degree of social inequality in society at large.

THE IMMEDIATE POLITICAL BACKGROUND: THE ADEBO COM-MISSION AND THE ROOTS OF CONFLICT

With the end of the civil war in January 1970, the Federal Military
Government (FMG) turned its attention to economic and social
problems exacerbated by the extended war effort. In particular, inflation was causing acute concern in some areas. In July 1970, the government responded to the situation by establishing the Salaries and Wages
Review Commission, under the distinguished chairmanship of Chief
Simeon Adebo. Its terms of reference limited it formally to the review
of public-sector incomes (Adebo 1971a), but the recommendations of
previous commissions had invariably been followed by private companies.

The setting up of the Adebo Commission raised workers' hopes of
economic improvement for a number of reasons. Chief Adebo and other
members of the Commission, unlike many prominent ex-politicians still
in powerful positions, had not compromised their reputations in such
a way as to detract from the objective and apolitical spirit their roles
demanded. Their concern for thorough investigation and amenability to
all shades of opinion quickly became apparent. Parallels were quickly
drawn between the Adebo Commission and the Morgan Commission
of 1964, which had not only recommended substantial wage increases but,
in its minority reports, had been severely critical of the increasing gap
between the rich and the poor and of the failure of the political class to
throw off the huge wage differentials of the colonial era (Morgan 1964).
The censorious tone of the Commission, and the minimum wage-levels
proposed, had thrown the civilian government into such confusion that,
by refusing to publish the report, a fourteen-day general strike had been
precipitated, which paralysed the whole country (Melson 1970). Certainly at Ikeja, the general strike contributed substantially to the demand
by workers for formal recognition of their right to form trade unions.

Only a handful of union leaders at Ikeja attempted to make a direct
contribution to the Commission's inquiries, and did so through the
United Committee of Central Labour Organizations (UCCLO). The
customary shortcomings of 'national' leaders of the Labour movement
were, however, quickly made as manifest as ever. In a lengthy memorandum to the Adebo Commission, UCCLO members calculated the

Minimum Living Wage of the average worker with a wife and child as being £116. 5s. 8d. per month (UCCLO 1970)! Although they cut this to an 'irreducible' £48. 10s., their stand was generally dismissed as attractive but preposterous. UCCLO's principal contribution was the call for an interim award, which caught the popular imagination. The Commission again demonstrated their sensitivity to public opinion, cut short their tour of the twelve states, and presented their first report to the FMG in Lagos.

The principal recommendation of the first report (several were planned) was an interim award of 1s. 7d. per day for daily-paid workers and £2 per month for wage- and salary-earners (Adebo 1971a). This cost-of-living allowance (*cola*) applied to all workers earning less than £500 per annum; those earning between £500 and £524 would receive increments to raise them to £524. All awards were to be backdated to 1 April, 1970, nine months in all. The award was thus relevant to the vast majority of Ikeja workers since most received between £10 and £25 per month. Only a very small minority of highly-skilled technicians and experienced administrative employees fell outside the upper limits stipulated in the report.

The *cola* award was given specifically in recognition of the prevailing inflationary situation. As Adebo expressed it in the report: 'In the circumstances, the award we feel able to recommend at this time is aimed only at relieving *intolerable suffering at or near the bottom of* the wage and salary levels' (emphasis theirs). As such it would be taken into account when the more general award to be given later was recommended.

On the general economic situation, the effects of the civil war and the sacrifices which this had required, Adebo commented:

'Such sacrifice would be easiest to bear, however, if it was seen to fall equitably on all sections of the population such that the least sacrifice was made by those in the lowest income group. From some of the representations made to us, it is clear not only that there is intolerable suffering at the bottom of the income scale because of the rise in the cost of living, but also *that suffering is made even more intolerable by manifestations of affluence and wasteful expenditure which cannot be explained on the basis of visible and legitimate means of income*' (emphasis theirs).

The immediate public response to the first report, which was exceptionally well publicized throughout the mass media, was favourable indeed. Further improvements were promised for the future and Ikeja workers could look forward to nine months backdated pay – almost two weeks wages for those just within the maximum limit of the award, around two months for those on the lowest income levels.

Clearly, the Commission planned to ameliorate conditions within the existing structure, rather than suggest radical changes to the structure itself. Its strategy was one of accommodation at the national level in the same way that the organization of industrial relations at Ikeja has sought to promote accommodation at the local level. Only five days after the award was announced circumstances changed drastically.

Following a meeting with the Nigerian Employers' Consultative Association (NECA), an organization dominated by the major expatriate concerns in industry and manufacturing, Chief Enahoro, the Federal Commissioner for Labour and a long prominent member of the political class, announced a significant qualification to the quite universal recommendations made by Adebo himself. NECA had argued that some of their members had made substantial wage increases since 1964; they could not be expected to pay the same increments now as companies that had paid none at all over the past six years, when minimum wage rates had last been laid down. In recognition of this 'injustice' Enahoro announced that where companies in the private sector had made wage adjustments since 1964 *on the basis of the cost of living*, which were equal to, or in excess of the *cola* award, such companies did not have to pay the Adebo allowance; where increases had been made but were less than the allowance, companies were expected to make up the balance; where there had been no such increase in wages, the full *cola* had to be paid.

Among Ikeja workers a general uncertainty prevailed on the subject of Enahoro's qualification. Details of management–house union negotiations were rarely known. But one worker, sitting in an Agege bar with friends the same evening, expressed a widely held view: 'Why is everyone surprised at what has happened? This is the government at work and Enahoro used to be a politician for many years, and you know what that means. Nothing goes for nothing in Nigeria!'

Whilst Lebanese, Indian, and Chinese companies at Ikeja paying the minimum wage rates had to agree to pay *cola* immediately, in several European companies, managements and unions were faced with the onus of establishing the influence of the cost of living in up to six years of joint negotiation. This was exceptionally difficult, for management often bargained on the basis of one set of considerations (e.g. the introduction of new job classifications and reallocation of the labour force), while the union bargained on others (from the cost of living to making daily-paid workers permanent).

Two weeks passed. Managements in different factories exchanged ideas between themselves and NECA on their possible stands, and union leaders conferred together on future strategy – especially in the light of Decree 53 which, with the country in a State of Emergency, forbade strike action or incitement to strike. Having covered the roots of the conflict, I turn to the sequence of events in two particular companies.

TWO CASE STUDIES IN PROTEST:

(a) Conflict in a Textile Company

Shortly after Enahoro's statement, J.O., the house union president, met the factory's personnel manager who simply told him that management had not yet made a decision on the payment of *cola*. Despite repeated efforts, no clearer response was forthcoming, and so after some two and a half weeks, the union executive called a meeting in a local hotel. In a company of over 3 000 workers divided between three shifts, comprehensive communication with the workers was difficult; general meetings were called when necessary. The core leadership was exceptionally popular, having ousted a corrupt and inefficient executive two years previously, and won two substantial all-round increments. J.O. was known at Ikeja as a dedicated and steadfast president, a well-earned reputation.

Although only about 200 workers attended the meeting, a lively debate was engaged. J.O., after filling in the background, complained that management were dragging their feet over a decision, aided by Government procrastination. He had called a meeting because 'the executive is only the voice of the workers'. He wished to prepare for the management's decision. He felt that he had been correct to follow established procedure, despite management's tardiness. Now he was looking for a mandate from the workers to continue in this vein but, as always when he had been in power, he would take directions from the workers themselves.

Eight workers in all rose from the floor to congratulate J.O. on his 'reasoned' approach. Management was always loathe to pay out money, said one worker, but J.O. had won increases for all workers nevertheless, and had not sold them out. If he felt that this was the right course, then he should continue. Other workers voiced much the same opinion. However, as the meeting drew to a close, M.L. stood up. He was a man well known for speaking his mind at such meetings, despite his limited English, the language of such formal meetings. He himself, he said, felt more direct action was required 'to push the management forward and give us *cola*'. Some workers in his section wanted to strike, but there were too many like himself who respected J.O. highly. 'Every worker in this company follows you alone, and even if you walk out of the compound and leave just the big men (i.e. the management) there, we will follow immediately. Government and management are out to cheat the workers every time so we must stand behind our leaders.' After shouts of approval, the meeting closed.

It was clear from this, and other scattered informal meetings, that the established negotiation procedure was generally favoured. But although J.O. received the mandate he sought, the limitations on such negotiations were becoming clear. J.O. privately admitted that he had expected the issue of more direct action to come up, but the possibility of government informers (a legacy of colonial rule) at the meeting had limited his public pronunciation on the issue. Now he felt that workers were satisfied with his position, and, during the next four days, he made several representations to the management but met with the same response. Workers became increasingly impatient, but the established framework continued to hold.

On the fourth day after the meeting, a Thursday, as workers on the morning shift arrived, they saw police on guard outside the sheetmetal factory opposite. It quickly became common knowledge that there, on the previous evening, management had announced their refusal to pay *cola*. During the night shift there had been a complete sitdown strike until the police cleared the factory of workers. As the morning shift in the textile company got under way, workers in the dye house ceased work. They walked around the factory and encouraged others to down tools. Workers gradually drifted into the open factory compound and assembled there in small groups.

At this point, the unpopular personnel manager in charge of negotiations over *cola* arrived. As he left his car, he was abused and beaten up by a group of young workers. Several elderly employees and security men intervened, but as other managers entered the factory compound, they too were subjected to threats and a decision was made to call the police. Before their appearance, J.O. entered and made a short speech. Workers could now return to their sections, he said, 'for now the management know we mean business and will listen to the executive with well-opened ears'. Production began again as members of the executive counselled patience.

But as the afternoon shift crossed with the morning contingent, several hundred workers stood around discussing the morning's events. J.O. again addressed the workers and allowed a senior manager to speak as the police entered the compound. Scarcely had he pointed out that management were still engaged in discussion with the Ministry of Labour than a chant of 'No work, pay us *cola* now' started. At this, police armed with clubs and dogs began to clear the compound. Several workers were beaten while the majority fled through the main gate or climbed over the compound perimeter. After discussions with police, the management declared a lockout for that day. As workers arrived at the factory the same evening and the following morning, to hear of the latest developments from the union leaders, fighting broke out with police as they tried to disperse the peaceful crowds of several hundred workers and observers.

The following morning, J.O., members of his own executive, and leaders from other companies in which similar protests had occurred were called to the office of the Commissioner of Police in Lagos. He read to them Decree 53, indicating that under this, he could imprison them for leading strike action. The leaders protested. The disputes were not of their creation. Indeed they had done all they could to prevent such disturbances, but the workers would not listen. He pointed out that, nevertheless, unless they brought the workers back into the factories, they would be prosecuted under the decree.

In itself, the threat had marginal impact. But when the union leaders returned to the textile factory, they effected a compromise with the management. Their respective cases would be submitted to the Commissioner for Labour and management would accept his decision as final. Having studied the previous agreements, management anticipated that they would have to pay. This, however, should not be regarded as a guarantee: only the Commissioner's judgement would be accepted. J.O. accepted this and decided to bring the workers back to the factory the same evening. The following day was pay-day, so the workers should be amenable to his instruction. In addition, during the course of the meeting, management had suggested that the executive had lost the respect of their followers and had allowed anarchy to prevail, a taunt which, although inaccurate, struck home.

F

As the night shift workers assembled to hear of the union's progress, J.O. was present to address them. He felt confident now, he said, that the award would be paid because 'workers have shown their power to the management'. It was only a question of time: workers should enter the factory and resume production. This was quietly received and there was general compliance. At this point, a management representative called J.O. aside. When he returned to the platform, he put the management's request that each worker should sign a guarantee against damaging company property.

Immediately after this was announced to the three hundred or so workers present, they began to shout 'No work, all go home!' and many workers rushed away. A majority remained, but when K.L., a popular worker, pointed out that such a demand insulted not only the workers but the union too – 'If the union says production should begin then that by itself should be enough for the managers' – everyone dispersed homewards.

Despite the fact that the following morning, Saturday, was pay-day, only a handful of workers arrived, and, after receiving their pay, were sent home. The vast majority of workers had evidently decided to stay at home over the weekend. J.O. had been unable to announce a general meeting before the Friday night meeting had dispersed, and, as a result, only sixty workers arrived on the Sunday. J.O. pointed out that success was now in sight, for workers and union leaders had co-operated well throughout. Though management were 'certain' to pay *cola*, they were cunning, especially when near defeat. The only way in which workers could avoid termination for going on strike was to follow the letter of the law.

Several workers exhorted the assembly to follow J.O. But K.L. brought the meeting to a close by pointing out that now, following the workers' major contribution, their protest had reached the point at which the expertise of the executive around the bargaining table *had* to be brought once again into play: 'We are all on the point of success. . . . The management will surely have to pay us all *cola* for we have all done a good job.'

On the Monday morning, no demand for workers' signatures was forthcoming from the management. Although the shift was incomplete, production started. Within two days, the full labour complement had returned and, four days later, the management agreed to pay *cola* to all the workers, albeit without approval from the Ministry of Labour.

This completes the account of events in the one company in which I have concentrated on the changing balance of power between the union, the management, and the workers. The position was, in broad outline, much the same within the second company described below, the beer company, and similarities will be taken for granted. In the second case study, I introduce the nature of external influences as opposed to internal ones, for these are of considerable importance to the form of class relationships within a neo-colonial economy.[6]

(b) Conflict in a Beer Company

As with the textile company, this was one of the earliest factories on the estate, and the British management had encouraged the duly elected union executive from the outset. The union had experienced a number of internal disputes due to mishandling of funds and personal rivalries. Despite its chequered history, the incumbent executive during the previous year had won wage increases of between 8 per cent and 13 per cent. Union–management relationships were cordial and clearly defined. The union had a sound internal organization built on an active body of shop stewards.

Although the leaders were under considerable pressure to force the management into making a decision, the sound organization of the union adequately encompassed the 500 permanent workers in the firm: leaders retained their clear-cut authority roles longer than elsewhere on the Estate.

But during the morning on which the textile workers finally resumed production, the management had sent for S.A., the union president, and complained to him of low production in the bottling section. On all shifts at least half the labour force was engaged here and industrial action in the section quickly disrupted the whole plant. S.A. and a fellow executive member visited the section, but reported back that machine breakdown was the cause. Since low production continued throughout the morning and afternoon shifts, management accused leaders and workers of collusion. Overnight, production fell to 10 per cent and, as the morning shift arrived, all shopfloor workers assembled in the factory compound. They were joined two hours later by the substantial clerical force as they arrived for work, although highly-skilled and supervisory staff continued to work. Older, respected workers also patrolled the compound to ensure that no workers damaged machinery.

When management and union met, the former declared that the shutdown of production was illegal. S.A. had not declared any breakdown in negotiating procedure; he should press the workers back to their sections. He replied that, while the union acknowledged that management were experiencing difficulties with the Ministry of Labour in obtaining a firm ruling over *cola* payment, the workers were tired of such malingering and had initiated action on their own account. The union had tried to avoid a show-down, but management had only themselves and the government to blame.

That afternoon, as strikers continued to wait for further developments, the Nigerian personnel manager asked them to leave the factory voluntarily. Valuable machinery could be damaged by 'hotheads' and the families of European technicians living inside the compound had to be protected. He was shouted down when several workers declared that management could interpret this as a walk-out.

Another worker commented: 'We have waited some days now for a management decision, despite what other workers have done on the estate. Look what has happened in the textiles. The workers struck there, and they must have won for they are working again today. Now we have made our strike we shall not give way at all.' Tempers were running high and verbal attacks were made against notably unpopular managers. The management called in the police and, after some violence, the compound was cleared.

The following morning, annoyed that European technicians inside the compound were continuing to service vital equipment, groups of workers began to picket factory entrances. S.A. and his colleagues attempted to persuade workers to return to their homes; but workers insisted that their presence was not interfering with the union's progress. The groups were later broken up by the police. To this point, management, union, and workers dominated the field of action. However, for this company, as with several others on the estate, the resolution of the conflict was determined elsewhere.

Since the beginning of the dispute, Ikeja managements had communicated with the Ministry of Labour through NECA. As worker protest emerged, NECA's official strategy had been to follow government directions as precisely as possible and to present a united front against what was considered to be the first indications of a state of anarchy among workers. But splits had begun to appear among the managerial class as to precisely where their interests lay.

NECA's core leadership accepted that, if one company gave in to workers' demands and awarded *cola* where, according to government policy it was unnecessary, the pressure on other companies would be so much the greater. As protest spread at Ikeja and elsewhere, this view hardened for in it was seen organized rebellion against the military regime. The reasoning behind this interpretation was somewhat unclear, but the FMG had recently announced their intention to rule for a further six years. A conspiracy between disgruntled politicians, ambitious trade unionists, and external bodies to discredit the regime was widely suspected. For NECA industrialists to submit to workers' demands would indicate a lack of confidence in the government itself, an intolerable position if they were to contribute to the post-war economy.

More immediately pressing considerations, however, faced Ikeja managers. In one cocoa-processing company, workers had, on the same morning as the textile strike, threatened to burn down the administration building with managers inside unless they signed a document to the effect that *cola* would be paid. After doing so, managers had been allowed to leave although they were abused and their cars stoned. The police arrived much later, when everyone had dispersed! This and subsequent incidents suggested that the managerial class could not rely on the government to provide a sufficient show of physical force, and they considered their plants to be in danger of destruction. The peak to this dilemma came when the general manager of another strike-hit company was injured by workers picketing his factory gates. Again no police were present to protect him.

At a heated meeting of NECA representatives soon afterwards, he announced his intention to pay *cola* without waiting for government approval; he could no longer risk his plant and ignore investors' interests for the small amount of profit involved in paying the award. Several other managers under such pressure agreed with this view and the earlier unity between managements and government collapsed.

Following this meeting, individual Ikeja managements could do little more than spread the announcement of their change of policy in order to avoid the impression of wholesale retreat. In the beer company, where workers continued picketing for a further three days, production was quickly resumed when management finally announced their readiness to pay. The company's personnel manager summarized developments in the following way:

'Once one company at Ikeja had decided to pay, all the rest had to follow. If the workers in our plant, where we were still holding out, had heard that others had got *cola* by their force and anarchy, (so) the violence inside our own company was much more possible. . . We have over £4 million of equipment to protect here, but the cost of paying the (Adebo) award was only £30,000 each year, nothing besides our usual profits. Had the government supported us with force, then we could have resisted all the workers' demands, but when we saw we could not count on that support we had to give in and protect the interests of our shareholders first and foremost.'

THE NATURE OF CLASS RELATIONSHIPS AND THE EXPRESSION OF CLASS CONSCIOUSNESS

Quite obviously, the essential outcome of events described here was that the Ikeja workers gained through their collective action the Adebo award which a combination of management and government had attempted to deny them. But considering the manner in which the government took away with one hand that which had been given by the other, some form of protest appeared fairly inevitable. This being the case, can one legitimately term the action described here as an expression of class consciousness which, as Lloyd points out '(implies) consciousness of the special interests of the class and activity directed towards preserving these interests' (Lloyd 1966a: 57)?

Objectively, this was certainly so. The Adebo award was applicable to all wage-earners in the public and private sectors, indicating them to be a special case; the Enahoro qualification then singled out workers within the private sector, defining their special interests even more clearly. Again, strike action originated on the shopfloor among those workers on the lowest wage rates in their respective companies and with most to gain by taking a stand. But to what extent did the workers themselves see their action in these terms?

The most immediate judgements centred on the £2 award, but as the following comment shows, behind this specific issue lay a number of other grievances:

'This is our right, the £2 per month increase and we shall fight for it to the end. What does the government think it can do to us the workers and the other poor people? . . . We have paid new taxes, we have paid NPF[7] and in the war we paid extra taxes to fight the Biafrans. Then there are all the duties to the government on imports so that the costs go up again. The war has ended, but how would we know when there has been no improvement for us?' (A young unmarried worker from Ibadan, aged 25 and earning about £15 per month)

At one level then, the protest was set against the background of the civil war and the manner in which the lower strata had borne its brunt, a fact recognized by Adebo himself. At another level, both the *cola* payment and post-war conditions were viewed in the context of economic and social inequalities rooted in the colonial experience but ingrained and cultivated throughout the period of Independence:

'All the prices are going up and we can do nothing. . . . Let us say this man is a director, you are a manager, and I am a worker. We all go to the same market and our wives buy side by side. But the manager and the director, they do not feel anything at all. They have free houses and cars and their children go to good schools paid for by their companies. But I, the worker, I have scarcely enough money to pay my bus fare. From my house on Lagos Island near Tinubu is 3s. each day. A bottle of palm wine or two is 2s. and chop from the petty trader here 2s. Then there is the rent for my one room which is £5. 10s. each month. . . . And the manager and director have their big fine houses *free*! All we want is £2!' (A junior supervisor earning £27 per month, aged 35 with five children)

And with a somewhat different emphasis on the present, workers viewed the *cola* issue as a clear illustration of the manner in which members of the political class, the managerial class, and other elites conspired to retain their monopoly of material rewards in Nigerian society, coming to terms among themselves to exploit the masses further:

'These big guns in Lagos, they are not interested in what happened to us, the labourers. The European managers have refused to give us the £2 owed to us, and the big men help them in this matter. Some of them used to be poor men, labourers, as we are now. But now they are at the top, they are *ogas*, (and) our conditions are the same as ever . . . . What does this £2 mean to a top government officer or an Ikeja manager? Some of them go out for the night with their wives and spend £50, £100, even £500 on a ceremony. We want only this £2, a miserable sum, and we the workers have the power and strength in our hands.' (Newly employed worker, aged 19, one wife and child; salary – £9. 16s. per month)

In sum then, not only were workers acting in protection of quite specific economic interests, which they share by virtue of their common class situation; they were taking advantage of the relative ease of mobilization allowed by such class experience to protest against a diversity of the exploitative economic and political processes to which the masses as a whole were subjected. Such processes, described in these and other comments made at the time, are not limited in application to the industrial order. They are manifest in the oppressive conditions facing the urban poor in general. This was not a protest by industrial workers solely against their position within the industrial system as such, but was against the prevailing inequalities within Nigerian society at large. The great majority of the urban masses have little possibility for such structured opposition: they look to the wage-earners to provide the leadership in protest movements, and of this the wage-earners themselves are acutely aware.

Where, beneath the veneer of social calm, the underlying resentment against the extent of inegalitarianism was as extensive as it certainly was at this time, then the protest even within this limited setting assumed the proportions of a minor insurrection against the prevailing order.

But, notwithstanding undercurrents of hostility and the fact that this was a crisis situation, there was little in the way of expressions by workers that indicate a vision of an alternative order radically different to the one prevailing at that time. On the contrary, most workers interpreted their action as a *variant on the normal processes of accommodation to the social order* which, during periods of social calm, were expressed through the channel of peaceful bargaining between unions and managements around the negotiating table. Far from being the condition of anarchy that many managers considered to obtain during this period, not only was this a highly-structured conflict situation, it was one that encouraged leaders and workers to adhere further to peaceful negotiation within their respective companies. Workers' own interpretations of the conflict in which they were involved and of subsequent developments give support to this view.

Essentially, the strategy developed by the workers at this time was viewed as a *complement* to the established procedure rather than a rejection of it, and one induced by the decree operative at that time forbidding strike action or incitement to strike. This is illustrated by the comment of one textile worker on the afternoon of the first strike action:

'What use for us if the executive were in gaol because they had called for a go-slow or even a strike to get our rights? Our leaders are good leaders. We know that because of our achievements. If they had not done well in the past we would surely have removed them by now! We, the workers, we have made the protest, and we can see that the

General Manager and his men are on the run. These managers, they are all so frightened at what we have done that they must give in soon. And yet our leaders remain quite free. When the manager comes to his bargaining table, they can be there to take over the whole business again. Then they can easily get the award written down, for they have experience of such things where people like myself do not.'

Certainly I would not suggest that all workers expressed the nature of their relationship with union leaders so precisely. But this comment does illustrate the acknowledgement that, faced with Decree 53, elected representatives, who look after workers' well-being from day-to-day, had unavoidable restrictions at that time on the way in which they performed their duties. The expertise for which they had been elected had been eliminated from the rules of the game during this critical period. But it could be drawn upon later when 'the management has been brought to its knees' – a common expression at this time.

Following the management's capitulation, union leaders did indeed employ their expertise in this fashion. It is such a close congruity of interests between union leaders and workers that indicated the major source of strength of house unions at Ikeja. In everyday affairs, the working relationship between leaders and followers is an integral element in accounting for house unions gaining wage increments and improved conditions of employment. Local union leaders and shopfloor employees see their national spokesman to be as remote and self-interested as members of the political class. Where successful industrial action occurs at the local level, then workers' attachment to their democratically-elected leaders is all the more heightened. So too is their short-term interest in supporting those institutional arrangements which indicate a general acknowledgement of the overall reward system generated by the present distribution of ownership of the means of industrial production. We can see this in the subsequent *dénouement* to the Adebo affair.

Despite the furore surrounding the government's handling of the first Adebo report, hopes of further improvements for wage-earners were high. But the recommendations of the second and final report presented seven months later were disappointing indeed (Adebo 1971). Far from narrowing the gap between rich and poor, the recommendations widened it substantially. General wage and salary increments were awarded across the board on a sliding scale. Workers earning less than £200 per annum were to receive an increment of £36, £24 of which they had already received as *cola*. For the lowest-paid workers this meant a £1 per month increase. In the upper echelons however, those with salaries between £2 000 and £2 500 were to receive increments of £240, whilst those with £2 500-plus were awarded £300 per year increase! This was an apparently incredible reversal of policy from a concern with 'the intolerable suffering at or near the bottom of the wage and salary levels' to a cossetting of the 'aristocracy' of public and private employment.

The predominant interpretations made by workers were that the government had either pressured Adebo to severely curtail his recommendations, or subsequently tampered with the report: 'The government top men have altered the report so they will get more money'; 'our bosses have bribed the government officials so that Adebo cannot give the workers more pay'; 'even though Adebo helped us before, it is always the big guns who win in the end'.

If, as I have argued, the handling of the first award provided a focus around which crystallized many of the undercurrents of resentment against the prevailing social structure, one might have anticipated that the final award would provide yet another catalyst for collective action. In fact no such action was forthcoming, nor even realistically contemplated by workers or union leaders.

This is to be accounted for by reference to the views workers held on the consequences of their earlier strike action. Workers in the companies affected calculated the prospects for future collective bargaining in the light of the demonstration of unity and strength of purpose which had been so manifest throughout the critical two-week period. Neither workers nor leaders were aware of the external influences I have described here, knowing little of the important interest divisions between managements and government.

In their view, managements had capitulated because of the threat to production they had caused by withdrawing their labour power. Faced with the possibility of some violence from over-eager workers but the certainty of enormous loss of profits in their capital-intensive plants, managements had been forced to capitulate.

Leaders and workers were, then, increasingly optimistic of the opportunities available to take advantage of their earlier demonstration of strength in the face of government's and management's rejection of their rights. Following the second report, one union leader commented: 'Our annual negotiation comes up in a month's time. Whatever increase I demand, the management will have to consider it very seriously. Now, in the light of the trouble *cola* caused them, they know precisely where (union) executive and workers stand.'

A protest movement against the 'adulteration' of the report, which many workers believed to have occurred, could have been no more than a political demonstration against the injustices of the Nigerian elite. By continuing to work as normal, in effect, the Ikeja wage-earners *were* engaging in social action on class lines. They were taking account of their relationship to representatives of other social classes with interests opposed to their own, and rationally calculating the avenues available to them for future economic improvement in collective terms.

An explanation of the solidarity of the lower-class within the industrial system can be attempted by describing the structure of relationships between leaders and followers within *that system*. Within the context of a neo-colonial society, however, where ownership of the means of industrial production is in the hands of those outside the society itself, such a clear-cut parameter cannot be drawn. The social anthropologist, examining the nature of class relationships at the micro-level can only point to the consequences of the domination of imperialist capitalist interests over such underdeveloped economies and the effects that such domination has for the articulation of internal class conflicts.[8]

At Ikeja, certain such effects were paradoxical in the extreme. Ikeja managers were faced with an unresolvable conflict of interests as intermediaries within a neo-colonial situation. Either they could look to the interests of the international financiers whom they represent, or act to buttress the incumbents of state office. They could not, in this situation, do both. In the event, they decided in favour of the former, and in doing so, they not only had to pay out the award, which their employees considered their right anyway, but they also created a situation that encouraged the workers to become further aware of their collective strength by virtue of their relationship to the means of production.

Such managers were, not surprisingly, extremely critical of the government's handling of the Adebo affair. They resented further the manner in which the government stood aside from the conflict, providing only a nominal display of physical force. This too, perhaps, is to be explained by the inherent conflicts in the processes of neo-colonialism.

As noted at the outset, the capital-intensive nature of expatriate industry and the profits derived from industrial enterprise place a premium on industrial peace rather than on rigid adherence to minimum wage-rates. However, relatively generous wage and salary increments by expatriate enterprise to safeguard sound union–management relationships not only can be passed on through price increases, they also prove extremely embarrassing to the largest employer of wage labour, namely

the government itself. It is the government above all other employers
that has vested interests in keeping wages at the absolute minimum.

But the government has difficulty in objecting to wage increases within private enterprise. These are usually justified on the basis of the rising
cost of living and increased productivity. The first is (as in the case of the
Adebo Commission) acknowledged by the government; the second is the
raison d'être for allowing expatriate enterprise to operate in the first
first place. In the light of the large differentials in wages and salaries
between the private and the public sector, open resentment to the fact
that 'the country's manufactures . . . remain a perpetual appendage of
foreign industrial complexes' (Nigeria 1970: 143) is on the increase.
Possibly then, it becomes necessary for the government to take advantage of confrontations between expatriate industrial managers and their
workers in order to demonstrate where power really lies, and what is the
most preferable balance of competing interests from the point of view of
the indigenous political class.

Such realignments within the power structure of Nigerian society are
essential to ensuring socio-political stability within the wider arena.
Periodic reassessments of the distribution of wealth and power between
the competing elites must not be allowed to upset the even more fragile
balance between the elites and the masses. In the case of the Adebo
affair we have some illustration of how this can be achieved.

Labour leaders and workers emerged from this conflict with a heightened sense of accommodation to the existing social order, and an
increased awareness of their ability to make certain economic gains
within that framework. In doing so they were perhaps making the same
point as Marx did over a century ago, that even members of the labour
movement require to develop and sustain a comprehensive and politically sophisticated level of organization before the possibility of imple-
menting an entirely different framework emerges.

A PERSPECTIVE SUMMARY

In this paper I have not regarded the existence of class relationships in
Nigeria as problematic. In that one has, at Ikeja, a clear division between
those who own and those who control the means of production on the
one hand, and those who only contribute to the production process by
selling their labour power on the other, then class relationships can be
said to exist in that system.

Here I have concentrated on the *form* that such class relationships take, the interpretation of events by those involved in conflict situations, and the congruity or conflict of interests between those in dominant and subordinate positions within only the industrial sector of the economy.

Nevertheless, the existence of social classes even in the African industrial context has been frequently denied. Sociologists and ideologues have arrived at essentially the same conclusions, albeit by different routes. In an early study, *The Third World*, Worsley (1967) writing with a distinctly Marxist perspective, comments of the wage-earners: 'These are not, then, modern industrial workers at all. They are people only beginning to transform themselves into permanent city dwellers, learning the habits of industrial and urban society, struggling to piece together a new identity and community out of the kaleidoscopic fragments of their lives' (pp. 160–1).

Having failed to establish the existence of a proletarian consciousness, Worsley turns to the peasantry as a 'potentially revolutionary force', 'potentially' because: 'Other social classes, to put it simply, are either not there or are only in the process of formation, or if they do exist, are impeded by a variety of factors from developing their own institutional ideological identity' (p. 163).

Such equivocal statements as this (and Worsley's is one among many) are obviously unsatisfactory. At the most elementary level, if they are not industrial workers, what then are they? But there are two major criticisms which can be directed at generalizations attempted in this fashion.

First, there is a failure to acknowledge that the very nature of uneven economic development of malintegrated neo-colonial societies allows the existence of highly-developed class relationships on the basis of one mode of production, but only marginally structured ones on the basis of another – and this within the same national polity.

Second, in the African context, class continues to be looked upon as a 'thing' with a set of attributes according to the possession of which it qualifies, or does not qualify, for the appropriate label. An indication of this is the manner in which the wage-earning force, the urban masses, the peasantry and so on, are presented as discrete categories with distinctive qualities; on this basis, and usually without examination of a single conflict situation, the existence of social classes has often been denied. But the analysis of class in the African context, as in any other, must proceed through the analysis of social relationships and social action, and the crucial class relationships are those determined by the mode of production.[9]

Within the limits of this paper, I have accordingly tried to avoid these pitfalls in two ways. First, I have taken the major arena in which social action takes place as the system of relationships based on the industrial mode of production, regarding this as conceptually expedient in providing a natural set of parameters within which the conflicts and contradictions inherent in that mode of production are most clearly displayed. Where economic development is exceptionally uneven and competing and complementary modes of production diverse (as is usual in a neocolonial economy), such a strategy is not only heuristically valuable but analytically essential in keeping attention focused on the specific mode of production around which class relationships are structured.

Second, I have taken as my subject a conflict situation in which class interests are most clearly demonstrated by individuals and groups acting in protection of such interests and with reference to the behaviour, actual and anticipated, of class members whose interests they perceive as being essentially opposed to their own. A conflict situation is a convenient issue, for it is at such times that what Weber calls the 'naked class situation' is most transparently exposed.[10] But class relationships are of the essence of ongoing politico-economic processes. The experience of direct class conflict, sporadic and ephemeral as it is, has important implications for the dialectical realignments of class relationships. And an integral part of explaining such consequences is an appreciation of the interpretations that class members themselves place on the conflicts in which they are involved.

Notes

1 Many friends and colleagues have been kind enough to make extensive comments on earlier drafts of this paper. I would particularly like to thank Peter Lloyd and Gavin Williams whose detailed criticisms have always proved quite invaluable at all stages of my research. The research upon which this paper was based was financed by a grant made by the Social Science Research Council to Dr. P. C. Lloyd, University of Sussex, for the study of social stratification among urban Yoruba.

2 Most of the points made in the introductory section are included in the following works: Lloyd (1967, 1971), Worsley (1967), Andreski (1968).

3 For an account of the Lagos labour force in historical perspective, see Cohen and Hughes (1971). On the success or otherwise of Nigerian

(and other African) workers in raising real wages, see Kilby (1967), Weeks (1968, 1971a) and Cohen (1971).

4 For a critique of Scott (1966) see Grillo (1969). Cf. too Epstein (1958).

5 See, for example, Zolberg (1966: 72) who points to the creation of:

> 'relatively large agglomerations of workers in towns or in neighbourhood within towns. Although unions are often very loosely structured and fragile, human ecology tends to facilitate rapid communications among workers and enables them to act as visible mobs.'

And Davies (1966: 125–5):

> 'If the English working class slowly evolved a mixture of institutions and programmes that produced some rough semblance of unity, the African working class has had its spontaneous outbursts and its tentative steps towards organization rapidly transformed into centralized institutions.'

6 For a valuable presentation of an ideal-type of a neo-colonial economy, see Williams (1970). Williams's interpretation is, in broad terms, the one followed here.

7 National Provident Fund contributions.

8 The complementary nature of different levels of analysis required to build up a composite picture of such a complex subject as neo-colonialism is well stated by Gunder Frank (1971: 15):

> 'The attempt to spell out the metropolitan-satellite colonial structure and development of capitalism has led me to devote very little specific attention to its class structure and development. This does not mean that this is intended as a substitute for class analysis. On the contrary, the colonial analysis is meant to complement class analysis and to discover and emphasize aspects of the class structure in these underdeveloped countries which have often remained unclear.'

I have sought to show how the processes of interaction at the micro-level, determined in their general outlines by the macro-level neo-colonial relations, dialectically develop a self-conscious labour movement, a development of considerable significance for the internal class structure.

9 To be fair, Worsley (1967) does admit to the need to see class as 'a *relationship* and not a thing' (p. 163), but this is little more than an acknowledgement of the problem rather than an attempt to come to grips with it.

10 Weber is in fact discussing the much broader position when he employs this phrase (Gerth and Mills 1967: 194):

'Every technological repercussion and economic transformation threatens stratification by status and pushes the naked class situation into the foreground. Epochs and countries in which the class situation is of predominant significance are regularly periods of technical and economic transformation.'

References

ADEBO REPORT 1971a. *First Report of the Wages and Salaries Review Commission*. Lagos: Federal Ministry of Information.

ADEBO REPORT 1971b. *Second and Final Report of the Wages and Salaries Review Commission*. Lagos: Federal Ministry of Information.

ALLEN, C. and JOHNSON, R. W. (eds.) 1970. *African Perspectives*. Cambridge: Cambridge University Press.

ANDRESKI, S. 1968. *The African Predicament*. London: Michael Joseph.

ARRIGHI, G. 1970. International Corporations, Labour Aristocracies, and Economic Development in Tropical Africa. In Rhodes, R. I. (ed.) 1970.

ARRIGHI, G. and SAUL, J. 1968. Socialism and Economic Development in Tropical Africa. *Journal of Modern African Studies* **6** (2): 141–70.

COHEN, R. 1971. Further Comment on the Kilby/Weeks Debate. *Journal of Developing Areas* **5** 155–64.

COHEN, R. and HUGHES, A. 1971. Towards the Emergence of a Nigerian Working Class: The Social Identity of the Lagos Labour Force, 1897–1939. Occasional Paper, Series D, Number 7. Faculty of Commerce and Social Science, University of Birmingham.

DAVIES, I. O. 1966. *African Trade Unions*, Harmondsworth: Penguin.

EPSTEIN, A. L. 1958. *Politics in an Urban African Community*. Manchester: University Press.

FRANK, A. G. 1971. *Capitalism and Underdevelopment in Latin America*. Harmondsworth: Pelican.

GERTH, H. H. and MILLS, C. W. (eds.) 1967. *From Max Weber: Essays in Sociology*. London: Routledge & Kegan Paul.

GRILLO, R. D. 1969. The Tribal Factor in an East African Trade Union. In Gulliver, P.H. (ed.) 1969.

GULLIVER, P. H. (ed.) 1969. *Tradition and Transition in East Africa*. London: Routledge & Kegan Paul.

KILBY, P. 1967. Industrial Relations and Wage Determination: Failure of the Anglo-Saxon Model. *Journal of Developing Areas* **1**: 489–520.

—— 1969. *Industrialization in an Open Economy: Nigeria, 1945–66*. London: Cambridge University Press.

LLOYD, P. C. 1966a. Introduction. In Lloyd, P. C. (ed.) *The New Elites of*

Tropical Africa. International African Institute and Oxford University Press.

—— 1966b. Class Consciousness among the Yoruba. In *The New Elites of Tropical Africa (op. cit.)*.

—— 1967. *Africa in Social Change*. Harmondsworth: Penguin.

—— 1968. Social Stratification in Western Nigeria. Unpublished seminar paper. London: Institute of Commonwealth Studies.

—— 1971. *Classes, Crises and Coups*. London: MacGibbon and Kee.

MELSON, R. 1970. Nigerian Politics and the General Strike of 1964. In Rotberg, R.I., and Mazrui, A. (eds.) 1970.

MORGAN REPORT. 1964. *Report of the Commission on the Review of Wages, Salaries and Conditions of Service of Junior Employees of the Federation and in Private Establishments*. Lagos: Federal Government of Nigeria.

NIGERIA (1970). *Second National Development Plan 1970–74*. Lagos: Federal Ministry of Information.

PARKIN, F. 1971. *Class, Inequality and Political Order*. London: MacGibbon and Kee.

RHODES, R. I. (ed.) 1970. *Imperialism and Underdevelopment: A Reader*. New York: Monthly Review Press.

ROTBERG, R. I. and MAZRUI, A. (eds.) 1970. *Protest and Power in Black Africa*. London: Oxford University Press.

SCOTT, R. 1966. *The Development of Trade Unions in Uganda*. Nairobi: E. A. Publishing House.

UCCLO (United Committee of Central Labour Organizations) 1970. *Equitable Demand for Economic Growth and National Prosperity* Ibadan: Government Printer.

WEEKS, J. F. 1968. A Comment on Peter Kilby: Industrial Relations and Wage Determination. *Journal of Development Areas* 3: 7–17.

—— 1971a. Further Comments on the Kilby/Weeks Debate: An Empirical Rejoinder. *Journal of Developing Areas* 5: 164–74.

—— 1971b. Wage Policy and the Colonial Legacy – A Comparative Study. *Journal of Modern African Studies* 9 (3): 361–87.

WILLIAMS, G. P. 1970. The Social Stratification of a neo-Colonial Economy: Western Nigeria. In Allen, C. and Johnson, R. W. (eds.) 1970.

WORSLEY, P. 1967. *The Third World*. London: Weidenfeld.

YESUFU, T. M. 1962. *An Introduction to Industrial Relations in Nigeria*. London: Oxford University Press.

ZOLBERG, A. 1966. *Creating Political Order*. Chicago: Rand and McNally.

PART THREE
Marginality

SEBASTIAN BRETT

Low-income Urban Settlements in Latin America: the Turner Model

INTRODUCTION

The growth of self-built squatter communities on the outskirts of Third World towns and cities must surely be one of the most striking and extraordinary social phenomena of the post-war world. Although a welter of statistical and descriptive studies have appeared in recent years, particularly on Latin American shanty-towns, systematic attempts to formulate a theory which would provide a general understanding of the phenomenon as a whole have been noticeably lacking. Only very recently have social scientists grasped the full complexity of the social processes involved, and this realization came about more by accident than by design. The tendency of disciplines to import their theoretical assumptions and substantive preoccupations into the field led in most cases to an eclecticism that only made the lack of a theory more embarrassing, as the comparability of discrete findings seemed increasingly questionable.

It is therefore perhaps more than a coincidence that the theory to be discussed in this paper was the work of an architect. John Turner has been engaged for more than ten years in a prolonged polemic against the almost wholly negative view of squatters taken, until very recently, by Latin American officialdom. Turner's work with voluntary organizations in the *barriadas* of Lima and his later appointment as architectural adviser to the Peruvian Junta Nacional de la Vivienda gave him a unique opportunity to observe the contrasts between popular and official conceptions of housing action. He became increasingly aware that the inadequacies of planning policy lay less in the shortage of capital and organizational capacity than in a failure of communication, which arose out of ignorance of the *nature* of popular housing needs in societies characterized by rapid urbanization, underemployment, and institutional marginality. There has always been a tendency for politicians, planners, and journalists, by the very nature of their professional roles, to distort social phenomena by the application of unquestioned normative assumptions; even sociologists and anthropologists, who have a great deal more intellectual autonomy, are often limited by their habituation to well-tried conceptual schemata. In relation to those academics whose chief interest in shanty-towns was the convenient 'universe' they provided for the study of urban poverty, acculturation, etc., the originality of Turner's work was to search in the shanty-town environment for the *intrinsic* logic of the process of unplanned urban settlement. The popular control of the housing process provided insights into the hidden or qualitative elements of the relationship between man and his dwelling environment. These elements, while matters of survival for the poor migrant, are largely invisible to those who depend for them on specialized institutions outside the housing context.

The first two sections of this paper are devoted to an exposition of the two major components of Turner's work: an analysis of the different housing needs of sub-groups within the low-income sector and a typology of settlements upon which an analysis of settlement 'trajectories' can be based. In the section that follows, some of the implications for the model of recently observed developments are drawn, and some critical points are made. In conclusion, I refer rather tentatively to some of the issues the model raises in relation to current conceptions of 'marginality' in the analysis of urban poverty.

As a cautionary note, the reader's attention is drawn to the dangers of over-systematization that often arise from the desire to present a writer's thought as succinctly and clearly as possible. This is a field in which generalization is particularly hazardous, and where *practical* immersion in the 'language' of housing action has proved to be vitally important. The focus on theory in this paper made it difficult, in the restricted space available, to provide adequate empirical documentation of the hypotheses discussed. While I do not wish to evade these criticisms, it should be pointed out that Turner has continually emphasized the tentative and pragmatic nature of his explorations into theory. It is enough to say that contemporary research into low-income urban settlements will continue to be greatly influenced, particularly in its methodology, by the insights of Turner and his colleagues.

EXISTENTIAL NEEDS AND HOUSING PRIORITIES

In his analysis of low-income housing needs Turner begins with a distinction between three features of every housing situation: *physical shelter and amenities, location,* and *tenure.* An 'optimal' housing situation would be one in which the quality of shelter approximated to 'modern' norms of layout, materials, and amenities, location provided cheap and easy access to the place of work, and security of tenure was guaranteed by freehold ownership. In practice, of course, most households have to 'choose' between these alternatives. Although the home is one of the vital resources of all urban households, its significance and function for the household can vary greatly both between societies and within them. Among upper-income groups, in both the advanced and the dependent poles of the capitalist world, housing can be primarily a vehicle for the expression of personal tastes, and function more generally as a reflector of social status or identity. For the poor, particularly in rapidly urbanizing societies, it can be a decisive determinant of short-term economic opportunities, and, in the longer term, act as a stabilizing factor in the consolidation and protection of achieved living standards. These three 'existential functions' of the home: *identity, opportunity,* and *security* will normally be expressed in terms of a selective emphasis being placed by the household on either the achievement of modern standards, or proximity to employment, or freehold tenure, in the evaluation of its housing situation. The broad correspondence between the material and legal aspects of housing and its existential functions is depicted below:

Material/legal aspect	*Existential function*
Modern standard shelter	Identity
Access to employment	Opportunity
Freehold tenure	Security

The existential priorities from which housing needs derive vary very widely indeed, according to the degree and nature of participation of households in the wider urban economic and social systems. For example, 'the achievement of modern standards and amenities for all' figures prominently in the public conception of housing needs in societies where employment opportunities and economic security are 'normally' guaranteed by the existence of a dynamic labour market and its public servicing institutions. The prevalence of a normative ideal of 'standards' reflects a general situation in which very few are compelled to sacrifice standards for considerations that are more fundamental and pragmatic – such as easy access to markets for labour contracted on a daily basis, which may mean the occupation of sites where modern standards are physically impossible. As we shall see, a characteristic of mass underemployment societies, such as those of the majority of Latin

American nations, is that low-income housing (and consequently the very physical expansion of cities) is tied to a basic and very pragmatic 'economic logic' of the poor, a function it has almost wholly lost in the societies familiar to the metropolitan-trained sociologist and planner.

The starting-point in Turner's analysis, then, is an examination of housing needs in the context of levels of involvement of low-income groups in the labour market and public institutions in Latin American cities. The wage-level and security of employment constitute the most important variables in this discussion. With respect to these factors, not only do we find very considerable differentials among low-income populations at a given point of time, but also that the position of an individual household of rural immigrants is likely to change significantly in a short time-period after arrival in the city.

Middle-income groups with relatively secure employment and some industrial bargaining power will tend to evaluate housing as an article of consumption, in terms of a simple trade-off of quality (approximation to a normative standard) against cost. The chief indicators of quality are typically the material standards and amenities of the home and the 'reputation' of the residential neighbourhood. This kind of demand will be relatively inelastic for these groups; to satisfy it they may be willing and able to sacrifice accessibility or freehold tenure (see *Figure 1* below). Such households are characterized by their relative integration and participation in the formal economy, institutions, and status hierarchy of the city.[1] In full employment economies with an 'integrated' working class, this category of households forms the great majority and consequently definitions of housing need tend to be rather homogeneous and uniform with the dominant emphasis on differentiation of material standards and status factors in residential selection.

In underdeveloped and rapidly urbanizing societies the situation appears to be quite different. The proportion of relatively stable industrial jobs in the low-income labour market is often extremely low and growing more slowly than the rate of rural–urban migration (Furtado 1970). Large and growing numbers are dependent on a casual labour market which is low paying, unstable, and normally highly competitive. A high proportion of incoming immigrants are semi-literate and possess only limited skills, while access to employment is normally restricted by particularistic constraints: patronage and kinship controls (cf. Strickon 1965 on Argentina), and, in the case of countries with significant indigenous populations, linguistic and cultural discrimination (e.g. Stavenhagen 1965, Mangin 1965). These controls often extend to the tertiary sector in which a wide range of small-scale commercial activities and forms of self-employment can be found with varying degrees of formality and organization. The structure of the migratory stream in terms of levels of education, skill, income levels, and aspirations varies enormously from city to city at both inter- and intra-societal levels (Balam 1969). The nature, type, and dynamism of the labour market is subject not only to a similar geographical variation, but also to severe fluctuations which are typical of dependent capitalist economies. Given the complexity and heterogeneity of this employment structure and the generalized poverty and underemployment that exists, we would expect to find widely varying housing needs, together with an increasingly rigid and inelastic set of housing priorities, as one moves down the socio-economic scale where the gap between family income and subsistence needs narrows (Turner 1971).

Under these conditions, it is a reasonable hypothesis that, for large numbers of incoming migrants, housing needs have to be subjected to the search for an income source to keep the family in a hand-to-mouth existence, and subsequently to the search for more secure and better-paid jobs. Since opportunities will depend to a large extent on being at the right spot at the right time, *location* of housing will be of overriding importance for the poorest newcomer to the city. Cramped living conditions, insecurity of tenure, the exploitative pressures of speculative landlords, disease, and endemic violence are the price the newcomer is forced to pay for the vital priority of *accessibility* to sources of casual employment – central market areas, construction sites, car parks, bus stations, etc. Against this must be set avoidance of transportation costs, the relatively low space requirements of families at the initial phase of the household-cycle (often single men or young couples), a recent memory of a wretchedly poor rural existence, often accompanied by a strong mobility consciousness (Germani 1964), and a view of present housing conditions as a temporary adjustment, a step on the ladder, rather than a permanent condemnation. Here, in other words, the slum is a condition of upward mobility, rather than, as in the case of the ghetto, a filter for the rejected or dispossessed.[2] The housing environment is selected and evaluated in terms of the *opportunity* it provides (see *Figure 1* below).

The commercial–industrial areas of rapidly expanding cities are characterized by a steepening gradient of land-values towards the centre (Leeds 1969: 72) and relatively intense competition between industrial, commercial, and residential land-users, which leads to a rapid rate of turnover, reconstruction, and renewal. The principle victim is normally old housing stock, particularly the multi-dwelling conversions of upper-income residences vacated by the middle-classes during an earlier period of urbanization, and the traditional slum-courts and tenements.[3] In the remaining 'recognized' slum areas, density is likely to increase, since rents must be low enough for the poorest households to be able to afford them, yet high enough in aggregate to provide profits that can compete with those obtainable from alternative land-uses. Normally, both density and rents will tend to increase leaving a significant proportion of migrants with no alternative but to settle illegally on pockets of vacant land or interstitial zones adjoining central commercial areas. Turner refers to such shanties as *provisional* or *bridgeheader* settlements, in order to convey the insecurity of their status and the impermanent and mobile nature of their populations. Where the 'official' slums normally have shared water and sanitary facilities, these clandestine bridgehead settlements frequently lack all amenities, but at the same time, may escape the drain of rent payments.

Despite these differences, Turner points to the similarity in the functions and population characteristics of traditional slum and central-city shanty-town. This point is obscured if the legal status of low-income housing is taken as an indicator of 'marginality'. In fact, the legal point of view would tend to put all squatters (who are viewed as those *excluded* from the formal housing market) below the socio-economic level of the 'official' slum-dwellers. If we view the phenomenon of intersticial squatting simply as a consequence of a deficient supply of recognized low-income housing stock, due to the physical and demographic rate of urbanization, there may be an argument for viewing bridgeheader squatters as a deprived or marginal group *in relation to the official slum-dwellers*. The concept of marginality should be applied only to the situation of groups who are involuntarily excluded from the range of choices that are available to others who share their basic existential priorities. Even at this level of poverty, we cannot simply *assume* that the bridge-header is *excluded* in this sense. The bridgeheader situation may be preferable to the incoming migrant in that rent-evasion, anonymity, and informality contribute to stem the drain of resources from the family, keep very restricted savings-margins liquid and options open, and consequently enhance mobility and opportunities to get out of that situation *and the situation of the official slum-dweller as well*. The fallacy of evaluating or even classifying the housing environment independently of the orientation and motivation of its users should be apparent (Turner 1967).

Legalistic criteria can serve to define the boundaries of the squatter universe, although even here there are complex gradations between wholly legal and wholly illicit tenures and settlements (Turner 1969a: 508). Yet the differences that can be found within this universe in terms of the functions of the housing-environment, socio-economic levels, and motivation are very great. Turner's central hypothesis is that settlements located on the *periphery* of Latin American capitals reflect the housing priorities of households whose position in the urban social and economic system can be clearly differentiated from that of the much poorer bridgeheader group, which normally resides on legal or illicit tenures in *inner-ring* areas. Many reports have emphasized the higher average family incomes, stabler populations, and considerably longer lengths of urban residence to be found in peripheral settlements in favourable locations (Mangin 1967). Yet with a low and precarious savings-margin, it may take considerable lengths of time for these differences to be reflected in a noticeable material improvement in the levels of construction and amenities. Given the difficulties of organization and politico-legal manoeuvring, the installation of regular urban services may be even longer delayed. The frequent use of phrases like *cinturón de miseria* indicates that due to a typical middle-class preoccupation with standards, these factors may lead to a popular confusion of peripherality with pauperization, exclusion, and a sense of hopelessness. An analysis of squatters' motivation and orientation to their environment is necessary to correct this distortion. An alternative, and equally incorrect, view is to typify such settlements as essentially rural enclaves *socially and economically* peripheral to the city. While this may have been an appropriate picture of the lower-class *barrios* of the pre-industrial city (Hansen 1934; Sjoberg 1960), it bears little relationship to the ecological and social processes occurring in cities at advanced levels of urbanization.

The phrase *cinturón de seguridad* is a more accurate description of the function of peripheral settlements. Turner argues, on the basis of evidence from Lima (1965), that a certain limited period of initiation and manoeuvre (say four to six years) is normal before 'insertion' into the labour market and the establishment of a reasonably secure source of income.[4] This period corresponds to central-city slum or shanty-town residence: it is one of special hardships. There is the constant drain of rent-payments and the fear of sudden eviction in the case of accident, illness, or temporary unemployment. The constriction of central-city

life – noise, pollution, and overcrowding, the risk of violence and arrest –
are particularly hazardous at a time when the number of dependents in
the household is likely to be growing. Furthermore, in a buyers' labour
market, subject to fluctuations, with ineffective, if any, union protection
job security is low. Where it exists, social security affords no protection
against the unavoidable mishaps that can befall the very poor at any
moment. The migrant's reaction to this panoply of uncontrollable threats
is to search for a single *controllable* factor, which can act *cumulatively*
as a pole for the investment of his meagre resources, and provide the
long-term security that is the essential medium of social mobility. This is
the basic existential logic behind the formation of organized squatters'
invasion groups, which, often at the risk of violent confrontations with
police or army, may establish *de facto* ownership of tracts of land often
miles from the city centre. Here the squatter can stake a plot and lay
down the skeletal outlines of his future home – goals which are so
important that families may endure great physical hardship to achieve
them.[5] For such groups of *consolidators* (see *Figure 1* below) the dominant
priority of housing is *de facto* freehold ownership at whatever levels of
material standards or amenities are within reach, and at the cost of considerable deductions from the household budget to pay for transportation.
Peripheral squatting is therefore normally a correlate of a process of
mobility within the low-income sector, which may have decisive consequences for the social trajectory of individual households. Although the
motivation for residential movement is normally highly pragmatic rather
than status orientated, the phenomenon has elements in common with
the process of middle-class suburbanization. Ecologically both phenomena represent a movement from central-city neighbourhoods to outlying residential areas, where greater space and flexibility create a more
favourable environment for bringing up children, keeping them 'out of
trouble', and augmenting the solidarity of the nuclear family. Equally,
both phenomena are the outcome of the exercise of *choice*, a choice that
is normally denied low-income sectors in developed countries where
urban growth and land-use are rigidly controlled.

Once a settlement population has established *de facto* ownership, the
relatively low values of marginal peripheral land decrease the likelihood
of eviction, creating a climate of some confidence in which gradual improvements in house construction and in the provision of community
services can go ahead. The rate and order of installations will vary
greatly and will be especially influenced by climatic and topographic
factors (Leeds 1969: 74–5). Successive inputs will however normally act

in such a way as to lessen gradually the probability of eradication and dispersal. Although numbers cannot be rigidly controlled and will increase as the settlement evolves, density levels are normally far lower than in the inner-ring shanties. This facilitates a relatively orderly layout with provision for community services (schools, recreation centres, etc),[6] while providing much more ground-space for the individual family.

The advantages of space are not only psychic. Space can be, and is, used speculatively (i.e. as an economic value) to supplement income or replace income lost as a result of redundancy or sickness. Sub-letting, conversion of house fronts into informal retail outlets and eating places have been widely reported. The process of consolidation and piecemeal investment itself generates an embryonic labour market, which enables those with specialized skills (even very 'informal' ones, like bicycle repairing) to find odd jobs. Groups of construction workers may derive their total income from contracted work within the settlement itself. Because settlement residents are self-selected the spread of income differentials is likely to be quite high, in striking contrast to the residents of government re-housing projects where homogeneity is imposed by costing procedures or political considerations (Turner 1967: 178). This factor tends to promote opportunities for development at least partly independent of formal credit and servicing mechanism.

Socio-economic status and residential differentials within the settlement will also tend to arise out of differences in length of residence, since incoming groups will normally be considerably poorer than 'consolidators' of several years standing. Again, given a relatively heterogeneous employment structure, fluctuation in the wider labour market may not hit the settlement population evenly or uniformly; dependency may be correspondingly reduced as the economically buoyant generate tiny sources of income for the unemployed. The relative stability of this environment provides practical as well as psychological support for the functioning of kinship. The view of kinship dependency as a drag on savings and a disincentive for material improvement is valid for the congested city centre, where there is little space and where household labour has little use other than in domestic chores. However, in the consolidating settlement, unemployed kin and dependents can be turned into producers, since the climate of opportunity and need and the inability to rely on formal urban services will create a series of tasks that enable support to be exchanged for productive labour. Thus small additions to the house are genuine investments in that they raise its value independently of the market, create a sense of ownership and security, and must

FIGURE 1

Existential needs and housing priorities: a comparison between middle-income groups, consolidators and bridgeheaders[7]

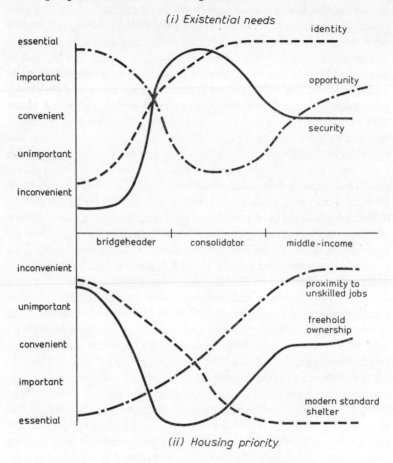

(i) Existential needs

(ii) Housing priority

therefore be considered an important factor, independent of occupational role and income, in shaping attitudes and expectations.

Under optimal conditions, these factors may interact to give birth to a gradual but cumulative trajectory of investment and growth in the peripheral settlement, culminating in juridical recognition, the provision of full urban services, and incorporation as a legitimate suburb of the city. Such a trajectory appears unfortunately to be the exception rather than the rule. In practice, a series of uncontrollable pressures tend to force the settlement off its original path, making it less and less able to fulfil adequately the expectations of the first settlers. A regressive cycle may gradually turn the settlement into a relatively homogeneous low-income slum with a general deterioration of dwelling standards and an increase in density levels. Alternatively, a 'composite' settlement may emerge with very significant differences in income-levels and material standards reflected ecologically in most cases, and with a declining sense of community identity and lowered levels of participation. In both cases, we would expect change to be reflected in a fairly complex process of residential movement in and out of the settlement.[8]

THE SECURITY-INPUT MODEL: A SETTLEMENT TYPOLOGY[9]

At a time when Latin American governments are having to come to terms, in one way or another, with the phenomenon of uncontrolled urban growth, a rational distribution of servicing and credit resources will come to depend increasingly on the ability to predict the growth-potential of different settlements at least approximately enough to achieve some kind of priority scale. In addition, future research into urban poverty will be of limited general value unless some attempt is made to check the representativeness of the population by reference to a typology of urban settlements.[10] The security-input model can be considered the first systematic attempt to fulfil both these requirements.

Turner begins with the assumption that the most crucial preoccupation of the squatter is security of tenure; some degree of security is essential if improvement is to proceed (1966a: 19). Security, however, may be gained in two principal ways: either by rapid initial investment in layout and construction, followed by successive inputs of labour and material resources, or, alternatively, by a simple physical increase in numbers, unaccompanied by significant fixed investment. In the case of central-city settlements, several variables that normally correlate with location make the second alternative more probable. High land-values and the pressures of urban land-use turnover will increase the initial risk of eradication even where there is *de facto* possession. Under these conditions the poor may be willing to risk their physical presence, but not their slender savings-margin. Space constriction and overcrowding also discourage investment by putting physical possessions at greater risk. Thus although *bridgeheader* settlements may achieve a measure of security due to high density and concentration and the economic and

political cost of removal, the general level of improvements originating
from the squatters themselves will remain quite low. This in itself will
tend to place a relatively low ceiling on the growth of security. Under
such conditions eventual eradication is a far more likely outcome than
legal incorporation or recognition. Peripheral settlements in favourable
locations will, by contrast, tend to exemplify the former alternative.
Given low land-values, a marginal site, and the relative absence of constriction by rival land-users, a relatively lower risk of eradication (once
the invasion 'crisis' is over) combined with lower density levels will tend
to produce conditions favourable to a relatively rapid initial investment.
According to the model, cumulative inputs of resources will enhance
security and provide a supportive atmosphere for further development.
The 'progressive' trajectory of the peripheral settlement, although more
'elastic' than that of the central or provisional settlement, will come up
against its own 'ceiling' if the demands for full legal integration and the
provision of regular urban services are frustrated. The blocking of legitimate legal and social status may cause those most able to invest to leave
the settlement; the rate of development would then slacken, confidence
and security would decline relatively to more successful settlements,
and typical slum conditions would begin to spread over the settlement as
a whole.[11]

By a simple cross-tabulation of the two parameters of degrees of
security of tenure and levels of physical development, a typology of settlements is obtained. The table is reproduced below,[12] the type in
CAPITALS representing those most commonly observed (*Table 1*).

Because settlements commonly change their status over time, this
chart can also be used to describe *stages* in the growth trajectory of settlements. After the initial invasion confrontation (where this occurs), most
Latin American squatter settlements will move relatively quickly from
'tentative' to 'established' squatter status. But this transition may or may
not be accompanied by incipient construction to potentially modern
standards. Following the logic of the security-input model, the progres-
sion of a *provisional* settlement will normally proceed *horizontally* from
left to right. For example, provisional settlements may achieve semi-
squatter status, but this will normally be a consequence of rising density
rather than of multiplying inputs. Initially, provisional construction
(poor lay-out, inferior building materials, and design) will make it unlikely for such settlements to evolve into acceptable urban environments. Settlements that begin as *incipient* may, however, jump up the
scale of physical development levels as they acquire greater security of

TABLE 1
A typology of settlements

Itinerant	Tentative	Established	Semi-squatter	Legal	LEVELS OF PHYSICAL DEVELOPMENT
				complete legal	*complete* structure and utilities to mod. standards
		incomplete squatter	IN-COMPLETE SEMI-SQUATTER	in-complete legal	*incomplete* structure or utilities but built to mod. standards
	incipient tentative	INCIPIENT SQUATTER	INCIPIENT SEMI-SQUATTER		*incipient* construction of potentially mod. standards
	PROVIS-IONAL TENTA-TIVE	PROVIS-IONAL SQUATTER	PROVIS-IONAL SEMI-SQUATTER		*provisional* construction of low standard and/or impermanent materials
nomad	TRANS-IENT TENTA-TIVE	transient squatter			*transient* temporary and easily removed shelter
Itinerant transient occupancy with no intention of permanent tenure	*Tentative* occupancy without any legal status or guarantee of continued tenure	*Established* de facto & secure possession but without tenure	*Semi-squatter* or semi-legal without full recognition but with some rights	*Legal* institutionally recognized forms of tenure	

DEGREES OF SECURITY OF TENURE

tenure, since the conditions of their layout, location, and population characteristics are, under favourable conditions, such that there need be no cumulative development as integral neighbourhoods of the city. They are, however, capable of regressing to *provisional* status if the inner-ring expands at a faster rate than the accomplishment of reasonable standards and legal recognition.

INTERPRETATIVE AND CRITICAL COMMENTS

Although Turner's work is documented with data from many cities and countries, it is necessary to point out that his practical experience (as adviser to the Junta Nacional de la Vivienda of the Belaunde government) is of Lima, and the majority of his examples are drawn from this city. A detailed case-study of one Lima *barriada*, Pampa de Cuevas, informs much of the material on the phases of peripheral consolidating development. In one article Turner (1968b: 357–60) analyses settlement growth by comparing three different settlements of varying age, assuming these to be representative of developmental stages in an ideal–typical sequence, a questionable methodological procedure. More doubts are raised by observations made by A. Leeds (1969) in a recent article which rests on the most comprehensive range of settlement data I have yet seen. Leeds notes the 'tendency for the physical quality of the settlement to improve as one moves away from the centre' (1969: 72) but he also argues that:

'Since one of the primary causes of squatment growth involves rational strategies relating residence to work area and to cost of transport . . . under conditions of depressed salary-high price ratios, it follows that a large per cent of squatment populations will live near enough to their work to walk (thus saving transport costs) and the second largest portion will live within a single bus-fare's distance. A minority will live two bus-fares' distance, *and virtually none with more expensive travel unless other factors are overwhelmingly influential* (1969: 76).

Leeds argues, on the basis of this assumption, that the nature and type of the adjoining labour market (measured in terms of the level of wages and job stability) will be the most reliable guide to the types and population characteristics of settlements. Other factors to which Leeds attributes importance are local ecology (especially presence of competing land-users), age, and size (which primarily affect the development of an internal labour market). The first observation directly contradicts Turner's analysis, while the second would tend to confirm it. The importance that Leeds attributes to size is significant because it indicates other respects in which peripheral sites (where large settlements are possible) have an advantage. First of all they may play a significant role in the siting of new industry, as in the case of Pampa de Comas, Lima (1969:

77). This is a 'feedback effect' nowhere mentioned by Turner. Second, there is a correlation between size and internal differentiation. Third, large settlements wield disproportionate political influence and get the lion's share of aid and benefits.

Further consideration needs to be given to topographic and political variables. However deductive their formulation, ecological models ultimately rest on a set of empirical generalizations regarding the correlation between central location and high land-values. This correlation can be affected by intervening variables such as topographical variation within the city, and political intervention, as, for example, in tax-induced siting of industry and decentralization. It might be argued that the flat or relatively gently sloping desert *pampas* in which the majority of the Lima *barriadas* are situated, combined with a very small rainfall, provide unusually favourable conditions for orderly peripheral development. Increasing density may give birth to problems on a different scale in hilly sites subject to subsidence or landslides, wooded areas with fire-risks, marshes or riverside locations prone to constant flooding. More important from the point of view of differences of settlement character-istics *within* the city are variations of topography *within* the metropolitan area which could cause considerable variation in the cost of housing construction and the levels of physical development possible. Paradoxic-ally, 'impossible' sites may offer an additional incentive to settlement in that their inaccessibility or unsuitability is likely to postpone reclamation by the city authorities. They may affect the rate and nature of construc-tion (which is highly flexible) rather than the motivation to move there, which appears to be considerably less flexible. The problem is complex because 'peripherality' is partially an economic, and partially a physical or topographic consideration. The crucial factor determining the *settlement* of peripheral sites is the low economic value of the land occu-pied, regardless of whether or not it is in fact located on the geographical periphery of the city. On the other hand the *growth-potential* of a settle-ment may be decisively affected by its topography. The sides of the intermontane valley in which Caracas is situated, and some of the hill-sides and marshes of Rio have been given as examples of 'internal peripheral' areas which are centrally located but which have, until recently, been of relatively low commercial value. These locations have, correspondingly, provided suitable conditions for both *bridgeheaders* and *consolidators*, and considerable contrasts in material standards and in-come levels can be found within them, the remoter and more precarious sites being selectively populated by *bridgeheaders* (Turner 1968a: 361).[13]

The relevance of the political factor can be seen where, as a result of government inducement, new industries are occupying peripheral sites where land-values are relatively low, and the pressures of land-use competition as yet weak. In this case, at least initially, the priority of access to employment and that of security and growth need not necessarily conflict.

Where it is occurring rapidly, radial city expansion will itself change the states of the variables which Turner postulates as determinants of settlement characteristics. It is therefore hazardous to base predictions on the existential priorities or choices exercised by the original settlers. At the city level, originally peripheral settlements will be influenced by the twin pressures of industrial/commercial expansion and municipal integration. The periphery created by *consolidators* in Mexico City in the early 1950s, for example, has already become part of the inner ring (Turner 1968a: 360). This process of 'encapsulation' is likely to make the *bridgeheader/consolidator* distinction increasingly difficult to apply, in that the match between individual settlements and the supposed 'shared' existential priorities of their inhabitants will become more and more questionable. The changing relationship of the settlement to the city-core is likely to be reflected in a tendency towards intra-settlement differentiation between original settlers and newcomers. Many of the earlier *consolidators* may move out, renting or sub-letting their homes to poorer newcomers squeezed out of the city centre, or to provincial migrants fresh to the city.[14] Where this happens, the selective out-migration of 'high-achievers' will tend to lead to a down-turn of the investment cycle, so that the peripheral settlements of today may become the slums of tomorrow. One would expect increasing income differentials, greater disparities of housing standards in different parts of the settlement, with a tendency to concentration of privileged areas. Above all, there will normally be differences in orientation to the settlement that will inhibit its ability to achieve collective organization and action. Those with longer lengths of residence, although better off, may experience a sense of disillusionment and loss of control, reluctantly viewing their housing situation as a permanent 'sentence'; the newcomers, on the other hand, may have the typical high aspirations of the *bridgeheader*: they will not yet have committed their savings and found their expectations frustrated.[15]

Turner mentions another trend which appears characteristic of cities at advanced stages of urbanization.[16] This is the tendency towards the rehabilitation and improvement of traditional slum areas (a preoccupation of recent urban policy in many developed countries) which leads to a rise in rents, a stabilization of the population, and a change in its composition towards lower middle-income groups. Where this is happening, 'intermediate' or 'encapsulated' settlements may begin to assume the functions of 'reception areas'. The outward expansion of industry and commerce and the growing concentration of administrative and office building in the city centre are developments that make this new tendency quite consistent with the basic assumptions of Turner's model of housing priorities.

The development of considerable labour markets *within* large 'consolidating' peripheral settlements provides another hypothetical instance in which the simple relationship between settlement type and housing priority may break down. As Leeds has stressed, the internal stratification of large low-density settlements normally grows with age and increasing investment. This may be caused partly by differential economic success among the original settlers, but more significantly, by an influx of lower-income groups attracted by opportunities for casual labour provided by a relatively prosperous core of residents. These incoming groups would be unable to own or build at the level achieved. They might however form marginal enclaves tangential to the settlement,[17] or produce a demand for rented accommodation within it. Turner found that subdivision and sub-letting was a significant factor in the older Lima *barriadas*. We would expect to find a reduction in the space needs of original settlers as their children split off and form independent households, and consequently some incentive for landlordism. Household space requirements would in fact typically decline as the general level of income and investment rise, thus increasing the potential for entrepreneurial space use over this period. The existence of *bridgeheader* enclaves within *consolidator* settlements makes an interesting and largely unexplored subject for research. In particular, information is needed on the nature of their tenure, their length of residence in the city, and the extent to which they draw, for their subsistence income, on the internal labour market of the settlement itself. In the remoter settlements, we would expect to find, following Turner's logic, a correlation between low income-levels or comparatively short length of residence in the settlement, tenant rather than owner status, and dependance on the internal labour market. There is very little reliable information on the internal differentiation and employment structure of growing settlements remote from urban labour markets.

One of the drawbacks of the security-input model is the rather mechanistic theory of the *determinants* of security of tenure. There is little mention of political factors. The correlation between security and population density is not supported empirically. Furthermore, if investment inputs were an automatic guarantee of security, Turner's justifiable polemic against city planners would be unnecessary. Second, it is quite possible to question whether or not the *perception* of security would in fact match the 'objective' security of any settlement, in so far as this could be ascertained at all. Yet, in as much as investment decisions and intentions of permanent residence are influenced by this factor, as Turner continually stresses, the model does in fact rest upon this assumption.

Third, it might be argued that this model contradicts Turner's analysis of relative housing priorities by assuming a universal motivation for security of tenure, and by placing all the emphasis on the 'objective' factors which limit or permit such potential. Close analysis of Turner's work reveals two distinct accounts of the settlement process, which stand in a rather uneasy relationship to one another, leaving an impression of circularity or over-determination. In the analysis of existential priorities, settlement characteristics seem to be broadly determined by motivational variables (the housing and vital needs of aggregate of persons in similar 'social situations') and the stress is placed on information and rational choice. In the security-input model, 'objective' parameters of the settlement (particularly its location) are assumed to affect and change the quality of motivation of its inhabitants (e.g. high density and low security reducing the will to invest). This apparent contradiction can be resolved by the introduction of a dynamic model, in which the housing action of groups of low-income settlers can be viewed within a wider context which is itself subject to change *independently* of the actions of the settlers themselves.

The replacement of static typologies with an analysis of process is the major innovation of a very recent paper in which Turner introduces a feedback model to elucidate the dynamic social context of housing action. He argues that any description of housing must include the actors, their actions, and their achievements. The housing process takes place in a *context*, part of which is provided by the achievements of past actions, which are interpreted by the actors in the light of their expectations and priorities (Turner 1971: 12). However, the *users* are not the only actors in the settlement process. We must also distinguish the commercial sector, motivated by speculative profit, and the public sector, in which considerations of political power and 'public' priority predominate. The interests and priorities of these sectors frequently conflict with those of the users (Turner 1971: 7-8), and, what is most important, they tend to exert, usually jointly, a *dominating influence over the total context in which housing choices are made*. In developed countries this power is often clearly visible as, for example, in urban re-location projects. As the power and capacity of the public sector increases, the context in which users can exert choice is correspondingly narrowed (as in Soviet Russia). This concentration of power is normally accompanied by ideological persuasion or advertising, so that expectations can be manipulated to 'match' the limited options made available. Where the capacity of the private and public sectors is very much reduced relative to the pressure of users' demands (as in Latin America), the housing context is likely to *appear* more open, and to permit a greater degree of choice, despite the massive overall constraints arising out of very low incomes. However, the housing context remains overwhelmingly controlled by sectors other than the users themselves, and is no less a product of a fundamental confrontation of interests. Without the socialization of land, this confrontation will persist regardless of even radical changes of government policy in favour of the squatters. At present such conflicts between the 'actors' in the housing process are seldom overt (except where the state or private landlords intervene directly through evictions, re-locations, or rent increases). They normally take the form of 'invisible' pressures, which to the user may appear, where he is aware of them at all, impersonal, objective, almost 'natural'. The most crucial examples are the rising land-values resulting from the 'competitive pressures' in the expansion of the city, which play so central a role in Turner's analysis of the potentialities and limitation of self-built housing. Rising land-value, quite regardless of the user's expectations, will tend to decrease the security of his investments, transforming the nature of his environment quite independently of his own actions. Yet given the existence in the lowest-income sector of *other* groups for whom investment and permanency are not relevant expectations, a close match between the changed environment and users' priorities is possible, assuming that information is available to fit choices to existential priorities. In this case the changed environment is reinforced by the expectations of the new user. Yet the environmental context is always likely to change again, quite independently of the users' expectations, through the actions backed by effective power of non-users adapting their speculative priorities to market fluctuations. The context will then again be brought into conflict with expectations, and so on. In other words, one man's choice is another man's frustration.

Stagnating settlements may, therefore, be of two kinds – those whose stagnation can be simply explained by the motivation of inhabitants who do not invest significance in the development of their stake, and second, settlements in which changes in land-values (the reaction of groups of non-users) have frustrated the expectations with which the users evaluate their housing action. In such cases, again assuming information and choice, we would expect a process of re-alignment to occur. This may take the form of out-migration on the part of those who have succeeded in retaining their expectations and 'matching' them with an 'alternative' environment. We might also expect in-migration of newcomers who have responded to the incentives provided by the changed conditions of the settlement (viewed, that is, from *their* relative scale of priorities). In such settlements we would also expect to find pockets of residents who have been unable to move out and have consequently been forced to re-adjust their expectations to a lowered ceiling, a situation that would seem most likely to produce strong feelings of discontent, bitterness, and cynicism.

CONCLUSIONS

The emphasis that Turner places on the productive and decision-making role of the urban migrant in the settlement process throws into question some of the basic assumptions implicit in the concept of marginality, and it may be profitable to raise some points as a basis for discussion.

1. The Status of Migrants as an Out-group with respect to City Natives

Recent research has drawn attention to the internal differentiation and stratification of the migratory stream in Latin American cities.[18] Turner's work has suggested, if it has not demonstrated, that peripheral settlement plays a functional role in the processes of social and economic adaptation and mobility of migrants new to the city. Especially where integration into the formal labour market is slow, the settlement process may contribute significantly to the differentiation of the migrant population in such a way as to diminish socio-economic differentials between the migrants as a group and city natives, while accentuating the differences between recent migrants and those of longer lengths of urban residence. Two factors, then, partially independent of the labour market, may contribute to the heterogeneity of low-income migrant populations: first, differences in income-levels, skills, education, and acculturation, which are found in the migratory stream, and which may be correlated with degree and nature of prior experience of smaller cities and towns, and second, differences that may be accounted for within the life-cycle of the newly settled household by the strategies of residential mobility. Since squatter settlements as a universe are not selectively populated by migrants, but may also include large numbers of city natives, the settlement environment would not *in itself* provide reinforcement for the identification and perception of migrants as marginal to the city.

2. The Status of Squatters as an Out-group with respect to the City

Where those living on illegal tenures form at least 40 per cent of the urban population, where many settlers are city natives in stable employment, and where squatters have in the past two decades been responsible for more city building than has been achieved in the past 400 years, the city-squatter distinction becomes at best sociologically trivial; at worst positively misleading. Turner's work suggests that legal low-income housing (the city-slum proper) is often populated by the *least* integrated and acculturated sectors; squatting, on the other hand, normally functions as a vehicle in the integrative process in that it reflects a *strategic* decision to avoid the formal housing market, and is only under certain conditions a consequence of *exclusion* from it. At least implicitly, the latter assumption informs the views of those who regard illegal settlements as an indicator of marginality.

3. The Reification of Legal Norms and Material Standards

The orthodox view of squatters tends to be both highly normative and static, a criticism that can be levelled equally at the current usage of the concept of marginality. Turner has shown that the housing needs of those living in conditions of underemployment and generalized poverty will frequently depart from the concern with legality and material standards typical of the middle classes who, often from the best motives, assume that the need for legal shelter is of *equal* importance for all strata of the urban population. Yet where desirable density-levels and location conflict with the legal status and 'acceptable' standards of housing, the poor will very frequently choose to sacrifice the latter. Who, then, are to be defined as marginal? Those who make this choice because it offers a chance of maximizing their opportunities for long-term social and economic mobility, or those whose voice is frustrated through the imposition of absolute standards with high opportunity costs by 'outside' agencies? The reification of legal norms and material standards may result in re-location projects which successfully 'integrate' the poor into the formal housing market while, as a result of space-restriction and loss of income and contacts, effectively blocking the opportunities that might have existed had they been left free to squat. 'Integration' from the point of view of the social engineer may mean 'marginalization' from the point of view of the poor. As currently used, the concept of marginality is by no means neutral – its *appearance* of neutrality derives from the tendency of power-holders to *universalize* the norms that reflect their own (relative) priorities and expectations.

At the methodological level, the reification of the shanty-town as a physical entity has led to a preoccupation with aggregate settlement data, rather than with the nature of the changing *relationship* between settlement and inhabitants. Such surveys tend to rest on the untested assumption that the settlement constitutes a relatively homogeneous universe. The observer is thereby desensitized to pressures of change and will underestimate the phenomenon of residential mobility (Mac-Ewen 1972). This shortcoming may be partly due to a confusion of levels: while poverty and the shanty-town environment may be relatively constant factors, despite the rapidity of urban and economic development, groups of poor households may be highly mobile. Complex processes of displacement and replacement may occur which are seldom clearly reflected in a *homogeneous* change in the physical or social aspects of settlements.

4. A Relational Model of the Settlement Process

An adequate sociological model of the settlement process must be based on the *actor's* changing definition of the 'housing situation' rather than on that of the 'observer'. A first requirement is investigation into the function of housing as it is selectively perceived by aggregates of low-income households with different, but relatively inelastic, needs and priorities; such needs and priorities are themselves subject to change within the life-cycle of the household, as a consequence of its growth and shifting relationship to the urban economic and social system.

Since the existence of a homogeneous housing demand differentiated solely on the basis of purchasing power cannot be assumed, settlement types cannot, without serious distortion, be classified independently of the orientations of their residents. On the other hand, it cannot be assumed that settlement types will simply correspond to, and indeed arise out of the effective choices made by distinct 'housing-demand groups'.

This may be true of the initial phases of settlement (the most important 'objective' variable, location, is after all *chosen* by the original settlers) but thereafter a close correspondence will be the exception, rather than the rule. It is in fact highly probable that situational pressures arising out of changes in the settlement, over which the original settler has no control (e.g. increasing density and competition for land in adjacent areas, encroachment), will have a considerable effect on motivation and expectations. In many cases this will lead to a destruction of confidence, a shifting population, and a deterioration of physical standards. I have suggested that, while considerable differences between settlements will remain, classification on the basis of location will be increasingly misleading as settlements evolve and change. For the process of 'encapsulation' will normally be accompanied either by further intra-urban migration or by increasing internal differentiation and heterogeneity of standards, income-levels, and aspirations. Indeed, as in every other field of competitive relations, squatters have to respond to changes that are the indirect effects of choices made in fields remote to them by actors with goals and interests very different from their own. This disguised conflict constitutes a structural limit to the 'autonomy' of the consolidating settler and the security of his property. It shows the fallacy of looking for a solution to the housing problem in the private enterprise of the squatter, when that enterprise can be ultimately negated by the same system that makes it possible.

Notes

1 In Latin American metropolitan cities, this group may not necessarily be middle class in the classical sense. It may include significant numbers of skilled workers in the 'modern' sector whose living standards and status conceptions are sometimes considerably closer to those of the *empleados* than to the unskilled or underdeveloped sectors. This analysis is developed in two papers: Turner (1968a and 1971).

2 This difference reflects the contrast described by Charles Stokes (1962) between 'slums of hope' and 'slums of despair'.

3 Each country tends to have its name for the slums: *vecindades, callejones, conventillos, corticos, turgurios,* etc. Oscar Lewis's work remains the best description of central-city slum conditions, but see also a descriptive account by R. Patch (1961).

4 See also two case-studies: Mangin (1963) and Turner's study of Pampa de Comas (1967: 170–76).

5 The Cuevas invaders lived out in the open for five weeks before they were allowed to settle the land. See Turner (1967: 172).

6 The phases of this process are analysed by Turner (1968b: 358). He shows that community facilities usually take precedence over urban services.

7 This table is based on the one to be found in Turner (1971). I have however replaced the simple income scale used by Turner with his own classification into social situations as used in the diagram in 1968a: 358.

8 The case of *Las Canaletas* analysed by Alison MacEwen seems to fit admirably (editors).

9 The fullest development of this is in Turner (1966a).

10 See, for example, Leeds's (1969) criticism of Oscar Lewis's work. The only study I know that has used Turner's typology is Goldrich *et al.* (1967).

11 Turner bases this analysis on observed contrasts between Cuevas and El Augustino, which are taken to typify an incipient-peripheral and a central-provisional settlement, respectively.

12 This table and its rationale can be found conveniently in Turner (1969a: 514). John Turner is thanked for his permission to reprint.

13 Leeds also gives examples from Rio and Lima (1969: 73).

14 Some cities may have laws to prevent this.

15 Many studies have stressed the likelihood that tension and unrest will increase among second generation migrants. (Again the MacEwen material in this volume is relevant – editors.)

16 The study referred to is that of Valencia (1965).

17 This happened, for example, in the case of Cuevas. See Turner (1967: 176).

18 See Balan (1969) on migrant-native socio-economic differences. See also Herrick (1965).

Acknowledgement

Table 1 is reprinted from 'Uncontrolled Urban Settlements: Problems and Policies' (p. 514), in G. Breese (ed.), *The City in Newly Developing Countries* (Engleword Cliffs, New Jersey: Prentice-Hall, 1969), with the permission of the author, John Turner.

References

BALAN, J. 1969. Migrant-native Socio-economic Differences in Latin American Cities: a Structural Analysis. *Latin American Research Review* **4** (1).

BREESE, G. (ed.) 1969. *The City in Newly Developing Countries*. Englewood Cliffs, New Jersey: Prentice-Hall.

FURTADO, C. 1970. *Obstacles to Development in Latin America*. New York: Anchor.

GERMANI, G. 1964. Migration and Acculturation. In Hauser P. (ed.) 1964.

GOLDRICH, D., PRATT, R. and SCHULLER, C. R. 1967. The Political Integration of Lower Class Urban Settlements in Chile and Peru. *Studies in Comparative International Development* (1967–8) 3.

HANSEN, ASAEL T. 1934. The Ecology of a Latin American City. In Reuten, B. (ed.) 1934.

HAUSER, P. (ed.) 1964. *Handbook for Social Research in Urban Areas*. Paris: UNESCO.

HEATH, D. and ADAMS, R. 1965. *Contemporary Cultures and Societies in Latin America*. New York: Random House.

HERRICK, B. 1965. *Urban Migration and Economic Development in Chile*. Cambridge, Mass: MIT Press.

LEEDS, A. 1969. The Significant Variables determining the Characteristics of Squatter Settlements. *America Latina* **Year 12** (3).

MACEWEN, A. 1972. Stability and Change in a Shanty-town. *Sociology 6* (1).

MANGIN, W. 1963. Urbanisation Case-history in Peru. *Architectural Design* (August) **33** (8).

—— 1965 The Role of Regional Associations in the Adaptation of Rural Migrants to Cities in Peru. In D. Heath and R. Adams, 1965.

—— 1967. Latin American Squatter Settlements; a Problem and a Solution. *Latin American Research Review* **2** (3).

—— 1970 (ed.) *Peasants in Cities*. Boston: Houghton Mifflin.

OLIVER, P. (ed.) 1970. *Shelter and Society: New Studies in Vernacular Architecture*. London: Barrie and Jenkins.

PATCH, R. 1961. Life in a Callejon: A Study of Urban Disorganization. *West Coast South America Series* (Peru) **8** (6): June. American Universities Field Service.

REUTEN, B. (ed.) 1934. *Race and Culture Contacts*. New York: McGraw Hill.

SJOBERG, G. 1960. *The Pre-industrial City*. Glencoe: Free Press.

STAVENHAGEN, R. 1965. Classes, Colonialism and Acculturation. *Studies in Comparative International Development* **1** (6).

STOKES, C. 1962. A Theory of Slums. *Land Economics* **38** (3).

STRICKON, A. 1965. Class and Kinship in Argentina. In D. Heath & R. Adams 1965.

TURNER, J. F. C. 1963. Dwelling Resources in South America. *Architectural Design* **33** (8): August.

—— 1965. Lima's Barriadas and Corralones: Suburbs *versus* Slums. *Ekistics* **112**: March.

—— 1966a. *Uncontrolled Urban Settlements: Problems and Policies.* Paper prepared for the United Nations Seminar on Development Policies and Planning in Relation to Urbanization. Pittsburgh, Penn.

—— 1966b. *A New View of the Housing Deficit.* Paper prepared for the Seminar on a Housing Policy for a Developing Country. University of San Juan, Puerto Rico (April).

—— 1967. Barriers and Channels for Housing Development in Modernizing Countries. *Journal of the American Institute of Planners* **33** (3): May. Reprinted in W Mangin (ed.) 1970.

—— 1968a. Housing Priorities, Settlement Patterns and Urban Development in Modernizing Countries. *Journal of the American Institute of Planners* **34**: November.

—— 1968b. The Squatter Settlement: an Architecture that works. *Architectural Design* **38** (8): August.

—— 1968c. With W. Mangin. The *Barriada* Movement. In *Progressive Architecture* May: 154–62. Reprinted in Paul Oliver (ed.) 1970.

—— 1969a. Uncontrolled Urban Settlements: Problems and Policies (shortened and revised version). In G. Breese (ed.) 1969.

—— 1969b. Alternative Interpretations and Alternative Policies for Low-income Housing in Transitional Economies. USAID Workshop on Squatter Settlements. Washington D.C. (November 3–7; revised February 1970).

—— 1971. Housing Issues and the Standards Problem. Paper delivered to the Rehovot Conference on Urbanization and Development in Developing Countries. Israel (August, unpublished).

VALENCIA, E. 1965. La Merced: Estudio Ecologico y Social de Una Zona de la Ciudad de Mexico. Serie de Investigaciones No. 11. Mexico D.F. Instituto de Antropologia y Historia.

ALISON M. MACEWEN

Differentiation among the Urban Poor: an Argentine Study

INTRODUCTION

The post-war urban explosion in Latin America which has manifested itself in the proliferation of vast numbers of shanty-towns in the major cities has raised dramatic questions at the level of theory and policy (cf. Economic Commission for Latin America 1963, 1970). In the main these questions have been approached through the concept of integration, both at the aggregate level (what structural changes are brought about by the development of a new or expanded stratum), and at the individual level (what personal adjustments are required for people to integrate themselves with urban life). An example of this approach is the work of Germani (1965). This has led to a type of theoretical analysis that relies on a hypothetical integration/non-integration axis (or varieties of it, viz. integration/disintegration, urban/rural etc.), in which the squatters are placed near the non-integration pole. Empirically it also has been the case, because of congestion in the jobs and housing markets, that the majority of squatters actually were experiencing various forms of distance from urban structures. This might take the form of unemployment, physical distance from the city centres, or segregation in urban social relationships (Hauser 1961; Mangin 1970). The perception of the visible aspects of shanty-settlement led to the formation of popular stereotypes that also assumed a situation of separateness within the city.

The term *marginality*, which has acquired popular usage in this context, tends to combine both empirical perceptions and theoretical assumptions that conceive the central problem of the shanty-towns as one of inadequate integration. It is used, on the one hand, in empirical research, which attempts to measure the degree of participation in urban structures by immigrant squatters and the extent of their assimilation of urban norms, and, on the other, in theoretical analysis, which examines the implications at the conceptual level of the presence within the city of quasi-autonomous cultures, economic sub-systems, and sub-proletarian class structures. Marginality then is a relational concept which refers, in different contexts and according to how the concept of integration is operationalized, to a situation of tenuousness and ambiguity, peripherality, or superfluity and redundancy (see ECLA, 1970).

Now, while the exact nature of that relation is an important area for clarification, one set of factors, which is consistently overlooked, is the definition of the entities that are being related to one another through the concept of marginality. On the one hand, we have such vague groupings as 'shanty-towns', 'low-income groups', 'marginal masses', and so on, and on the other, even more elusive aggregates such as 'urban society', 'the city', 'the system of production', 'the elite', etc. It must be obvious that clarification of the nature of both the 'marginal' and the 'integrated' is essential, not only for increased empirical validity and theoretical clarity, but for the essential adequacy of any statement about the nature and causes of marginality itself. Nevertheless, there are considerable problems involved here which arise from first, the difficulty of operationalizing the concept of integration and its opposites, and second, the problem of actually identifying the characteristics of the group which, in empirical terms, is considered to be marginal.

About twenty years ago, when shanty-towns first began to appear in quantity around major Latin American cities, it seemed possible to restrict the frame of reference to the squatter population of any given city. There were two main reasons for this, first because there appeared to be a great deal of social homogeneity and common migratory history within the shanty-towns, and second, because the ecological and social processes of the city seemed at that time to be so synchronized as to aggregate most of the occupants of the lowest socio-economic stratum and most immigrants into ecological areas that could be identified both physically and legally as shanty-towns (illegal land-tenure, improvised housing, lack of public utilities, etc.). Furthermore, the social and ecological factors were seen to be causally rather than coincidentally linked by a common weak bargaining position in the job and housing markets.

Since then, however, the results of empirical research have begun to show that the picture was not as simple as was thought and, in any case, during the lag that appeared between investigation and analysis, those very social and ecological processes have themselves become more complicated. First, there has been considerable differentiation within the socio-economic stratum concerned, introducing varieties of economic skill, income levels, style of life, political affiliation, urban experience, and so on. Second, the population in many shanty-towns is by now largely native born and has few immigrants from the interior. Third, those areas that were identified as squatter-settlements on the basis of physical and legal criteria have been differentiated by both internal change (individual improvements in material welfare, notably housing) and external intervention by public and private bodies (legalization of tenure, provision of physical amenities, etc.). Time has introduced differentiation along a number of different dimensions and has added further differentiation by not introducing those changes uniformly.

For these reasons then it has become increasingly difficult to identify social class or migratory history with ecological grouping. At a more general level this has accentuated the problems of distinguishing characteristics that will be of universal applicability in an empirical or analytical definition of marginality. This is not a particularly new assertion: in 1967 William Mangin published a mammoth review of material on shanty-towns which served to destroy the generalizations and oversimplifications embodied in popular stereotypes and myths on the subject, and, more recently, Anthony Leeds (1969) has produced another survey of factors affecting squatter-settlement, which is based precisely on variations rather than similarities between different forms of settlement.

In view of the complexity that has arisen in this area, it is clearly of considerable importance to make detailed studies of forms of differentiation within the stratum that constitutes the urban poor, giving due attention to both social and ecological sources of variation. There are a number of reasons why the analysis of differentiation is important: first, and most obviously, in order to validate or modify general statements about social or ecological aggregates within the city; second, in order to establish any structural–functional relationships between different groups within the city. Work along these lines has been largely provided by urban ecologists and architects, notably John Turner, who has shown that different areas within the city serve different social and economic purposes for low-income population, and thereby recruit differentially. Central areas, for example, provide crucial contacts for those who rely on contracting work on a casual basis – usually the newcomers, the most impoverished, and so on – while outer areas provide 'suburban' settlement functions for those who, having acquired more economic stability, wish to consolidate their position within a particular class or status group (1969: 507–34). Turner's contribution is further discussed in Brett's paper in this volume.

A structural–functional analysis, however, gives a false notion of stasis to particular social situations and ignores the processes of movement which give rise to differentiation in the first place and probably continue constantly within those situations. Unless differentiation is the simple product of the establishment within an area or social grouping of persons of heterogeneous social origins, then evidence of differentiation is in itself a probable indicator of movement and change, especially in cities that are noted for their dynamism rather than for their stagnation. This brings me to the third reason why differentiation is of such importance for the understanding of the phenomenon of marginality. Not only does differentiation bring with it the assumption of change and movement, but also of the possibility of an order to that movement: a pattern according to which differential characteristics are related to one another, a system of distribution according to which they are allocated, and a set of values which legitimizes all of these things.

Now these assumptions, if true, are of considerable importance, for if there is in fact a pattern to differentiation and a distributive system which ranks those differentials and makes possible a degree of movement between ranks, then there immediately arise two possible implications regarding the relation of that group to the wider society. First, that the systems of internal ranking and mobility are relatively autonomous from the wider society, in which case considerable weight can be given to the argument that shanty-towns constitute separate structures and cultures within the city, with a consequent internal hierarchy and leadership. Second, that the internal ranking system is not exclusive but does in fact plug into the stratification system of the wider society, with the consequent assimilation of stratification values and loss of internal leadership that this implies. The condition of marginality in this case might apply in varying degrees to aggregates of individuals within a broad stratum, but would not indicate a condition of structural or cultural separatism which affected them on a group basis.

I shall try to show how, by examining in detail the internal structure of a shanty-town, it was possible to discover the processes of internal stratification and mobility, and in particular, the way in which locational variables combined with social structure in the system of differentiation. This pattern of internal differentiation had important influences on the leadership structures and capacity for political organization (to the extent that competition for status created fragmented and mutually hostile groups and drew off leaders into the town), and also for the more day-to-day social relationships of the squatters. The ranking system within the shanty-town provided a mirror image of that of the wider society – the categories of differentiation, the criteria for their allocation, and the mechanisms for their distribution were based on the stratification system of the town.

These data show very clearly the dynamism of social change in a shanty-town and demonstrate vividly the difficulties that pertain to the demarcation of ecological areas on the basis of social characteristics. At the wider level, this study raises a number of questions about the internal structure and organization of the urban working class, and, in particular, points to the importance of status aspiration and achievement as a mechanism whereby the urban poor are integrated into the urban culture and structure.

METHODOLOGY

The shanty-town studied was one of three which surrounded a small, riverside town in the province of Buenos Aires, about 190 miles from Buenos Aires, the capital of Argentina. This town, San Pedro, which in 1960 had a total population of around 25 000 was the administrative centre for the county (*partido*) of the same name, which had a further 7 000 inhabitants. It served as the principal marketing centre for cereals, fruit, and livestock from the hinterland, some of which were exported directly from the port on the edge of the town. San Pedro also had a few manufacturing establishments, which were in the main derivative of agriculture (fruit-canning, jam-making, etc.), although its economy was based largely on commerce and administration.

The shanty-town selected for study, which was popularly called *Las Canaletas* (from the chutes – *canaletas* – used for loading grain at the time when this area was used as a port), had a population of 1 168 squatters. Most of the families there worked in the town or countryside in manual, unstable, and poorly paid jobs. The poverty that ensued from their economic situation was reflected both in the area in which they had settled (peripheral public land unsuited for housing because of liability to flooding, with consequent lack of public amenities such as roads, water, street lighting, sewerage, or rubbish disposal), and in their style of life (largely mud shacks with little household equipment).

The research was carried out by the author over a period of four years between 1964–8. Methods of investigation during the two years of field-work (1964–6) consisted of two questionnaire surveys (a 94 per cent census and 50 per cent sample survey of attitudes), participant observation, collection of detailed case histories, depth interviews, documentary research, and experimental studies connected with a community development project currently in operation in *Las Canaletas*. The last two years consisted of analysis, which was followed up by a return visit during the summer of 1968.

One of the objects of this paper is to point out the importance of the analysis of differentiation among the poor, yet this kind of work in itself is particularly difficult for sociologists. First, because amongst the poor, almost by definition of their situation of poverty, substantial material differences of the kind that would lend themselves to statistical quantification are rare, and second, again because of poverty, there tends to be low status-crystallization and thus a low correlation between the various items of status in given individual cases. This is not to say that status ranks are not discernible within the shanty-town, nor that individuals cannot consolidate their status on the basis of aggregation, but rather that the subjective meaning that is given to status differentials allows them a greater weight than their intrinsic value. Within the shanty-town, for example, there is all the difference in the world between a mud and a brick house, an illiterate person and one who has been to primary school, even if only for a few years. The proof of this is that each minor acquisition of status gives rise to comment amongst the squatters and, in the case of status-consolidation, sets off a process of re-grouping which may involve the rupture of social ties with people who have come to be identified as inferior.

In addition to the usual problems connected with the carrying out of research in semi-literate and impoverished communities (which in my view can only be overcome by supplementing survey techniques with depth interviews, an elaborate procedure of cross-checking information, and a lengthy period of participant observation) this situation calls into question the whole role of verification by quantification and interpretation through observation. In my opinion, no observer can be wholly outside a situation, nor can he share perfectly the perceptions of the actors, no matter how fully he has participated in their way of life. Subjective perceptions are no less real to the actors in a situation than the conditions observed by a computer, even where there is a discrepancy between the two. Thus the artificial distinction between 'actors and observers models' is abandoned here.

In this study, differentiation was quantified on the basis of indicators which were used by the actors in defining their situation and which were observed by the researcher in survey analysis. The meaning given to differentiation could only be investigated in depth interviews and portrayed in analysis by illustrative description.

SOCIAL AND ECOLOGICAL STRUCTURES IN SAN PEDRO

Before commencing the description of internal patterns within the shanty-town studied it is necessary to locate the characteristics of the group as a whole within the wider social and ecological structures of the town, since the process whereby they are differentiated as a distinct social group and an ecological area provides the basis for internal social and ecological differentiation.

(a) Class in San Pedro

While supporting a large proportion of the population of the county, San Pedro found its economic base either directly or indirectly in agriculture. As one would expect, there was a high degree of rural–urban continuity. Furthermore, because of a number of factors in the development of the region (high degree of commercialization, extensive capitalization, a history of continuing prosperity, etc.), the class structures of the town and countryside were not only closely intertwined but had in common the characteristics of fluidity, heterogeneity, and lack of polarization. As a result of successive booms in livestock, cereal, and fruit farming, there has, over the last 180 years, been a steady process of intensification of agricultural production and fragmentation of farm holdings. The social relations of agricultural production have, from early days, been based on tenancy and wage labour, in which there was a severe shortage of manpower. This allowed not only a general increase in the share of the surplus from the land by those who worked it, and hence a rise in their levels of living, but also occupational movement between categories of labour on the land, and movement laterally between the rural and urban social classes. Thus not only did some farmers and farm workers reside in the town, but some actually moved into urban occupations there.

The principal features of the class structure in this area then were as follows: first there was a narrow range of occupations connected with farming, marketing, commerce, small industries and crafts, and public services. It lacked extremes of wealth in terms of ownership of capital resources and personal incomes, giving rise to two main strata differentiated from one another on the basis of the manual or non-manual nature of work. The upper stratum, which identified itself as a middle class (using a national rather than a local frame of reference) had the characteristics of a *petite bourgeoisie* – merchants, small businessmen, public employees, white collar workers, and a few professional men such as doctors and lawyers. The other stratum, which identified itself as a lower-class was distributed mainly in the primary and tertiary sectors of the economy. Both of these strata were heterogeneous and lacked internal organization.[1] Second, there was within both strata a range of status groups, distinguished from one another by flexible and non-ascriptive criteria directly related to various manifestations of income expenditure. Concretely the criteria were income, occupation, education, style of life, and associational patterns. There were no cultural, ethnic, or linguistic differences between middle and lower classes either in the town or in the countryside. The relationship between status groups was emulative and, within them, competitive.

Manual labourers in both town and countryside were differentiated both internally and externally by levels of income and work conditions, differences in style of life, reflected particularly in material possessions and educational levels, and by social distance. According to these criteria the entire population of the shanty-town studied fell within the *clase baja*. Furthermore, because of their employment in unskilled manual work, the extremely low and unstable incomes, the impoverished style of life, and the general low level of educational attainment, they were marked out as members of the lowest status group within that class. Their patterns of association whether informal (kin and neighbours) or formal (membership of social clubs) also gave them a certain social exclusivity, and finally, their residence in an area that lacked basic amenities gives visible symbolism to their identification as the 'urban poor' (*los pobres*), or the squatters (*los intrusos*).

(b) Ecological Distribution in San Pedro

As is common in most Hispanic forms of settlement the city was organized on a rectangular grid pattern around the geometric centre which comprises the commercial district, government buildings, church, transport terminals, and so on. Thence settlement radiated out to the periphery with status and land values correlated in such a way as to distribute the wealthiest families on the most expensive property nearest to the centre and conversely the poorest on the cheapest land at the periphery, where private dwellings merged into *quintas* (market-gardens) and thence into the fruit-farming belt.

Proximity to the city centre thus functioned as the primary factor in the allocation of land values. Even within the cheapest sectors of the private housing market, however, it would not be possible for the poor to find accommodation. As is usual in such cases, they were forced to seek residence on sites outside the private market and invade public property or areas where freak topographical features have given land low economic value and a certain indeterminancy about ownership. In San Pedro, there was a narrow strip of public land between the foot of the bluffs left by the Paraná and the present-day river's edge. This area, although commanding considerable scenic beauty, and being situated relatively near the city centre, was not used for building because of the threat of floods and the considerable problem of drainage.

Since residential location fused two important status variables – style of life and associational patterns – it itself became an item of social definition, further consolidating the complex of variables that mark out the squatters from the others in their class.

The social, economic, and ecological processes in San Pedro have thus fused in such a way as to place those who occupied the most inferior and unstable occupational roles, and who were thus also the groups with lowest social prestige in the town, in areas that did not form part of the private housing market, and that consequently lacked all the usual public facilities and amenities.

At the same time it is necessary to point to certain processes over a period of years which have involved some socio-economic change amongst the urban squatters. In the first place, fringe areas of the shanty-town have shown considerable improvement by virtue of the fact that the families living there have been able to raise their economic status and consequently their levels of living. This has blurred the boundary between shanty-town and town. Second, some of these families have been able to enter the private housing market and have left the shanty-town for better areas. Thus where once one could state that the entire *clase baja* of San Pedro lived in shanty-towns, recently it has been more correct to say that those who occupied the *lowest* positions, i.e. the most impoverished, tended to do so, but even within shanty-towns there were a number of variations in levels of poverty.

DIFFERENTIATION WITHIN THE SHANTY-TOWN

As already stated, differentiation within the shanty-town studied, henceforth referred to as *Las Canaletas*, followed the same pattern as that in the town, being based on occupation, income, education, style of life, and associational patterns.

(a) Occupation and Income

In general the occupations of the working population in *Las Canaletas* were manual, unskilled, and arduous. Although there appeared to be little persistent unemployment as such, there was extensive under-employment (i.e. jobs with low productivity lasting less than a full working-day), and the remuneration was, with few exceptions, low and irregular.

Most personal incomes fell between US $56 and $224 per month, although there were wide differences between the lowest incomes ($28–42) per month and the highest ($280).[2] When individual incomes were spread over families the differentiation is even more noticeable; 8 per cent of the squatter families had a monthly income of between $28 and $56, where although most of these families were childless or lived alone, some had families of five, six, and seven children. At the other end of the scale, nearly 5 per cent of the families had a monthly income of $280 and $477 and while a third of these had families of nine and ten, nearly half had four to six members in the households. *Table 1* below (based on census information) sets out household size and monthly income.

The poverty of the shanty-town dwellers can be illustrated by two figures. The overall *per capita* income in *Las Canaletas* was approximately $30. The *per capita* incomes for the largest group of families (namely those with five to six members) was approximately $20. This contrasts with a national figure for Argentina in 1965 of $64 (Banco Central, 1965).

Related to the earnings associated with certain jobs were the conditions of employment, particularly the form in which income was derived from certain types of work, which, in turn, was related to job stability.

The most common form of employment (40 per cent of the total; see *Table 2*) was the unskilled *jornalero* who contracted work on the basis of a daily wage (*jornal*). The wages of skilled workers (mechanics, bricklayers, etc.) were calculated on a fortnightly or monthly rate, and they thus identified themselves as salaried workers (*empleados*) even though their work might be manual. *Empleados* could earn double or treble the income of *jornaleros*, and their employment was also stable. They constituted 22 per cent of the employed.

TABLE 1

Monthly income of households (in pesos and US $) and size of household (census)

Monthly income	Number in household							Total
	1-2	3-4	5-6	7-8	9-10	11-12	13-14	
0–10 000 pesos $0–$55	15	3	2	1				21
10–20 000 $56–111	34	31	28	9	5			107
20–30 000 $112–167	3	8	15	7	7	2		42
30–40 000 $168–223	9	13	11	5	5	1		44
40–50 000 $224–279	1	7	7	1	2	3		21
50–60 000 $280–335			1	1	3			5
60–70 000 $336–391		1			1		1	3
70–80 000 $392–447			4					4
Total	62	63	68	24	23	6	1	247

Contrasted with these two categories of workers, whose income would be regular as long as they were employed, were the self-employed and the odd jobbers, whose income was subject to immense fluctuations in quantity and stability. The odd jobber (*changarin*) contracted odd jobs of work (*changas*) on a piece-work system from an assortment of employers. They were extremely unskilled and among the poorest workers in the shanty-town (31 per cent of the total). The self-employed (*cuenta propia*) were distinguished from the odd jobbers by the fact that they owned some capital equipment (a store, traps, a lorry, etc.) which enabled them to carry out a form of entrepreneurial activity. They were not dependent on employers or wages and thus had a degree of auto-nomy, but also of risk, which other workers did not have, and their incomes could embrace the total range of personal earnings of the

entire shanty-town ($28–280 per month). They were a small group:
only 7 per cent of all employed.

The third variable which affected income levels was the location of
employment. As already mentioned, roughly half of the employed
population in *Las Canaletas* worked in the countryside and half in the
town. Even within the categories outlined above incomes would tend to
be higher if they were urban rather than rural, although some jobs such
as skilled trades and service employment were obviously less prevalent
in the countryside than in the town. The relationship between these two
variables is set out in *Table 2* below.

TABLE 2

Type and location of employment (census)

| Type of employment | Location of employment | | | |
	Urban	Rural		Total
Skilled wage earner (*empleados*)	75 100%	0	0%	75 100%
Self-employed (*cuenta propia*)	19 79%	5	21%	24 100%
Unskilled wage earner (*jornaleros*)	57 43%	75	57%	132 100%
Odd jobber (*changarines*)	39 38%	64	62%	103 100%
Totals	190 57%	144	43%	334 100%

One hundred and forty-four persons, or 43 per cent of the employed
labour force in *Las Canaletas* worked in a rural environment; of these
just over a quarter worked in the islands of the Paraná, fishing and
trapping *nutria*.[3] Almost all of the latter were self-employed, although
considering their lack of capital equipment and poverty it has been
considered more appropriate to classify them as odd jobbers (*changarines*).

The rest of the rural workers were employed on the fruit farms,
where sequential periods of harvesting and planting for each type of
fruit ensured a more or less stable demand for labour as long as the
harvests were good. In addition, there was some work with cereal and
potato farming. In general the work was organized through a union
which received the requests for labour from the farmers and then
distributed the work to the men according to a rota which was worked
through in order. In this way the members of the union were ensured a
full day's work most days of the week, although if demand fell, they were
likely to be called less regularly. During the period of research an oversupply of labour had given an element of risk to union employment and
therefore rural workers preferred to bypass this method and arranged

jobs directly with farmers through patronage. Thus they claimed to have more stability of work, but usually had to put up with lower wage rates and longer working hours from which unionized workers were protected. Of all agricultural workers seventy-five were classified as *jornaleros* in that they had, either with the union or a patron some sort of arrangement by which work could be obtained over relatively long periods (albeit with occasional short-term unemployment); twenty-nine were *changarines* in that they had no such arrangements and would turn up for odd jobs of work whenever the will took them; two were self-employed, one of them owned a lorry, which he hired out, and the other had a small market-garden and raised poultry.

Rural work, both in the islands and in the countryside, had low occupational prestige, not only because the incomes were lower and more unstable but because the work was harsher. While questions about job satisfaction did not show evidence of great discontent, but rather of resignation and apathy, examination of the aspiration of fathers for their sons showed an overwhelming desire to acquire jobs in the town.

Urban work had a greater variation of types of job, levels of remuneration, and consequently of occupational recruitment and career mobility. A brief examination of the urban economy is relevant in this respect. The principal characteristic that concerns us here is its extreme fragmentation; by this I mean a proliferation of similar small economic units which have varying degrees of economic autonomy and perform similar activities.

With regard to the manufacturing sector, the largest factories employed under a hundred men, and some as few as twenty-five. The construction industry was divided up into a number of independent groups of four or five tradesmen. The eighty dockers who worked in the small river port, and who were organized on the basis of a co-operative, formed the largest single economic group. Below this level there was a proliferation of small cottage industries and crafts, such as sawmills, brickmakers, boat-menders, and so on. The broom-making industry in San Pedro was an extreme example of this fragmentation – brooms were made in the town for sale nationally – and lay in the hands of seventy-five broom-makers, each of whom had a small *taller* (workshop) and employed between three to six men.

The same situation existed in the commercial sector: there were numerous small shops, hotels, bars, *almacenes* (stores), most of which employed about half a dozen people, many of whom were members of a nuclear family, and some of which were owner-operated, single-handed.

The only exceptions to this fragmented structure were the regional offices of nationally organized administration and commerce: the municipality, the hospital, schools, the post office, the *Asistencia Publica* (government welfare agency), and the national and provincial banks.

The most important consequences of this fragmentation have been first, the extension of economic independence to a great number of people, which is reflected in the large numbers of self-employed workers; second, the creation of structural differentiation within each little economic unit or segment, thus forming an internal hierarchy from the self-employed patrons through a series of wage levels to the lowest rungs of apprenticeship. While possibly permitting a greater absorption of the labour force, this also created underemployment and helped to keep wages down.

Although it is possible to classify the urban work force of *Las Canaletas* by sector the usefulness of this classification can be undermined by the phenomena of fragmentation and underemployment already described. For comparative purposes, however, it is included here and set out in *Table 3* below.

TABLE 3

Classification of urban workers in Las Canaletas by sector (census)

Sector	Number	Percentage
Market-gardening	2	1·1
Industry and manufacturing	33	17·4
Construction	21	11·0
Transport	32	17·0
Commerce and services	76	40·0
Unspecified (odd jobbers)	26	13·5
Total	190	100·0

Differentiation of urban employment has been created both by the juxtaposition of secondary and tertiary sectors and also by the internal hierarchy within economic units in both sectors. The aristocrats of the working class were the dockers who were organized in the form of a closed-shop co-operative which had a restricted labour force of eighty people. The men worked six-hour shifts for which they received 1 600 pesos ($8.40) per day and on Sundays the rates were doubled. At the end of each year profits were divided out to the members of the co-operative in proportion to the number of shifts worked. In addition, they received the traditional New Year Bonus which constituted 8·3 per cent of shifts worked. Provision was made for superannuation, accident insurance, family allowances, free medical assistance, and holiday pay (6 per cent). The co-operative also provided short-term loans to its members and helped out in times of crisis, such as in 1966, when a flood destroyed the homes of some of the dockers who lived in *Las Canaletas*. Thus, in addition to more sophisticated forms of economic stability and insurance, the wages at the port could reach as much as $280 per month.

Those who had trades (bricklayers, plumbers, mechanics, carpenters, etc.) were able to command higher wages than other workers, and were also able to combine wage-work with self-employment. All other categories of workers were subject to low wages and instability of employment, though, in the case of public administration, employment was more stable.

In summary, urban jobs had a greater differentiation of income and stability than rural ones and thus provided more opportunities for economic advancement. At the top of the list of manual occupations it was possible to identify groups that were relatively privileged – those who worked in manufacturing and transport, and those who had trades – all of whom could earn as much as three times the wage of those employed in menial services, the economic condition of the latter group being only a marginal improvement on rural employment.

(b) Style of Life: Material Possessions

In view of the general low level of income in *Las Canaletas* the range of variation in material possessions was rather limited. Nevertheless, they clearly formed the most important indicators of status because of their visibility. Three classes of material possessions could be distinguished:

(i)   the type of dwelling, its size, aspect, and construction
(ii) household equipment and furnishing
(iii) personal items.

(i) *Type of dwelling*

The traditional form of house construction for the poor in Argentina is the *rancho* form of dwelling, particularly noted for its small size, lack of windows, and small number of rooms. The *rancho* is usually built of cheap and improvised construction materials and lacks internal plumbing. In *Las Canaletas* the basic structural characteristics of the *rancho* were maintained whatever the variation in building materials or household equipment, hence the strong visible demarcation of the area as a whole from the rest of the town where principles of construction followed quite different patterns. There was, however, a considerable range of variation in the more superficial aspects of building and equipment.

The principal variation was constituted by the nature of building material, the poorest huts being made of mud mixed with straw and reeds, the 'richest' being of bricks and mortar. In between these two extremes, which represented 49 per cent and 31 per cent of all dwellings respectively, there was a series of combinations in which efforts were made to give the impression of brick construction, either by white-washing the mud walls in a way that made them appear to be rendered, by laying the bricks in mud rather than mortar and subsequently white-washing them, or by constructing the front wall which faced the roadway of bricks and making the others, which were out of public view, of mud.

There was a similar variation in the provision of latrines, which ranged from an improvised hole in the ground surrounded by an assortment of sacks, rags, tins, and so on, to sturdy brick constructions with proper septic tanks and lavatories. Differentiation in types of dwelling was reflected in the cost of materials, and even more, in their price in the squatter housing market. In general, expenditure on housing varied directly with income, and represented in most cases approximately two or three months' wages. The unofficial price of houses to some degree reflected relative proximity to or distance from the city, as we shall see below, but in general, the price of mud houses fell within a range of $56 to $112, while brick houses were at least double this. During the period of my research a brick house with only two rooms was sold for $448, another went for $840, and one very large house on the urban periphery cost over $2 800.

(ii) *Household equipment*

Household equipment varied widely in price and thus served as a basis for status differentiation. The most important of these was concerned with water, since the urban water supply did not reach *Las Canaletas*. The cheapest method of obtaining water was from open wells which required a depth of one to three metres to reach the first water level.

However this was generally recognized as insanitary because of inadequate coverage and infiltration from nearby latrines. Electrical and mechanical pumps solved this problem, especially if they were driven to the lower water level which lay twenty metres below the ground, but they were costly ($70–140). For those families who lived higher up on the bluffs the problem was accentuated by the fact that it was impossible to dig wells even to the first water level and many families therefore did not have their own water supply. Of all the families in *Las Canaletas* only 4·5 per cent had electric pumps and running water, 26·5 per cent had mechanical pumps, 37·5 per cent had open wells, and 31·5 per cent had no water supply at all.

Provision of light varied similarly. There was no official supply of electricity for domestic consumption although there was a small line of street-lighting which extended to a few commercial establishments (stores and workshops) half-way along the shanty-town. Some families tapped these lines illegally for use in their homes, and others who were situated on the urban fringe adjacent to the town had the benefit of the domestic lines there. Together this gave about 27 per cent of households electric light, while others used tilley lamps and the very poor, oil wick lamps and candles.

The availability, by whatever means, of electricity made possible the purchase of electrically operated domestic appliances, and there was a very small privileged group of families (6 per cent) who had electric cookers, refrigerators, washing machines, and electric fans. Half a dozen families even had television (2·5 per cent). Compare this level of equipment with the others who did not have access to electricity; even among these there were varying levels of poverty. As regards cooking, for example, besides the 6 per cent who had electric stoves, some families used calor gas (11 per cent), some kerosene stoves (32 per cent) and the rest, 51 per cent, cooked over an open fire or brazier supplemented with a primus stove.

There was an infinite range of variation in household furnishings which is difficult to portray in aggregate terms, therefore I shall briefly describe the condition of two families whose style of life is easily distinguishable, and who can be considered typical of the relatively wealthy and relatively poor families within the shanty-town.

The first family, which had a stable and relatively good income derived from the father's job in construction, lived in a brick house with glass fitted windows, a tiled floor, and full array of electrically operated domestic appliances, including television. The bedrooms, of which there were two, were furnished with an attractive suite of cupboards and wardrobes, and the couple and each of the three children had beds of their own. The main room, an all-purpose kitchen-cum-living-room had a three-piece suite made of a strong, brightly coloured plastic, commonly fashionable amongst the lower class. The room was adorned with pictures and artificial flowers, apart from the usual ditties to the Virgin Mary, Peron, and the mother of the family.

The other family, where the head of household was sporadically employed in harvest work, and which had eight members, lived in a mud shack with two rooms, each of which had mud floors and small open windows protected only by boards or rags. In the bedroom there was one old iron bed in which the couple slept with the younger children. The rest of the family slept on the floor on blankets and mattresses which were rolled up during the day. In the main room there was one large table and a bench. The constantly burning brazier was kept at the door so that it could be easily moved inside or out according to the weather, and the walls of the main room were blackened by its smoke. There was nowhere to hang clothes or keep other possessions and these were kept in a disorderly heap in a corner of the bedroom or under the mattress. There was no form of internal decoration.

(iii) *Personal items*

Most working clothes, of course, were rough textured and well used, and poverty was shown in the degree to which working clothes were used in leisure time. The wealthier families would change after work into leisure clothes and some might even have a set of 'best' clothes, for special occasions. Among the very poor there was no such distinction. The wealthier families were pre-occupied with a number of items of personal adornment such as ties and tie-pins, nylon stockings, high heels, cosmetics, jewellery, and so on, while the very poor were not.

In general it can be seen that the degree of variation in style of life (measured here in terms of material possessions) was directly related to income. This in turn was related to occupation, as can be seen by the fact that 71 per cent of rural workers lived in mud huts and 77 per cent of urban workers lived in brick or brick combination dwellings. Similarly, 84 per cent of the skilled wage earners and 80 per cent of the self-employed lived in brick houses while 60 per cent of the *changarines* lived in mud huts. Home furnishings and items of personal adornment further consolidated this pattern of association, expenditure on small but highly visible luxuries occasionally making up for large inadequacies.

(c) Education

The general level of education in *Las Canaletas* was low. Of the adult population only two people (0·2 per cent) had ever attended secondary school, 43 per cent had completed only three years of primary schooling, which, together with the 24 per cent who were functionally illiterate, made up 67 per cent of the total, leaving the other third which had completed the full primary cycle, but not advanced beyond it. Among the school population there were high rates of absenteeism and drop-out; in 1966 seventy-three children entered the first primary grade, while only four were still at school in the final, sixth grade.

The overall low level of educational attainment suggests a number of problems, of which the chief is that, until recent years, schooling has not only been unrelated to occupational performance but is directly competitive with certain career structures of the poor. The two most obvious cases of this are first, the case of the semi-nomadic harvest workers, whose need to follow economic opportunities often conflicts with the desire to keep a child at school, or at least at the same school, and second, and more importantly, the case of the urban workers whose entry into a trade depends on a period of apprenticeship which begins at an early age, with a wage that could only be tolerated by a person of that age, namely a ten- or eleven-year-old.

In recent years, however, the completed primary school cycle has become more of a necessity amongst the lower class, since some industrial establishments require this in their formal recruitment to vacancies, and in the tertiary sector, especially in the large public bureaucracies, it is seen to be an advantage. Under these circumstances a completed primary school cycle has come to acquire an element of economic value (and thus also of prestige) among the poor. This is reflected in the levels of educational attainment of the younger workers, especially those who occupy the highest occupational grades among the lower class: 46 per cent of those employed in the town had completed the cycle as compared with 19 per cent of the rural workers, and of the latter, 34 per cent were illiterate compared with 9 per cent of the former. Of urban workers, performance was highest among the skilled wage earners of whom half had completed the primary school cycle and had only an 8 per cent illiteracy rate. These workers, incidentally,

H

tended to have a less random age distribution, being clustered around the twenty to thirty age group.

The increasing pre-occupation with schooling as a means of enhancing occupational opportunities and social prestige was reflected in a rather curious phenomenon; the concern about the social status of the school attended. *Las Canaletas* had a school of its own situated at the top of the bluffs at a distance that was convenient for most children. This was attended by the majority of the squatter children, especially those who came from the outer edge of the shanty-town which was the poorest quarter. Consequently the school had acquired a reputation as one which provided for the very poor and had tremendous problems of absenteeism and truancy, as it, indeed, did. Parents who became seriously concerned with the performance of their children tried to avoid sending them to this school, first, because they feared that their children would come under the 'bad influence' of the others, and second, because they wished them to associate with the children of 'better' families. Thus a little over a quarter of the squatter schoolchildren attended a school which lay on the periphery of the town, near a more affluent working-class area, and a fifth attended one in the centre of town which also catered for middle-class children. The prestige of the school attended was thus directly associated with the status position of the child's family, being high on all dimensions.

(d) Associational Patterns

Patterns of association were of considerable importance for the establishment of social status in a social situation that was riddled with patronage and personalism, and in a community where social ties had a high degree of visibility. This was especially the case since large numbers of patrons were not only members of the lower class but very often lived in the same area, thus combining their economic role with that of neighbour, kinsman, clubmate, and so on. Social groupings were thus important not only because internal relationships could, at appropriate moments, be mobilized to fulfil certain functions concerned with the acquisition of social status (establishment of patron–client relations, loans of money to purchase status items, and so on), but also because association with persons who were known and seen to be of high status became itself an item of prestige.

The two general principles of association were kinship and status parity. The most intimate and regular forms of social interaction between squatters were usually maintained within the kin group. Kinship, however, is basically an ascriptive form of grouping and was occasionally brought into conflict with the principle of status parity, which lead to the rupture of kinship ties (see MacEwen 1973).

The other form of grouping was the peer group which was non-ascriptive, and was composed primarily of workmates who might at the same time be neighbours and kinsmen, where they were of similar status. Peer groups were based on informal interaction and had a diffuse structure which was centred around leisure-time activities, particularly the frequenting of certain clubs, bars, and support for particular football teams. The most tight-knit structure was that of the adolescent gang (the *barra*), which had a high insistence on internal equality and thus controlled recruitment in such a way as to exclude a person who could not afford the types of entertainment indulged in by the *barra* or the style of dress of the members or, alternatively, to exclude a person considered too 'posh'.

The neighbourhood served as the basis for a more generalized form of association, and is relevant to the question of differentiation since the various elements of social status which I have described to this point were not only associated together but also clustered together in certain residential areas. Discussion of the locational groupings will therefore provide a useful transition to the discussion of the internal patterning of differentiation in *Las Canaletas*.

THE INTERNAL STATUS HIERARCHY OF LAS CANALETAS

Since most families in *Las Canaletas* have always been dependent on the town, either for employment or for transport to the countryside, proximity to the city has operated as the principle basis for valuation of residential sites in the shanty-town. During the eighty years or so that *Las Canaletas* has existed as a residential area for the poor, the pattern of settlement has operated in such a way as to place the first migrants in the area close to the town, and later ones successively farther out into the countryside. Thus there has developed an association between proximity to the town and length of residence.

Most migrants who came to the shanty-town were first employed in rural labour, with the accompanying characteristics of present-day rural labourers, such as low and unstable incomes, an impoverished style of life, and illiteracy. With time, however, the older residents, or their children, were able to find employment in the town and thus initiate a process of status-mobility. Thus the pattern of differentiaton within the shanty-town closely followed the association between length of residence and residential location. This concentration of status-mobility in the urban fringe area of the shanty-town has been continued by a process of individual residential movement whereby families from the poorer areas, who did manage to improve their situation, moved towards the more affluent parts, thus contributing to the collective up-grading of the urban-fringe area and accentuating its difference from the poorer areas.

Because of the previously mentioned principle of status parity in social relationships, the existence of internal differentiation meant that social groupings also tended to be structured around differentiated areas of the shanty-town concentrating social relationships within areas of broadly similar status. On the basis of a procedure whereby the 'best friendships' (measured in terms of shared confidences and exchange of loans) of a 50 per cent sample of households were mapped sociometri-cally, it was possible to discern five distinct areas in the shanty-town within which friendship ties overlapped and between which there were few such relationships (see *Figure 1* and *Table 4* below). When the

FIGURE 1

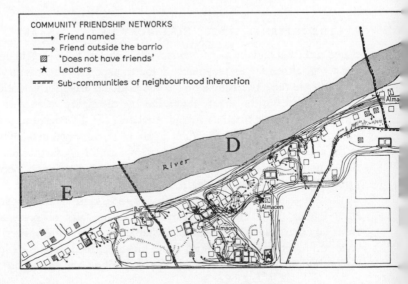

aggregate status of each 'neighbourhood' was assessed it could be seen that the geographical ordering of the neighbourhoods (nearness/distance from the town) was closely associated with the patterning of differentiation (high/low status) (see *Figure 2*).

Several points should be observed here: first, although the predominating influence on the allocation of status-values in *Las Canaletas* was urban employment, even in the highest status-areas there was still a significant number of rural workers there (30 per cent), and similarly there were a few urban workers living on the rural fringe, the low status-area. Second, although most of the items of status were distributed in the same way with regard to location in the shanty-town, some indicators were less differentiated by location than others; high-quality building materials for example were markedly clustered around the urban fringe area of the shanty-town and fell off sharply half-way along the road giving way to mud huts, while education did not differentiate so sharply between the areas. Thus, although there was differentiation within the shanty-town, the outer margins of that differentiation were not widely separated. Furthermore, although there was some association between the different dimensions of status, the correlations were not high.

On the face of it this immediately raises questions about the meaning

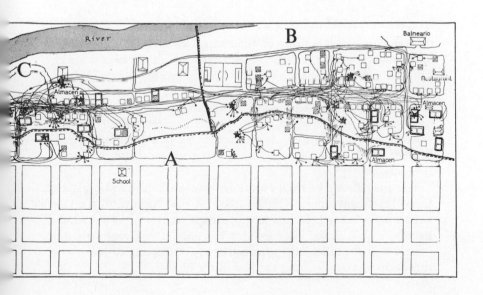

Alison M. MacEwen

TABLE 4

Location of friendship links (sample)

		No.	Percentage
A to rest of shanty-town		2	3
A to within A		21	35
A to outside shanty-town		37	62
	Total	60	100
B to rest of shanty-town		4	4
B to within B		70	70
B to outside shanty-town		26	26
	Total	100	100
C to rest of shanty-town		13	16
C to within C		48	61
C to outside shanty-town		18	23
	Total	79	100
D to rest of shanty-town		6	6
D to within D		70	67
D to outside shanty-town		28	27
	Total	104	100
E to rest of shanty-town		4	18
E to within E		6	27
E to outside shanty-town		12	55
	Total	22	100

that can be attached to forms of differentiation whose statistical significance would appear to be slight. At the beginning of this paper, however, I pointed out that it was the subjective perception of status differences which gave them added meaning within the context of poverty. This was of importance in affecting the way in which social relationships among the poor were structured since status parity required not only that relationships were maintained between peers but that distance be placed between superiors and inferiors and references constantly be placed vertically.

This was reflected best in the attitudes between the high and low status areas of the shanty-town: Neighbourhood A was separated from all the other neighbourhoods in that it was situated at the top of the bluffs. Because it was on the same level as the town it was considered the nearest to it. Families here were constantly attempting to show their superiority to those living at the foot of the bluffs:

FIGURE 2

Distribution of status-values in sub-neighbourhoods of shanty-town

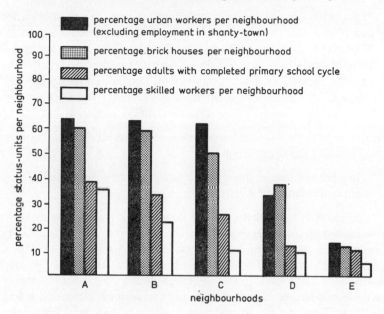

'I wouldn't live *abajo* (on the lower level) even if they had paving and electric light.'

'Those who live *abajo* don't want to change, they are very ungrateful for any help you give them.'

'Those people are dreadful, all they want is enough wine to get drunk.'

Neighbourhood B was the nearest to the lower level to the town and had a high proportion of urban workers, most of whom had a high standard of living relative to the others. Some of the oldest members of the shanty-town lived here and there a high percentage was native born. The need to assert their superiority over the other areas in the shanty-town is exemplified by their attempt to consider themselves part of the town rather than the shanty-town: they emphatically referred to their area as 'postal district number two', as opposed to *Las Canaletas*. People who lived in this area declined to participate in a community development project which was aimed at raising the standard of living of the entire shanty-town population, on the grounds that it meant identifying with the poorer areas of the shanty-town, referred to as the *fondo* (the outback):

> 'That project is fine for the people in the *fondo*, they need help, we don't.'
> 'The people from the *fondo* are lazy. Ten years ago our area was full of mud huts, but now everybody here is pulling their weight to improve themselves, I don't see why they cannot do the same.'
> 'Here in this area there is no trouble and never has been; in the *fondo* it's quite another thing, there are always drunkards and fights.'

In the *fondo* there was some recognition of the social distance between their area and the urban fringe:

> 'They are not like us those people, they are all well-off snobs, they don't understand the problems of the poor.'

The social distance that obtained between areas of the shanty-town also existed at the interpersonal level, so that even within neighbourhoods of the shanty-town, there was a constant momentum of critical gossip which was used as a mechanism for the projection for each individual's status level. In this there was always a combination of envy of those who had relative advantage and disassociation from those who had less. Thus one would find neighbours who had been friends for years suddenly ceasing to speak to one another because one had built a brick house; parents distressed because their daughter had married a rural labourer and set up house in a not too good part of the shanty-town rather than up on the urban fringe; adolescent youths used to roving together split up by the acquisition by one of them of a good job, and so on.

In this atmosphere of intense status competition each minor improvement would be observed, commented on, and acted upon, hence discrepancy between subjective and objective assessment of status differences. Not only did the possession of status items affect the social relationships of the squatters but also the aspirations towards mobility, and strategies for its achievement.

In summary then, the processes of differentiation and movement among the poor, while scarcely discernible to the outsider, were of crucial importance to the people involved. As far as residential relationships were concerned, the intense status competition that was produced by limited mobility and the stress on manifestation of appropriate status-symbols produced a strain towards conflict and tension within the neighbourhood rather than one of solidarity; reference groups tended to be located among the strata immediately above the persons concerned and social relationships structured accordingly, which prevented the formation of community leaders and the organization of collective goals. In short, 'mobility' produced a strain towards individualization of the poor, placing them in competition with one another, thus depriving them of a basis for collective leadership and consciousness.

CONCLUSIONS

The basis for differentiation in the shanty-town was the same as that which existed within class groupings in the wider society: social status. As in the rest of the town the criteria of status differentiation comprised four elements: occupation and income, style of life, education, and associational patterns. The extent of differentiation, while considerably exaggerated by the inhabitants of the shanty-town, did not present wide extremes and the degree of association between the different status values was not particularly high. Such differentiation as did exist, however, gave rise to a system of internal ranking and mobility, similar to that of the wider society.

The mechanism for the distribution of status differentials within the shanty-town was also the same as that in the town, occupational mobility. The movement from rural to urban jobs, and from unskilled wage earning to skilled jobs or self-employment involved not only enhanced occupational prestige, but also increased economic stability, and a rise in income levels. These jobs, however, were increasingly linked with educational attainment, particularly literacy over illiteracy, and a completed primary school cycle over an incompleted one. The increased wealth which accrued from occupational changes made possible an improvement in style of life, particularly regarding the home, and eventually a residential move to 'better' areas of the shanty-town or even out of it altogether and into the town. The rate of this movement into, through, and out of *Las Canaletas* was, however, slow. Between 1964–8 twenty new households were established by immigrants, five families moved their houses from a lower to a higher status-area within the shanty-town, and twenty-eight families left. Of the emigrants, it is to be noted that only a small number achieved some mobility through moving, since the majority, eighteen families, moved off to other areas in the countryside.

Since all of these changes were dependent on occupational movement, the pattern of differentiation depended ultimately on the characteristics of the labour market and the form in which occupational mobility took place. As we have already seen, the structure of the labour market in San Pedro concentrated workers into small economic units, which were mostly in the commercial and services sector. The capacity for expansion in this labour market was to some extent tied to the growth in demand for those services, which in turn was related to agricultural productivity, and not, as in metropolitan cities, to a rise in industrial investment and production. The area around San Pedro, however, has experienced a series of agricultural booms in the post-war period (mainly from fruit) which has permitted a slight expansion of the labour market and hence occupational mobility among the poor.

Such occupational mobility as did exist was carried out within the small economic units described – the shop, the small construction group, the small workshop, and so on, rather than in large factories or state bureaucracies. The small scale of operations of these units produced a tendency for patronage and personalism in recruitment and working relations. This placed a constraint on occupational mobility in that it depended on the creation of patron–client relations and long apprenticeships which, in turn, made for inter- rather than intra-generational mobility. It gave a disproportional advantage to the young who, being free of dependents, were able to subsist on the low wages commanded by apprenticeships. They also had access to a wider range of social relationships through which patronage links could be forged.

The existence of patronage in the labour market created the necessity for vertical links which militated against lateral solidarity. The relative scarcity of jobs placed a high degree of competitiveness among workers and they were constantly constrained to disassociate themselves from their status inferiors and orientate themselves towards their superiors. The transparency in social relations which was brought about by the overlapping of social roles (workmate, kinsmen, neighbour, etc.) created a high pressure for the exhibition of correct status symbols associated with status peers and superiors. This was seen at both interpersonal and group level, and in the neighbourhood resulted in the creation of a hierarchy of status groups which were both emulative and competitive.

The divisive influences of this internal status structure were stronger than the affinity which could be expected from a common situation of occupational and housing insecurity. One important implication of this is the absence of leaders who, as one has seen in other situations (Lima,

Caracas), have been of such importance in organizing invasions and occasional mass participation in political events. In a stratified situation, leadership is usually based on possession of elements of power and prestige, and this is especially the case in a society dominated by patronage and personalism. Within the shanty-town, however, aspirations for mobility prevented people from taking up leadership roles within the community, since as soon as they were in a position to fulfil the conditions of leadership, their own references were placed outside the community, often followed closely by a residential move to another part of the city.

It should not be forgotten that the high degree of status competitiveness was created not only by the fragmentation and differentiation of the labour market writ large, but also by the relative scarcity of jobs, and the low overall rates of occupational mobility. The movement of the few, in other words, was conditional upon the marginality of the rest. But while the majority remained in a situation of relative instability and poverty, the mobility of the minority constituted a source of legitimacy for differentiation, and hence also of relative deprivation.

The discussion in this paper has been structured around the argument that evidence of social differentiation breaks down a number of assumptions about the homogeneity of those residential areas in which the urban poor are concentrated. This argument has one important bearing on discussions about the urban poor in Latin America and that has to do with their relationship within the wider cultural and structural systems of urban society. In the first place, a system of occupational mobility which penetrates so deeply into squatter neighbourhoods must indicate a degree of structural integration beyond that suggested by the talk of mass unemployment and marginality. Second, the infiltration of a set of processes as fundamental as social mobility carries with it the accompanying value system which serves as the basis for integration at the cultural level. Thus, whether or not the poor are able to achieve the degree of social mobility which they would wish, the fact that they conceive it as a desirable end binds them to the urban class culture. In the light of these observations then it cannot be maintained that the poor exist in a separate or quasi-exclusive culture, nor that they constitute separate structural entities within the city.

Notes

1 The lack of an industrial base in San Pedro makes for difficulties in the selection of proper class terminology, too lengthy to be properly discussed here. The terms used here of middle and lower class are based on the self-identification of the Sampedrinos. The latter category includes the terms *obreros* (workers), *empleados* (salaried workers), and *peons* (labourers); it also includes the group referred to as *los pobres* (the poor). Where there is a need to distinguish the squatter group, who constituted the lowest category within the lower class (*clase baja*), from the rest of that class, I shall use the term 'squatters' to avoid confusion.

2 All figures refer to 1966 prices.

3 *Nutria*, a rodent similar to the otter, whose pelt is valuable for the fur trade.

References

BANCO CENTRAL DE LA REPUBLICA ARGENTINA, 1965. *Boletin Estadístico.*

BREESE, G. (ed.) 1969. *The City in Newly Developing Countries.* Englewood Cliffs, N.J.: Prentice-Hall.

ECONOMIC COMMISSION FOR LATIN AMERICA 1963. *El Desarrollo Social de America Latina en la Postguerra.* Buenos Aires: Solar/Hachette.

—— 1970. *Social Change and Social Development Policy in Latin America.* New York: United Nations.

GERMANI, G. 1965. Asimilación de inmigrantes en el medio urbano. Notas metodológicas. *Revista Latinoamericana de Sociología* 1 2: Julio.

HAUSER, P. 1961. *Urbanization in Latin America.* Paris: UNESCO.

LEEDS, A. 1969. The Significant Variables determining the Character of Squatter Settlements. *America Latina*, Ano 12 (3): Julio-Set.

MACEWEN, A. M. 1973. Kinship and Mobility on the Argentine Pampa. *Ethnology* 12 (2): April.

MANGIN, W. 1967. Latin American Squatter Settlements: a Problem and a Solution. *Latin American Research Review.* II (3).

MANGIN, W. (ed.) 1970. *Peasants in Cities.* Boston: Houghton Mifflin.

TURNER, J. F. C. 1969. Uncontrolled Urban Settlement: Problems and Policies. In Breese, G. (ed.) 1969.

PART FOUR

Dependence

PHILIP ELLIOTT AND PETER GOLDING

Mass Communication and Social Change: the Imagery of Development and the Development of Imagery[1]

I

Simple models of direct media effect on attitudes and behaviour, at last being questioned in research on mass communication in industrialized societies, still dominate research on communication and development. The economist M. F. Millikan's claim, that 'of all the technological changes which have been sweeping through the traditional societies of the underdeveloped world in the last decade ... the most fundamental and pervasive in their effects have been the changes in communication' (Millikan 1967), is an uncompromising example of the importance typically attached to the media as indices of development or crucial catalysts of change.

In the course of this paper we shall challenge this established view, first by critical appraisal of work carried out in this research tradition, second by substituting an alternative view of the media, stressing their integration into both national and international social and economic systems. It is our contention that this integration has important consequences for the image of development presented in the media in both developed and developing countries. Later in the paper we have attempted to sketch some aspects of this image and to identify its basis in the structure and process of the media, illustrating the case with data from Britain and Nigeria.

Our argument against the established view is not that the media are unimportant, but that the attempt to explain their importance in terms of direct influence for change is misconceived. It is misconceived as a statement about the way modern media operate in developed and developing countries. It is also misconceived in the assumptions it

229

makes about the likely origins and course of social change in developing countries.

Instead of stressing the role of the media as autonomous agents of change within a particular nation-state, our aim is to show how national media are involved in an international media network. Such connexions are at various levels, from those of economics and organization, to the production and presentation of all types of media content. This paper concentrates on news and the news media.[2]

News is not simply a collection of raw facts about the world, reflecting events with debatable but empirically determinable accuracy. Rather is it an important part of the cultural system of modern society, particularly concerned with providing, in a preliminary fashion, frameworks for handling new and recurring problems for society. This handling is done in various ways – by directing attention towards some types and aspects of conflict and change, and ignoring others, by complementary concentration on particular mechanisms of social control and conflict management, and by elaborating continuing perspectives and images on particular topics so that each new event is incorporated into an on-going plot.

These processes may be observed not only in the domestic news of any western country,[3] but also at an international level through the development of news as a marketable commodity throughout the world. At this level, the culture to which news, and other aspects of the international media system contribute, is not related to any single society or social structure so much as to that network of economic interests and organizations that is international corporate capitalism. Increasingly the growth of the international media system enables the news media to play broadly the same ideological role at an international level as is already apparent nationally in particular developed countries. The international media system is one mechanism by which developing countries are brought within the common cultural hegemony of western capitalism.

II

The research tradition we are criticizing finds its roots in a series of assumptions about the nature of social change. Concepts like modernization, problematic in their teleology and often ethnocentric in connotation, have provoked much debate over the characteristics of 'traditional' and 'advanced' societies. The change from one to the other has generally been portrayed as a shift from static, agricultural, primitive, rigidly ascriptive societies to dynamic, industrialized, urbanized, rational, and socially mobile nation-states. Three such approaches have dominated social change theory and underlie discussions of the role of the media. They are, first, the index theory of development and the correlation theory of the media and change; second, the differentiation theory and psychological approaches to the role of the media; and third, theories of exogenously produced change and diffusion approaches to the role of the media.

The index theory of development asserts that certain indices such as Gross National Product (GNP) *per capita*, the percentage of the population in non-primary sectors of production, numbers of radios, telephones, and so on, are simple unitary indicators of development. Two correlation theories of the media and development have emerged from this basic approach – the simple association and the causal. Unesco (1961), among others, have drawn up league tables of various modernization indices including urbanization, literacy, and GNP. Rank order correlations between these indices and media consumption figures show very close associations between the two sets of data. This approach sees modernization as a composite of distinct developments. Indices such as urbanization are expanded rubrics covering a wide variety of possible instances. *Per capita* indices of income include no account of income dispersion and distribution, while measures of media artifacts *per capita* give no indication of media use.

The simplest causal models, as in the work of Daniel Lerner (1957), present figures showing the percentage of urban dwellers required for literacy to develop to a point where the media too can join in the promotion of development.[4] More sophisticated models have come from political scientists concerned with the emergence of democracy and its antecedent conditions. McCrone and Cnudde (1967), for example, erecting causal pathways from prediction equations based on correlations, suggest that education and literacy require urbanization and then contribute to the growth of the media, so that 'democratic development occurs when mass communications permeate society'. In other words, peasants come to town, learn to read, study the newspapers, and vote wisely. Apart from the explicit caveats of the model-builders, among which are the exclusion from debate of all other possible variables and the assumption that political development is a dependent variable, there is the further question of the meaning attached to the indicators. Education is the number in school, not a system of cultural transmission; mass communication is the number of radios, with no concern for consumption or content. Democracy is defined by the vote. The fallacy of such sequential imagery is, of course, to conceive the polity as a distinct institution dependent on other institutions for its form and effectiveness. Literacy, education, and mass communications are as much the result of decision-making, i.e. dependent on 'the polity', as they are antecedent conditions for its democratic construction.

Differentiation theories of social change portray modernization as the emergence of role-segmentation, institutional differentiation, and the adoption of new values appropriate to such changes. This view takes vertical cleavages and value-systems to be paramount in the dynamics of social change. Roles in traditional societies are portrayed as particularistic, ascriptive, and functionally diffuse. Modernization is the slide to the other end of the pattern variables.

It is worth questioning how far role-specificity is a characteristic of 'modern' society as distinct from an important part of its mythology, and, conversely, to what extent is a lack of institutional separation actually characteristic of traditional societies?[5] But acceptance of differentiation theories has led media researchers to concentrate on the use of the media to promote 'appropriate' values for modernity, normally the industrial work ethic and the universalistic slogans of free enterprise in partial disguise.

The key concern has been with the ability of the individual to project himself into the role of another, conceptualized as 'empathy'. The media must expand the imagination of transitional man by 'giving him a high capacity for identification with new aspects of his environment' (Lerner 1958). A mobile psyche creates a mobile society. Apart from methodological objections to research using this concept,[6] research in developed societies has shown that the urban poor are equally low on empathy scales, suggesting that the perception of structural constraints mitigates against upward mobility far more than does an inert imagination.[7]

A third approach to change sees external stimulation as the cure for a static society. The stranglehold of apathy, stoicism, fatalism, and simple idleness is held to have gripped the peasantry of the Third World until brought to life by external aid, knowledge, assistance, and the induction of new ideas. The general influence of such theories on media research has been to concentrate on the role of ideas in social change and the part the media can play in conveying stimulative images from the technically-advanced to the inert, unimaginative Third World. Everett Rogers's (1969) work on the diffusion of new ideas about agricultural technology has been particularly influential in this area.

All these theories can be criticized theoretically and empirically in much greater depth than we have space for here in a brief overview. First, they are all grounded in psychological theories of change. Development is conceived as a process of individual enlightenment, an aggregate of personality adjustments producing new types of people. Seminal to this conception are the theories of Hagen (1962) and McClelland (1961), emphasizing child-rearing and the 'mental virus' model of innovativeness as an individual characteristic, and innovative individualistic entrepreneurship as the dominant role in social advance.

The need for change in the individual psyche is a recurrent theme in media research. Pool suggests that 'it is only that kind of internal change in the latent structure of his [i.e. the peasant's] attitudes that would produce self-sustaining movement towards modernization' (Pool 1963). Millikan emphasizes the point when he says that 'the dramatic upheavals in the economics, the politics, and social structures of the new nations . . . all have their origins in a radical alteration in the perceptions of the average man'. He concludes '. . . economic development requires the substitution of a built-in propensity to innovate for the more traditional view . . .' (Millikan 1967).

Second, communication and development theories adopt the notion of deferred gratification, the middle-class idealization of individual mobility reaping its just rewards, as the central value the media can convey. Lerner remarks that 'by consistently and vividly associating reward with effort, communication can give shape to the transformation of life-ways required for genuine development' (1967). He is echoed by Schramm (1967) who claims that communications 'must mobilize people to tighten their belts and harden their muscles, work longer and wait for their rewards'. The peasant view of 'perceived limited good' – the world has only so much to offer so why try – must be reformed into the mobile worker view – 'the world has infinite riches to offer if only I work hard enough to deserve them'. Lerner (1970) makes this quite explicit when he sermonizes on how communications 'will have to teach many millions of simple folk around the world to associate personal reward with personal effort, to acquire a work ethic appropriate both to what they want and what they get'. The danger he fears is that 'wants' will outstrip 'gets', so communicators should also restrain intemperate demands.

A third strand running through these theories is the ethnocentric identification of a western middle-class life-style with that deemed appropriate for emergent peoples. The media should portray incentives to stimulate the effort modernization requires. Pool, for example, remarks that 'the media show what opportunities exist for using new commodities such as electricity, refrigeration, or automotive transportation (1966a). In Pool's case, the need to beat the communists at their own life-style promotion in the Third World is paramount. It ought also to be questioned whether the media portray 'what opportunities exist', or whether they portray what opportunities ought to exist.

A fourth and related assumption of such media theories is that communications foster the values of individual entrepreneurship. Yet if capital accumulation has been difficult for the indigenous population in colonial countries, even where a commercial tradition exists, the restraints of colonial control provide a more convincing explanation than lack of initiative.

Fifth, Pool, Schram, Lerner, and other researchers who have looked at media content in this area have been criticized for ignoring the 'action frame', for concerning themselves with discrete images and isolated messages rather than 'the role of the communications media in defining broad types or forms of action' (Peacock 1969). This is, of course, a general criticism applicable to much content analysis. But in the development field it is a direct result of the assumptions that the goals of modernization and the role of the media in defining and diffusing them are beyond dispute, and that the concern of analysts can thus be limited to the particular forms and instances of such diffusion.

Finally, and more generally, these approaches share an ahistorical view of development, a view which takes two related forms. The first is the conception of developing countries emerging from static isolation, requiring an external stimulus to shake them into the twentieth century. The incompatibility of this view with the history of underdeveloped countries, many of which have regressed under external rule from advanced and sophisticated civilizations, has not eliminated the attitude from media research. The functionalist search for the pre-requisites of the modern nation-state systematically skirts around the existence of an international social system, initially of colonialism, subsequently of economic imperialism, to which these separate states are tied. The second form of the ahistorical vision is to conceive the future as a bigger version of the present – the liberal theory of progress–modernism is the accumulation of more consumer goods and the adoption of values and ideals tried and tested in the western world. Findings about the media in advanced countries are extrapolated and adapted to circumstances elsewhere, which are themselves perceived as mere embryonic microcosms of western capitalism.

III

The history of colonialism had an equal impact on the growth of the international news media. Towards the end of the nineteenth century the newly established European news agencies concluded a series of cartel agreements by means of which they divided the world between them, according to the prevailing imperial spheres of influence. These first links in the international media system set a precedent for much that was to follow as the media in developed and developing societies alike became progressively more involved in the corporate capitalist economy. In recent years many individual media have been absorbed into large-scale, multi-functional corporations, diversified vertically, like Reed-IPC, through the various production processes, or horizontally, like EMI, through a whole range of leisure activities.

For many of the corporations in the media and leisure industries success in overseas markets has become an increasingly important cornerstone of their survival and profitability. As the Chairman of EMI has said 'the market for entertainment . . . is transcending national frontiers more and more. The Group and its artists can no longer regard Britain, the United States or even, for that matter, the continents of Europe or North America as the only sources for their audience' (EMI 1971). However, the most profitable overseas markets may still be within the developed world, as trade between developed countries takes an increasing share of the total flow of world trade. An additional factor to be considered here is the political hostility towards foreign ownership expressed in many newly independent countries. This has encouraged British media companies to withdraw from capital involvement, leaving the media they established in government hands. A pattern has begun to emerge in Africa, which may well vary in other areas of the Third World, whereby the foreign company has recouped its initial investment and withdrawn, retaining only links with the media organization by servicing it and the market it has created.

One such service, which Keith Buchanan (1972) has identified as a major part of the 'culture offensive' of imperialism, is the syndication of television programming throughout the world. Newly founded broadcasting organizations, lacking resources in money and personnel, cannot afford not to buy popular American films and series. These are available very cheaply throughout the Third World owing to a system of charging what each national market will bear (Schiller 1969: 88–9). In 1965 it was estimated that ABC could reach 60 per cent of all world television outside the US, while NBC syndicated 125 film series in 83 countries to more than 300 television stations. One of these, Bonanza, was seen each week by over 350 million people in 60 countries. By comparison with the American networks the British television companies and the BBC at present play only a small part in the international programme market.

British organizations have been more closely involved, however, in another aspect of the 'cultural offensive' – the establishment of indigenous media organizations and the provision of education and training facilities for indigenous media personnel. Most of the radio services in ex-British territories were initially founded and run by seconded BBC staff who transplanted BBC styles of organization and programme-making. Experience of the BBC World Service, and the possibility of training in Britain, encouraged indigenous staff to concentrate on the BBC as a model. Such activities can be interpreted as disinterested philanthropy. A statement by J. M. Coltart of the Thomson Organization makes the point on behalf of his organization's investments in the Third World and of the Thomson training schemes in Cardiff and Glasgow for foreign editors and journalists.[8]

One consequence of such activities, however, is the establishment in developing countries of production styles and techniques founded on experience in the developed world. Programme-makers and journalists in underdeveloped societies are drawn into a common international media culture. This contains models and standards for the 'good' or 'successful' story or programme, based on examples from British and American media. The result is that even the indigenously produced parts of the press and broadcasting output tend to follow the pattern set by established western media.

Journalists are usually drawn into the international media system after training by 'stringing' as part-time correspondents for European or American media. Such jobs carry both financial reward and prestige. Prestige comes from writing for a western medium, thus ensuring once again that similar standards and approaches are adopted. 'Stringers' are at the bottom of the complex international network for newsgathering. Common definitions and criteria for news are necessary to make the various parts of this network – stringers, correspondents, agencies, the foreign desks of recipient media – articulate together.

The five international news agencies – two American, one British, one French, one Russian – occupy a central place in the network. One of the reasons behind the establishment of national agencies in Europe in the nineteenth century was to ensure that the views and interests of the nations concerned were represented on the international scene. More recently studies have shown that the international agencies, with the exception of Agence France–Presse (AFP), still concentrate on news from their country of origin (Schramm 1964; Adams 1964). Throughout the world, news organizations, even the better staffed prestige newspapers, rely heavily on agency reports for breadth and depth of coverage. But agency correspondents are not evenly distributed over the surface of the globe. For example, Associated Press (AP) has 111 bureaux in the USA, twenty-five in Europe, sixteen in Asia, thirteen in Central/Southern America, five in Africa, and one in Australia. Reuters has seven bureaux in the USA, fifteen in Western Europe, five in Russia and east Europe, thirteen in Asia, eleven in Central/Southern America, eleven in Africa, and nine in the Middle East. The agencies' aim is to serve the national news organizations, their customers. But the familiar question arising from discussions of mass media output, that of the relative primacy of supply and demand, applies also to the agency services, especially in the case of developing countries whose market position is generally not strong enough to give their organizations a say in deciding the news they get. With the introduction of television, the news agencies' services have been supplemented by the syndication of news film from the American television networks and from two film agencies, Visnews and UPITN (a co-operative venture run by United Press International and Independent Television News), centred on London.

This geographical concentration is reinforced by the underlying pattern of physical communications. Initially, in the late nineteenth and early twentieth century, cables were laid to link the colonial powers to their territories in the developing world. These links are only slowly being supplemented by overland links between adjacent Third World countries (Hachten 1971; Ainslie 1968). In most cases it is still necessary for news copy or agency film material from one country in the Third World to travel through the news capitals of Britain or America before it can reach an adjacent developing nation. The developing nation's dependence on particular news capitals has been further encouraged by discriminatory cable and freight rates. These have the additional consequence of making the outward flow from such centres cheaper than the inward, thus helping to make the news flow from the developed world to the developing larger than that in the opposite direction or that between developing nations themselves.

In these various ways the press and broadcasting media of the developing world are bound into the international media system. To call this a 'cultural offensive' is misleading only in so far as the phrase implies too large an element of coherent planning behind a system that is largely made up of a variety of organizations pursuing their own economic interests.

IV

These features of the international media system, especially those involved in the gathering and distribution of news, also have important consequences for the image of the developing world which it is possible to derive from western media.[9] As shown in *Table 1* (opposite), staff correspondents of the British news media tend to be concentrated in the same American and west European capitals. The distribution of correspondents to the American news media follows a similar pattern. In 1969 Kliesch found that of the 1 462 newsmen employed overseas, 793 were stationed in Europe, 332 in Asia and Australasia, 169 in Latin America and Canada, 76 in the Middle East, and 92 in Africa (Hachten 1971: 53). Of the last group only twenty-four were staff correspondents. Apart from 'stringers' and correspondents permanently stationed abroad, the British media have come to rely more and more on sending out teams from home to cover 'important' stories as they break. Such teams are able to exploit the same physical means of communication, the airline and cable routes, which play such a large part in determining the communication pattern within the Third World itself.

The same set of social, organizational, and occupational factors lie behind the production of foreign as of domestic news. Foreign news is a special case, in so far as it originates from a different range of sources and is processed and transmitted by specialized agents. Galtung and Ruge (1965) have provided one of the most concise accounts of the general characteristics of foreign news. They also relate these characteristics to some of the organizational and occupational factors that account for them, in particular those connected with the visibility and acceptability of different events to news organizations and their staff. Events and personalities make news, for example, rather than structures and processes. Negative events are generally more visible than positive, but to be acceptable they must come within the realm of the expected

TABLE 1

Location of foreign correspondents to the British daily news media
(May 1971)

	USA	W. Europe	Russia and E. Europe	Middle East	Asia and India	C. and S. America	Africa‡	Australasia
Newspapers:								
The Times	5	5	2	1	3	1	2	1
Guardian	3	2	—	2	—	—	—	—
Daily Telegraph	8	10	1	1	3	1	2	1
Financial Times	4	6	—	—	—	—	—	—
Daily Express	8	8	—	1	1	1	1	—
Daily Mail*	2	1	—	—	1	—	—	—
Daily Mirror	5	8	—	—	1	—	—	—
Sun		No Information						
Broadcasting:†								
BBC	4	4	1	3	3	1	1	—
ITN	1	—	—	—	—	—	—	—

* After absorbing *Daily Sketch* (11 May 1971).

† Bureaux rather than individuals.

‡ Four of the six British correspondents in Africa are stationed in South Africa, one is in Rhodesia, one has a roving brief.

and the possible. In a sense news are 'knowns'. Elite people and elite countries make news.

The close attention given to some areas of the world and the little given to others are the most characteristic features of the limited amount of foreign news which appears in the British media. A small-scale content analysis of four British and three Nigerian media for two weeks in November 1971 showed proportions of international news of just over one-fifth for the *Daily Mirror*, just over one-third for the two television networks' main bulletins and just over two-fifths for *The Times* (see *Table 2* opposite). The definition of international news included not only stories with a dateline abroad but also those with a predominantly foreign reference. Thus, for example, the announcement of the proposed Rhodesia settlement in the House of Commons occurred within this two-week period. This story provides a particularly clear example of a sub-type of international news – 'foreign news at home' – including cases where decisions, speeches, or actions are made at home but relate to the affairs of a foreign country, or where a foreign national visits the home country. Another sub-type – 'home news abroad' – is the mirror-image. Cases such as decisions being taken in America which affect British industry (Rolls-Royce and the RB211 engine) or such as ministerial trips overseas (like Sir Alec Douglas Home's visit to Rhodesia) are examples which occurred within this period. Emphasizing the domestic connexions of foreign news is one way of trying to combat audience disinterest in the subject.

A large proportion of the foreign news in all four British media came from the United States or western Europe. In general it seems that the less space a medium gives to international news, the more its coverage is likely to show the typical characteristics of foreign coverage in exaggerated form. The *Daily Mirror*, for example, showed the greatest concentration on the USA and western Europe. The same paper and the two television networks provided almost no news from Africa except for the Rhodesia settlement story. The relatively high proportion of international news coming from South Africa/Rhodesia and from Asia, excluding China, illustrates another characteristic of foreign news, that, given a crisis or a military conflict (the India–Pakistan war broke out during this period), resources can be mobilized to cover it. Even so, other factors will be important in deciding the level of mobilization, in particular, the historic connexions of empire and the contemporary connexions of trade and political or economic influence (Ostgaard 1965).

TABLE 2

International news in selected British and Nigerian media :
percentage of news hole for two weeks in November 1971

| Media | International news | Of which | | | No. of international stories |
		Foreign news at home	Home news abroad	Real foreign news	
Daily Mirror	23·6	29·6	19·2	41·9	173
The Times	43·1	2·8	5·8	91·3	367
BBC TV	38·7	12·5	29·3	58·2	58
ITN	35·0	38·5	21·5	40·0	49
Daily Times	30·6	14·8	4·9	80·2	208
NBC Radio	41·3	24·6	4·2	71·1	65
NBC TV	64·3	6·8	9·1	84·1	110

Definitions

International news: All stories from non-domestic locations or about non-domestic persons or institutions.

Foreign news at home: Story event located in media country, but with reference to an overseas news event, or involving foreign nationals in the media country.

Home news abroad: Overseas location involving media country nationals or referring to events in the media country.

Real foreign news: News events occurring outside media country not classified as home news abroad.

News hole: Space (in time or column-inches) available to news, less advertising, cartoons, editorial, features, and, in the case of the British media, sports.

The distinctive image of developing nations in the British media is a combined result of the low, selective attention given to them and the characteristic features of news through which events are perceived. The first component of the image is that of nations subject to repetitive political or military crises. Independent Africa is fast joining South America as another continent of military coup and counter-coup. This is not to say that such coups do not take place but that they provide some of the few circumstances in which a developing nation surfaces into the consciousness of the developed world. This image has important consequences in contributing to a particular view of development.

A second component of the image is that attention is given to direct British or western interests, be they political, as in the case of Rhodesia, military, as in the case of Malta, or economic, as in the case of both. Economic stories tend to emphasize the obvious distribution of exports, aid, or the provision of technical facilities and assistance in a more personalized way. In the few cases, such as oil, where developing nations have been able to threaten the interests of the western world, the issue has been translated in the media into a threat to western consumers' interests. Economic stories make up a very low proportion of total foreign news output but aid, dependency, and economic interests tend to emerge as themes within the context of more overtly political stories, as, for example, in the reporting of the 1972 Ghana coup.

Attention to specific interests shades off into a third component of the image, a more general tendency to view developments in the Cold War perspective of east/west conflict. Aid from a communist country attracts considerable interest, especially if it is backed by personnel, as in the case of the Chinese building the Tanzam railway. Again, however, the clearest examples occur in relation to political crises, when the pedigrees of those involved are assessed and events examined for their similarity to other successful and unsuccessful communist coups. Theodore Draper has argued, for example, that in the reporting of the Dominican crises of 1965, reporters from the American media grasped the opportunity to report events as a 'communist takeover', partly because they were led in that direction by diplomatic briefings and partly because that was what they expected following on from Cuba (Draper 1965).

A fourth component of the image, a component that appears in a variety of guises, is the tendency to simplify the political and social structures of the country concerned. The media's focus on the political leadership of a country in foreign news reporting is clear enough in the case of the USA or western Europe, but becomes even sharper in the case of countries in the Third World. Generally speaking, only the national leader of most developing countries receives any regular attention, and then the point made above should remind us that that is often only in the context of the coup in which he was replaced. Conflicts which are not palace revolutions but involve large numbers tend to be interpreted in terms of manifest symbols such as tribalism or religion, without reference to the underlying structure of divergent interests. Such conflict is likely to seem futile and pointless since the key concepts and categories necessary to understand developments are missing. The war between the Bahutu and the Batutsi in Rwanda in 1959 is one case in which the presentation of conflict as tribal directly obscured its nature as a revolt of peasants against a landed aristocracy.[10] Tribalism also confused the issue in the reporting of the recent Nigerian Civil War, a particularly good example of various aspects of the image of development.[11] The Biafran authorities were quick to spot ways in which they could exploit the news values of the western media by supplying human interest photographs and atrocity stories directly to correspondents and through the Markpress Agency in Switzerland.

Simplification can also be found in the use of national, regional, or racial stereotypes which can be invoked as explanations of developments, whether important or trivial. It is well known, for example, that excitable Latin Americans mob referees at football matches, that picturesque Africans dance for the Queen, and that the Japanese are suicidal, homicidal, or unscrupulously industrious.

The fifth component of the image of development is less a characteristic of the type of news than a property of the stories over time. Foreign stories, just like domestic stories, tend to follow predictable story cycles. Himmelstrand (1968) has pointed out the way in which 'self-infatuation cycles' develop in the coverage of particular stories. At the first stage fragmentary information is available to the western media which they are likely to interpret in terms of apparently similar events; for example, in the recent Ghana coup the tendency was to see Busia as another Nkrumah. This sets the pattern for subsequent selection and interpretation so that the initial perspective becomes established and finally passes into history. The range of such perspectives is itself very limited, however, in accordance with the other components of the development image.

A second aspect of story cycles appears in the way that foreign events are translated into domestic issues ('foreign news at home'), by asserting or assuming that the national interests of the developed country are at stake. In the two weeks covered by the content analysis, the India/Pakistan war story became a story about the possible exercise of British influence after only a few days of rumoured fighting. More startling, however, was the story cycle which occurred at an earlier stage of the same crisis when cholera broke out among the refugees from East Pakistan. On 1 June 1971 *The Times* led on the epidemic; nine days later it had become a British parliamentary story – 'Labour Clash on Bengal Aid forces Commons Debate Today'. By the following day, British influence had taken effect – 'Britain's Response to Cholera Crisis astounds India as Deaths Fall'. Even when they cannot be translated into 'foreign news at home', the affairs of developing countries are often dealt with on the assumption that the important decisions are taken in the capital of one of the great powers.

This account of the image of development has shown the various ways in which the affairs of developing nations are simplified and kept at a distance by the British media. The image is founded on an assumption, usually implicit, that the normal course for a developing country is to aspire to western economic and political standards with the help of aid and trade.

V

The conventions, traditions, and structures which have produced this imagery in the media of the developed world have been reproduced in those of the developing countries. The different colonial traditions of England and France in West Africa are reflected in the emergence of the mass media in their respective territories. So-called indirect rule in the anglophone countries permitted early use of the press as an instrument of nationalism and a far looser hold over communications than existed in the tightly centralized, predominantly expatriate media of francophone Africa. The African media have in many ways gone through a similar but compressed cycle (of political patronage, editorial entrepreneurship, to a final basis in international industrial finance) to the media in the United Kingdom, with the variation of more direct government control at this last stage.

Newspapers had been introduced fairly early on into many territories for missionary and educational use, as well as to serve the needs of resident Europeans. But it was the nationalism of the educated indigenous elites, particularly in British West Africa, and in north Africa, which provided the greatest stimulus to the growth of the African press.[12] The success of the nationalist press was commercial as well as political, attracting the financial interest of European media groups. The International Publishing Corporation, for example, bought the Nigerian *Daily Times* in 1947, and furthered its interests with the *Daily Graphic* and *Sunday Mirror* in Accra, and the Freetown *Daily Mail*. The Thomson Organization was also deeply involved in the African press but is now concentrating its efforts on television.

The post-independence period has seen increasing intervention in and control of the press by newly independent African governments. Broadcasting has in most cases been a government monopoly *ab initio*. The prestige of television, the concern with foreign ownership of the press, and the belief in the power of the media for rapid mobilization of nascent political support for the new regimes have all contributed to this development.

Radio developed in Africa in the inter-war period largely as a 'news-from-home' service for Europeans. The boom in broadcasting, however, had to await the transistor in the 1960s. Between 1951 and 1961 the number of radios on the continent increased from 350 000 to nearly twelve million (Hachten 1971: 19).

The philosophy of government involvement ostensibly suggests some autonomy for African media both from domestic commercial pressures and from external controlling interests in the international media corporations. But this is to misunderstand the nature of the dependence of these media on the international system, both in terms of the organization of the flow of material through the system and its effects on the routines of production within the dependent nation. The effects are particularly clear in news and current affairs.

As a result of their training by western experts or in western centres the traditions and occupational ideologies of Nigerian journalists are essentially those of their counterparts in the developed world. Their definitions of a 'good news story' and appropriate journalistic methods and attitudes are virtually identical to those of Fleet Street. Part-time work for European agencies or media is a potent attraction for poorly paid African journalists and their perception of the requirements of these organizations sharply focuses the shape and content of their daily news production.

Western training and influence bring with them, however, a journalistic credo including commitments to occupational autonomy and freedom of expression, which find themselves in sharp opposition to the situation in which the African journalist works. Tensions develop between his aspirations and the opportunity to fulfil them, which are resolved by the adaptation of the former. In Nigeria, for example, government control is not dictatorial or absolute, but it none the less represents a real invasion of professional autonomy for the journalist trained in the fourth estate ideology. By concentracting on good 'professional' treatment of government handouts or by accepting the definition of the situation as one of national crisis, the journalist is able to modify his occupational ideology without rupturing it. In any case, the expression of autonomy is in conventional European terms and forms.[13]

The journalist also suffers from a situation of role-conflict where his acceptance of development goals as a citizen and political actor in a developing country, including the instrumental use of the media to further these goals, is irreconcilable with his trained belief in news as an objective capture of the world's events and in the news media as honest brokers of non-purposive material. One possible way of resolving the issue is by a sharp division in the output he produces, news from features, or bulletins from current affairs. This solves the journalist's dilemma; it does not, however, emancipate him from the constraints of the material available to him.

Technology is a further factor defining the routines of news presentation. Television is a visual medium and news-film a crucial input. For the Nigerian Broadcasting Corporation, as for most other African television stations, Visnews is their only regular source of foreign news film. The availability of Visnews film is often the crucial factor in selecting what news events to present and the news coverage will often revolve around the film item and the commentary supplied with it from London. The influence of Visnews is also seen in the high percentage of time devoted to foreign news by Nigerian television. Far from being unable to convey news of the international scene, the media in an underdeveloped nation tend to carry a high percentage of world coverage, even though few, if any, have their own foreign correspondents. As *Table 2* shows, over 64 per cent of NBC-TV news time was devoted to international news, by far the highest proportion in any of the media analysed.

One cause of this is the comparative difficulty in acquiring domestic news. Staff shortages, communications deficiencies, and in many cases, political sensitivity make home news problematic while foreign news is flowing in from the agencies. Most newspapers and broadcasting organizations subscribe to at least one of the major news agencies. The high cost of the service plus its simplicity in usage help to ensure that maximum use is made of it. Where time is scarce and trained and proficient staff are in short supply, the temptation to use ready-made copy looms large.

The mapping of the world provided by the client media follows closely the distribution of agency correspondents and the interests of their major western customers. The content analysis showed that the Nigerian media devoted more attention to the developed world than they did to other countries in Africa, Asia, or Latin America. Nigeria's francophone neighbours, for example, received scant attention and even the anglophone areas of West Africa fared little better.

Virtually all foreign news in the Nigerian media is provided by agencies, but even before it reaches Nigeria it has gone through considerable editing. The agencies provide special services for Third World customers, preparing, for example, a West Africa file to be sent to recipients in this area comprising an edited version of their full world service. This includes items that the agency headquarters believe will be of interest plus a digest of world events as the agency perceives their relevance to the customer. Inevitably the selection and interpretation is through European or American eyes.

Given the congruence in organization and the dependence in the relationship between the media of the Third World and of the developed nations, it is no surprise to find that the characteristics of news are the same in both. In a study of the Tanzanian press Condon (1967) has noted that news of other African countries, sparse as it is, follows the western focus on crisis, violence, and the superficial forms of political disruption and instability. Similarly, in the Nigerian media, the largest number of stories was devoted to the actions of political leaders, endlessly recording their minor speeches and airport statements, their travels, meetings, and ceremonial activities. Thus, as in the west, political action is defined and portrayed by activities of incumbent elites, and international relations by the public trappings of diplomacy. Conflict and drama are provided by the familiar concentration on events and personalities.

Through transposition, however, the leaders portrayed are those of the major powers. At least as much attention is given to political leaders in the United States and Europe as to those in other Third World countries. The legacy of Cold War imagery can be found in much of the material supplied, particularly by the American agencies. Minor elections in east Europe, Kremlinology, trivial meetings between minor communist officials, reports on technological or military developments in the eastern bloc, all crop up with surprising frequency in African media served by American agencies. Agency coverage of Third World areas is often in terms of the Cold War struggle for influence. As Tom Mboya has written 'the news . . . is often, if not always, related to the already biased and prejudiced mind that keeps asking such questions as 'Is this pro-East or pro-West?' Very few, if any of the world's press ask such logical, in our view, and simple questions as: 'Is this pro-African?' (International Press Institute 1964.)

Where coverage of other countries in the Third World is extensive, it is entirely the result of renewed western interest. In the two-week period we analysed, attention to Asia, normally much neglected, rose considerably due to the India–Pakistan war. African media cover African news assiduously, but only as it is provided and interpreted by the London, Paris, or New York news desks of the agencies.[14] African

I

journalists' awareness of common purpose and problems among countries in the Third World is only able to find expression through extensive coverage of the UN. By concentration on the quasi-parliamentary UN, international relations are contained within the comfortable western imagery of international democracy. The management of conflict and dissent is thus handled in the international context in a way exactly parallel to that applied to deviance, dissent, and change within a single society.

VI

The conflict between the conventional ideals of journalism and the varying visions of its role in developing societies frequently emerges as a contrast between government intervention and a free press. Thus Nkrumah's strictures that the press 'is an integral part of our society, with which its purposes are in consonance', and that 'we do not believe that there are two sides to every question . . . we are partisan' (IPI 1965), are in fundamental opposition to the freedom of the press concept, with its connotations of laissez-faire and free trade in information.

The notion of a free press and the free flow of information, like the analogous arguments for free trade, presuppose a system whose members participate with equal opportunity and power. This is no more true for news than it is for other commodities. The rhetoric of the free press and the free flow of information is ideologically congruent with the interests of its proponents and is a persuasive rationalization for the continued satisfaction of those interests. The relationship between the slogans of free trade and the triumph of international private enterprise is precisely that between the commercial base of the media and the symbols of press freedom. So far as the developing country itself is concerned, however, the argument for a free press draws partly on the fourth estate ideology derived from the philosophy of western democracy, and partly on simple theories of development.

Such an attempt to win the argument every way is apparent in much of the traditional social scientific approaches to media and development discussed above in section II. For the most part researchers have assumed that media output is directly instrumental for development goals. In making this assumption they seem to have closed their eyes to actual media content or to have concentrated on the few explicitly educational sectors that are generally marginal to the overall media output. Interest in the type of media organization and production has generally taken the form of assessing such western characteristics as professionalism, technical efficiency, audience penetration, and political independence. A residual argument remains, however, for those who recognize the predominance of commercial entertainment. Such entertainment is also characteristic of developed societies; therefore it must have latent functions for development, if only through the presentation of a consumption-oriented life-style.

In the course of this paper we have argued that the conventional definitions of news and the routines of newsgathering make the media not so much catalysts for social change, as cultural mechanisms for maintaining social order. At the broadest level news can be explained as part of the cultural system of modern society, a mechanism whereby developing conflicts are surveyed and a preliminary attempt made to assimilate them or handle them as part of continuing social experience. In a narrower perspective, news is gathered, processed, and presented in a variety of organizations by a variety of occupational groups. Organizational processes and occupational cultures related to the ends of the particular groups and organizations in question mesh together within the peculiar commercial and political situation of the news media, to ensure that the news output fits into the political culture. This can be exemplified within the boundaries of one country by examining domestic news to show how deviance and dissent, which are a threat to the status quo, are characterized as the actions of ephemeral minorities outside the political system or as assimilable within that system through such institutions of conflict management as parliament and the other machinery of consensus. By concentrating on foreign news in the developed and developing world the analysis has shown that the social order being maintained is not confined within the boundaries of a particular nation-state. The culture of the international media system is consonant with the requirements of the international capitalist economy of which it is a part.

Some of the ways in which the production of news contributes to this mechanism of control have emerged from the discussion of the reciprocal images of developed and developing societies in sections IV and V above. In various ways news output tends to neutralize social conflict. For example, the concentration on events and personalities suggests that solutions are to be expected from the actions of established leaders. Preoccupation with negativity and human interest leads to the view that all men of goodwill can unite to abhor violence.[15] The tendency to focus on symbols, to the exclusion of structure and process, is exemplified by a concern with violence rather than with conflict. As they become visible, conflict and change are referred to the agents of social control and conflict resolution. These include such international bodies as the UN but are predominantly the various western leaderships. Foreign stories are transposed into the institutions of conflict management of the developed countries, for example, in Britain, parliament.

Alongside these general mechanisms, specific consequences can be identified in each type of society following on from the image provided of the other. In the western world developing societies appear as the backward fiefs of individual rulers, dependent on western aid and support, whose affairs should be managed by the great powers in view of their wisdom and experience. In developing countries news output also tends to obscure national interests and the interests of different classes within nations, helping to attach economic and social elites to western society and culture. The scope for developing countries to share interests and problems and develop a common culture among themselves is severely limited.

In concentrating on news this paper has focused on a particular organizational and occupational system available within society for the production of knowledge. Much work needs to be done on how this production is carried on, but in general, the type of knowledge is a product of organizational and occupational routines set within particular economic and political conditions. In the course of the paper attention has also been given to an alternative knowledge-producing system, that of academic social science research. Much of this research shows the prevalence of similar assumptions about development that are to be found in the media; for example, that it is based on individual rather than social change, that it is induced and directed from outside. Many have looked to academia as the last haven of the free-floating intellectual, detached from the concerns of the political and economic system. This view seems particularly inapplicable to the academics whose research we have examined and it seems likely that a closer analysis of this particular part of the academic knowledge-producing system would show that it is bound in as closely to the economic and social structure as is the production system for journalistic knowledge.[16]

Nevertheless, it is possible for alternative paradigms to be generated through academia. There has also been the development in the media in recent years of various 'alternative' forms of communication following approaches explicitly in contrast to that of the 'conventional' media. These developments, however, are highly insecure and marginal to the main output. Such considerations point to a final flaw in the traditional account of communication and modernization. The argument has been that modernization involves a progressive differentiation and specialization of functions in society including the agents of socialization and cultural diffusion. The alternative account would suggest that these agencies, including the media, produce functional and plausible accounts of events in society. In spite of organizational differentiation, these agencies are integrated into and dependent on the power structure in society and their output helps to maintain the stability of that structure. In the production of knowledge, specialization does not lead to autonomy.

Notes

1 This is an abbreviated version of the paper given at the 1972 BSA Conference. The content analysis described was originally presented in full tabular form and inquiries about it should be addressed to the authors.

2 Our concentration on news reflects work we have been doing on the production and content of news in three countries. This paper is a preliminary statement of the approach adopted for that study and draws on data already available from it.

3 For a case study at this level see Halloran *et al.* (1970).

4 Schramm and Ruggels (1967) were unable to replicate Lerner's figures but do not question the theory.

5 These questions have been influentially explored in Frank (1971).

6 For other criticisms of empathy research see, *inter alia*, Grunig (1969) and Smith (1971, Ch. 5).

7 Gans (1962) study of American slum-dwellers, for example, shows his 'urban villagers' scoring poorly on empathy scales.

8 He remarks that, 'As we in the Thomson Organisation have moved through country after country we realise this is not a profit-making venture but a service we must render' (Coltart, 1963).

9 This paragraph and the following section draw on Elliott and Golding (1973).

10 See Hachten (1971: 82). The same imagery of 'tribal massacres' was resurrected in 1972 in the Burundi troubles in June, providing a picture of a sudden flaring of primitive inter-tribal hatreds. 'Background' pieces referring only to 1959 and 1965 merely re-emphasized the impression of recurrent and irrational tribal fighting. It is arguable that the portrayal of the Northern Ireland conflict by the British media has followed similar lines, emphasizing available symbolizations of

conflict, in this case religion, rather than deeper structural conflicts of interest.

11 For opposing views on the coverage of the Nigerian Civil War by the world's news media see Forsyth (1969) and Himmelstrand (1969). We are grateful to Professor Himmelstrand for allowing us to read an English translation of his book. See also Himmelstrand (1968).

12 E. W. Blyden, a Virgin Islander, was preaching political autonomy in his *Lagos Weekly Record* as early as 1891, and fifty Nigerian newspapers were registered before 1937, nearly half of them with the word 'Nigerian' in their masthead (Coleman 1963; Coker 1960). The nationalist press in Africa was a training ground and important tool for men like Azikiwe, Nkrumah, Bourguiba, Kaunda, and Nyerere.

13 In one incident observed in Lagos, journalists were poorly treated by a Federal Commissioner at an over-abrupt and unhelpful press conference. On his return the Lagos newsmen boycotted the arrival and its attendant press conference in retaliation. A brave action given the Nigerian situation, but one nevertheless accepting the conventional view of news and the airport arrival or statement, however insignificant, as a news event.

14 Probably the biggest African news event during our content analysis period was the Rhodesia settlement negotiations. These were covered extensively in Nigerian media, via Visnews film and agency wires, including all the human interest stories on Sir Alec's days off. The 'African viewpoint' eventually emerged in severe editorial condemnation of the settlement terms, but news pages continued to use uncut agency coverage of the 'successful completion' of the talks.

15 Coverage of the Nigerian Civil War again provides a prime case. A more topical illustration was the editorial in the *Sunday Times* of 2 April, 1972, linking the deaths of three innocent victims of violence in a plea for an end to 'moral indifference to violence'.

16 Ithiel de Sola Pool, a central figure in communications research, has argued strongly for the closer alliance between academic social science and the political establishment (1966b). Much American communications research in developing areas has been financed by agencies such as the Defence Department, and examples of the service-research it has provided can be seen in the accounts in House of Representatives (1967).

References

ADAMS, J. B. 1964. A Qualitative Analysis of Domestic and Foreign News on the AP TA wire. *Gazette* 10: 285.

AINSLIE, R. 1968. *The Press in Africa*. New York: Walker and Co.

BUCHANAN, K. 1972. *The Geography of Empire*. Nottingham: Spokesman Books.

COKER, I. 1960. *The Nigerian Press 1929–59*. Ibadan: Ibadan University.

COLEMAN, J. S. 1963. *Nigeria: Background to Nationalism*. Berkeley: University of California Press.

COLTART, J. M. 1963. The Influence of Newspapers and Television in Africa. *African Affairs*: July.

CONDON, J. C. 1967. Nation Building and Image Building in the Tanzanian Press. *Journal of Modern African Studies* 5 (3): 335–54.

DRAPER, T. 1965. The Dominican Crisis. *Commentary*: December.

EMI 1971. Annual Report and Accounts.

ELLIOTT, P. and GOLDING, P. 1973. The News Media and Foreign Affairs. In Groom and Boardman (eds.) 1973.

FORSYTH, F. 1969. *The Biafra Story*. Harmondsworth: Penguin.

FRANK, A. G. 1971. *The Sociology of Development and the Underdevelopment of Sociology*. London: Pluto Press.

GALTUNG, J. and RUGE, M. H. 1965. *The Structure of Foreign News*. Journal of Peace Research 1: 64–90.

GANS, H. 1962, *The Urban Villagers*. New York: Free Press.

GROOM, J. and BOARDMAN, B. (eds.) 1973. *The Management of Britain's External Relations*. London: MacMillan.

GRUNIG, J. E. 1969. Information and Decision-making in Economic Development. *Journalism Quarterly*: 565–75.

HACHTEN, W. A. 1971. *Muffled Drums: the News Media in Africa*. Ames: Iowa University Press.

HAGEN, E. 1962. *On the Theory of Social Change*. Illinois: Dorsey.

HALLORAN, J. D., ELLIOTT, P. and MURDOCK, G. 1970. *Demonstrations and Communication: a Case Study*. Harmondsworth: Penguin.

HIMMELSTRAND, U. 1968. The Problem of Cultural Translation and of Reporting Different Social Realities. In Stokke 1968.

—— 1969. *Världen, Nigeria och Biafra: Sanningen som kom bort*. Stockholm: Aldus/Bonniers.

HOUSE OF REPRESENTATIVES. 1967. *Modern Communications and Foreign Policy*. Papers of the Sub-Committee on International Organization and Movements of the Committee on Foreign Affairs, 90th Congress, 1st Session. Washington.

INTERNATIONAL PRESS INSTITUTE. 1965. *IPI Report*. Zurich. October.

LERNER, D. 1957. Communications Systems and Social Systems. *Behavioural Science* 266–75.

—— 1958. *The Passing of Traditional Society*. New York: Free Press.

—— 1967. Communications and the Prospects of Innovative Development. In Lerner and Schramm 1967.

—— 1970. Book Review in *Public Opinion Quarterly*. Summer 311.

LERNER, D. and SCHRAMM, W. (eds.) 1967. *Communications and Change in the Developing Countries*. Honolulu: East-West Center Press.

MCCLELLAND, D. 1961. *The Achieving Society*. Princeton: Van Nostrand.

MCCRONE, D. J. and CNUDDE, C. F. 1967. Towards a Communication Theory of Political Development: a Causal Model. *American Political Science Review*: 72–9.

MILLIKAN, M. F. 1967. The Most Fundamental Technological Change. In Lerner and Schramm, 1967.

OSTGAARD, E. 1965. Factors Influencing the Flow of News. *Journal of Peace Research* 1965: 39–56.

PEACOCK, J. L. 1969. Religion, Communications and Modernisation, a Weberian Critique of Some Recent Views. *Human Organisation*, no. (1): 35–41.

POOL, I. DE SOLA, 1963. The Mass Media and Politics. In Pye 1963.

—— 1966a. Communication and Development. In Weiner 1966.

—— 1966b. The Necessity for Social Scientists doing Research for Governments. *Background 10*: 2.

PYE, L. W. (ed.) 1963. *Communications and Political Development*. Princeton: Princeton University Press.

ROGERS, E. 1969. *Modernisation among Peasants – the Impact of Communications*. New York: Holt, Rinehart and Winston.

SCHILLER, H. I. 1969. *Mass Communications and American Empire*. New York: Kelley.

SCHRAMM, W. 1964. *Mass Media and National Development*. Stanford: Standford University Press.

—— 1967. Communication and Change. In Lerner and Schramm 1967.

SCHRAMM, W. and RUGGELS, W. L. 1967. How Mass Media Systems Grow. In Lerner & Schramm 1967.

SMITH, A. D. 1971. *Theories of Nationalism*. London: Duckworth.

STOKKE, O. (ed.) 1968. *Reporting Africa*. Uppsala: Scandinavian Institute of African Studies.

UNESCO. 1961. *Mass Media in the Developing Countries*. Paris: UNESCO.

WEINER, M. (ed.) 1966. *Modernisation: the Dynamics of Growth*. New York: Basic Books.

RONALD FRANKENBERG AND JOYCE LEESON

The Sociology of Health Dilemmas in the Post-colonial World: Intermediate Technology and Medical Care in Zambia, Zaire, and China[1]

I INTRODUCTION

It is a commonplace realization that the so-called developing countries suffer a double disadvantage in the field of health. Not only do they have a greater mortality and morbidity but their medical care services are more inadequate. In this paper we shall seek to define their problems more precisely in economic and medical terms and to suggest an analysis in sociological terms which aims to answer the question – why are the obvious solutions not applied even when they are perceived? Health in non-industrial countries (and perhaps elsewhere) is not, we shall argue, to be seen in medical and economic terms alone; all the traditional concerns of sociology such as role, class, age, sex, stage in life-cycle, conflict, and reference group are also involved. In order to advance this argument we shall combine the distilled wisdom of King (1966, 1971, 1972), Gish (1971a, 1971b), the Intermediate Technology Development Group (1971), and others, with our own experience in Zambia, as researchers, medical education administrators, and teachers of preventive medicine and medical sociology.

Politics and human values will also be involved, for it must be stated at the outset that although the thesis seems plausible, there is not, in our view, any evidence as yet (Elliott, forthcoming?) that improving the health of a nation advances its economy. It is, however, quite certain that human beings wish to be healthier, and do not, in general, welcome the early deaths of themselves or their children. Furthermore, our researches lead us to note the existence and effect of imperialism and neo-colonialism in general and specific medical varieties of these phenomena in particular. Finally, by way of introduction, we want to state our view that anyone writing honestly in this field must not only praise the practice of the People's Republic of China (which one of the authors has visited recently), but must also recognize a consistency between their medical practices and other aspects of their social system.

II THE PROBLEM

Medical and Demographic Aspects

One of the difficulties involved in discussing the subject with any precision is the absence of really detailed information on disease, birth, and death patterns in developing countries. In Zambia, for example, there was no registration of births and deaths among the African majority. (A South African African friend who sought to register the birth of a child was told 'you are not very black, would you like to register him as coloured'.) Since even the births of children to ministers and permanent secretaries could receive no official recognition, the permissive clause enacted in May 1914 may soon be put into force, and birth registration established, once the inter-departmental disputes have been resolved, as to whether the Ministry of Justice, of Labour and Health, or Home Affairs should be responsible.

However, even without national vital statistics, sample surveys and censuses make the general picture clear. A very large proportion of the population (about 42 per cent in Zambia) of a developing country will be under eighteen, a third of the population will be under ten years of age, and half or more of all deaths will be of children under five (Leeson 1970a). Infant mortality (0–1) is likely to be four or more times that of industrialized countries, and childhood mortality (1–4) may be more than forty times as great (Gish 1971b). Children die from gastro-enteritis, malnutrition, pneumonia, and (in Zambian towns, above all) measles. The general rule that it is better to prevent disease than to seek to cure it once it has occurred is especially true of these particular causes of death and ill-health and the social conditions surrounding them.

Between 50 and 90 per cent of the population live in rural areas that have poor communications (either electronic, or in terms of transport) with towns. The rapidly growing urban populations live mainly in shanty-towns on the outskirts of the cities, and their integration with, and possibility of getting to, the centre may be limited in all sorts of ways.

The rate of population increase (2·5–3 per cent per annum) in developing countries is much greater than in industrialized countries where the rate is 0·5 to 2 per cent (Gish 1971b). This fact may well be paradoxically connected with the high childhood mortality (King 1971: 29–30). Women (and men) who want children take account of the expected death of most of them; they are therefore unlikely to wish to limit the number to which they give birth, until they are confident that those who are born will not be buried prematurely.

Economic Dimensions

King (1971: 26) reports that in 1967 the Gross National Product per head of Zambia was US $310 (about £130). The government of Zambia spent about 1 per cent of the gross domestic product on health, which amounted to nearly 6 per cent of the government's total recurrent expenditure. In 1969 this was about 4·8 dollars (or £2) per head. In the same year, King (1971) estimated that there was one doctor per 11 900 persons in Zambia and 3·58 in-patient beds of all kinds per 1 000 of the population. (The limitations of these as measures will become apparent later.) For comparison, it can be noted that the British government spends about 5 per cent of its much greater GNP on the National Health Service, which in 1969 was equal to about £40 per head of population. There is one doctor per 860 of the population, and ten beds per 1 000 (Gish 1971b). Malawi, to take the other extreme, has one doctor to 53 000 population.

It is clear, then, that merely in statistical terms, Zambia and other developing countries (which are often even worse off) spend a smaller proportion of a smaller quantity of economic resources on a greater number of worse problems. We now turn to the social resources available.

III THE RESOURCES

Doctors

In 1965–6, according to the Zambian government, there were 275 physicians and surgeons in the country, of whom eleven were classified as 'African by race' (Manpower Report 1966: 78). There were at that time thirty-four Zambians on medical courses abroad and seven more doing pre-medical science studies in the United States.

Since then a University Medical School has been set up (in 1968) which should produce its first fourteen or fifteen medical graduates in 1973 and output will eventually rise to 150 per year.

By 1969 there were 340 doctors in the country (Davies 1971). About half these doctors were employed in government service and half were not; presumably a large proportion of the latter were working either for the mining companies or for the missions. Furthermore, as elsewhere in the developing world, they were concentrated in the towns; especially in Lusaka, in Ndola, and the other Copperbelt and line of rail towns where some were in lucrative private practice. (For the pattern of medical care in Lusaka see Leeson 1967.)

Medical Assistants and Nurses

In 1966, at the time of the publication of the First National Development Plan (FNDP), there were 138 Medical Assistants in the country, the stock of whom was increasing by about twenty-five per year (FNDP 1966: 64). The FNDP estimated that it would be necessary to raise the yearly output of Medical Assistants to seventy-two in order to keep pace with the planned increase in the number of rural Health Centres. To achieve this it was proposed to establish an additional Medical Assistants' training school at Ndola on the Copperbelt. The training for new entrants consists of a two-year course, and Senior Medical Assistants do a further one-year course, including rotation in several hospital departments. Graduates from the one-year senior course may take charge of rural Health Centres and, in some cases, rural hospitals. The ideal role of such medical auxiliaries is discussed below, as are the difficulties involved in fulfilling it. The World Health Organization Consultants' report on the medical school said 'the training is intensely practical and gives a very favourable impression' (Jessop and Vine 1966: 10). It went on to propose that the Lusaka school, which had been established since 1950, should be moved away from the capital in order to avoid resentment and status confusion between the new Zambian doctors and the old style Medical Assistants (cf. Craemer and Fox 1967).

There is a marked discrepancy in the figures for numbers of Medical Assistants in training and in post between the FNDP (July 1966) and the WHO Report (May 1966) which appears to arise out of the fact that the FNDP classifies female Medical Assistants as either State Registered Nurses or 'Zambian Enrolled Nurses'. This classification may be undesirable but is socially and practically realistic, since it reflects their own view of their professional position (Jayaraman 1970). Its implications are discussed further below.

In 1966, at the time of the FNDP, there were 230 enrolled nurses, twenty Zambian SRNs, 200 female Medical Assistants, and 750 untrained dressers. The plan envisaged the disappearance of the final 750 and the other 450 were considered to make up about a sixth of the number required. What was then the annual increment of 130 in all three grades just about maintained the *status quo*, whereas the plan estimated that 520 nurses needed to be trained each year but that even this would only provide two nurses for each rural Health Centre instead of the target three. The Statistical Year Book for 1968 lists a total of 515 in 1966 which jumps to 1 378 in 1967, suggesting either that the target was being met, or that one should not take the figures too seriously.

There was the additional problem of the mismatching of training and careers. In the mid-sixties the paradox obtained that Medical Assistants (especially male but also female) were trained to work independently in rural Health Centres but remained, frustrated and discontented with their status, subordinate to expatriate SRNs in the large hospitals in the towns along the railway line, whereas enrolled nurses, trained to work in hospitals were looking after rural Health Centres.

Other Health Workers

Apart from the categories directly connected with the provision of medical care listed above, there are at least three more types of occupation connected with the provision of help. These are: first, Laboratory Technicians and Radiographers, whose functions are fairly clear; second, Health Inspectors and Health Assistants; and third, Traditional Healers. We will now consider these last two in turn.

Health Inspectors and Health Assistants

King (1966: 3, 6) describes their functions (from Kenyan experience) by saying that they are ideally centred on a dispensary or health sub-centre.

'They are responsible for providing safe water by digging wells and protecting springs, and often have a mason to help them in these tasks. These Health Assistants also provide latrines and see that these are used [sic], they advise on improvements in indigenous housing, they assist in measures against diseases such as malaria, and they help to trace the contacts of infectious cases. They inspect meat and supervise markets. Like other members of staff, Assistant Health

Inspectors and Health Assistants go into the patients' homes where their work is particularly valuable in times of epidemic, because it is then that the villager is most susceptible to advice and instruction.'

He continues (perhaps over-optimistically): 'All the health staff are taught to be active workers with their *hands* as well as their *heads*, and are encouraged not to be afraid of getting their hands dirty' (italics in original).

We note the absence of any concept of meeting felt needs and of self-help in community action in this prescription, which may reduce its efficacy, even in the unlikely event of its being closely followed. Another factor militating against its success is the tendency for industrialized society to elaborate a division of labour and social stratification in such a way that the man who uses his head may think it beneath him to use his hands. This is particularly disastrous for progress in developing countries and is incompatible with the Intermediate Technology ethos.[2] China is a contrast in this respect as in many others. One of the authors asked in a Chinese rural hospital who gave the anaesthetics, and was told it was the radiographer, who had become competent at both as a result of interest, motivation, and two short six-month courses at a hospital in Shanghai. There are, of course, no craft-protective organizations or professional competitiveness to hinder such initiative in the People's Republic of China.

Traditional healers

We have analysed the social characteristics of traditional healers in Lusaka elsewhere (Leeson and Frankenberg 1972) and have material on the pattern of consultation which has yet to be examined. It is impossible to estimate the numbers of part-time or full-time professional traditional healers (*MaNg'anga*) in Zambia, or to know how many of them justify the title of witch doctor and how many of herbalist. They certainly outnumber any category mentioned so far, although they are not included in the Manpower Report. We are unable to express an opinion on whether there is in Africa, as (in Mao's words) in China, a 'treasurehouse' of traditional medicine, with many effective remedies waiting to be incorporated into general use. Three things, however, are quite sure. First, that everyone in Zambia can get access to traditional medicine more readily than to any other source of primary medical care – although it is certainly more expensive than free medical care through the government, and often more expensive than private 'western'

medicine. It has, however, the advantages of being available close at
hand without involving any expensive or lengthy journey, and of
working with a 'payment by results' system. Second, there is no reason
why more orthodox (in the 'western' view) treatments should not be
added to the traditional and such healers involved in dispensing
'scientific' advice or medicine. Indeed, one of us (J.L.) had some success
in persuading some healers to add skim milk to anti-witchcraft and anti-
adultery medicines traditionally used in the treatment of kwashiorkor
and marasmus, two forms of protein-calorie malnutrition (see Mitchel
1968). Third, the sharp distinction that we as so-called educated
westerners make between different forms of healing is not necessarily so
sharply made by Africans (educated or otherwise). They may, in contrast, have a more sophisticated view of the events which take a patient
to the doctor and which we simplistically call 'disease' (Frankenberg
1968). Evidence that continuity between, and even fusion of, traditional
and modern medicine is possible is provided from Zaire (formerly
Congo Kinshasa) by Craemer and Fox (1968: 13, 14):

'In exploring the life histories of Medical Assistants one is also
struck by the role played by Congolese values and traditions which
antedate the arrival of Christian Missionaries in the country. A few
Medical Assistants come from families which have *ng'anga* and
guerisseurs (medicine men and healers) among their members. In
the context of the traditional Bantu cultures in which they functioned,
such healers occupied a highly respected, valued and even sacrosanct
position; the state of health of an individual and that of his family was
an important concern. It was regarded primarily a consequence of
magical and religious forces, and the treatments administered by the
traditional practitioner were based on fundamental super-natural as
well as natural considerations.

Dr. Moke, for example, originally was destined to succeed his
father as chief and healer. However, his elder sister, who was also a
healer, felt he had the intellectual qualities to go far in his studies and
become the practitioner of a modern profession. Dr. Usafi, whose
mother cared for ill people of her region with traditional plants,
taught him her art when he was a boy. "Mama played an important
role in my medical vocation", Dr. Usafi explained. "But I wanted to
practice medicine in a way that was better than that of the past . . .
medicine that was more adapted and more *evolué* . . ." It is characteristic of many Medical Assistants to have been motivated to serve

their people in a traditional role of high prestige and religious associations, with the added benefits of advanced education and modern science.'

Although neither Jayaraman nor ourselves stress this continuity of approach, we would consider that the last view is shared by many Zambian traditional healers. As Craemer and Fox point out, the attitude to injections is another example of this combination of values (1968: 16–17). Our observations confirmed this. Private doctors told us that patients did not regard themselves as having been treated unless they had an injection. A *ng'anga* acquaintance called scarification procedures 'African injections' and got the best of both belief worlds.

We wish to close this discussion of the human resources available for medical care by referring to the people in general, independently of specialist roles. It is, of course, precisely through the mobilization of 'the masses' own desire to be healthier that the achievements of China and other successful developments in health care have been possible, as Kreysler (1970) found in Tanzania. King (1966: Chapter 6) and others have emphasized that the roles of health worker/educator are merged in practice in developing countries. The Chinese lesson would be to modify the title to 'health worker/educator/learner'. The health worker has a certain technical knowledge and expertise which he can contribute to the solution of health problems. The masses, however, know the problems and the limiting factors which will constrain possible solutions, better than anyone else can know them. The health worker/educator who is unwilling to learn from the people is unlikely to be able to work effectively with them for the goal that all share, namely better health.

Health Care Units

We now turn briefly to the capital resources actually deployed by, or potentially available to, the health services in Zambia. The basic unit is the rural Health Centre which is ideally run by a Medical Assistant under the supervision of the Provincial Medical Officer. These are mainly concerned with out-patient and preventive services but most have some in-patient provision. In 1969 there were 276 government and seventy-five mission rural Health Centres, providing 3 660 in-patient beds and 420 cots. Over half of these organized under-five clinics. In towns, urban clinics numbered sixty-four government-run and twenty-eight Mining Company centres (Davies 1971: 100). This rural and urban provision represents a 48 per cent increase on the 1964 (independence year) figure. The number of District Hospitals has also increased. In 1969, there were fifty-six District Hospitals – twenty government, twenty-six mission, and ten mines' hospitals, with 6 600 beds and 620 cots. The mines' hospitals have facilities comparable with those of central and general hospitals, and some District Hospitals have fee-paying as well as free provision. The District Hospital

'provides fully qualified doctor services, in-patient wards, maternity beds, operating theatre, X-ray and laboratory facilities and an outpatient department. A centre of referral for health centres and clinics, it is run by one or more Medical Officers and registered nurses with Medical Assistants and enrolled nurses. . . .' (Lilli Stein in Davies 1971).

There are three central, two general and three specialist hospitals in Lusaka, Livingstone, Kabwe, Kitwe, and Ndola (the line of rail and the Copperbelt). These are staffed by forty-five specialists and seventy-five other doctors. They have 2 950 beds and 250 cots. The largest in Lusaka is the University Teaching Hospital (Davies 1971: 100). These hospitals are supposed to serve the whole of Zambia but judging from the experience of Mulago Hospital in Kampala, Uganda, the great majority of their patients are likely to be local (Hamilton & Anderson mimeo quoted in ITDG 1971: 15). At Mulago in 1964, 93 per cent of all admissions came from the surrounding district of Mengo (98 per cent of all obstetrics and gynaecology, 88 per cent of all other cases). If, as seems likely, this pattern of hospital care also applies in Zambia, 120 of the 170 doctors in government service are at the service of less than 30 per cent of the population. Also serving these town-dwellers are about fifty doctors in mine hospitals, and ninety in private practice. Hence 260 out of 340, or 76 per cent, of Zambia's scarce doctors are concentrated in urban areas.

A further consideration is the capital and recurrent cost of these large town hospitals, as compared to the services accessible to the rest of the population. King has pointed out (quoted in ITDG 1971) that the cost of four beds in the Lusaka Teaching Hospital could provide a Health Centre which would be a base from which the health needs of 20 000 people could be met. The capital cost of the whole hospital would provide 250 Health Centres, thus covering the whole population of Zambia. Furthermore, the recurrent costs of a Health Centre are

£10 000 per annum or 50p per patient served. We do not yet know the exact recurrent costs of Lusaka Teaching Hospital, but Uganda once more may give an indication: in 1968, 60 per cent of the entire health budget of Uganda went on its teaching hospital. The early predictions for Zambia's Teaching Hospital of 4 million Kwacha a year represented 36 per cent of Zambia's health budget (King 1966. See also the then Soviet Dean of Medicine's reply: Elizarov 1968. Part of this is quoted below). Part of the argument for such an extravagant use of resources is, of course, the need for a high standard of medical education. This has sociological concomitants which will be discussed below.

Before turning to this, one must mention two marginal but highly expensive additional facilities, the Zambia Flying Doctor Service and Mission Medic-Air. The former administered twelve airstrip clinics in remote areas, manned by an orderly and visited two or three times weekly by a doctor and a qualified nurse. One estimate in 1968 was that this service saw eleven patients a day on average throughout the year, at considerable cost to the Ministry of Health. Mission Medic-Air is a recent innovation manned by volunteer doctors and pilots, which treats in-patients at mission hospitals at weekends, and has the virtue of being independently financed by charities.

IV TOWARDS A MORE APPROPRIATE HEALTH CARE SYSTEM

The implications for health care of the combination of factors outlined above have been most recently and clearly stated by King in his closing address to the Kampala Conference on the Teaching and Practice of Family Health, in November 1971 (King 1972). They are rarely contested in words but even more rarely put into action. Zambia has done rather better in this respect than many other countries. King begins with a quotation from David Morley:

> 'Three quarters of our population are rural, yet three quarters of our medical resources are spent in the towns where three quarters of our doctors live. Three quarters of the people die from diseases which could be prevented at low cost and yet three quarters of medical budgets are spent on curative services.'

King goes on to suggest as practical characteristics of desirable health services:

'1. the maximum use of auxiliaries,
  2. the intensive development of health services,

3. "Pushing tasks down the skill pyramid" through effective delegation,

4. no expensive prestige projects,

5. the doctor as leader, teacher, and administrator of the health team,

6. bonding of medical graduates'.

The Republic of Zambia was committed to many of these by the First National Development Plan, yet they proved difficult to put into practice. Despite King, as Professor of Social Medicine, one of us (R.F.) as a leading administrator, a sympathetic Vice-Chancellor and Deputy Vice-Chancellor, a friendly Ministry of Health, and WHO backing, it was not possible to establish medical education on an appropriate basis. This requires sociological as well as historical explanation. In the remainder of this paper we shall look at some of the reasons why so little progress has been made towards a more desirable and appropriate health care system. We shall begin with a detailed examination of the role of medical auxiliaries and of the status problems encountered by them in the present circumstances.

The Auxiliary, or Medical Assistant, and his Role

Katharine Elliott (ITDG 1971: 32–3) summarizes the desirable characteristics of a medical auxiliary which were set out in more detail in King (1966):

'A medical auxiliary should be able to:
1. Undertake the care of the sick, wherever necessary, in local conditions: e.g. in the community or at a health centre or hospital.
2. Either treat the sick himself or else arrange for them to be referred to someone more skilled; he must know enough to judge how urgent is the need for referral.
3. Think about the community as a whole, assess its problems and needs in order of priority and suggest solutions making the best use of limited resources.
4. Understand the value of, and be able to undertake, health education with the aim of improving the health of the community, not just of treating the sick.
5. Apply to his work an open, inquiring mind, receptive to new ideas without necessarily rejecting all tradition.
6. Understand what a physician does and how his own work relates to the doctor's role.'

J. P. Vaughan in a useful recent article has gone some way to operationalizing these ideal prescriptions with specific reference to Medical Assistants (Vaughan 1971: 269). He states:

'1. There is a continuum of knowledge and diagnostic skills among health workers from the aid post orderly or dispensary attendant to the specialists. Consequently it is impossible to draw a hard and fast line on who should be allowed to treat patients. It is a matter of the prevalent diseases, and the training and supervision of the available staff.

2. Not all developing countries have felt the need for the Medical Assistant category of health worker, but he is capable of relieving the doctor of much routine work, and thus freeing him for other duties. He can also be a very effective worker in rural and preventive medicine. Two of the Medical Assistant's advantages over the doctor are that he is cheaper to employ, and that he is culturally and socially less removed from the people he is working amongst. Consequently he has a much better understanding of their problems, and is more likely to be happy working in the rural areas.

3. The duties of the Medical Assistant must be seen in the context of total health planning and not in isolation from other members of the health department.

4. The factors modifying the training programme in one country are not necessarily applicable in another, and the objectives of the training programme for the particular country concerned must be stated with reference to the definition of the duties and capabilities of the Medical Assistant.

5. Criteria for admission to the training programme will have to depend on the availability of suitable applicants and on the definition of the duties of the graduated Medical Assistant.

6. Three years would appear to be a suitable maximum length for the basic training programme.

7. Supervision and retraining are vital to the morale of the Medical Assistant who is often working in isolated rural areas and out of contact with other members of the health department.

8. The Medical Assistant must see himself as an auxiliary worker and not expect automatic upgrading towards the fully qualified medical officer level. Training programmes producing a sub-professional doctor or an assistant medical officer have nearly always run into difficulties over professional status.

9. The Medical Assistant should not be allowed to assume greater responsibility than that which he was trained for and he must be made to realise the limits of his ability and responsibility. This equally applies to the doctor as well.

10. A good career structure, incentives and adequate salary scales are as important to the Medical Assistant as they are to the professional worker, and much dissatisfaction with his work could be avoided by attention to these factors.

11. There is an overwhelming and immediate problem in many of the developing countries, due to their economic transition. What is right today may well be wrong in the future, but not to do what is possible in the future is shelving the problem, but offering no solution.'

Kenneth Hill realistically recognizes in his contribution to the ITDG booklet that there are difficulties in the Medical Assistant's role, but he is unable to understand them. He writes (1971: 27–8):

'Although the use of intermediary personnel is on the increase, resistance to their recognition continues and this is often even stronger in developing countries than it is elsewhere. It is hard to understand the rationale of such opposition. It is true that there is a remote danger of people with less advanced training developing inflated ideas of their own capabilities, but such people can only be relatively few and they will be found at the fringe.'

It is, in fact, as both Craemer and Fox in Zaire and Jayaraman in Zambia have shown, only too easy to see the rationale, and general knowledge of Zambia gives the sociologist still further insight. There is, of course, the conservatism and craft exclusiveness of the fully trained physicians, which may cause them to oppose the existence of Medical Assistants from the outset, or (as with the University of Lovanium in Zaire) to object strongly to their upgrading. But perhaps the major contributing factor is that the role of Medical Assistant itself is full of internal contradictions.

We have already drawn attention to the change of terminology between Jessop and Vine's WHO report (May 1966) and the FNDP (July 1966). In fact, once Zambian Enrolled Nurses began to be trained, female Medical Assistants were no longer so designated. Those who had qualified on the same basis and in the same school as men were forced to accept this change of designation. This sometimes led to further complications. The right to give injections being allowed to Medical Assistants but denied to ZENs led to the temporary closure of one Health Centre in May 1970 because women patients refused to be injected by men and the government was not able or willing to provide an SRN, the lowest grade of women allowed to give injections. A similar problem, of health workers with inappropriate status, arose when women refused the services of young girls as midwives (*Zambia Mail*, May 1970). According to Jayaraman, however, the distinction that was made between men and women with the same two years' training actually reflected the reality of hospital life, since the female assistants did regard themselves as part of the nursing hierarchy and therefore subordinate to the white, or South African black, or coloured Sister, while the men considered themselves as part of the clinical hierarchy and subordinate only to the physicians and surgeons.

The resulting ambiguity in the relationships between expatriate nurses and male Medical Assistants was a constant source of friction in Lusaka Central Hospital. Like so many relationships in Zambia, this was complicated by coincidence of ethnic and status division. Brown (Indian) doctors, white sisters, black Medical Assistants and black patients was the modal occurrence. The fact that, except for a few Rhodesian Shona, the Medical Assistants in Zambia were Zambian – and rarity of rarities, could sometimes speak to patients in a language that the latter could understand – gave them much power and a key role in the hospital. This may have led to their not being sent to man rural hospitals and Health Centres, but being kept in Lusaka, where, like doctors trained in urban hospitals, they wished to stay, but where their skills were underused. Their key, intercalary position certainly also added to resentment aimed at them by both patients and other staff when things went wrong (Gluckman 1949).

A further contradiction arose, particularly in rural areas, in defining just how far the competence of a Medical Assistant extended. A passage in Craemer and Fox (1968: 37–8) spells this out very clearly for Zaire:

'Medical Assistants have never claimed to be the equal of physicians. [A] passage of the memorandum written by a group of Medical Assistants in July, 1957, affirms:
"Even though the studies of a Medical Assistant are calculated on the basis of those of a physician, his training has gaps in it of varying degrees in different branches of medicine. The Medical Assistant is inferior to the physician, and no one has ever contested it.' "

Later they continue:

'The longer a Medical Assistant practised medicine, the more aware he was likely to become of all he did not know and was not qualified to do for patients, that would have been within his competence and rights were he a physican. This problem was a particularly frustrating and sometimes even tragic one for the Medical Assistant working in a Bush country dispensary that was visited only occasionally by a physician. Sometimes he was faced with a case of complexity and gravity beyond what he was legitimately trained to handle. A Medical Assistant describes a typical case of this sort:
"Suppose you are alone in a dispensary in the Bush country, with only nurses and nurses' aides to help you. The physician under whose supervision you work visits the dispensary every month, or two months, or even three. A pregnant woman who is about to deliver prematurely and whose placenta is not normal, arrives at the dispensary. Under ordinary circumstances, the obstetrician can do a caesarean in a case like this, and safely deliver the child without endangering the mother. The Medical Assistant is not qualified to carry out such a surgical procedure, and it is supposedly illegitimate for him to try to do so. Under these circumstances, one of the only alternatives left to the Medical Assistant is to send the woman out of the interior to a larger medical center. But in so doing, he would be subjecting her to a journey over primitive bumpy roads, and he would run the real risk of jeopardizing the lives of both the mother and the baby. It is in this kind of situation that the Medical Assistant most wishes he were a physician who, without hesitation, could carry out the indicated procedure on the spot".'

This sort of dilemma is inherent in a system that leaves a Medical Assistant, or indeed any medical worker, on his own to cope with all medical problems without means of communication, either by radio or road, with those who should support him and guide him through difficulties.

We were doubtful about the wisdom of transferring the Medical Assistants' school away from Lusaka merely to separate them from the 'real' medical students, and we remain doubtful about Vaughan's prohibition of further training to the level of physician, which we would not rule out for some, at least, until the manpower position eases. We recognize, however, the unavoidable difficulties of the role of Medical Assistant in a status-ridden, highly competitive, incipient capitalist, neo-colonialist, dominated society. There are, in fact, two further contradictions here. First, the role was created in both Zaire and Zambia as a subordinate colonial one – Medical Assistants, before independence, were in the highest status job for Africans in the Belgian Congo, and the highest attainable within the health services for Africans in Northern Rhodesia. Both Craemer and Fox and Jayaraman claim that their change from a high position in the prestige system to just one among many, imposes a particular strain upon post-independence Medical Assistants who are, moreover, denied the possibility of further mobility. (We remain somewhat unconvinced about the high status of Medical Assistants in pre-independence Northern Rhodesia.)

We feel that these difficulties in the role of Medical Assistants need to be more frankly acknowledged than they have been up to now – but we do not feel this is a reason to abandon the category as appears to have happened in Zaire, since, for most people in countries like Zambia, the only alternative in the foreseeable future to a health service based on Medical Assistants is no service at all (Gish forthcoming).

V THE IDEOLOGIES OF THE MEDICAL AND POLITICAL ELITES

King in his most recent paper refers to red and blue opinions which are tabulated in *Table 1* opposite. The medical school in a developing country, such as Zambia and elsewhere, has to recruit expatriate medical teachers who are chosen for their specific skills. The required anatomists, physiologists, biochemists, neurologists, surgeons, and physicians of various specialities come from a wide variety of backgrounds and countries, but they have been trained mostly in advanced industrial countries, in modern teaching hospitals. Like most of us in higher education, such teachers usually consider their own education to have been ideal and seek benevolently to allow others hitherto less fortunate to share in it. Their education was arguably unsuitable even for their own country; in the case of the Soviet experts in Zambia it even lacked the historical perspective of their own country's very recent great achievements in overcoming in a mere fifty years many of the same problems now facing Zambia. The blue opinions of these expatriates tend to be strongly reinforced by the immediate apparent consumers – the urban educated elite, civil servants, and others, themselves often educated in advanced industrial countries.

Just as Zambia's airport and parliament building had to be prestigious and grand, so, in the view of vocal pressure groups, had the Teaching

TABLE 1

Reds and blues

Question	Answers	
	Right blue	*Left red*
How important is Community Medicine in the curriculum?	What is it?	Vital
What can medicine give the rural poor?	Their needs are economic	Much
Should students' training be different?	We must maintain standards and comparability	Radically
How important is rural field-work?	Complete waste of time	Essential
Should there be bonding?	Infringement of liberty	Why not, the cost of their education is borne by the poor
Doctor's car?	Mercedes	VW
Responsibility for whom?	Patients who request our services	For those who ask and those who don't
Medical School to train whom?	Doctors	Whole health teams
Is teaching hospital essential?	Yes	Modify district hospitals
Conditions – costly to treat?	Let's be a centre of excellence	Compassionate palliation
Should writing basic texts be an important academic activity?	Gram described his stain about 1880. No need to do it again	Yes

Freely adapted from King 1972.

Hospital. They planned only from the point of view of consumers like themselves – affluent townsmen. They belonged to medical aid schemes which allowed them privileged conditions within Zambia, and they resented, at the same time as they asserted, the occasional 'necessity' for shipment outside. One individual civil servant had to be flown to a London kidney unit where he remained until a kidney unit was specially built and equipped for him in Zambia (he died shortly after-wards). A well-known chief delayed treatment until a plane could be provided to take him to South Africa (he refused to go to England) and died as a consequence. It seemed scandalous to nationalist politicians that Zambia should be dependent on medical services overseas, and self-evident that 'the best' should be available in the capital. They had been assimilated into the international travelling circuses of diplomats, experts, advisers, and civil servants. Their reference groups were their opposite numbers from neighbouring states, and the whole world. In less than a generation they had genuinely forgotten the circumstances of life and death as experienced by the ordinary villagers that they, or at least their parents, had been. It is significant that Mao in China characterized the Health Ministry at the beginning of the Cultural Revolution as the Ministry of Urban Overlords (see below).

It would not be reasonable to place heavy blame on the Zambian elite. They were victims of an international system of exploitation that had created not only the situation but also their attitudes. The only system of 'western' medicine they had encountered was colonial hospital medicine, and since it was evident that the standard of this available to the people of Lusaka was poor, it was not surprising that they demanded its improvement. Their medical advisers are the ones who might have been expected to make a more informed evaluation of national needs.

Elizarov's defence of the teaching hospital, in 1968, certainly reflected the view both of an influential section of the Zambian elite and the expatriate medical specialists.

'The planned teaching hospital will not only be used for teaching but will serve the people of Zambia with medical care of a very high standard. For example, all the most complicated surgical operations on the heart, lungs, kidney, brain, etc., will be performed in Lusaka and therefore Zambians will not need to go to other countries for these operations.'

(The Dean who replaced Elizarov was an eminent Soviet neurosurgeon.) However, he concedes (in a situation where many of the men admitted slept on the floor, waiting for a bed above them to become vacant): 'It may be too luxurious to build rooms for 1, 2 or 4 patients: it might be more reasonable to create rooms for 4, 6, 10 or 12 patients' (Elizarov 1968).

As mentioned above, a further obstacle to improving the supply of medical personnel for the ordinary people was the restrictive practice behaviour of the, largely expatriate, Zambia Medical Council. It refused, for example, for a long time to recognize the degrees of Czech doctors who had volunteered to man rural hospitals with the support of their government and the government of the Republic of Zambia, on the grounds that degrees from the Charles University in Prague were suspect. (There was a similar incident regarding Soviet-trained Ghanaians in Ghana in 1968.)

VI MEDICAL IMPERIALISM

Training doctors in the Lusaka Teaching Hospital, and not bonding them effectively, may well lead to the same conditions of brain drain that caused the number of doctors per head of the population to fall, rather than rise, between 1962 and 1965 in twelve anglophone and twelve francophone countries (Vysohlid (1968) quoted in ITDG 1971). Nor will doctors so trained be likely to move willingly to rural areas.

The Third World is exploited medically by Britain, the United States, and other powers in two ways. First, through 'cultural imperialism' and pressures towards inappropriate patterns of medical care in the Third World itself, as in the part played in the creation of teaching hospitals in Uganda and Zambia, cited above. Second, as Gish (1971a: 28–53) has shown, by a classical 'ragged trousered philanthropist' apprentice system, in which cheap labour is acquired, and craft restriction maintained by the pretence of training. We will content ourselves with two quotations from Gish. He reports that the conference of Deans of African Medical Schools seeks to stem 'the drain of postgraduates to Europe and North America where they learn sophisticated techniques and engage in research which is completely unsuited to African conditions' (31). (That is, of course, if they learn anything at all in understaffed provincial hospitals with no teaching facilities.) One out of every four hospital doctors in Britain works in a teaching hospital: however, of British-born doctors it is one in three and of overseas doctors one in six (mostly from former Dominions). Half the British doctors in registrar grades are in teaching hospitals – one-sixth of those from overseas. In house-officer grades one-third of British doctors are in teaching hospitals; one-tenth of immigrants (Gish 1971a: 49). Gish sees a contradiction in the attitude of the profession in supporting compulsory assessment for Commonwealth doctors:

'On the one hand it is implicitly understood that many of the prerogatives enjoyed by senior members of the profession could not go on but for substantial continued immigration, and yet many (if not most) of these same professionals are deeply concerned about the implications for medical care in this country of such continued large scale immigration. This is not to say that the medical profession is totally unaware of certain of the adverse effects in the new Commonwealth countries resulting from the present pattern of medical migration.'

It is, of course, by now well known that the National Health Service could not exist without the 60 per cent of junior hospital doctors coming from abroad (Gish 1971a: 52). No doubt, once the Zambian Medical School gets under way, Zambia too will pay its tribute to the UK, and perhaps the USA. At least the Soviet Union's non-competitive profession and the continued use of *feldshers* (Medical Assistants) make it unlikely that they will seek to drain off medical graduates from developing countries.

VII IS THERE A VIABLE ALTERNATIVE TO THE NEO-COLONIALIST PATTERN?

An approach that one of us (R.F.) has recently encountered is that adopted by the Chinese, the concept of 'barefoot' or 'peasant' doctors. The significance of these health workers is that they do not constitute a separate professional category at all. Peasants (often women), recommended by their comrades, are trained for a number of four-month periods during agriculturally slack times; they then return to their previous jobs and act as sources of first-line medical care for prevention and treatment, when required to do so.

It is not our purpose here to describe Chinese medical practice in detail (see Horn 1969; Frankenberg 1972; Rifkin and Kaplinsky 1973). We should, however, point out that peasant doctors operate within a framework of medicine in abeyance in the years preceding the Cultural Revolution and which emerged again after the denunciation of the Ministry of Health as a Ministry of Urban Overlords. It is based on the four principles:

1. lay stress on medicine for the workers, peasants, and soldiers,
2. preventive work comes first,
3. unite western and traditional medicine,
4. medical workers must be integrated with the masses.

The aim, which appears to have been successful, is not so much to create a profession, as to mobilize the whole population. This clearly is the long-term answer.

CONCLUSION

In this paper, we have tried to achieve three main tasks. The first two were neither original nor difficult. They were to outline, by using

Zambia as an example, the kinds of health problems that beset a developing country, and the rational way of solving them.

As our many predecessors have pointed out, the problems of such countries arise from their young malnourished populations. It is the children who die, and they die of infectious diseases like measles, malnutrition, and of gastro-enteritis. Even more clearly than is the case in developed countries, the disease pattern is one that lends itself to effective control by preventive rather than curative measures. However, such countries are poor, both in financial resources and medical manpower. A solution cannot be achieved by creating fully trained doctors in the western style. In the first place, the training of such doctors is not appropriate to the conditions in which they would be required to work; second, economic resources are not sufficient to train enough; third, the few that are trained are likely to remain in, or move to, either towns, or worse still, metropolitan countries like the United States and the United Kingdom.

It is clear that an alternative to fully trained physicians is required and experience in both the colonial west and in the Soviet Union suggests that medical auxiliaries of various kinds will provide this. We added our own more unusual but nevertheless not entirely original suggestion that traditional healers could also be used.

There are, then, three characteristics of a suitable health programme that have been widely recognized, namely:

1. the training of doctors as educators and preventers of disease,
2. the widespread use of local materials and people – Medical Assistants and rural Health Centres,
3. the concentration of effort on prevention of disease in rural areas.

These requirements are simple, the arguments for them cogent and convincing, and the costs relatively small. Yet they are rarely put into effect and those who advocate them are ignored almost to the point of persecution.

Our third task was to seek to suggest an explanation for this contradiction between the apparently rational and the events of the real world. This contradiction appeared particularly sharp in Zambia, since there was government and university support for rational policies, and yet great difficulty in carrying them out.

Our explanations for this failure were based on an attempt to understand the social position of doctors (both in the undeveloped country and elsewhere), of decision-takers, and of medical auxiliaries. We suggested that doctors in metropolitan countries condoned a brain drain because it benefited them, and that as expatriate advisers, their too effective socialization and vested interests led them to seek (often successfully) to impose an inappropriate large-scale technology. Furthermore, they found ready disciples in local elites, who, as well as being urban and western educated, saw medicine in terms of national prestige and their own curative needs. Their reference groups were their peers in other countries rather than their own rural (or for that matter, urban) poor. Large capital projects were easier to point at than improvements in health.

Finally, we tried to show that the position of medical auxiliaries themselves was fraught with conflict. In Zaire, where it has been well documented, and in Zambia, it suffers from its association with colonial rule. Soviet experts who could show its alternative association with socialist medical services fail to do so. It is further complicated in Zambia by considerations of status based on ethnic divisions, gender, and medical hierarchy.

We believe that these characteristics of social positions in ex-colonial societies are supported and reinforced by a world situation in which China, virtually alone, is at present exceptional and we discussed briefly the different outlook and practice of China since the cultural revolution.

In fact, we feel it is clear that the opposition that Professor King and others of like mind have met in applying their ideas in practice is not accidental but is bound up with the whole structure of post-colonial societies in a world that remains predatory, imperialist, and neo-colonialist. As long as competition, profit, and self remain the guiding motives, and nations are organized by emerging urban bourgeois elites, there will be no easy solution to medical problems through the appropriate intermediate technology – Health Centre, District Hospital, and auxiliary. That, however, does not excuse doctors and administrators from trying, nor sociologists from helping to overcome the difficulties.

Notes

1 We are grateful to the Nuffield Foundation for support in Zambia and since. Our debt to Professor Maurice King will be evident throughout; our debt to Dr Felicity (Savage) King, although more cunningly concealed, is nevertheless as real and as great. Our debt to the people and the University of Zambia is also evident.

We would like to acknowledge the inspiration we have received over the years from the published works of Professor Titmuss and especially his study of the health services in Tanzania.

2 We use Intermediate Technology as a summary term to mean the perception of problems in small-scale terms and their solution through locally available resources of men and materials. Further discussion of its implications will be found in Intermediate Technology Development Group 1971.

References

CRAEMER, W. DE and FOX, R. C. 1968. *The Emerging Physician*. Hoover Institution Studies, 19. Stanford, California.

ELIZAROV, V. 1968. Common Sense about Health. *Business and Economy*. (4) May: 24–5. Lusaka.

DAVIES, D. H. 1971. *Zambia in Maps*. London: University of London Press.

ELLIOT, C. (forthcoming). *Constraints on the Economic Development of Zambia*. Nairobi: Oxford University Press, East Africa.

ELLIOTT, K. 1971. Using Medical Auxiliaries: some Ideas and Examples. In ITDG 1971: 29–46.

First National Development Plan. 1966. Lusaka: Office of National Development and Planning.

FRANKENBERG, R. 1968. The Beginning of Anthropology. *Proceedings VIIIth International Congress Anthropological and Ethnological Sciences, Tokyo* 2: 73–7.

—— 1969. Man, Society and Health. *African Social Research* 8: December. Lusaka.

—— 1972. Two Means a Thousand. *China Now*: March.

GISH, O. 1971a. *Doctor Migration and World Health*. Occasional Papers in Social Administration, no. 4. London School of Economics.

—— 1971b. Towards an Appropriate Health Care Technology. In ITDG 1971: 11–28.

—— (forthcoming). *Lancet*.

GLUCKMAN, M., BARNES, J. A. and MITCHELL, J. C. 1949. Village Headmen in British Central Africa. *Africa* **XIX** (2): 89–106.

HAMILTON, P. J. S. and ANDERSON, A. 1965. *An Analysis of Basic Data on Admission in 1963 and 1964 to Mulago Hospital, Kampala* (mimeo). Cited in ITDG 1971.

HILL, K. R. 1971. Intermediate Technology In Medicine. In ITDG 1971: 24–8.

HORN, J. 1969. *Away with all Pests*. London: Hamlyn.

—— 1971. Experiments in expanding the Rural Health Service in People's China. In Wolstenholme, G. and O'Connor, M. 1971.

INTERMEDIATE TECHNOLOGY DEVELOPMENT GROUP. 1971. *Health, Manpower and the Medical Auxiliary*. London.

JAYARAMAN, R. 1970. The Professional Medical Assistant in Zambia. East African Social Science Conference Paper. Unpublished.

JESSOP, W. J. E. and VINE, J. M. 1966. *The Establishment and Development of a Medical School within the University of Zambia*. WHO: Regional Office for Africa.

KING, M. (ed.) 1966. *Medical Care in Developing Countries: a Symposium from Makerere*. London: Oxford University Press.

—— 1971. The New Priorities in Tropical Medicine. In Wolstenhome, G. and O'Connor, M. 1971.

—— 1972. Medicine in Red and Blue. *Lancet* (1): 679–81.

KREYSLER, J. 1970. Health, Water Supply and Self-reliance in a Maya Village. *Journal of Tropical Paediatrics* 16: 116–23.

LEESON, J. E. 1967. Paths to Medical Care in Lusaka, Zambia. Conference Paper: Dakar (mimeo).

—— 1970a. Lusaka Deaths, 1967. *Medical Journal of Zambia* 4 (3): 85.

—— 1970b. Traditional Medicine – Still Plenty to Offer. *Africa Report* 15 (7) October: 24–5.

—— 1972. Lusaka Mothers and their Children. *Medical Journal of Zambia* 6 (6): 173.

LEESON, J. E. and FRANKENBERG, R. J. 1972. Association of Social Anthropologists Conference Paper.

Manpower Report. 1966. Lusaka: Cabinet Office.

MITCHEL, W. E. 1968. The Doktaboi: a Mediant Medical Role in New Guinea. *Proceedings VIIIth International Congress Anthropological and Ethnological Sciences: Tokyo* 1: 242.

RIFKIN, S. B. and KAPLINSKI, R. 1973. Health Strategy and Development Planning: Lessons from the People's Republic of China. *Journal of Development Studies* 9 (2): 213–32.

STEIN, L. 1971. Medical Facilities: Health and the Prevention of Disease. In Davies, D. H. 1971: 100–2 and 127.

VAUGHAN, J. P. 1971. Are Doctors always necessary? A Review of the Need for the Medical Assistant in Developing Countries. *Journal of Tropical Medicine and Hygiene* 74 (12): 265–71.

VYSOHLID, J. 1968. *Health Manpower in the African Region*. E/CW 14/ WP 6/19. UN Economic and Social Council (mimeo).

WOLSTENHOLME, G. and O'CONNOR, M. 1971. *Teamwork for World Health*. A CIBA Foundation Blueprint. London: Churchill.

IAN CARTER

The Highlands of Scotland as an Underdeveloped Region

Scotland is *terra incognita* for British sociology. Little work has been done by sociologists on Scotland, rather than in Scotland. This situation is to be explained by a number of factors. The first is that departments of sociology are of relatively recent growth in Scottish universities.[1] Consequently, the vast majority of sociologists working in Scotland today were neither born nor trained in the country. A second factor is the marked centripetal tendency among British sociologists; English conurbations, and above all London, draw them inexorably, for this, after all, is where the action is (and the consultancies to government departments). A third factor leading to the small amount of sociological work on Scotland is an assumption of British homogeneity;[2] if all parts of Britain exhibit similar social structural features (even if some parts are lower down the evolutionary scale than others), then there is no point in going to distant parts to do research that could be done more quickly and comfortably within a fifteen-mile radius of Hampstead.

Two consequences typically have followed from the operation of these factors; sociologists have either ignored Scotland or they have misunderstood Scotland. An example of the strategy of ignorance is Johns's textbook on the social structure of modern Britain; the book contains no index reference to Scotland, and the sole reference that I can find in the text is a footnote in which we learn that the average Scotsman gets one-half as many official holidays as the average citizen of the USA (Johns 1965: 123). Examples of the strategy of misapprehension are legion; the most usual kind is the assumption that Scotland is an antediluvian province of England, demonstrating social structural features once present in more 'advanced' parts of England but long since superseded by rationality and modernity. This assumption, which can lead to effigy-burning in Princes Street, is not unknown – sad to say – among British sociologists of development (Dore 1965: 379).

Such errors of omission and commission would not matter if it were true that Scotland may adequately be described as a province of England explicable solely in terms of English history and social structure. But this is not in fact the case. The Union settlement of 1707 contained explicit safeguards against English assimilationist tendencies for the Roman Law based Scots Law, for the Presbyterian Kirk, and for the relatively egalitarian (and European-influenced) Scottish educational system. Some degree of assimilation to English forms has occurred.[3] But the dearth of work on the sociology of Scots Law and, perhaps even more importantly, on religion in Scotland, makes it difficult to see just how significant are these institutional differences which still divide Scotland from England and how these institutions work themselves out in the social life of Scotland (Kellas 1968: 230–1).

But we are not only concerned here with the fact that generalizations about Britain, which are really based on England, may be invalid if they fail to take into account significant and on-going differences between England and Scotland. Scotland presents some sociological problems that are not to be found in England. Chief among these, for my purposes, is the matter of the Highlands. Hobsbawm notes (1969: 98) that one of the casualties of the Agricultural Revolution in England was the peasantry:

'By 1790 landlords owned perhaps three-quarters of the cultivated land, occupying free-holders perhaps fifteen to twenty per cent, and a peasantry in the usual sense of the word no longer existed.'

As so often happens with empirical statements about the historical course of social and economic change in the later eighteenth century in England, this statement is mirrored by generalizations about the consequences of change in agrarian societies:

'In the modern world peasants are anachronisms, and it is inevitable that they disappear. Peasants themselves have demonstrated time and time again that they prefer a different, and what they believe to be a better life' (Potter 1967: 378).

The crofters of the west Highlands and Islands form a peasant group that obdurately refuses to die, to the discomfort and annoyance of planners and economic geographers. Darling says of Lewis, in the Outer Hebrides, that it 'is almost unique in the modern Western world in its being a society still inseparable from its peasant agriculture' (1955: 142). Collier noted the extremely low division of labour characteristic of the crofter's life and of crofting communities, and the way in which economic functions are highly integrated with the family (1953: 35). How did these peasants survive in Britain, arguably the nation in which the most complete of all destructions of the peasant sector took place (Hobsbawn 1969: 15–16)? No sociologist has thought it worth his while to ask the question.

My concern in this paper is with a different question, although crofting will reappear in the argument. I am principally concerned with the Highlands and Islands Development Board and its strategies for the economic development of the Highlands.

THE HIGHLANDS BOARD: REMIT AND INTERPRETATION

The Highlands and Islands Development (Scotland) Act of 1965 gives very wide powers indeed to the Board constituted under its terms 'for the purpose of assisting the people of the Highlands and Islands to improve their economic and social conditions and of enabling the Highlands and Islands to play a more effective part in the economic and social development of the nation'. The Board is to prepare, concert, assist, and undertake measures for the economic and social development of the crofting counties.[4] It may acquire land, by compulsory purchase if necessary, and it may hold, manage, and dispose of land. It may erect buildings, provide equipment and services, and hold or dispose of these buildings and services. It may establish businesses and then, if it pleases, dispose of them. It may train people, produce publicity about the Highlands and the activities of the Board itself, and use a wide range of methods to bring jobs to the crofting counties. It may give grants or loans, on unspecified criteria, to anybody carrying on commercial or industrial operations that would promote the economic and social development of the area. It may also charge for its services, accept gifts, commission or undertake research, and borrow money. The finance for the Board's activities comes from the Secretary of State for Scotland, and it is to him alone that the Board is answerable.

This is a formidable list. No other agency engaged in regional development in Britain has been presented with such an armoury. But the breadth of its powers merely reflects the breadth of its remit. Two features of this remit deserve notice. First, *pace* Lugard's dual mandate, the Board is to promote both the development of the crofting counties and of the nation as a whole. This is common to all British regional development policies. Second, the Board is to promote both economic and social development simultaneously. Apthorpe has noted the hegemony that one university discipline – economics – enjoys in development planning. Any interdisciplinary approach in this field is, he suggests, more of a horse and rider relationship, with economics in the saddle, rather than a relationship of equals (Apthorpe 1970: 4–7). So it is with the HIDB (Carter 1972, 1973). The Board has an implicit definition of social development as 'non-economic development',[5] and identified non-economic objectives in the first annual report as the prevention of outmigration from the crofting counties as a whole, the maintenance of population levels in peripheral areas, and 'adding another perfectly possible way of life to that in the great cities' (HIDB 1967: Foreword). But it is clear that economic criteria have primacy over non-economic, and when a conflict occurs – as between the need to maintain population levels in 'remote' areas and the pull migration implicit in a growth centre policy – it is the economic policy that wins out.

The Board's economic orientation is shown in the way in which 'the Highland Problem' is conceptualized. Just before the Board was established, D. I. MacKay published an analysis of the economic prospects of the Highlands. He saw no solution to the economic problems of the area in any development of the staple primary industries; both agriculture and fishing would continue to decline absolutely in importance. Forestry offered some long-run employment opportunities, but these would be relatively few in number. The only safe long-term bet for the regeneration of the Highland economy would be a large-scale development of manufacturing industry. But the high cost of such industrial development would involve the sacrifice of economic opportunities in more favoured locations elsewhere in Britain and hence would not be justified on purely economic grounds (MacKay 1965: 79–81).

The first annual report of the HIDB outlines the agency's strategy for the Highlands. It shows a high level of agreement with MacKay's gloomy prognosis. There are some differences of detail – tourism is seen to have important short-run possibilities, for example, and fishing is seen to have development potential in those few areas of the crofting counties where it retains some vitality – but by and large, the Board, like MacKay, plumped for manufacturing industry as the salvation of the Highland economy (HIDB 1967: 3–4). This industry was to be concentrated in growth centres, where inter-industry linkages and the most effective use of infrastructure would minimize the effect of the disadvantageous situation of the Highlands, far from major British markets.

The Board's policy commitments derive from an assumption about the category of economic region into which the Highlands fall. McCrone puts the Highlands in a class of poorly developed rural regions (1969: 14):

> 'Agricultural regions, untouched by industrialization, which, as national income rises, cannot provide their population with living standards comparable to the rest of the country.'

The HIDB brackets the Highlands with the Mezzogiorno in Italy, North Norway and parts of Holland and Eire, as a problem region of this kind (1967: Foreword):

> '... Areas of their countries that the various revolutions in agriculture, industry and technology have passed by.'

The basic problem of the Highlands on this definition is not geographic remoteness, compounded by bad communications and a convoluted terrain, but isolation from those market forces that govern the rest of Britain and that would transform the Highlands if once they came to operate there. Thus the economic development strategy for the Highlands is to bring the area into the 'modern' economy. The creation of strong nexi of manufacturing industry is intended not only to alter the sectoral distribution of economic activity in the Highlands, but also to produce spread effects of economic growth and growth-mindedness throughout the crofting counties. The HIDB's view of the nature of 'the Highland Problem' and its strategy for the solution of that problem, assumes that the Highlands are an 'archaic', 'lagging' economic sector isolated from the cold winds of market forces. Thus the Highlands are seen to be an 'archaic' sector of a dual economy.[6] It is this that we will be questioning.

HIGHLANDS AND LOWLANDS BEFORE THE EIGHTEENTH CENTURY

From the time of the rise of clanship as the organizing principle of Highland social structure between the twelfth and fourteenth centuries (Grant 1961: 23) until the destruction of clanship in the eighteenth century, a clear division existed between the Highlands, the Lowlands, and the North (Mitchison 1962: 4). The exact geographical position of

FIGURE I
Definitions of the Highlands

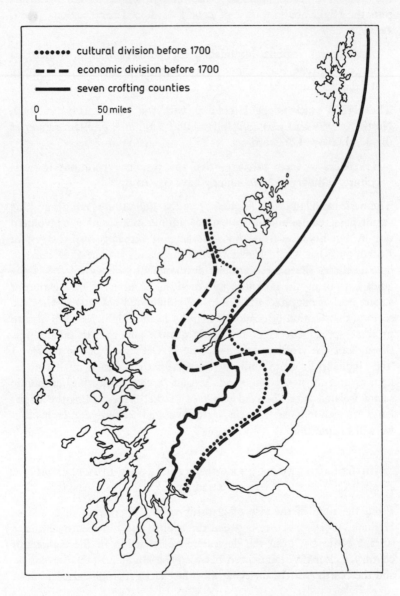

•••••• cultural division before 1700

＝ ＝ ＝ economic division before 1700

——— seven crofting counties

0   50 miles

the division depends to some extent on whether one uses economic or cultural criteria in distinguishing Highlands from Lowlands – as *Figure 1* shows – but historians are unanimous in telling us that such a division existed and was perceived to be important by Highlanders and Lowlanders. The Highlands formed a relatively autonomous social and political sector within Scotland; a point which may be demonstrated through an analysis of elite marriage patterns. Marriages of the heads of the main line and septs of Highland clans and Lowland families were political actions, in that they forged and maintained alliances, until the decentralization of political power in Scotland was brought to an end by the triumph of Royal authority in Lowland areas and the military conquest of the Highlands by the Hanovarian government after the '45. An analysis of elite marriage patterns should thus demonstrate the area within which Highland clan chiefs and Lowland lairds thought it worth while to make political alliances through marriage.

TABLE 1

Marriage patterns of Clan MacDonald, 1500–1880

	Origin of wife (per cent)		Total (per cent)	N
	Highland	Lowland		
1500–1699	93	7	100	46
1700–1880	66	34	100	80

Source: Calculated from data in Mackenzie 1881.

TABLE 2

Marriage patterns of Clan MacKenzie, 1500–1900

	Origin of wife (per cent)		Total (per cent)	N
	Highland	Lowland		
1500–1699	92	8	100	59
1700–1900	62	38	100	69

Source: Calculated from data in Warrand 1965.

Tables 1 and *2* show that in the case of the MacDonalds and MacKenzies, two important west Highland clans, elite marriages were contracted almost exclusively within the Highland area[7] before 1700.

TABLE 3

Marriage patterns of the family of Burnett of Leys, 1500–1900

| | Origin of wife (per cent) | | | |
	Highland	Lowland	Total (per cent)	N
1500–1699	0	100	100	16
1700–1900	0	100	100	18

Source : Calculated from data in G. Burnett 1901, C. Burnett 1950.

Table 3 shows that the elite of the Lowland family of Burnett of Leys, living close to the Highland Line in Aberdeenshire, contracted no marriages with Highland partners before 1700. After 1700, however, while the Burnetts retained their firm resolve not to marry across the Highland Line, a greatly increased proportion of MacDonald and MacKenzie clan gentry contracted marriage with Lowland partners.[8] This one-way flow of influences across the Highland Line reflects the increasing hegemony of the Lowland aristocracy, and through them the English aristocracy, throughout Scotland in the eighteenth and nineteenth centuries and was one of the more subtle forms of the institutional incorporation (Pearse 1971: 75) of the Highland social sector.

The data presented above suggest that the Highlands formed an autonomous social and political sector before the eighteenth century. This conclusion is supported by other evidence. The central authorities, the Scottish kings, were unable to control the Highlands on a continuing basis as late as the reign of James VI and I in the early seventeenth century (Grant 1930: 528–42; Smout 1969: 106–7). The customary strategy applied to the Highlands by the central authorities – divide and rule – increased division in the area without promoting centralized rule.[9] Contemporary accounts emphasize the narrow and hostile stereotypes held by Lowlanders of Highlanders and vice versa. James VI and I held the characteristic Lowland attitude to the Highlanders, albeit in a strong form:

'As for the Hie-lands, I shortly comprehend them al into two sorts of people: the one, that dwelleth in our maine land, that are barbarous for the most part yet mixed with some shew of civilitie: the other that dwelleth in the Iles and are alluterlie barbares . . . reform and civilize the best inclined among them, rooting out or transporting the barbarous and stubborne sort and planting civilitie in their roomes' (James VI and I, *Basilikon Doron*, quoted in Smout, 1969: 111).

Samual Johnson noted the unfavourable attitudes towards Lowlanders held by Highlanders as late as 1770:

> 'By their Lowland neighbours they would not willingly be taught; for they have long considered them a mean and degenerate race. These prejudices are wearing fast away; but so much of them still remains, that when I asked a very learned minister in the islands, which they considered as their most savage clans: *"Those,"* said he, *"that live next the Lowland."*' (Johnson 1775: 31 – original emphasis).

We are dealing here with a case of two ethnic groups, in Barth's sense of the phrase: groups formed through self-ascription or ascription by others, based on a perception of shared meanings (Barth 1969: 10). Economic exchanges across the Highland Line (which we will consider below) need not represent on this argument an attenuation of differences between the ethnic groups of Highlanders and Lowlanders: rather, by demonstrating the lack of shared meanings between Highland and Lowland actors, such exchanges could reinforce the differentiation (Barth 1969: 15–16). Barth notes that the persistence of a poly-ethnic system – such as the Scotland of Lowland, Highland, and North sectors which we are considering – depends on relatively high stability in the cultural features associated with ethnic groups; although this does not mean that there is no crossing of the cultural and ethnic group boundary on an individual level (1969: 21).[10] This high stability existed between Highlands and Lowlands,[11] reinforced not only by cultural differences but by economic, religious, and social differences.

Gaelic was the language of the Highlands and the Lordship of the Isles gave rise to a Gaelic high culture. The destruction of the Lordship in the fifteenth and sixteenth centuries began 'the degradation of the old Gaelic civilization to a folk culture' (Grant 1961: 27). In the Lowlands, however, Scots was the language and the Great Tradition (in Redfield's phrase) which Lowland peasants copied was the culture of pre-industrial Scottish cities such as Edinburgh and Glasgow.

The economic structure of both Highlands and Lowlands was based on the runrig joint farm. A number of tenants, with their sub-tenants, if they had any, worked a single farm with a high degree of co-operation in tasks such as ploughing. The arable land was divided into 'infield', which was intensively manured and intensively cropped, and 'outfield', which was manured less (if at all) and bore infrequent crops. Each tenant was allocated a number of 'rigs' of infield and outfield, on which he grew his subsistence crops – oats to eat and barley to drink, and was allocated a 'souming', the right to graze a specified number of beasts on the common grazings. The land was periodically reallocated. Rents, amounting to a third or a half of total produce, were paid to domain-holders in a mixture of cash, kind, and labour services.

In Lowland areas joint tenants paid rent directly to the laird. In the Highlands, however, tenants usually paid rent to a tacksman who lived on the difference between rents aggregated from a number of joint farms and rents paid to the chief. The differences between Lowland and Highland social structure are elusive. Smout summarizes the differences thus: 'Highland society was based on kinship modified by feudalism, Lowland society on feudalism modified by kinship' (1969: 44).

This raises some conceptual problems. A feudal society marked by strong vertical kinship relations is a contradiction in terms for Coulborn (1956: 196–7). What Smout seems to mean is that the land tenure system in the Highlands and Lowlands was feudal in a sense that most authorities would accept. Under *wardholding*, the chief or laird held his lands of the king and leased the land either directly to joint tenants or to tacksmen who then leased to tenants. Rents were paid in cash, kind, or labour, as we saw above, but the main obligation of an inferior to a superior under wardholding was not economic but military – the obligation to follow the superior if called 'out'. Thus the clan system was capable of being transformed at a moment's notice from an economic to a military institution. The chief was transformed from a landlord to the leader of the clan in battle. The rentier tacksmen became the *duine uaisle*, the lieutenants of the clan, fulfilling a crucial role in organizing and controlling the clan host. The tenants and sub-tenants became the clansmen, the foot soldiers of clan warfare.[12] Runrig was an essential part of this military arrangement, for the periodic reallocation of land allowed an increasing population, and therefore more fighting men, to occupy a given amount of land up to the limit set by subsistence. It thus represented a finely tuned adaptation to a situation, common to both Highlands and Lowlands before the centralization of political power, where a paper title to land was worthless without the military force to support it.

When one considers the nature of the relationships within this system, however, the idea of feudalism seems rather less appropriate. Perceived kinship links between a superior and an inferior seem to have had some importance in Lowland 'families'; among Highland clans they were of crucial importance. 'Clan' is a translation of 'children'. The chief was not only a landlord; he was a kinsman. This provided an affective element in the vertical, multi-stranded relationship between chief, tacksman, and clansman, which is far removed from the contractual relationship of classic feudalism. It was the reneging of chiefs on their kinship obligations to tenants, as the tenants saw it, that gave such bitterness to the reaction to the Highland Clearances. Furthermore, the 'feudal' rule of primogeniture was, on occasion, supplanted in the Highlands by tanistry, whereby any chosen male heir could become chief (Grant 1930: 477).

Although the runrig joint farm was common to both Highlands and Lowlands, in one respect the economic structure of the one differed from the other. The Highlands were a pastoral area – producing a cash crop of black cattle as well as a subsistence crop of oats and bere, while Lowland agriculture was basically arable.[13] Exchanges took place between the two areas, with Highland exports of black cattle paying for needed imports – grain in dearth years, timber, and manufactured goods (Gray 1957: 42–3). The sale of black cattle was critically important for the Highland economy, since the cash product of such sales provided the bulk of rent payments. This, and a cultural preference in the Lowlands, for wages in kind rather than money, produced a paradoxical situation in the early stages of agricultural improvement, when rents were paid in money more frequently in the 'archaic' Highlands than the 'modern' Lowlands.

The passage of time accentuated the differences between Highlands and Lowlands. From the sixteenth century wardholding gave way to feuferme land tenure. Under this form of feudalism, if we can call it feudal, an inferior's obligations to his superior were (and are) economic rather than military. 'Feuing was primarily undertaken as a method of increasing revenue. The cash nexus was predominant' (Grant 1930: 279–80). The spread of feuferme thus represents an attempt at the commercialization of agriculture, since feu duties were originally set at the level of economic rents. But wardholding remained as the landtenure arrangement of the Highlands, giving rise in Lowland breasts to fears about the implications of the continued existence of such a 'martial society'. These fears were reinforced by further fears about the religious and political adherence of Highlanders. The triumph of Presbyterianism in the Lowlands following the Reformation and the Convenanting Wars, and the subsequent development of parish schools throughout the Lowlands, threw into higher relief the continuing Catholicism of some Highland areas, the (to Presbyterian Lowlanders) heathenism of the rest, and the lack of formal educational facilities throughout the Highlands. The willingness of at least some Highland chiefs to come 'out' in support of Jacobitism – or in opposition to Whig royal agents in the Highlands – made the Highlands politically suspect.

This, then, is the background to the market incorporation of the Highlands. I have argued elsewhere that one should take the institutional incorporation of the Highlands to be anterior to market incorporation (Carter 1971), but what I wish to consider here is the account of the nature and process of market incorporation given by economic historians of the Highlands.

LIBERAL ECONOMICS AND THE MARKET INCORPORATION OF THE HIGHLANDS

In 1776 Adam Smith published his *The Wealth of Nations*. In the course of his discussion of the influence of towns in the improvement of agriculture he provided a potted economic history of the Highlands. He noted the essentially 'feudal' nature of Highland society before the eighteenth century:

'The occupiers of land were in every respect as dependent upon the great proprietor as his retainers. Even such of them as were not in a state of villanage, were tenants at will, who paid a rent in no respect equivalent to the subsistence which the land afforded them. A crown, half a crown, a sheep, a lamb, was some years ago in the highlands of Scotland a common rent for lands which maintained a family. In some places it is so at this day; nor will money at present purchase a greater quantity of commodities there than in other places. In a country where the surplus produce of a large estate must be consumed upon the estate itself, it will frequently be more convenient for the proprietor, that part of it be consumed at a distance from his own house, provided they who consume it are as dependent upon him as either his retainers or his menial servants' (Smith 1776: II, 199).

Smith is arguing that the Highland economy was only weakly influenced by trade, if at all, since the surplus economic produce must be consumed on the estate itself. Further, the estate owner (clan chief or, if the two offices were not held by a single individual, feudal superior) used the economic surplus from his estate to maintain his economic, social, and political control of the local area. This situation was not changed, Smith argues, by the imposition of the feudal law by central authorities. The local autonomy of chiefs remained very high.

'But what all the violence of the feudal institutions could never have effected, the silent and insensible operation of foreign commerce and manufactures brought about. These gradually furnished the great proprietors with something for which they could exchange the whole surplus produce of their lands, and which they could consume themselves without sharing it either with tenants and retainers. . . . For a pair of diamond buckles perhaps, or for something as frivolous and useless, they exchanged the maintenance, or what is the same thing, the price of the maintenance of a thousand men for a year, and, with it the whole weight of authority which it could give them' (Smith 1776: II, 203).

Two hundred years of political economy and, latterly, economic history have not added greatly to this basic story. The clan system is still seen to have been oriented to social needs rather than economic needs until the abolition of wardholding land tenure in 1747 knocked away the prop to this martial society.[14] Smout argues that the clan system inhibited the market incorporation of the Highlands:

'Undoubtedly social factors impeded the penetration into the Highlands of the economic forces that could have changed them. The surplus the Highlanders tried to sell outside was black cattle, but the widespread social institution of stealing cattle from a neighbouring clan was so prevalent that it seriously reduced the profitability of ranching within the hills, and thus limited the impact that market forces could have upon the Highlands until they were completely reduced to law and order' (Smout 1969: 341).

Thus the Highlands were only weakly linked to trade until the quaintly named 'pacification of the Highlands' by Hanoverian troops after the '45.[15]

Smith's description of an effete elite selling its patrimony for a diamond buckle is mirrored by more recent accounts of the rising debts loaded on Highland estates as chiefs adopted increasingly expensive consumption habits, shifting their reference group from other chiefs and clansmen to the Lowland and English aristocracy (Gray 1957: 149).

But more recent writers rest their analysis of the economic transformation of the Highlands on much firmer evidence than was available to Smith and recognize more factors in this transformation than just impersonal economic forces. The institutional incorporation of the Highlands, particularly the legal changes that followed the '45, are seen to have some importance (Smout 1969: 343-4); but impersonal economic forces are still, as with Smith, the major explanatory variable. The commercialization of Highland agriculture through extensive sheep-farming, and the consequent eviction of tenants to make way for sheep, and the Highland Clearances of the late eighteenth and nineteenth centuries, are seen to have been the result not of human action but of the Invisible Hand:

'But, although it was a situation in which the rich and the ruthless had the best chance of survival, it would be mistaken to put the blame for the resulting clearances simply upon greedy or malign landlords, for they were really the results of impersonal forces beyond the control of either landlords or tenants of "the total impact of the powerful individualism and economic rationalism of industrial civilisation on the weaker, semi-communal traditionalism of the recalcitrant fringe".' (Gaskell 1968: 26, quoting Gray 1957: 246)

Furthermore, the definition of what constitutes agricultural improvement in the Highlands is very specific. The model is improved agriculture in the Lowlands, where runrig joint farms were abolished and replaced by consolidated farms. Subsistence production was replaced by production for the market and efficiency was raised through new cropping arrangements – the rotation of arable crops with turnips and leys, for example – and technical innovations such as drainage and the steel plough. The vertically articulated social structure of laird and joint tenants was replaced by a polarized structure of capitalist farmers and industrialists on the one hand, and landless labourers on the other (Smout 1969: 347). Smout notes that some marginally Highland areas – parts of Perthshire, Angus, Aberdeenshire, Banffshire, and Cromarty, that is, the eastern fringe of the Highlands – did see an evolution towards such a 'modern' agrarian system. By contrast, in the north and west Highlands, peasant society was not destroyed (a necessary condition for 'modernity'), but merely changed to a different kind of peasant society. Runrig joint farms were abolished, to be sure, but crofts took their place. Crofts were (and are) small, consolidated arable units, individually tenanted, and carrying the right to a souming on common grazings. The crofting system allowed population levels to increase up to the level set by subsistence through subdivision of crofts. This system is seen as 'the one instance in Scotland of the improvers' failure to improve' (Smout 1969: 347). It was only with the mortality crisis of the potato famine of 1846–7 that the crunch came for many west Highland estates and they were cleared, or sold, and then cleared, for the creation of 'modern' capitalist sheep-farms'[16]

Opposition to clearance for sheep-farms and later for deer forests, strangely muted in the early nineteenth century, eventually resulted, partly as a result of contemporaneous land reform agitation in Ireland and Wales, in the establishment of the Napier Commission to examine the conditions of Highland crofters and, in 1886, in the Crofters Holdings Act. This Act gave a high degree of security and heritability of tenure to crofters within the seven crofting counties[17] who could satisfy a number of conditions. Current economic thinking suggests that this was a mistake in that it froze the economic structure of west Highland and Island areas; the HIDB described crofting as 'a stultifying form of land tenure' (HIDB 1967: 4). Farquhar Gillanders goes further. He regards the Crofters Holdings Act as a disaster:

'It is my belief, however, that the 1886 legislation heralded the death of crofting as a way of life, insulating it almost completely from normal economic trends and *legally* ensuring that crofting land could not now be developed into viable economic units' (Gillanders 1968: 96–7 – original emphasis).

The solution for the ills of the Highland economy follows from this premise:

'The real hope for the Highlands today . . . cannot be in tourism but in the simple courage to implement proved economic principles. The Highlander must cease to regard himself as a member of a chosen race to whom normal economic laws do not apply' (Gillanders 1968: 148).

Thus whether one believes that the agricultural revolution never touched the Highlands (HIDB 1967: Foreword; McCrone 1969: 14) or merely that it was rendered incomplete by the 1886 legislation (Turnock 1970: 108, 114), the policy conclusion derived from this analysis of the Highlands as an 'archaic', 'feudal', 'subsistence-based' economic sector is similar – open the subsistence sector to the market forces of the 'modern' economy.

LIBERAL ECONOMICS AND LATIN AMERICA

The consensual view of Latin American agrarian history is that, like the history of the Highlands reviewed above, it represents an incomplete transition from a 'traditional', 'archaic', 'feudal' structure to a 'modern', 'capitalist' structure. I will illustrate this argument with material from the highly regarded introductory text by Jacques Lambert.

Lambert argues that the *encomienda*, which delegated part of the sovereign's rights to individuals and gave rise to mutual personal duties on the part of masters and dependents, became associated with land ownership and produced the feudal *latifundio*, 'the fundamental institution of Iberian colonialism' (Lambert 1967: 59). *Latifundios* are defined as 'large estates operated under archaic methods and only partly put to use' (Lambert 1967: 59). Such estates are multifunctional institutions, providing economic, social, and political functions for a local region. The *latifundio* proved to be an admirably adapted institution for the solution of the basic problem of Iberian colonization: how to control large tracts of land with a relatively small number of Iberian colonists. But as the market forces of the 'modern' economy began to impinge on the Latin American economy, the *latifundio* became dysfunctional. The political genesis of the *latifundio* as a means of controlling a given area of territory is reflected in the owner's interest in upholding his political position; this means maintaining the isolation of his estate, as far as possible, from the market forces of the modern economy.

The *latifundio* is feudal, for Lambert, in that the relationships on the estate are based on reciprocal rights and duties and not on the cash nexus.[18] But not all estates in Latin America are *latifundios*. Estates exceeding 2 500 acres occupied 73 per cent of the agricultural and cattle-raising lands in 'modern' Argentina in 1945 (Lambert 1967: 61-2) and earned a large part of the foreign exchange of that country. But these were, in the main, 'modern' plantations, highly efficient and highly capitalized, employing wage labour rather than tenant labour (Mörner 1970), and not 'feudal' *latifundios*.[19] The total involvement of plantations in cash crop production for the market means that motives of economic maximization predominate in plantations. In *latifundios*, by contrast, agricultural production is set at a level that provides a barely sufficient subsistence for the 'feudal' dependents, plus a surplus which the owner can use to satisfy his consumption demands and dominate the local political structure (Chonchol 1965: 84). Social needs have precedence over economic needs. Lambert's prescription for economic (and socio-political) development in Latin America thus includes, as a major element, the full involvement of 'feudal' *latifundios* in the money economy and their consequent and inevitable transformation into 'modern' plantations. The dual economy in Latin America, created as in Boeke's classic formulation by the introduction of mature capitalism into a pre-capitalist economic system (Lambert 1967: 60), must give way to economic modernity in a final triumph of capitalism.

THE FRANK THESIS AND THE 'LATIFUNDIO'

This dual economy account of the nature of the Latin American agrarian sector has recently been challenged by a number of Marxist economists and sociologists, notably Frank (1967, 1970); Vitale (1968); and Stavenhagen (1968). The members of this school have their differences. But they all tell the same story about the origins of Latin American underdevelopment, if not about solutions.

The basis of the argument is that the Iberian conquest was impelled by commercial motives. Vitale goes further in claiming that late fifteenth-century Iberia was in the process of transition from feudalism to capitalism, and that the conquest stemmed from specifically capitalist motives (1968: 36–7). Other authors take the conquest to have been mercantilist rather than capitalist (Stavenhagen 1968: 16; Frank 1967: 242), but one of the problems of this school is that the difference between mercantilism and capitalism is never clearly specified – if, indeed, they accept the existence of such a difference (Riddell 1972: 93). Regardless of the precise label which we attach to the motives for conquest, however, they were, it is argued, undeniably commercial, and the development of large agricultural estates was similarly commercial. The growth of the Mexican *hacienda*, as of estates in other mining areas, took place in pursuit of profit, first by providing food for the 'growth pole' of the silver mines (Furtado 1970: 13–16) and for export crops and then, with the decline in profitability of mining in the seventeenth century, as a more profitable economic enterprise than mining. The desire to monopolize land and income which might be used by competitors or independent producers (Frank 1970: 234–7) gave rise to the particular form of the estate – occupying vast tracts of land but using very little of it for productive purposes.

Furtado argues that *latifundios* were established in pursuit of profit, but that later they became feudal institutions (Furtado 1970: 53). This, for Frank, is a nonsense. Both the dual economy account of the movement from an 'archaic' economy to the 'modern' economy and the Marxist account of the transition from feudalism to capitalism are evolutionary and cannot handle regressions. The view of *latifundios* as feudal institutions, when the genesis of such estates was mercantilist or capitalist, is based on the illegitimate inference from the existence of non-cash nexus relationships within the *latifundio* that the *latifundio* as a socio-economic system is pre-capitalist (Frank 1967: 239). The genesis of the *latifundio* was commercial for Frank, so it remains commercial. There is no analytical difference between a *latifundio* and a plantation; both exist to maximize profit for the owner, but in the *latifundio* this purpose is concealed by the seemingly non-commercial relationships between owner and peasants. But the very non-commercial nature of these relationships is determined by market forces; payment oscillates between cash and non-cash according to the economic interest of the owner (Frank 1967: 234–5, 266). Even the modes of production within the *latifundio* can be altered in 'feudal' directions if it is to the advantage of the owner so to do. Increased demand for wheat led to free producers on Chilean wheat *latifundios* being transformed into 'feudal' peons (Frank 1970: 244).

A corollary of Lambert's view of *latifundios* as large estates within the 'archaic' sector is that the *latifundio* is, at best, weakly linked to national and international trade. For Frank, on the other hand, trade with national and European markets brought the *latifundio* into being. But this is an exploitative relationship; economic surplus is sucked out of the 'remote' areas and consigned along chains of metropolitan-satellite relationships through the 'modern' sector and then to an overseas metropolis. This process continues until the surplus arrives at a highest order world-capitalist metropolis.[20]

'Moreover, each national and local metropolis serves to impose and maintain the monopolistic structure and exploitative relationship of this system ... as long as it serves the interests of the metropoles which take advantage of this global, national, and local structure to promote their own development and the enrichment of their ruling classes' (Frank 1970: 6–7).

Three consequences follow from this. First, the dual economy model, with its assumption of two dynamics in one society – an economic dynamic in the 'modern' sector and a non-economic dynamic in the 'archaic' sector – is clearly inadequate (Frank 1970: 221–30). The 'archaic' sector, like the 'modern' sector, is the result of a single historical process – the penetration of capitalist modes of production and motivations to the 'remotest' areas of Latin America (and Asia and Africa).[21] Second, evolutionary accounts of economic development, which are based on extrapolations of the historical experience of now developed nations (usually Britain and the USA), will give misleading predictions in the context of underdeveloped countries, for the developed countries may once have been *undeveloped* – in a primal economic state – but they were never systematically *underdeveloped* through the establishment and maintenance of exploitative metropolitan–satellite relationships (Frank 1970: 4). Finally, the policy prescription derived from dual economy premises – to open the 'archaic' sector to the cold winds of the market economy – would, on the monopoly capitalism argument, increase underdevelopment rather than promote development, since present underdevelopment is itself the result of just those market forces that dual economy theorists see to be an economic panacea.

THE FRANK THESIS AND THE SCOTTISH HIGHLANDS

We have seen that the consensual view of Highland economic history before the growth of capitalist sheep-farming shares many features with Lambert's views on Latin America. In both cases one has an agrarian structure based on units engaged in extensive agriculture (runrig joint farms and *latifundios*) and the prevailing motivation underlying agricultural production is, in both cases, non-economic; enough wealth must be produced to satisfy the consumption demands of the owner, whether 'latifundist' or clan chief, but beyond this the interest of the owner lies not in maximizing economic production and profit but in maintaining his social and political domination of the local area. The dual economy policy prescription in both cases is to open up this 'feudal' sector to the play of market forces; to bring *latifundios* and Highland estates within the 'modern' economy.

Do Frank's arguments about Latin America have relevance to the Scottish context?[22] How adequate is the view that, before the commercialization of Highland agriculture through sheep-farming, the Highlands formed a precapitalist economic sector?[23] R. H. Campbell asserts that high prices for black cattle and kelp during the Napoleonic Wars inhibited the penetration of market forces to Highland areas 'by enabling an anachronistic economy to continue to exist still longer' (Campbell

1965: 36). Thus Highland estates engaged in producing cattle and kelp were outside the 'modern' economy; economic motivations were subsidiary to social and political motivations for owners of such estates. How adequate is this view?

The trade in black cattle, the staple cash crop of Highland agriculture, was of very great importance to the Scottish economy before the Union:

> 'By the middle of the seventeenth century the cattle trade to England had, despite all handicaps, grown to such proportions that Scotland was described as little more than a grazing field for England' (Haldane 1952: 18).

But this trading relationship was asymmetrical. With the reorientation of Scots trade from Europe to England after the Treaty of Edinburgh of 1560 and the Union of the Crowns in 1603 (Smout 1965: 456–7), the Scottish economy became increasingly dependent on exporting cattle (and, to a lesser extent, linen) to England, while England, although dependent on imported supplies to satisfy the demand for beef, had alternative sources of supply in Wales (Bonser 1970: 78) and Ireland. The closing of the Border to the cattle trade by the English in 1704 was thus a highly effective economic sanction (Hamilton 1963: 88); it was followed three years later by the Act of Union which represented the end of Scottish pretensions to a political and economic policy independent of that of England.

The Union established free trade throughout Britain. One of the greatest immediate beneficiaries of this was the cattle trade, which increased in scale throughout the eighteenth century. It was calculated that in 1794, 60 000 beasts were sold at the central tryst in Falkirk, at an average price of £4 sterling (Hamilton 1963: 96). As the trade grew in volume, so the links with England were strengthened. The central tryst was moved from Crieff to Falkirk in the eighteenth century, partly to ease access from south-west Highland areas, but also because of the greater accessibility of Falkirk for English buyers (Hamilton 1963: 91). The cattle trade had an important influence on the economic development of the Lowlands, since the need for credit on the part of cattle drovers was one spur to the development of the Scottish banking system, which Campbell sees to have been one of the necessary preconditions for the growth of manufacturing industry in the Lowlands (Campbell 1965: 68–73). The Highlands derived some profit from the sale of cattle, but most profit was made by drovers and graziers outwith the Highlands. The price for cattle in the Highlands rose as high as £5 or £6 per head during the Napoleonic Wars (Hamilton 1963: 96): in 1812 the Navy victualling yards paid an average price of £15 per head (Haldane 1952: 175). The lucrative trade of salting beef was entirely confined to England (Hamilton 1963: 96). Thus the Highlands produced relatively low-value primary products; the profits from converting these products went into other hands.

But, of course, some profit did accrue to the Highlands, and it was extremely important in the Highland economy. Cash derived from the sale of cattle formed the major part of rent payments from tenant to landlord. Hamilton argues that:

'In the Highlands the livelihood of laird and peasant depended on the sale of cattle at remunerative prices. . . . This industry thus lifted the economy from mere subsistence to farming for profit' (Hamilton 1963: 89).

Note the assertion that the rearing of black cattle was a commercial operation. Nor were chiefs adverse to taking a part in the risky business of financing the droving trade.

'The cattle dealers of the eighteenth century found it necessary to "engage a co-adventurer in an intended speculation". The names of Highland chieftains and Lowland lairds appear little less frequently than those of graziers, cattle dealers, merchants and businessmen of the cities in the story of this hazardous trade' (Haldane 1952: 61–2).

It is difficult, on these grounds, to see the Highland economy as non-commercial. The failure of landlords to innovate with new methods of agriculture and with improved breeding (Bonser 1970: 78) could be seen not as an economically irrational decision based on the precedence of social needs before economic, but as a rational economic decision in a situation where landlords were already enjoying profits from the cattle trade and in which new methods would have involved heavy capital outlay for an uncertain economic return. The kelp industry presents a similar picture.

Kelp is an alkaline ash obtained by burning seaweed. In demand as a fertilizer and for soap-making and glass-making, the price of kelp rose from about £2 per ton in 1750 to over £20 in 1810 (Gray 1951: 197–8). This astronomical rise was due in part to the cutting-off of supplies of Spanish *barilla* during the Napoleonic Wars. The rise in price led owners of kelp estates, the Clanranald estates on the west coast and in the Hebrides, for example, to become increasingly dependent on kelp

manufacture for their income; in 1823 the Clanranald factor wrote that
'it is entirely a kelp estate' (Gray 1951: 206). This growing dependence
of the landlords' income on the process of gathering and burning kelp
had two major effects. First, since kelping was a labour-intensive
industry, it was in the interest of the landlord to have a large population
on his estate. Emigration was discouraged, and it has been suggested
that landlords encouraged immigration to the kelping areas (Prebble
1963: 248). Land tenure was reorganized: the old runrig joint farms
gave way to a system of small, consolidated, individually tenanted crofts,
which provided work for the crofter and his family for only two or three
days a week, leaving them the rest of the time for kelping. The subdivision of crofts was allowed, to enable the largest possible population
to live at subsistence level. The change from the joint farm to crofting
reduced the differentiation among tenants, consigning all to a similar
position (Caird and Moisley 1961: 89). Clanranald introduced the potato
to South Uist in 1743 – the potato gave a higher subsistence crop yield
than oats[24] – and coerced his tenants into accepting it (Graham 1899: 1,
172).

The second major effect had to do with profit. Since the costs of
producing kelp rose less steeply than the selling price, kelp production
became increasingly profitable. At the peak price of £20 per ton in 1810
the landlord's profit was £16 (Gray 1951: 202). As the profit rose, so
did the landlord's involvement in the productive process. From letting
out kelp rights to entrepreneurs, landlords moved on to contracting
directly with kelpers (tenants) for the disposal of their product. Monopolistic control was established by making tacksmen market their
tenants' kelp through the landlord. Tenants became wage labourers,
standing in a dual relationship to the landlord: tenant to landlord and
employee to employer.[25] Rents were set at a level where they creamed
off the whole cash product from kelping, leaving the tenant the occu-
pancy of his croft as the reward for his labours (Gray 1951: 200–1).
When the price for kelp crashed at the end of the Napoleonic Wars with
the renewed importation of *barilla*, tenants could not pay their money
rents. The landlord therefore took the whole cash product from kelping,
taking rent from tenants in the form of wage labour. Landlord–tenant
relationships settled down into a form of demonetized tenant labour,
with tenants subsisting on produce from their crofts and on relief from
the landlord. This relationship lasted on the Clanranald estate until
1838, when the estate was sold to Gordon of Cluny, 'one of the most
ruthless removers in the Isles' (Prebble 1963: 250).

The view that it was only with the clearance of kelping estates for extensive sheep-farming that these areas were incorporated in the capitalist economy is surely wrong. The driving force of the kelp industry had been the desire of landlords to maximize profit. The emphasis on production of a single cash crop for markets outwith the highlands, with the greatest possible profit to the landlord, makes the kelp-estate just as capitalist an operation as the monocrop sheep-estate which followed it.[26] The seemingly 'feudal' nature of kelp-estates after the price fall is the result, as in Frank's interpretation of the *latifundio*, of a process whereby a capitalist operation, once closely integrated into the capitalist economy, has been left beached by the receding of those market forces that brought it into being. To regard kelp-estates as 'anachronistic' and, by implication, pre-capitalist (Campbell 1965: 36); to regard the crofting system as 'the one instance in Scotland of the improvers' failure to improve' (Smout 1969: 347) because it meant merely a change from one kind of peasant society to another kind, instead of a total destruction of the peasantry, is to do two things. First, as we have seen, it means misinterpreting the nature of the cattle trade and the kelp industry, and therefore the nature of the Highland economy in the eighteenth and early nineteenth centuries. Second, such arguments demonstrate the tyranny of Lowland, and through them of English, models in Highland economic history. Only those changes which produce a polarized social structure of capitalist farmers and landless wage labourers are to count as 'improvement'. Yet if one takes the critical feature of improvement to be not particular social structural outcomes but the turn to commercial agriculture, then the English and Lowland experience becomes only one of several possible ways of 'modernizing' agriculture (Moore 1967: 413–83). The kelp industry is a paradigm case of what Moore calls *conservative modernization*:

'. . . The landed upper class will use a variety of political and social levers to hold down a labour force on the land and make its transition to commercial farming in this fashion' (Moore 1967: 420).

The particular form which this took in the case of the kelp-estates is similar to Moore's description of Japan, where:

'A landed aristocracy may maintain intact the pre-existing peasant society, introducing just enough changes in rural society to ensure that the peasants generate a sufficient surplus that it can appropriate and market at a profit' (Moore 1967: 433).

The fact that the attempts of kelp landlords to develop their estates took a different form from the attempts of Lowland landlords, and had different consequences, does not disguise the similarity in the underlying intention in both situations – to maximize profit.

Where does this leave the policy of the Highlands and Islands Development Board? First, it is clear that the Highlands may be underdeveloped, but they are not undeveloped. The 'ecological devastation' of large parts of the Highlands (Darling 1968: 37–8) is the result of the removal of indigenous woodland cover, and subsequent overgrazing by sheep, which removed the residual fertility formerly locked in the land by the tree cover. This overgrazing is clearly the result of the search for maximum profit in sheep-farming, but the destruction of the woodland stemmed in large part from similar causes. Some cutting took place in order to remove refuges for wolves, footpads, and rebels before the eighteenth century, but thereafter the major reasons were, to produce charcoal for the smelting of iron by English ironmasters who had largely exhausted wood stocks farther south, to improve grazing for sheep and, in the nineteenth century, to make birch bobbins for Lowland and Lancashire cotton mills (Hamilton 1963: 189–92; Darling and Boyd 1969: 70–4).

Second, any view of the Highlands as an area 'that the various revolutions in agriculture, industry and technology have passed by' (HIDB 1967: Foreword) is patently mistaken. The Highlands today are not independent of such processes – they are the result of them. A number of consequences follow from this on Frank's assumptions. Any attempt to strengthen the links between the Highlands and the 'modern' economy through a large-scale exploitation of indigenous Highland raw materials (*pace* the HIDB's determined efforts to promote the development of the mineral resources of the crofting counties) will increase the underdevelopment of the area by reinforcing the satellization of the Highlands. Alternatively, the growth of industry based on imported raw materials – British Aluminium's Invergordon smelter is an obvious example – would result in a metropolitan rather than a satellite industry. But the smelter is unlikely to have a great positive impact on the economic life of the Highlands for three reasons. First, it is highly capital-intensive, and despite its high capital cost, around £37 million, will create relatively few jobs. Second, it is unlikely to act as the propulsive industry in a growth pole spatially located in the Highlands, since metal fabrication industries are typically sited close to markets.

Third, to return to the monopoly capitalism argument, since the smelter is owned outside the Highlands (and, indeed, outside Scotland) the profits from its operation will leave the area. This contrasts with the growth of Lowland industry in the late eighteenth and nineteenth centuries, which was very largely Scottish owned.[27] It is quite possible, however, that the smelter (and the most recent panacea for the Highlands – the oil boom – which has important locations in the Inner Moray Firth area) could have serious negative consequences for the Highlands. In the time when the British navy was a force to be reckoned with, two of its major bases were at Scapa Flow in Orkney and Invergordon in the Moray Firth. The closing of these two bases caused severe economic and social dislocation in the areas concerned. There is no evidence that, after the exploration and development phases of the oil boom are completed, which seems likely, at present, to be a fairly short period, the same fate will not overcome those areas which believed that oil would bring permanent prosperity.

Finally, one might see metropolitan–satellite processes at work within the crofting counties. We noted above the contradiction between a growth centre policy and an attempt to maintain given population levels in areas outside the growth area. The HIDB is committed to both these policies, but the *Economist*, that objectification of economic rationality, noted in 1970 that it was arguable whether any economic purpose was served by having remote parts of the Highlands inhabited all year round, since the profitable enterprises – tourism, forestry – could be worked by seasonal labour (*Economist* 21 February 1970, XXXI). Even discounting such radical suggestions as this, which lies in the same tradition of hard-headed liberal economic thinking about the Highlands as the Sutherland Clearances, a centralist economic development policy is likely to have a devastating effect on the crofting areas,[28] which are the last toehold of the Gaelic language and culture in Scotland. It all depends on what you mean by development.

Notes

1 This does not mean that sociological, or at least proto-sociological, concerns did not occupy Scottish academics in the past. But the Scottish Moralists – Smith, Hume, Reid, Hutcheson, Stewart, Ferguson, Millar, Lords Kames and Monboddo among them (Schneider 1967) – did not call themselves sociologists. Their speculations in this

field grew out of their professional concerns as lawyers and – the Scottish academic catch-all – moral philosophers (Davie 1964).

2 One of the most striking assertions of British homogeneity of recent years is Alford's thesis that class membership is now the only social factor exercising a significant effect on British voting behaviour. Nationality, regional loyalties, and religious affiliations used to be significant but are no longer: Britain is psephologically homogeneous (Alford 1963: 108–9, 144–5). No better example could be adduced of the way in which social science is discomfited by events; the upsurge of Welsh and Scottish nationalism and the events in Ulster make Alford's thesis seem, at best, quaint. Even before these events, however, it had been demonstrated that Scottish political behaviour was not consistent with Alford's thesis (Budge and Urwin 1966: 132).

3 For Scots Law see T. B. Smith (1963, 1970); for university education see Davie (1964: 7–8). The problem in considering assimilationist tendencies is to distinguish between changes that are the result of a conscious (or taken for granted) application of English patterns and changes coming from a simultaneous adaptation to new circumstances in both Scotland and England. For the latter see MacCormick (1966: 201–4) and Withrington (1970).

4 For the definition of the crofting counties see *Figure 1*.

5 The Board's annual statistics include a category labelled 'non-economic'. When challenged to say what they are doing to promote social development, Board spokesmen invariably point to this category. Between 1965 and 1970 non-economic grants constituted 2 per cent of the amount of money disbursed by the Board in grants and loans (HIDB 1971: Appendix X).

6 I take Belshaw's summary as my definition of a dual economy:

'The notion of dual economy implies that, within one political framework, there is one sector which operates according to the principles of modern capitalism. This sector is commercially sophisticated, linked with international trade, dominated by motives of maximization, and in the colonial context, almost entirely in the hands of aliens or residents of alien extraction. . . . Opposed to this sector and separated from it is the traditional peasant economy, which according to the puristic form of the theory, is conservatively oriented, interested in security and continuity rather than change, not concerned with maximisation of profit or of resource use, oriented towards the satisfaction of social needs rather than reacting to international forces, and incapable of engaging dynamically in trade and commerce. Except for a very small minority of Westernised natives who have left traditional society, the indigenous population lies in this sector' (Belshaw 1965: 96).

7 Defined as in the cultural definition in *Figure 1*.

8 In this analysis 'Lowland' is a residual category, embracing all areas outside the Highlands and the North.

9 Cregeen argues that one of the main factors leading to the decision of clan chiefs in the south-west Highlands to support the Jacobite Rebellion in 1745 was their opposition to the expansionism of the Dukes of Argyll, who were the chiefs of Clan Campbell and Royal agents in the south-west Highlands (Cregeen 1965: 159–60).

10 A celebrated example of such crossing was Alexander Stewart, 'the Wolf of Badenoch'. A younger son of King Robert II, the Wolf 'went native' and descended on Elgin in 1390 with his 'wild Wykked Hel-and-men' and burned the burgh and Cathedral (Kermack 1957: 62).

11 'The pendulum has swung back, and once more it is not easy to realise how utter and how clear-cut was the dividing line between the Highlands and the Lowlands during the four hundred years between the fourteenth century and the eighteenth century' (Grant 1930: 149).

12 It is possible to make an analytical distinction between these economic and military aspects of land tenure, but this distinction did not exist for the actors themselves, as the prevalence of cattle-reiving in the Highlands demonstrates.

13 This pastoral–arable division explains the divergence between the economic and cultural divisions in *Figure 1*. The Aird – the district around Inverness – and the east coastal strip to Caithness were arable areas within the Gaelic sector. Cattle stocks were held in some Lowland areas, notably Aberdeenshire and Galloway.

14 In at least one area, the Argyll estates, important economic changes preceded the '45. Leases were being offered by competitive bidding in 1710, and hereditary tacks were abolished in 1737 (Cregeen 1965: 169–70).

15 Disarming Acts were imposed on Highlanders after both the '15 and the '45. On both occasions cattle drovers were specifically excepted from the provisions of the Acts.

16 For a very concise statement of this view, and the derived conclusion that the Highland elite was dancing to a social tune and disregarded economic opportunities, see Hobsbawm (1969: 301–3).

17 The crofting counties were identified in 1886 as the most convenient administrative area for handling the problems of crofting. Their subsequent reification as 'the Highlands and Islands' makes little sense on economic, cultural, historical, or development policy grounds.

18 'Thus, in different ways, a large proportion of the rural population came to be scattered in small structural units, self-sufficient from the viewpoint of the organisation of production, subject to tutelege, whether direct or indirect . . . of a ruling class that extracted from it a

surplus in a manner resembling the pattern generally known as *feudalism*' (Furtado 1970: 16 – original emphasis).

19 Part of the confusion over *latifundios* and plantations is the result of conflicting definitions of the difference between the two. Furtado does not make this distinction. He defines a *latifundio* as an estate employing more than twelve workers in a permanent capacity, whether in the 'modern' or the 'archaic' sector (Furtado 1970: 54–8). Chonchol distinguishes between traditional estates and modern plantations, but argues that both make very inefficient use of land and labour (Chonchol 1965: 83). Stein and Stein echo Lambert's distinction between the 'feudal' *latifundio* and the 'modern' plantation. The *hacienda* is seen as a patriarchal social nucleus as well as a unit of agricultural production, while the plantation is defined historically as 'an independent economic unit, created to produce staples for external, that is, European consumption' (Stein and Stein 1970: 39, 40).

20 Laclau criticizes Frank for making the presence or absence of a link with the market the criterion for the existence of capitalism (1971: 20). This leads, he asserts, to Frank having an excessively wide conception of capitalism which does not allow him to distinguish between capitalism, in the Marxist sense, and other modes of production. Indeed, Laclau sees the crucial failure of Frank to be his unwillingness to define capitalism, with Marx, as a mode of production (1971: 25). These criticisms of Frank, although well founded, are not central to my argument, since Laclau accepts Frank's demolition of the dual economy thesis (1971: 24), and it is with this that we are here concerned.

21 'The regions which are the most underdeveloped and feudal-seeming today are the ones which had the closest ties to the metropolis in the past' (Frank 1970: 13).

22 Buchanan has attempted to explain the upsurge in support for Welsh and Scottish nationalism in the mid-1960s as a response to economic satellization, using Frank's terms. Unfortunately, however, he assumes that the Highlands and Scotland are co-extensive (Buchanan 1968: 38–9) – an interesting form of the strategy of misapprehension. His argument depends on the Lowlands standing in the same satellized situation to the English metropolis that I am here arguing for the Highlands; and the argument will not hold. Lowland industrialization was the result of the English allowing a place in the metropolitan sun for certain specialized heavy industries, provided that they were complementary with the English economy and not competitive, and Scottish capital was invested abroad – three-quarters of the foreign investment in ranching in the United States in the 1870s and 1880s was Scottish (Campbell 1965: 79). See also Nairn 1968: 45.

23 Marx certainly believed that the Highlands were pre-capitalist. Indeed, in one of his swingeing attacks on the Sutherland Clearances he categorizes the clan system as not just pre-capitalist but pre-feudal ('The Duchess of Sutherland and Slavery' in Bottomore and Rubel, 1963: 131–2). Once again one sees the categorical problems that the Highlands present to sociological typologies; the clan system contained feudal elements such as wardholding land tenure and elements drawn from the kin-based social structure of pre-feudal Scotland and Ireland, such as tanistry.

24 On the influence of the potato in Highland and Lowland Scotland see that monument of comparative sociology Salaman 1949: 344–408.

25 Thus the kelp industry counts as a capitalist enterprise on Laclau's criteria: the labourer's sale of his wage labour (Laclau 1971: 24).

26 Although the price of kelp fell after 1815, production on the Clanranald estate did not fall. In 1815 the estate handled rather more than 1 100 tons; in 1838 it handled 1 300 tons (Gray 1951: 201, 202).

27 But no longer. American-controlled businesses alone accounted for over 10 per cent of total employment in Scottish manufacturing industry, for 12 per cent of total output, and for an estimated 27 per cent of Scotland's manufactured exports in 1968 (Johnston, Buxton and Mair 1971: 88). Nor is the definition of what constitutes a 'Scottish company' unambiguous. The largest company registered in Scotland is Burmah Oil. See the fund of data, from turnover and profits to chairman's salary, for the fifty largest Scottish-registered public companies in Hawthorn 1971.

28 The population of the crofting counties rose by 6 443 between 1961 and 1971: a significant event, since the population previously had been falling continuously since 1841. But the population of the burgh of Inverness alone rose by 5 143 between 1961 and 1971. Population growth at the centre is accompanied by decline at the periphery.

References

ALFORD, R. 1963. *Party and Society*. Chicago: Rand McNally.

APTHORPE, R. 1970. Development Studies and Social Planning. In R. Apthorpe (ed.), *People Planning and Development Studies: Some Reflections on Social Planning*. London: Cass.

BARTH, F. 1969. Introduction. In Barth F. (ed.), *Ethnic Groups and Boundaries: the Social Organization of Culture Difference*. Boston: Little Brown.

BELSHAW, C. 1965. *Traditional Exchange and Modern Markets*. Englewood Cliffs, N.J: Prentice-Hall.

308 *Ian Carter*

BONSER, K. 1970. *The Drovers, Who They Were and How They Went.* London: MacMillan.

BOTTOMORE, T. and RUBEL, M. (eds.) 1963. *Karl Marx: Selected Writings in Sociology and Social Philosophy.* Harmondsworth: Penguin.

BUCHANAN, K. 1968. The Revolt against Satellization in Scotland and Wales. *Monthly Review* **19** (10): 36–48.

BUDGE, I. and URWIN, D. 1966. *Scottish Political Behaviour: a Case Study in British Homogeneity.* London: Longmans.

BURNETT, C. 1950. *The Burnett Family, with Collateral Branches.* Los Angeles.

BURNETT, G. 1901. *The Family of Burnett of Leys, with Collateral Branches.* Aberdeen: New Spalding Club.

CAIRD, J. and MOISLEY, H. 1961. Leadership and Innovation in the Crofting Communities of the Outer Hebrides. *Sociological Review* **9**: 85–102

CAMPBELL, R. 1965. *Scotland Since 1707: the Rise of an Industrial Society.* Oxford: Blackwell.

CARTER, I. 1971. Economic Models and the Recent History of the Highlands. *Scottish Studies* **15**: 99–120.

—— 1972. The Highlands Board and Strath Kildonan. *Catalyst* **5**: 21–2.

—— 1973. Six Years On: an Evaluative Study of the Highlands and Islands Development Board. *Aberdeen University Review* **45**: 55–78.

CHAPMAN, R. W. (ed.) 1924. *A Journey to the Western Islands of Scotland.* Oxford: Oxford University Press.

CHONCHOL, J. 1965. Land Tenure and Development in Latin America. In Veliz, C. (ed.) 1965.

COLLIER, A. 1953. *The Crofting Problem.* Cambridge: Cambridge University Press.

COULBORN, R. 1956. *Feudalism in History.* Hamdem, Connecticut: Archon Books.

CREGEEN, E. 1965. The Changing Role of the House of Argyll in the Scottish Highlands. In Lewis, I. (ed.) 1965.

DARLING, F. 1955. *West Highland Survey.* London: Oxford University Press.

—— 1968. Ecology of Land Use in the Highlands and Islands. In Thomson, D. and Grimble, I. (eds.) 1968.

DARLING, F. and BOYD, J. 1969. *The Highlands and Islands.* (Revised edition.) London: Collins.

DAVIE, G. 1964. *The Democratic Intellect.* (2nd edition.) Edinburgh: Edinburgh University Press.

DORE, R. P. 1965. Land Reform and Japan's Economic Development: a Reactionary Thesis. In Shanin, T. (ed.) 1971.

FRANK, A. 1967. *Capitalism and Underdevelopment in Latin America:*

Historical Studies of Chile and Brazil. New York: Monthly Review Press.

—— 1970. *Latin America: Underdevelopment or Revolution.* New York: Monthly Review Press.

FURTADO, C. 1970. *Economic Development of Latin America: a Survey from Colonial Times to the Cuban Revolution.* Cambridge: Cambridge University Press.

GASKELL, P. 1965. *Morvern Transformed: a Highland Parish in the Nineteenth Century.* Cambridge: Cambridge University Press.

GILLANDERS, F. 1968. The Economic Life of Gaelic Scotland Today. In Thompson, D. and Grimble, I. (eds.) 1968.

GRAHAM, H. 1899. *The Social Life of Scotland in the Eighteenth Century.* (Two volumes.) London: A. & C. Black.

GRANT, I. 1930. *The Social and Economic Development of Scotland before 1603.* Edinburgh: Oliver & Boyd.

—— 1961. *Highland Folkways.* London: Routledge.

GRAY, M. 1951. The Kelp Industry in the Highlands and Islands. *Economic History Review* 4: 197–209.

—— 1957. *The Highland Economy.* Edinburgh: Oliver & Boyd.

HALDANE, A. 1952. *The Drove Roads of Scotland.* Edinburgh: Nelson.

HAMILTON, H. 1963. *An Economic History of Scotland in the Eighteenth Century.* Oxford: Clarendon Press.

HAWTHORN, J. 1971. Top Scots. *Scotland.* (November): 17–27.

HIGGINS, B. 1968. *Economic Development.* (2nd edition.) New York: Norton.

HIDB (Highlands and Islands Development Board) 1967. *First Annual Report.* Inverness: HIDB.

—— 1971. *Fifth Annual Report.* Inverness: HIDB.

HOBSBAWM, E. 1969. *Industry and Empire.* Harmondsworth: Penguin.

JENKINS, R. 1971. *Exploitation.* London: McGibbon & Kee.

JOHNS, F. 1965. *The Social Structure of Modern Britain.* Oxford: Pergamon Press.

JOHNSON, S. 1775. *A Journey to the Western Islands of Scotland.* In Chapman, R. W. (ed.) 1924.

JOHNSTON, T., BUXTON, N. and MAIR, D. 1971. *Structure and Growth of the Scottish Economy.* London: Collins.

KELLAS, J. 1968. *Modern Scotland: the Nation since 1870.* London: Pall Mall.

KERMACK, W. 1957. *The Scottish Highlands: a Short History.* Edinburgh: Johnston & Bacon.

LACLAU, E. 1971. Feudalism and Capitalism in Latin America, *New Left Review* 67: 19–38.

LAMBERT, J. 1967. *Latin America: Social Structures and Political Institutions.* Berkeley: University of California Press.

LEWIS, I. (ed.) 1965. *History and Social Anthropology*. London: Tavistock Publications.

LICHTHEIM, G. 1971. *Imperialism*. London: Allen Lane.

MACCORMICK, D. 1966. Can Stare Decisis be Abolished? *Juridical Review*: 197–213.

MACCORMICK, N. (ed.) 1970. *The Scottish Debate: Essays on Scottish Nationalism*. London: Oxford University Press.

MCCRONE, G. 1969. *Regional Policy in Britain*. London: Allen and Unwin.

MACKAY, D. 1965. Regional Planning for the North of Scotland. *Aberdeen University Review* **41**: 75–83.

MACKENZIE, A. 1881. *History of the MacDonalds and Lords of the Isles*. Inverness: A. & W. MacKenzie.

MAGDOFF, H. 1968. *The Age of Imperialism*. New York: Monthly Review Press.

MILLER, K. (ed.) 1970. *Memoirs of a Modern Scotland*. London: Faber & Faber.

MITCHISON, R. 1962. *Agricultural Sir John: The Life of Sir John Sinclair Of Ulbster, 1754–1835*. London: Bles.

MOORE, B. 1967. *Social Origins of Dictatorship and Democracy*. Harmondsworth: Penguin.

MÖRNER, M. 1970. A Comparative Study of Tenant Labour in Parts of Europe, Africa and Latin America, 1700–1900. *Latin American Research Review* **5**: 3–15.

NAIRN, T. 1968. The Three Dreams of Scottish Nationalism. *New Left Review* **49**: 3–18. Reprinted in Miller, K. (ed.) 1970.

PEARSE, A. 1971. Metropolis and Peasant. In Shanin, T. (ed.) 1971.

PETRAS, J. and ZEITLIN, M. (eds.) 1968. *Latin America: Reform or Revolution?* Greenwich, Connecticut: Fawcett.

PHILLIPSON, N. and MITCHISON, R. (eds.) 1970. *Scotland in the Age of Improvement*. Edinburgh: Edinburgh University Press.

POTTER, J. 1967. Peasants in the Modern World. In Potter, J., Diaz, M. and Foster, G. (eds.). 1967.

POTTER, J., DIAZ, M. and FOSTER, G. (eds.) 1967. *Peasant Society*. Boston: Little Brown.

PREBBLE, J. 1963. *The Highland Clearances*. Harmondsworth: Penguin.

RIDDELL, D. 1972. Towards a Structuralist Sociology of Development? *Sociology* **6**: 89–96.

SALAMAN, R. 1949. *History and Social Influence of the Potato*. Cambridge: Cambridge University Press.

SCHNEIDER, L. (ed.) 1967. *The Scottish Moralists on Human Nature and Society*. Chicago: University of Chicago Press.

SHANIN, T. (ed.) 1971. *Peasants and Peasant Societies*. Harmondsworth: Penguin.

SMITH, A. 1776. *The Wealth of Nations*. Three volumes. (2nd edition.) Dublin: Whitestone.

SMITH, T. 1963. Legal Imperialism and Legal Parochialism. *Juridical Review*: 39–55.

—— 1970. Scottish Nationalism, Law and Self-government. In MacCormick, N. (ed.) 1970.

SMOUT, T. C. 1965. The Anglo-Scottish Union of 1707: the Economic Background. *Economic History Review* **16**: 455–67.

—— 1969. *A History of the Scottish People, 1560–1830*. London: Collins.

STAVENHAGEN, R. 1968. Seven Fallacies about Latin America. In Petras, J. and Zeitlin, M. (eds.) 1968.

STEIN, S. and STEIN, B. 1970. *The Colonial Heritage of Latin America: Essays on Economic Dependence in Perspective*. New York: Oxford University Press.

THOMSON, D. and GRIMBLE, I. (eds.) 1968. *The Future of the Highlands*. London: Routledge.

TURNOCK, D. 1970. *Patterns of Highland Development*. London: MacMillan.

VELIZ, C. (ed.) 1965. *Obstacles to Change in Latin America*. London: Oxford University Press.

VITALE, L. 1968. Latin America: Feudal or Capitalist? In Petras, J. and Zeitlin, M. (eds.) 1968.

WARRAND, D. 1965. *Some MacKenzie Pedigrees*. Inverness: Carruthers.

WITHRINGTON, D. 1970. Education and Society in the Eighteenth Century. In Phillipson, N. and Mitchison, R. (eds.) 1970.

L

PART FIVE

Perspectives on the Future

W. F. WERTHEIM

The Rising Waves of Emancipation - from Counterpoint towards Revolution[1]

If the dream of an imminent world revolution was torn to pieces at the end of the First World War, then the dream of 'modernization', as a gradualist policy on a world scale, has been cruelly disturbed since the end of the Second World War. For sociologists the latter disillusion, rather than the former, will be a traumatic experience. Sociologists have generally not been over-concerned with revolution, but they have pinned all too many hopes on modernization. The sociologists' belief in modernization was the 'modern' version of evolutionism; the latter had become less fashionable since Berthold Laufer (1918) had declared it to be 'the most inane, sterile, and pernicious theory in the whole theory of science'. Laufer considered the theory inane because of its unilinear simplifications. I do not know to what extent he considered the theory pernicious because it had been made an article of faith by the Marxists who, at the time of his writing, had just gained power through a revolution in Russia. Lenin, for one, wrote as late as 1919 that one could rely, even in detail, on Friedrich Engels's *The Origin of the Family* as a scientific basis.

In the Marxists' view, evolution had become mixed up with revolution. In contrast, western sociologists, terrified as they were by the prospect of revolution, first rejected evolutionism lock, stock, and barrel. Since the Second World War, however, they have developed a new type of evolutionism fully dissociated from the idea that revolution could ever be a thing to be applauded. This was where the modernization concept came into play. Modernization theory really stood for plain evolutionism. In its crudest unilinear form modernization, as elaborated by Daniel Lerner (1958), was a process moving from tradition, via a 'transitional society', towards the Valhalla of modern society - and modern society was, of course, identical with American society.

In a less crude form unilinear evolutionism appeared in disguise whenever terms such as development and underdevelopment were used

315

in common parlance or in economic jargon. The anti-revolutionary
undertones of the gradualist approach became particularly apparent
whenever the term development was applied as 'community development' to the villages of the Third World. Phillips Ruopp made the
political implication explicit:

> 'The developmental differs radically from the cataclysmic, with the
> latter's delusive appeals to violent action. Development is gradual,
> but it is not a gradualness that lends itself as an excuse for inaction. It
> means growth, but it must be growth cultivated by unequivocal and
> constant witness to justice, liberty, and compassion' (1953: 18).

For those who thought like this India was expected to show that gradual
development could occur in this democratic, humanitarian sense, and
that revolution of the Chinese, cataclysmic type could be dispensed
with.

Since the end of the Second World War there have been other types of
evolutionism in disguise. The bias against revolutionary upheaval was
implicit in Walt Rostow's (1960) version of evolutionism in the economic sphere, as expressed in his 'stages of economic growth'. It is
significant that he calls his book a 'Non-Communist Manifesto';
evidently he wants to stress the point that 'development' is a process
determined by purely quantitive factors which operate independently of
politics. In Russia, says Rostow, the take-off had already occurred
before the First World War. The Russian Revolution was superfluous
to the initiation of the next phase: 'the drive to maturity, the process of
industrial differentiation, the advance to modernization on a wide
front'.

Modernization, as conceived by its advocates, is largely a process
initiated and directed from above. In the past such modernization processes actually have taken place and have propelled the societies concerned towards higher levels of production and economic maturity. A
striking example is Japan, where modernization was initiated from
above by a social group narrowly allied with the establishment, without
the occurrence of any revolution, that is to say any mass movement
from below. Japan's modernization process started after the Meiji
restoration, as early as the late sixties of the nineteenth century. To
quote the Polish economic historian Witold Kula (1960: 24): 'The last
time the "take-off towards economic growth" which Rostow and Ger-
schenkron hope to find in the history of each capitalist country actually
occurred, was in Japan'. Since the turn of the century there have been

no more cases of smooth 'modernization' processes. What we have witnessed time and again is what Eisenstadt (1964, 1966) has termed 'breakdowns of modernization'.

For Eisenstadt modernization implies a gradual process. In western Europe the process was initiated by the upper and middle classes in the late eighteenth and nineteenth centuries. Only gradually was it extended from the centre to the periphery, towards wider groups and strata, owing to the slow pace of urbanization and industrialization. Broadly speaking the process was, in his view, a smooth and harmonious one. The primacy of economic and cultural innovation had produced a 'flexibility of the existing political structure' at the centre. Consequently, there was 'a strong absorptive and integrative capacity within society in order to meet all kinds of political demands'.

In the new nations of today, however, the trick does not work. The process of industrialization lags behind. Evidently, according to Eisenstadt's diagnosis, the breakdown is due to the fact that broad layers of the society, including those on the periphery, put forward far-reaching political and social demands, and aim at a say in the central institutional framework, before the society has reached a certain maturity in the economic and educational field. In Eisenstadt's analysis, accordingly, the 'revolution of demands' among the broad masses is a purely negative factor in the total modernization process. True modernization, in his view, implies a gradual spread of modernity from an urban elite towards the broader masses on the periphery of each society; and the process is being confounded whenever the masses put in too early their political and other claims (1966: 114–17).

Other sociologists are equally worried about the breakdown of modernization in many new nations. In dealing with Java, Clifford Geertz speaks about a 'permanently transitional society'. He wrote (1965: 152): 'Both tradition and modernity seemed to be receding at an increasing rate, leaving only the relics of the first and the simulacre of the second.' Whereas Eisenstadt speaks about a 'breakdown of modernization', Geertz describes Java as 'a society stranded'. René Dumont (1966) writes about the 'false start in Africa', whereas Myrdal (1968) has coined the term 'Asian Drama'.

In my view the basic weakness of these modernization theories – which are among the best of the type – is the neglect of the international economic environment and power structure in which the new nations are forced to operate. In his book on modernization, Eisenstadt only deals with factors within each society, as though they were decisive for the specific course modernization has taken. That strikes me as incomplete. Certainly since the turn of the century one has to take account of the dominant position of huge world concerns and world powers. These effectively block the type of gradual industrialization, based on the efforts of private entrepreneurs, that was typical of the nineteenth century. Eisenstadt, in his otherwise judicious study, does not touch upon the impact of these external factors. Yet it is precisely these factors that, as I shall point out in the course of my argument, generally prevent the so-called elites of the new nations from operating as true 'problem-solvers' in a largely agrarian environment.[2] Too often these elites sometimes unwittingly stand not for 'development', but for what Frank (1969) has scathingly called the 'development of underdevelopment'. As a consequence of the innumerable failures of the elites in their attempts, sincere or alleged, to start true economic development of the type that would benefit the broad masses, it is, therefore, only too logical when the rural masses often react in a negative way, by saying *no* to the type of modernity imposed by these urban elites. Is this a breakdown of modernization, or is it only a breakdown of the *ideology* of modernization, including its implicit assumptions?

The concept of modernization, then, needs to be fundamentally reconsidered. It is too easily assumed that modernization is largely a one-way process, initiated from above by a leadership that derives its qualifications from its acquaintance with western concepts and western techniques. But any social process is a two-way affair of interaction – that much is obvious from historical experience accumulated during centuries. No process started from above takes root without actual involvement of the people, who therefore have to be 'mobilized' in order to take an active part therein. On the other hand, there are many historical instances of processes in which the initiative came to a large extent from below, although (mostly urban-oriented) leadership is always required to canalize the initiative into coherent action. If one wants to define the processes that could be assessed as constituting the totality of social evolution, 'emancipation' rather than 'modernization' is the appropriate term. Emancipation – in the sense of liberation, both from natural and man-made shackles – is a process which does not develop in a unilinear, unambiguous way. It is mostly a dialectical process, which advances in successive waves. Only as a dialectical, emancipatory process on a world-wide scale can human evolution be understood as a viable analytical concept.

In order to detect the sources of human emancipation, we have to disengage ourselves from the concept of human societies as nicely integrated units. The different modernization models, including Eisenstadt's, over-stressed the integrative functions of modern societies. Integrative–functionalist interpretations of societies accentuate their adaptive qualities. Evolution, in the integrative conception, is largely reduced to adaptive processes.

Personally, I cannot endorse the integrationist model. In the past fifteen years, this model has been disputed by quite a number of critics such as Lockwood (1956), Dahrendorf (1959), and Rex (1961). It seems to me, however, that the criticism of the integrationist model can be carried farther and directed against some of the basic tenets of sociology as it stands. Reification of geographically circumscribed societies, as conceived by Durkheim, was the original sin of western sociology; and Radcliffe-Brown was the devil's advocate. If one is to understand how human evolution, viewed as a relentless, although basically dialectical, process of emancipation actually proceeds throughout history, one has to start from a different societal model: one into which the seeds of dissatisfaction, unrest, and change have been built from the outset. In all social units there are value dissensions, although they are not always manifest. One distinct value-system may dominate, adhered to by the holders of political power, the 'establishment'. But usually one can discover disguised countervalues, which function as a kind of counterpoint to the dominant values. Such counterpoints express themselves, for example, in religious values opposing the existing hierarchy of power, status, and wealth. They can also assume the apparently more innocuous form of folk tales in which the prevalent social order is more or less reversed (as when the poor swineherd marries the beautiful princess), or of myths in which the weaker groups may recognize themselves as masters of yesterday and victors of tomorrow (as, for example, in the widespread animal fables).

Hidden and institutionalized protest of the counterpoint type may act as a safety-valve and serve the ultimate interests of the establishment in making the repression easier to bear. Thus the royal buffoon served to mitigate the rigidity of court etiquette. But the urge for emancipation usually does not stop here. Social protest, embodying countervalues carried into the open, assumes many different shapes – all the way from movements basically accepting the prevalent social and political order, to movements questioning the legality of the established power structure.

There have been periods in human history when emancipation

movements from below were able to effect social change in a gradual way through lawful action. There have been other periods when sections of the establishment have stimulated emancipation, at least partly, through mobilizing the masses, as for example in Japan after the Meiji restoration. Situations do, however, also exist where the prevalent political order is so completely dissociated from popular forces that its aims are squarely opposed to anything that could directly contribute to further emancipation. We have to ask ourselves whether such a condition is not nowadays prevalent in most of what we are used to calling the Third World.

Changes introduced from above tend to be frustrated through the social, political, and economic climate in which the agents of change have to operate. A good example is provided by the community development projects, so in vogue during the fifties. In India these projects mostly amounted to a method of relying on the so-called progressive farmers. These farmers possessed a sizeable plot of land, sufficient capital to be able to experiment with new agricultural techniques, and a general outlook influenced by an urban orientation, so that they were willing to transform their farm into a kind of experimental station. The underlying strategy was that this group would introduce the kinds of innovations advocated by the district or village level social workers; the other villagers, having observed the splendid results with their own eyes, would then follow suit. In Indonesia a similar method was used by the agricultural extension service and called the oilstain effect. Unfortunately, it was far from easy for those without sufficient land or capital to follow suit and introduce the innovations. In practice, relying on the progressive farmers – a system which I have called 'betting on the strong' (1964) – has not produced a strengthening of community ties and greater equality, but has led to a polarization within the Asian villages, with the poor peasantry losing their lands and becoming the victims of 'modernization' introduced from outside.

Similar problems arose in the past few years in connexion with attempts to introduce purely technological innovations from above. It appears that the 'Green Revolution' is not producing cornucopia, but is turning into Pandora's box, as was foreseen by some critics (Wharton 1969). 'Modernization' within the boundaries of the prevalent social and political order may spell wealth and increased production for some – it does not revolutionize rural society as such. In time, the advocates of miracle rice will look for other panaceas, which will again prove ineffective. The same has earlier been the case with panaceas such as birth control or the formation of co-operatives.

Similarly, as Myrdal and others have convincingly shown, agrarian reform legislation is bound to fail in a society (such as India) where social inequality permeates the entire political structure. No 'modernizing' effect on the peasantry as a whole can be expected if such legislation is introduced from above, without any sign of a peasant emancipation movement forcing the establishment to take such a step. The authorities called upon to put such reform legislation into effect are generally too strongly allied with the gentry, against whose privileges the legislation is directed, to take a strong stand in favour of the poor. Usually, when the peasantry starts to move in an attempt to emancipate itself from the fetters of landlordism and exploitation, the 'soft state' drops its softness and proceeds harshly against those who try to wrest concessions from the obstinate elite. Soft the officials are only towards their social peers – the high and the mighty, practising fraud and corruption – or towards the foreign interests with enough power to call the tune.

In *The Challenge of World Poverty* Myrdal (1970) gives a devastating criticism of the way in which officialdom in underdeveloped countries and foreign interests have thus far misused their power. It is, therefore, somewhat puzzling to find in the same book a plea for other types of reforms and foreign aid to be introduced and brought into effect by exactly the same authorities and external forces. Evidently, Myrdal does not believe in emancipation forces from below, for the countries of south and south-east Asia.

It is true that the peasantry in most of the countries of that region do not yet move on a massive scale. But, as we have already observed, they have a response of their own to the attempts at modernization from above. For the moment that response is negative: they say *no* to all those who try to manipulate them. Let me elaborate.

Bailey (1957) has described the negative reactions on the part of Indian peasants towards those who are deemed to represent the state: 'They' do not understand 'our' problems. 'They' make unreasonable demands. The whole relationship between peasantry and government is dominated by a deep feeling of mistrust on the part of the villagers, a feeling rooted in lifelong negative encounters. The government officials, in their turn, have stereotypes of the villagers. 'The peasant is stupid, indolent and greedy' . . . 'They' do not know what is good for them. 'They' want things for nothing and will not help themselves. The attitude of the villagers is interpreted as 'resistance to change', springing from a strong sense for tradition. This concept of resistance to change is at the root of several theoretical approaches to the problem of modernization. Foster (1965) attributes the resistance to the 'Image of the Limited Good'. Banfield (1958) holds that the lack of co-operative spirit among the southern Italian peasants is due to 'amoral familism'. Erasmus (1968), in contrast, argues that the Mexican peasants lack a sense of individualism, an urge to keep up with the Joneses: the normal peasant jealously watches his neighbours who might push ahead and 'keeps the Joneses down'.

Erasmus does not realize that the absence of individual aspirations does not preclude a willingness to get ahead collectively. The peasant distrust prevalent among so many rural populations is not necessarily an expression of lack of civic sense, of a resistance to change, especially if it benefits only the happy few, the 'progressive farmers'. One has to consider whether they also reject overall change, which holds the promise of an ulterior improvement of their life as a group.

Huizer (1973) has attempted to prove, in a study of peasant unrest in Latin America, that peasants are by no means averse to action, if they feel that their interests are really involved. Whenever the 'culture of repression' prevalent in so many *hacienda* areas is relaxing, the peasants are prone to form organizations defending their rights and advancing claims for radical land reform or for the removal of all kinds of grievances. Such claims are advanced in a legal way, but if they are not taken seriously the organization may resort to illegal action such as land occupation. The usual consequence then is repression, with the landlords getting support from the government. In these circumstances solidarity on a class basis, which hold a promise for future revolutionary action, can develop.

Depending on the reaction of those in power, emancipation movements may, therefore, assume different forms. It is impossible simply to dismiss such movements as 'breakdowns of modernization'; and if the peasants mostly reject piecemeal change, the so-called 'elite', supported by external economic forces and held in power through what is called 'development aid', are opposed to wholesale change. Non-participation in the modernization process, as initiated by the establishment, could be a pre-condition for collective action liable to bring about social and economic innovation of a more comprehensive kind. If saying *no* on the part of the peasantry is a distinct phase in the emancipation process, and action within the legal boundaries does not help, the next, conclusive phase could be a peasant revolution. 'If you want the people to be conservative, then give them something to conserve', once said a conservative leader in Britain Stanley Baldwin. Asian peasants have nothing to conserve – they have nothing to lose but their chains. This is why they are, potentially, a revolutionary force.

However, certain scholars doubt whether peasant revolutions are still on the agenda. We have to ask ourselves whether their prospects are still as promising as they seemed to be shortly after the Second World War.

Are the waves of emancipation actually rising? Barrington Moore (1966) has tried to analyse the reasons why a peasant revolution did occur in China, and not in India. Although he is fully aware that 'in the backward countries today, there continues the suffering of those who have not revolted', his conclusion is that the factors which opposed such a revolution in India in the past will prove an obstacle to revolution also in the future. Moore admits that, in view of the deteriorating food situation, 'a political upheaval of some sort will become highly likely. But it will not necessarily take the form of a communist-led peasant revolution. A turn to the right or fragmentation along regional lines, or some combination of these two, seems much more probable in the light of India's social structure'. And then he adds: 'The situation in India leads one to ask whether the great wave of peasant revolutions, so far one of the most distinctive features of the twentieth century, may not have already spent its force' (1966: 482-3). A similar view has been taken by Kiernan (1970: 9), who suggests the possibility 'that the phase of modern history that made socialism through peasant revolution pure and simple a possibility, is a limited phase only, and confined to special areas – just as the period of possible working-class revolution pure and simple was a limited one'.[3]

I would certainly agree that it would be absurd to suggest that revolutions in which a peasantry is actively engaged arise easily under circumstances of extreme rural poverty. We have to take full account of the social forces that oppose such revolutionary action on a large scale on the part of the peasantry, such as the protective function of patron-client relationships, prevalent in any peasant society where a gentry can be clearly distinguished from the peasantry. In India, for example, all kinds of inter-caste relationships of a ritual as well as economic nature have always provided a measure of protection. On the other hand, caste divisions in India have seriously obstructed the growth among the peasantry of a broad solidarity on a class basis.

However, I would not agree with the view of Moore and Kiernan that 'the great wave of peasant revolutions may have spent its force'. I shall try to make my stand clearer by taking, as a starting point, Moore's comparison of India and China.

In Moore's view, what distinguished Chinese rural society from that in India was 'the weakness of the links that bound the peasantry and the upper classes'. According to Moore 'the clan and patrilineal lineage emerge as the only important link between the upper and lower strata in Chinese society' (1966: 207–8). I doubt whether Moore's argument is conclusive. In China, patron–client relationships outside the clan did prevail. In his work *Fabric of Chinese Society* Morton Fried has paid a good deal of attention to the *kan-ch'ing* institution, which operated as a patron–client type of relationship outside the realm of kinship ties, and was often connected with tenancy bonds. Nor does a clan structure preclude the existence of patronage relationships within a clan or lineage. A member of the gentry had a certain latitude within which to decide to which poor members of the clan or lineage he would extend favours or protection, and whom he would ignore as a clan member.

Therefore, I am not at all convinced that the difference between the situations in China and India can be reduced to structural differentials. It could just as well be argued that the difference between the two developments is largely one of phase in a generally parallel process.

In China a peasant revolution on a large scale did occur, in India it did not. Why could we not argue that in India it has *not yet* occurred? Moore posits that in India, for the moment, a turn to the right is more likely. Here I fully agree. The way in which the Indian government dealt with leftist movements in West Bengal, its intervention in East Bengal (Bangla Desh), and the constant pressure from the extreme right (the Jan Sangh) point towards the possibility of such a development in the next decade. But this could mean that through such a turn to the right India would come nearer to a large social revolution. In China, under Sun Yat-sen, an amount of democratic freedom was still prevalent, and emancipation along legal lines still seemed to be in the picture. At that time the chances for a revolution under communist leadership proved to be scanty. But after Chiang Kai-shek had introduced a harsh military dictatorship, mainly based on landed interests and foreign support, a largely rural social revolution got its chance, and a great number of intellectuals gradually defected from an establishment that seemed to offer no prospect for further emancipation. But an accelerator – the Pacific War – was needed to weaken the military machine of the Kuomintang sufficiently to enable the communists to make a bid for power.

I am aware that the assumption of a fixed sequence of evolutionary stages does not take sufficient account of the dialectical character of the evolutionary process nor of the basic uniqueness of any single historical constellation (Johnson 1966: 91, 98). But perhaps the Chinese sequence does present a model for further developments in India and elsewhere. There is much evidence to show that in the 'New Nations', at first, more or less democratic 'populist' regimes arise, and that later, professional military people are likely to stage a counter revolution or a *coup d'état* and establish a regime with many of the characteristics of a military dictatorship. In Asia the sequence occurred in Indonesia, Burma, and Cambodia, and also in Africa there are several instances. And although it is hardly a 'New Nation' we should not forget Brazil.

It is, therefore, incorrect to assume that the situation in the Third World is more or less static, and that one could content oneself, as Barrington Moore appears to do, with the diagnosis that a peasant revolution either did or did not occur. Dynamic forces are operating, which Frank has attempted to summarize in the formula 'development of underdevelopment'. In the rural sphere a growing polarization occurs between the few wealthy (a gentry transformed into a class of rural capitalists) and the numerous poor. Even in areas such as Java, where in a former phase the social process could better be described as an agricultural involution, leading towards a 'sharing' of poverty, a growing opposition between landowners and landless people crystallized during the nineteen-fifties.

But under a populist regime, popular discontent may still express itself in legalized forms, and mobilization of these popular forces remains one of the main aspects of such regimes, mostly led by 'solidarity makers' of the Sukarno or Sihanouk type. The Sukarno regime, for example, initiated a land reform in the early sixties which was far from radical, but which still caused alarm among the landowners' class and their allies. In such a situation a communist take-over, either as a consequence of a social revolution or as a culminating point in a gradual radicalization process of the populist government, is highly improbable, as the actual history of the past few decades proves time and again (Spain before the Second World War, and in the post-war period, countries such as Greece, Indonesia, Cambodia, Ghana, and Brazil) – although the rightist opponents of the regime keep claiming that such a take-over is imminent. This assertion then serves as a rationalization for a military take-over, putting an end to most aspects of emancipation along legal, evolutionary lines. The new military regime mostly resorts to brute repression, as occurred under Chiang Kai-shek and as now occurs in Indonesia and Cambodia, and leans heavily on foreign aid. In such a situation patronage-like relationships, providing a modicum of protection to some of the poor, tend to dwindle. This strengthens the potential for organization of the poor peasantry along lines of class solidarity not weakened by patron–client relationships. Nevertheless, in most cases 'accelerators' of some sort will be needed to transform this potential for organization and ultimately for social revolution into a reality.

Overall development is an arduous affair, especially in a world where vested interests, despite all pronouncements to the contrary, are opposed to it. This is why I must conclude that, in many countries, there is no outlook for true development except through a radical social revolution.

But even after a social revolution has occurred, development remains a nearly superhuman task. After such a social revolution much becomes truly possible – family planning, radical agrarian reforms, a green revolution, co-operative farming, or educational reforms of a radical kind. But if such measures are to prove successful they must not be regarded as panaceas, and it must be fully realized how difficult and all-embracing such innovations are, and how much depends on the genuine and active participation of the masses. Mental factors, implying full devotion to the revolutionary cause, are as basic to a total transformation of the social fabric as a radical remoulding of the material production relationships. The Chinese experience since 1949 may serve to show the importance of these mental factors. The mental factors have operated beside the material ones throughout human history. Emancipation has been proceeding, in waves, from counterpoint towards revolution. But after a revolution mental factors maintain an enormous significance as a driving force to prevent a relapse into Thermidor, and to forestall the potential threat that the revolution would end in a restoration, without having produced anything sizeable but a 'circulation of elites'. The Chinese cultural revolution was a heroic attempt to prevent the operation of Robert Michels's 'iron law of oligarchy'.

My conclusion would be that World Revolution, in the sense of a world-wide, at times retarded, at times accelerated, process of emancipation, need not be scrapped off the agenda. What needs to be scrapped is modernization from above on a world-wide scale.

Notes

1 This paper deals with some of the main themes of the author's book: *Evolution and Revolution: the Rising Waves of Emancipation*.
2 Feith (1962: 117) distinguished between two types of 'elites': the 'solidarity makers', exemplified by the late President Sukarno, and the efficient 'administrators' who stress 'problem-solving' as the main task in an underdeveloped country. The distinction between the two types of 'elite' has been endorsed by several sociologists and political scientists, including Eisenstadt (1966: 137).
3 For a contrary view, as far as Latin America is concerned, see Hobsbawm (1970).

References

BAILEY, F. G. 1957. *Caste and the Economic Frontier: a Village in Highland Orissa*. Manchester: Manchester University Press.

BANFIELD, E. C. 1958. *The Moral Basis of a Backward Society*. New York: Free Press.

DAHRENDORF, R. 1959. *Class and Class Conflict in Industrial Society*. London: Routledge.

DUMONT, R. 1966. *False Start in Africa*. London: Andre Deutsch.

EISENSTADT, S. N. 1964. Breakdowns of Modernizations. *Economic Development and Cultural Change* 12: 345–367.

—— 1966. *Modernization: Protest and Change*. Englewood Cliffs, N.J.: Prentice-Hall.

ERASMUS, C. 1968. Community Development and the Encogido Syndrome. *Human Organization* 27 (1): 65–74.

FEITH, H. 1962. *The Decline of Constitutional Democracy in Indonesia*. Ithaca: Cornell University Press.

FOSTER, G. M. 1965. Peasant Society and the Image of Limited Good. *American Anthropologist* 67: 293–315.

FRANK, A. G. 1969. *Latin America: Underdevelopment or Revolution*. New York: Monthly Review Press.

FRIED, M. H. 1969. *Fabric of Chinese Society: a Study of the Social Life of a Chinese County Seat*. New York: Octagon.

GEERTZ, C. 1965. *The Social History of an Indonesian Town*. Cambridge, Massachusetts: MIT Press.

HOBSBAWM, E. 1970. Guerillas in Latin America. In Miliband, R. & Saville, J. (eds.) 1970.

HUIZER, G. 1973. *Peasant Rebellion in Latin America*. Harmondsworth: Penguin.

JOHNSON, C. A. 1966. *Revolutionary Change*. Boston: Little.

KIERNAN, V. G. 1970. The Peasant Revolution. In Miliband, R. & Saville, J. (eds.) 1970.

KULA, W. 1960. Les débuts du capitalisme en Pologne dans la perspective de l'histoire comparée. Address delivered at the Polish Academy in Rome, 1960.

LAUFER, B. 1918. Review of R. H. Lowie, *Culture and Anthropology*. *American Anthropologist* **20**: 90.

LENIN, V. I. 1965. Lecture delivered in 1919, reprinted in *Collected Works*, Vol. 29. Moscow: Progress.

LERNER, D. 1958. *The Passing of Traditional Society: Modernizing the Middle East*. Glencoe, Illinois: Free Press.

LOCKWOOD, D. 1956. Some Remarks on *The Social System*. *British Journal of Sociology* **7**: 134–46.

MILIBAND, R. and SAVILLE, J. (eds.) 1970. *The Socialist Register, 1970*. London: Merlin Press.

MOORE, BARRINGTON, JR., 1966. *Social Origins of Dictatorship and Democracy: Lord and Peasant in the Making of the Modern World*. New York: Beacon Press.

MYRDAL, G. 1968. *Asian Drama: an Inquiry into the Poverty of Nations*. London: Allen Lane.

——— 1970. *The Challenge of World Poverty: a World Anti-poverty Programme in Action*. London: Allen Lane.

REX, J. A. 1961. *Key Problems of Sociological Theory*. London: Routledge and Kegan Paul.

ROSTOW, W. W. 1960. *The Stages of Economic Growth. A Non-Communist Manifesto*. London: Cambridge University Press.

RUOPP, P. (ed.) 1953. *Approaches to Community Development*. The Hague: Van Hoeve.

WERTHEIM, W. F. 1964. *East-West Parallels: Sociological Approaches to Modern Asia*. The Hague: Van Hoeve.

WERTHEIM, W. F. 1973. *Evolution and Revolution: the Rising Waves of Emancipation*. Harmondsworth: Penguin.

WHARTON, C. R. 1969. The Green Revolution: Cornucopia or Pandora's Box. *Foreign Affairs* **47** (3): 464–76.

KRISHAN KUMAR

The Industrializing and the 'Post-industrial' Worlds: on Development and Futurology

INTRODUCTION

The purpose of this paper is not to predict the future relations between the 'developed' and the 'underdeveloped' societies. Less grandly, it is to consider some of the attempts that have been made in that direction, with a view to assessing their value for the sociology of development. For some years now, and especially during the last decade, a number of social scientists in all the major industrial countries of the world have been engaged in what many of them have been pleased to call 'the futurological enterprise'.[1] They have been attempting to discern the main structural outlines of future industrial society. They have conjectured, many of them, that industrial society is entering a new phase of its evolution, marking a transition as momentous as that which a hundred years ago took some European societies from an agrarian to an industrial social order. They have called this new society variously: the 'post-industrial society' (Daniel Bell), the 'post-modern era' (Amitai Etzioni), 'post-civilization' (Kenneth Boulding), 'post-economic society' (Herman Kahn), and – to vary the phrase a little – 'the knowledge society' (Peter Drucker), 'the technetronic era' (Zbigniew Brzezinski), and, more modestly, 'the service class society' (Ralf Dahrendorf).[2]

Very few of these theorists deal extensively or in detail with the likely framework of relationships between the 'post-industrial' and the industrializing worlds. Their focus, as with so much social theory in the past, is on the intrinsic mechanisms of societal change. Consequently their interest is in the new society in the making, as it expresses itself in the various stages of formation in the different industrial societies of the developed world. We are largely left to make our own inferences as to the probable impact of the new type of society on its environment, especially as that is constituted by other societies outside the 'post-industrial' pale. Perhaps this lack of curiosity reflects no more than the indifference commonly displayed by the strong to the weak. But it is obvious that the developing societies cannot respond with a similar indifference. The industrial societies only too promptly, massively, and forcibly manifest themselves as an active presence in the environment of these other societies, who are constantly required to adjust to changes induced by the continuing evolution of their host societies.

Thus the sociology of development cannot ignore the work of the futurologists. If, as they declare, the industrial societies are moving into a radically new era, with different demands and requirements from the present, then the developing societies will equally radically be affected. The forces shaping their internal evolution will have taken on a new character. To be able to say anything about the direction of that evolution we shall need to know something about those new forces.

I

That development theorists and futurologists are strangers to one another appears all the more unjustified when we consider that development theory and futurology taken together constitute one of the best examples of convergence and complementarity in the history of social theory. They both, in their different spheres, re-establish the study of social change as the central pre-occupation of their studies, following a period of over half a century of neglect of that topic.

One hardly need elaborate these days on the extent to which the heroic period of sociology was dominated by the awareness of social change. Saint-Simon, Comte and Spencer, de Tocqueville and Marx, Weber and Durkheim all wrote and theorized under the overwhelming impression that a 'terrible beauty' was born. A new society, 'the industrial society', was in the making, fraught equally with hope and despair. Whether they were struck most by the process of industrialization, or democratization, or rationalization, and whether inspired with more hope or more gloom, the nineteenth-century sociologists conceived their task as the description and explanation of the great transformation taking place before their eyes. And however much they may have been concerned with re-establishing the bases of social order – as Robert Nisbet claims for the whole sociological tradition (Nisbet 1967) – it was an order seen as lying beyond and based on an acceptance of the current changes. Those changes had to be put in a systematic framework that gave them a past as well as a future.

Their sociologies were therefore pre-eminently evolutionary and developmental. To accomplish their task they had to do two things: they had to give an account both of the mechanisms of change, and of the directions of change. In both areas their accounts became the decisive source for the later conceptualizations of development theorists and futurologists. As to the mechanisms of change, they had recourse to a tradition of thinking as old as recorded western thought itself. The 'conjectural histories' of the Greeks, the idea of 'the Great Chain of Being', the widespread use of the 'organic metaphor' relating the structure and functions of individual organisms to the structure and functions of society; later the idea of progress, the uniformitarian method in the new geology of the nineteenth century, and finally, a loosely held notion of biological evolution; all these, consciously or not, were compounded into a view of social change that has continued to exert an irresistible fascination for social theorists.[3]

In this conception, change is due essentially to forces intrinsic to the thing changing. Change is constant, cumulative, and coherent. It takes the form of evolution by stages, each stage arising out of the preceding one, and, in its turn, being pregnant with the next, and each expressing a 'higher', more developed, and more complicated state of the system. Thankfully, not many theorists allowed themselves to be committed to all the implications of this view. In particular, they were interested in only a relatively small number of the stages of social evolution, and especially those that seemed to have been the recent antecedents of their own novel stage. Hence the many dichotomously expressed evolutionary stages: from *gemeinschaft* to *gesellschaft*, 'status' to 'contract', 'folk' to 'urban', etc. But the underlying mechanisms of change still remained the basically organic ones of growth, differentiation, and maturation.

As to the directions of change, the nineteenth-century sociologies offered us broadly the 'convergence' thesis: that under the impact of industrialism all societies were moving towards one basic type, 'the industrial society'. Even where, as with Marx, it was felt that the new order had not yet reached its final, stable, form – that was to be the accomplishment of socialism – it was still considered that the destiny of all societies was to tread the path mapped out by the industrial nations, and to incorporate their institutions and culture as a necessary stage in their evolution. As Marx put it in the preface to the first edition of *Capital*: 'The country that is more developed industrially only shows, to the less developed, the image of its own future.'

Sometime near the beginning of the twentieth century, social change ceased to be the chief pre-occupation of social theory. The reasons were many, and cannot be gone into here.[4] At the purely theoretical level, historians and anthropologists attacked the evolutionist character of social change theory as providing bad history and inadequate conceptualizations of the movement from one state of society to another.[5] The weaknesses of evolutionary social thought were traced, by Malinowski and Radcliffe-Brown, to an insufficient concern for how, at any given time, a society actually worked and maintained itself in being. As Radcliffe-Brown put it, 'we cannot successfully embark on the study of how culture changes until we have made at least some progress in determining what culture really is and how it works' (Radcliffe-Brown 1931: 22). The functionalist approach in sociology and social anthropology was one of the consequences of this view.

But of course the functionalists did not abandon a view of social change. They merely put the topic in cold storage for a time. In fact, their concepts overlapped heavily with some characteristic assumptions of the evolutionists.[6] Their approach represented a sort of 'frozen evolutionism'. Herbert Spencer, after all, had combined a thorough-going evolutionism with a thorough-going functionalism. When the thaw came, and functionalists turned their attention to large-scale problems of historical and societal change, it should not have surprised anybody to find that they reverted almost without modification to the basic form of nineteenth-century evolutionism.[7]

The important point is that no serious revision was made of the classic sociological conception of social change. In the first half of this century the systematic study of social change was left to the philosophers of history, to the Spenglers, Sorokins, and Toynbees. Their approaches, for good or bad, did not impinge much on the sociological consciousness.[8] When, therefore, the anti-colonial movements of the post-Second World War era brought into being a host of new states, and the problem of the future development of these societies became too pressing for sociologists to ignore questions of social change, social theory had to fall back on its evolutionary past.

The sociology of development, as it grew from the early fifties, did represent a return to some of the characteristic concerns of the 'founding fathers', and that, I hold, is something to be welcomed. But the sons imitated their fathers in ways far too automatic and uncritical for the attempts to be reassuring.[9] There was the invoking of the old notion of stages of evolution, with the assumption of each 'undeveloped' society as an enclosed, self-contained entity, propelled upwards through the various stages of growth by some entelechy called 'the will to be modern'. The stages of the earlier evolutionists were bundled together into the two polar types, 'traditional' and 'modern' (or 'undeveloped' and 'developed'), and the process of development or modernization conceived as the movement from the first to the second. Furthermore, there was little doubt from where the model for the ideal-typical modern society came. It was the industrialized, democratized, bureaucratized, and rationalized society seen by the earlier sociologists as the ideal-typical 'industrial society', and now almost naturally identified with Anglo-American society of the nineteen-fifties.[10]

The resurgence of interest in social change did not, interestingly enough, extend to the societies of the industrial world. Quite the contrary – there seemed, in the social science view of those societies, quite simply the belief that all important structural change had come to an end there. These, the fifties, were the halcyon days of the 'end of ideology' thesis. Industrial society appeared to have come of age, to have matured with remarkable fidelity along the main lines outlined by the nineteenth-century sociologists. Even the spectre of the unpleasant shuffle at the end, predicted by Marx in the form of the socialist revolution, had ceased its haunting. The conflicts bred of inequality had largely been resolved, and without the need of recourse to revolution. All the industrial societies, of both east and west, had evolved into rational, 'managed' societies, and in doing so had 'got over the hump'. No further major institutional changes should be required in the process of applying the fruits of steady economic growth and a rapidly expanding technology to clear up the marginal pockets of poverty and deprivation.[11]

Views of this sort are still seriously held, of course. But enough happened in the sixties, in all industrial societies, to shake the firm belief in the consensus, and the view that the industrial societies had resolved all their outstanding problems. The result was a renewal of interest in the future of industrial society: the project known as futurology. Certainly it has not been as widespread an enterprise as the sociology of development, nor so coherent, nor so academically respectable, but it parallels it in some striking respects. It is markedly interdisciplinary in character: more so, perhaps, in that it involves a large number of natural as well as social scientists.[12] It is global in its tendency, both with regard to its field of study and to the organizations involved in that study.[13] More significantly, it has picked up nineteenth-century social change theory in its almost pristine form. Like development theory, futurology was stimulated into existence by pressing developments in the real world. Like development theory, futurology, in casting around for a suitable conceptualization of large-scale societal change, found only the evolutionary schemes of the past to hand and, in some cases, quite consciously adopted these for its own purposes.

In doing so, the futurologists have recommenced the characteristic task and pattern of nineteenth-century sociology. We might call their position the 're-convergence' thesis. They accept that the nineteenth-century scheme in its strict form will no longer do. 'Industrial Society' as it has been known hitherto cannot be taken as the fulfilment and final end of social evolution; but all one has to do is to add another stage to the sequence. The old story is given a new chapter with a new ending, rather as Marx had tried to do, and after him, James Burnham. But formally the pattern remains the same. The present is once more seen as transitional, as metamorphosis: not now from feudal agrarianism to industrialism, but from the industrial society to the 'post-industrial society'. The driving-force of this transformation is also of the same character as in the past. It is technology, 'the great, growling engine of change' as futurologist Alvin Toffler puts it (1970: 25).[14] Instead of the power loom, the steam engine and the railway, we have computers and the electronic media of communications. The futurological enterprise is frankly Saint-Simonian, and a comment by Edward Shils on what he calls 'the generously stimulating tyranny of our classics' seems apposite here:

> 'One of the great difficulties is that we cannot imagine anything beyond variation on the theme set by the great figures of nineteenth- and twentieth-century sociology. The fact that the conception of 'post-industrial society' is an amalgam of what Saint-Simon, Comte, de Tocqueville and Weber furnished to our imagination is evidence that we are confined to an ambiguously defined circle which is more impermeable than it ought to be' (Shils 1970: 825).[15]

Shils's remark points to one of the main problems associated with the 'post-industrial' idea: the problem of conceptualizing novelty in the terms, and with the basic schema, of nineteenth-century evolutionary social theory. Nevertheless, proponents of the 'post-industrial' thesis are making a number of assertions about current social changes that need to be taken very seriously. Development theorists, in particular, need to examine them because, if true, they have profound implications for strategies of development. I turn now, therefore, to the lineaments of the 'post-industrial' society and its possible consequences for other types of society. As I have remarked before, the futurological literature is particularly thin in treating the issue of the future relations between the industrial and the industrializing societies.[16] Briefly put, the tendency is to think of the future of the industrial societies with optimism, sometimes positively with euphoria, and to be pessimistic about developments in the non-industrial world. We are left largely to infer for our selves future transactions between these two worlds. But one student at least, Johan Galtung, has applied himself systematically to this issue. In what follows, I have found it convenient to employ Galtung's framework for considering the future of the international system (Galtung 1969), bringing in other authors and materials by way of elaboration, confirmation, and assessment.

II

Galtung distinguishes four societal forms: the primitive, the traditional, the modern, and the neo-modern (the last also called the post-industrial) (see *Table 1* below). Following in the Fisher-Clark-Fourastié tradition, these distinctions are based on the factors of agricultural productivity – i.e. the number of families one family doing farming can feed – and the general distribution of the population in primary (mainly agricultural), secondary (manufacturing or industrial), and tertiary (services) sectors. Behind these, in turn, are the variables that have to do with technology, particularly the technology of production and of communication – the latter added to Marx's emphasis on 'means of production' as a factor of primary importance.

Our concern at the moment is with the neo-modern or post-industrial form. Galtung, along with Kahn and Wiener, Brzezinski, Bell, and others, argues that some industrial societies are already clearly in the process of being transformed into the predominantly post-industrial type. The sort of evidence presented to back up this assertion varies a good deal; but the most systematic account has been given by Bell, whose pre-eminence in the elaboration of the post-industrial concept is, in any case, generally acknowledged. Bell (1971a: 168) identifies[17] five dimensions of the evolving post-industrial society.

TABLE 1

Stages of socio-economic development

	Primitive (P)	Traditional (T)	Modern (M)	Neo-modern (N)
Economic sectors	Primary	Primary / Tertiary	Pri-mary / Sec-on-dary / Terti-ary	Tertiary
Nature of stratification	High / Low	High / Low	High / Middle / Low	Post-tertiary education / Tertiary education / Secondary education / Primary education
Term for the transition	← Urban revolution	← Industrial revolution	← Automation revolution	
Population profiles				
primary sector	100 90	80 75	50 20	5 0
secondary sector	0 5	5 10	20 30	5 0
tertiary sector	0 5	15 15	30 50	90 100
Agricultural productivity	1:1 and less	1:1.25 1:1.33	1:2 1:5	1:20 and higher
GNP/capita	up to $50	$50–$600	$600–$4 000	$4 000 and above
Communication				
goods, persons	walking, running rowing	animals, wheels sailing	steam engine combustion engine	jet rockets
information	eye and ear	dispatches	post, telegraph telephone	tele-satellite
Economic system	subsistence economy	barter economy	money economy	credit economy
Domain	group, clan, tribe	village, city-state	nation-state	region, world state
Magnitude	10^0–10^2	10^2–10^5	10^5–10^8	10^8–10^{10}

Source: J. Galtung (1969: 16)

1 Economic Sector: the Shift from a Goods-producing to a Service Society

Colin Clark himself had argued, in *The Conditions of Economic Progress*, that there was a trajectory along which every nation would pass, once it became industrialized, whereby, because of the sectoral differences in productivity and the demand for health, recreation, and the like as national incomes increased, the greater proportion of the labour force would inevitably move to the service sector. The first dimension of the post-industrial society is that the majority of the labour force is no longer engaged in agriculture or manufacturing but in services, which are defined residually as trade, finance, transport, health, recreation, research, education, and government. This shift, it is generally accepted, is occurring in all the industrial societies. The United States is the only one yet to have actually made it: at some point in the 'fifties the US became the first 'service economy' – 'that is, it became the first nation in which more than half of the employed population was not involved in the production of food, clothing, houses, automobiles, or other tangible goods' (Fuchs 1966: 7). The service sector there already accounts for more than half the gross national product. By 1975 it is expected to absorb about 60 per cent of the employed population. The evidence from other industrial countries suggests that they too are moving speedily in that direction.[18]

2 Occupational Slope: the Predominance of the Professional and Technical Class

While the overall growth and predominance of the service sector in the post-industrial economy is important, even more significant is the differential rate of growth of the various occupational groups within the service sector. The fact is that the growth in professional and technical employment has been at a rate twice that of the average. For the United States, in 1940 there were 3·9 million such employees in the society; by 1964 the number had risen to 8·6 million; and it is estimated that by 1975 there will be 13·2 million professional and technical persons, making it the second largest of the eight occupational divisions of the country, exceeded only by the semi-skilled workers. Moreover, within that category of professional and technical employees, a particular group – the scientists and engineers – have been developing even faster. While the growth rate of the professional class as a whole is twice that of the average labour-force rate, the growth rate of the scientists and engineers is triple that of the working population as a whole.[19]

The distinctiveness of this specialized trend has prompted some students to distinguish between a more narrowly defined tertiary sector and a 'quaternary' sector, and to suggest that the more noteworthy phenomenon in the transition to the post-industrial society is the rapid expansion of the quarternary sector (Kahn and Wiener 1967: 62–3). The tertiary sector is restricted to the area of the classic services, common enough in the capital cities of pre-industrial societies – commerce, financial services, administrative departments. Expansion in this sector seems to be a preliminary phase to a more fundamental phase of expansion of the quarternary sector; indeed, according to the old law of 'the privilege of backwardness' it may be possible for the phase of service expansion to be severely abbreviated or truncated, using the already existing innovations and technology of 'leader' societies. It has been noted that the curve of the explosive expansion of the service sector in the United States is already flattening out, under the impact of better use of management systems and cybernation; while, for instance in Sweden, commerce, finance and clerical occupations account for a much smaller proportion of the overall service sector than in the United States, and a relatively larger share is taken by welfare, health, education, and cultural services. Moreover, the share of the routine white-collar services is beginning to shrink more rapidly than in the United States. Thus the key occupational category of the post-industrial society would comprise two main 'quaternary' groups: one concerned with science, research, and development, the other with the area of 'human welfare', especially education and cultural services, the health services, social welfare, and recreation (Richta *et al.* 1967: Vol. I, 32–6).

3 Technology: the Rise of a New 'Intellectual Technology'

4 Pattern of Change: Self-sustaining Technical Growth

5 Axial Principle: the Centrality of Theoretical Knowledge

These three dimensions of the post-industrial society are really all aspects of the final one. The post-industrial society is organized around knowledge, or rather, around a special type of knowledge, since knowledge has been necessary for the existence of any society. 'What has now become decisive for society,' writes Bell, 'is the new centrality of *theoretical* knowledge, the primacy of theory over empiricism, and the codification of knowledge into abstract systems of symbols that can be translated into many different and varied circumstances. Every society now lives by innovation and growth; and it is theoretical knowledge that has become the matrix of innovation' (Bell 1967: 28–9). One can see this in the changing relations of science and technology, for instance. In the nineteenth and early twentieth centuries, the great inventions and the industries that derived from them – steel, electric light, telegraph, telephone, automobile – were the work of inspired and talented tinkerers, many of whom were indifferent to the fundamental laws which underlay their inventions. But if we look at an industry such as chemistry – which has good claims to be considered the first of the 'modern', post-industrial type industrics we find a case where the inventions were based on theoretical knowledge of the properties of macro-molecules, which were 'manipulated' to achieve the planned production of new materials. We have here an example of what Radovan Richta has called 'a law of higher priority' in the evolution of the productive forces in the post-industrial era: 'the precedence of science over technology, and of technology over industry' (Richta *et al.* 1967: Vol. I, 28).

Similarly, the development of macro-economic theory makes it possible for governments, by direct planning, monetary or fiscal policy, to seek economic growth, to redirect the allocation of resources, and to maintain balance between different sectors. More generally, the growing sophistication of computer-based simulation procedures – simulations of economic systems, of social behaviour, of decision problems – allows, for the first time, the possibility of large-scale 'controlled experiments' in the social sciences. These, in turn, will allow us to plot 'alternative futures', thereby greatly increasing the extent of our choice and the ability to control matters affecting our lives. All such applications of theory are seen as resulting from the rise of the new 'intellectual technology' – constituted by such techniques as linear programming, systems analysis, information theory, decision theory, games, and simulation which, when linked to the computer, allow us to accumulate and manipulate large aggregates of data of a differentiated kind so as to have more complete knowledge of social and economic matters. Such a technology, Bell suggests, 'may by the end of the twentieth century be as decisive in human affairs as the machine technology has been for the past century and a half' (1968b: 156–7).[20] Taken altogether, finally, these developments are making possible continuous, planned technical innovation: partly through the systematic linking of science and technology through the institutionalization of research and development sections in private and public organizations, and partly through the new techniques of technological forecasting, which lay out the future areas of development, and allow industry, or society, to plan ahead systematically in terms of capital possibilities, needs, and products. Technical growth in the post-industrial society is therefore self-sustaining.

We may note, in passing, what is considered to be the dominant group and the dominant institutions, of this evolving post-industrial society. Bell writes: 'If the dominant figures of the past hundred years have been the entrepreneur, the businessman, and the industrial executive, the 'new men' are the scientists, the mathematicians, the economists, and the engineers of the new computer technology.' And the dominant institutions will be the institutions they inhabit, in their roles as seekers, elaborators, and codifiers of the theoretical knowledge that is the ganglion of the social system of the future: such institutions as universities, research corporations, industrial laboratories, and experimental stations. As Bell, again, puts it, no doubt with much satisfaction: 'Perhaps it is not too much to say that if the business firm was the key institution of the past 100 years, because of its role in organizing production for the mass creation of products, the university will become the central institution of the next 100 years because of its role as the new source of innovation and knowledge (Bell 1971b: 15). 'Not only the best talents, but eventually the entire complex of social prestige and social status, will be rooted in the intellectual and scientific communities' (Bell 1967: 30).[21] Relationships with other groups, especially the politicians, are likely to be problematic, but there seems little doubt about which way the lines of influence will run. The making of decisions, whether to do with business production in the private sector or political goals in the public sector, 'will have an increasingly technical character', shaped and constrained by the 'information' supplied by the masters of the new intellectual technology. The dream of Saint-Simon, of an industrial order ruled in rational, positivist fashion by a 'natural elite' of technocrats, seems at last to be on the point of fulfilment – not, it is true, in the industrial society, but in the 'post-industrial' society.

III

It is in these terms that the future of most current industrial societies is being spelled out. Only the United States is held by anyone to have travelled to any significant extent along the road to post-industrial status. Other industrial societies exhibit aspects of it with varying degrees of clarity, just as they also contain various aspects of 'pre-industrial' life and culture. (Japan is perhaps the best example of the hybrid made out of the simple threefold typology, 'pre-industrial', 'industrial', 'post-industrial'.). But, just as Marx thought that nineteenth-century England showed to less-developed societies the image of their future, so the United States is seen as mapping out the path of development of the industrial societies.

I have followed Bell in specifying only the most novel and, in a sense, pivotal features of the new society in the making. To be more comprehensive, I should have included some account of other, more familiar, trends: continuing urbanization, leading perhaps to the growth of 'megalopolises' ('Boswash', 'Chipitts', 'Sansan' in the US, for instance); continuing increase in affluence and leisure, with continuing uneven distribution of both; continuing secularization and 'rationalization' in all areas of cultural and moral life. These trends – which Kahn and Wiener identify as the 'Basic Long Term Multifold Trend' of western civilization[22] – are continuities – expansions and intensifications – of processes which brought about the first set of industrial societies in the west; whereas there is a real sense in which the changes selected by Bell express fundamental discontinuities with the earlier processes of industrialization.

This is not the place to attempt a detailed critique of the post-industrial idea.[23] It is, as I have already suggested, basically utopian in conception, closely akin to the industrial utopias of St Simon and Fourier. It is grounded in the belief in the primacy of technology and administration, and hence disdains the autonomous claims of politics. It does not ask what might be the private interests or the political ideologies of the technocratic group it singles out as the emergent elite: such a group is regarded as the neutral and disinterested servant of the new order. More concretely, it takes the fact of an increase in the number of scientists *in* government and industry as an expression of the influence of science *on* government and industry: a dubious inference even were there not such ready examples as Concorde, or the siting of the third airport in Britain, to create suspicion. It may even be the case, as suggested in different ways by Jean Floud and Noam Chomsky, that the features of American society picked out by Bell as indications of an emerging post-industrial society may be no more than the expressions of the abnormal growth forced upon America by its massive military commitments (Floud 1971; Chomsky, 1969). At any rate, so long as politics within and between nations continues, as still seems true, to be dominated by the struggle for power between competing interests, we might fairly expect the next thirty years to be more rather than less like the last thirty years of this century – only, as it were, writ large.

But it is perfectly possible to be sceptical about the claims for the emergence of a new form of society while remaining impressed by the importance of the trends identified by Bell and co. So far as the 'Third World' is concerned, the effects of these trends are not diminished by their being refused the title 'post-industrial', and the Third World has reason to be concerned about those trends, for they are not re-assuring (when, for the Third World, have trends ever been?). Summarily, they point to an increasingly integrated and increasingly autonomous industrial and post-industrial sector of the globe, more or less able to determine its future irrespective of the wishes or requirements of the non-industrial world. Conversely, for the Third World they indicate a situation analogous in many respects to that of the American blacks within American society: that is, of a population desperate but dispensable, in an economic sense. If the future promises the industrial societies the self-sustaining, self-sufficient economy of post-industrial civilization, it seems to condemn the Third World to the limbo of 'global ghetto-ization'.[24]

This stark divergence is not the only possibility nor, of course, is it inevitable. It is simply a strong possibility if we extrapolate from current trends, and if nobody does anything about them. To consider these trends in the context of the broader international system, and the varying responses that might be expected to them, we can return now to Galtung's framework (Galtung 1969). Having distinguished the four societal forms – primitive, traditional, modern, and neo-modern or post-industrial (see *Table 1*, above) – Galtung adds two assumptions for the purposes of analysing changes in the world system of states. The first is the assumption of development – that primitive societies tend to develop into traditional ones, traditional into modern, and modern into neo-modern (although the development may take place in jumps and, while not necessarily linear, is more linear and more rapid the higher the level of communication between societies at different levels of development). The second assumption is that of the nation-state as a general pattern – that the surface of the world is divided into generally continguous territories called nation-states, and that some nation-states are composed of societies at various levels of development, and thus have dual or triple economies; others may coincide with one social order at a particular level of development; and still others are segments within one society comprising more nation-states (Galtung 1969: 15–17).

These two assumptions lead, says Galtung, to 'what we see as the basic structural condition for change in the international, or global, system: the consequences of the incompatibilities between state and society, between the nation-state and the social orders it contains or is contained in' (Galtung 1969: 17).

Furthermore, it is not just any nation-state that has become the norm of the international system: it is a nation-state formed in principle according to the model of nations that are societies at the level of development characterized as 'modern'. In order that interaction between nations can take place, certain uniformities of structure come to be impressed upon them. In particular, as Galtung points out,

> 'they have to be organized in a relatively equal manner at the top to respond to at least some of the demands made by international interaction, to participate in the international game. This will facilitate the emergence of modern and even neomodern segments at the top of many nations, which in turn has the consequence that the "internal development distance" between the least and most developed segments is higher, the less developed the nation is . . . making the less developed nations less cohesive' (Galtung 1969: 18–19).

Since all nations have to have at least some modern segment, and since all nations contain at least some segments at different levels of societal development, the typology of four types of society can be translated into two types of nation-states. There is type PTM which has primitive, traditional, and modern segments, and hence is *less developed*; and type TMN, which has traditional, modern, and neo-modern segments, and hence is *more developed*. (Using such indices as the percentage not working in the primary sector, which also correlates highly with *per capita* GNP, this distinction corresponds essentially to the familiar division between rich and poor, developing and developed nations.)

We can consider now the trends in the 'more developed' and the 'less developed' worlds, and the likely future interaction between them. Characteristic of the more developed world, says Galtung, is the manner in which societies with increasing development are *growing out* of their nation-states 'which even become like strait-jackets for them' (1969). This pattern follows basically from the post-industrial developments surveyed earlier. For an increasing fraction of the nation,

M

especially those employed in the quaternary sector, the nation-state becomes perceived as being of decreasing relevance. Their typical cast of skills, education, culture, and political ideology militates against national identification. When we consider the key occupational groups of the post-industrial sector: the educationists, teachers, and students; the specialists in health, welfare, and recreation; the professionals of the communications industry; the experts in world welfare (Galtung predicts particularly rapid increases in 'international peace specialists' and 'international development engineers'); above all, the scientists, mathematicians, economists, and engineers of the new computer technology, it is clear that these are the groups that are least likely to find the nation-state a satisfactory arena for their activities. As professionals of a particular kind, they will share more in terms of interests, values, and lifestyles with similar professionals in other countries than with other groups in their own.[25] To a degree never before attained, their skills will be 'universalistic', valid in all post-industrial segments in any country. Finally, the fact that these groups belong to the 'top' of the nation, located in its most advanced and creative areas, means that their influence will offset the nationalism of other groups whose interests still call for a national identification.

The post-industrial groups will, therefore, look for forms of non-national identification: although, for some time to come, the limits to their internationalism may well be set by the area of the more developed world. Evidence for this trend comes at a number of levels. At the lowest level there is the rapid growth of the multi-national business corporation, with a 16 per cent growth rate, and, as Peter Drucker has stressed, increasingly multi-national in its management personnel and in its scientific and technological foundations.[26] Next comes the growth of the non-profit international non-governmental organizations (INGOs), which, at present, number about 1 600 and have a growth rate of about 10 per cent. Examples of these are the international professional organizations, international political/ideological movements, such as the anti-Vietnam war movement, and international age-set movements, created by the rapidly-increasing conflict between the generations in the post-industrial society (due to obsolescence of skills, rapid rate of social change). Finally, there is the growth of the international governmental organizations (IGOs), of which there are about 600 at present, 'with a very high growth rate'. Examples of these are the economic IGOs, such as the EEC, co-production schemes, military alliances, and various institutions of the UN.[27]

It would be easy to overstate, and to idealize, the internationalism of these developments. There is a strong whiff of the international jet-set in the accounts given by Galtung and others; and the 'internationalism' of development experts and 'international peace specialists' seems closer to David Frost than to the average professional of the 'post-industrial' sector. Moreover, it should not be unexpected if calculations of national self-interest, however misguided, continue to interrupt the process of integration among the developed nations. De Gaulle may have been archaic, but no sociological law seems to prevent political atavisms. Nevertheless, it does not seem unrealistic to interpret the evidence as pointing to a growing interpenetration of the advanced industrial nations; although it is an internationalism of a self-interested, military-industrial type, rather than of the more disinterested UN type.[28] Conversely, we should note the tendency for the more developed world to become not merely integrated and inclusive, but autonomous and exclusive. The corollary of the growing attraction of the industrial nations for each other is their repulsion of the non-industrial Third World.

This would follow from the long-term projection of some familiar trends. First is the changing pattern of world trade. As Andrew Shonfield has said, 'the most notorious divergence from the historic norm is the vast increase in trade between advanced industrial countries selling each other manufactured goods'.[29] For more than half a century the greater part of the increase in the sales of capital goods was taken up in trade between the industrial and the non-industrial countries. In the early 1950s there first occurred a reversal of this pattern. Primary products (food, fuel, and raw materials) which accounted for 54 per cent of world trade in 1953-4 had fallen to 42 per cent in 1965-6, only a dozen years later. Moreover, *within* the total trade of primary products, the Third World's share has fallen from 45 to 40 per cent. The counterpart of this has been the dramatic expansion of trade in manufactures between industrial countries. As Dudley Seers says, 'even in the short period from 1953 to 1969, world trade has become predominantly trade between rich countries. In these sixteen years, internal trade within the bloc of rich countries quadrupled, while trade between rich countries and poor doubled' (Seers 1971: 19–20). There seems no good reason to expect an interruption of this trend and, given the developments within the industrial nations already noted, we may well expect an intensification of them.

The changed patterns of trade have been made possible through the industrial societies' improved techniques in manufacturing and agriculture (which have meant an increasing economy in the use of raw materials), and the substitution of synthetics for many natural products. Kenneth Boulding has put the position as follows:

'One by-product of the technological revolution is a diminution in the bargaining power of the poor countries as against the rich. The whole impact of technology in these days is towards self-sufficiency of smaller areas. There is a tremendous increase in the number of substitutes for practically everything. The only economic bargaining power which the tropical belt possesses in relation to the developed temperate countries lies in its ability to withhold supplies of tropical products. These, however, seem to be becoming less and less essential to the economic systems of the temperate zone. We now have synthetic rubber, synthetic camphor; synthetic coffee and cocoa may be just around the corner, and the tropical belt may be left with very little in the way of comparative advantage' (Boulding 1964: 113–14).

The industrial societies, comments Boulding, have learnt the lesson that 'the highest pay-offs in these days comes from staying home and minding one's own business successfully' (1964: 115). This results not so much from exasperation at the unbusinesslike ways of foreigners, nor of a late conversion to Cobdenism, but from an awareness of the changed environment for economic activities in the industrial world. The Third World is, quite simply, becoming less relevant to those activities. In an economic sense, it is becoming dispensable, something to be cast away once its riches have been plundered and its cultures smashed, like a child throwing away a ruined toy. As the industrial societies take on increasingly post-industrial features, their characteristic interests, concerns, and problems will make them even more decisively inward-looking. Their demands will be framed in the context of the tertiary and quaternary sectors, not that of manufacturing. Their focus will be on personal services, education, science policy, leisure; their problems will be pollution, noise, crowding, bureaucracy. In none of these things will the Third World seem relevant – except perhaps as an area for tourism, or for the siting of some of the more polluting industries of the industrial world.[30]

This development throws some doubt on some of the more firmly-held beliefs about the relationship between the industrial and the nonindustrial world, especially traditional Marxist beliefs. The Marxist category for exploring that relationship has generally been one of exploitation. The Third World was 'underdeveloped' by western capitalism, its economy and social structure distorted and stunted to provide cheap raw materials for western industry, and to create a market for western industrial products. This seems a fair account of what happened in the past.[31] It will not, however, help us to understand the future. The industrial societies of today, and *a fortiori* those of tomorrow, are not those of Marx's day, or even of Lenin's and Luxemburg's day. The chain of exploitation linking exploiters and exploited seems in the process of dissolution, and this largely through the voluntary actions of the beneficiaries under the original scheme of exploitation. Peter Worsley has commented, in this connexion, on the attempt to draw Marxist parallels along the lines of 'proletarian' and 'millionaire-capitalist' nations, and to predict a Marxist-style overthrow of the latter by the former. As he says, 'the problem for these "proletarians", increasingly, is that the "millionaires" are less and less interested in exploiting them. Today's "super-profits" are being made in Western Europe, not the Third World' (Worsley, 1964: 261).

We should note, finally, certain other possible developments that would strengthen the tendency towards the creation of a future global system marked by vast 'ghetto' areas (Third World nations), which are less and less capable of affecting the activities of the rich, powerful, and increasingly autonomous post-industrial area. Aid and intervention in underdeveloped societies have been to a considerable extent an incident of the Cold War. The relaxation of that war, taken with the other changes already noted, may make that involvement both less necessary and less attractive. The political instability of many areas of the Third World makes foreign investment precarious, and so may discourage involvement of the purely profit-making sort. The prospect may then be that feared by the Algerian delegate to the UN Economic and Social Council, when he commented at its Geneva meeting in 1966: 'Even as the detente in the Cold War has permitted an attenuation of the conflict between blocs with different social systems, one must fear that the East–West opposition will revolve on its axis and become an antagonism of North against South' (Brzezinski 1970: 51). Boulding, along with many others, has expressed the same apprehension (1964: 23): 'Perhaps one of the greatest dangers we face today, assuming that the East–West relationship can be solved and that the Cold War is put in permanent cold storage, is that the developed nations will form in effect an alliance against the underdeveloped against which the poor countries of the tropical belt will be powerless for many generations to come'.[32]

IV

The less-developed world, although it could well be ignored by the more developed, cannot but be affected by it. Just as in the earlier process of industrialization the progress of some societies acted to constrain, retard, or distort the development of others, so as the rich societies move into a newer phase of their evolution will they continue to have an impact on the rest of the world, although their sins may now be those of omission rather than of commission. The international system imposes some measure of interaction on all nations. At the same time it is strongly hierarchical in structure, in a form that Galtung has termed 'feudal' (1966). That is to say, there is a high degree of interaction at the top (between the wealthy and powerful TMN nations), a lesser degree between top and bottom, and a very low level of interaction between nations at the bottom (the less-developed PTM nations). The future of the less-developed world turns to a considerable extent on the implications of that structure. Since the relevant features are very well known to developmentalists and many others, I shall review trends in the less-developed world only briefly, and mainly as a corollary of the changes in the industrial nations.

Galtung suggests that characteristic of the less developed world is the manner in which the societies are *growing into* their nation-states, at the same time as societies of the more-developed world are growing out of theirs. The use of the comforting organic metaphor, which is consistent with the a-political evolutionism of most futurology, disguises the fact that societies of the Third World are being beaten, battered, and bludgeoned into nationhood (as, at the very least, any Kurd or Biafran knows). Moreover these are, and are likely to continue to be, nations marked by a high degree of incohesiveness and unbalanced development, as compared with the past of western nations. These features are strengthened by the fact that the 'leader' societies in the global system, as they go their own way, continue to cast their long and baleful shadow.

First, it is likely that the problem of the 'dual economies' of the less-developed world will get worse. We might, by the end of the century, reach a situation of massive unevenness: the large cities exhibiting many features of post-industrial society, borrowed from the post-industrial world, with a trend towards tertiary and quaternary occupations; while the rest of the society, especially the rural areas, will be slowly moving out of what Kahn and Wiener call 'modified sixteenth century' – modified by the addition of the bulldozer, electric lights, the transistor radio, etc. The 'over-development' in the cities, particularly as regards the impact of automation and cybernation, will produce post-industrial style problems (e.g. the displacement of large numbers of routine white-collar bureaucrats), but will be exacerbated by the lower level of development of the society as a whole.

Next, we can expect an intensified feeling of frustration and resentment on the part of certain key groups, as a result of the revolutionizing of the 'subjective environment' of the Third World, mainly through the rapid spread of education and communications. As Brzezinski has put it (1970: 35–6):

> 'In a world electronically intermeshed, absolute or relative under-development will be intolerable, especially as the more advanced countries begin to move beyond that industrial era into which the less developed countries have as yet to enter. It is thus no longer a matter of the "revolution of rising expectations". The Third World today confronts the spectre of insatiable aspirations . . .'[33]

This, again, will strengthen other familiar tendencies. There will be more dissatisfied graduates and other trained personnel, unable to find work compatible with their expanded expectations. There will, more significantly, be the deepening phenomenon of the formation of alienated elites in Third World societies: 'Foreigners at home, foreigners abroad' – as Alexander Herzen described a much earlier westernized elite in nineteenth-century Russia – they will have been socialized into the culture, life-styles, and aspirations of the ruling-classes of the industrial and increasingly post-industrial societies. Their tendency will be to emigrate, either vicariously, into the 'post-industrial enclaves' of the developed parts of their society, or directly, in pursuit of a variety of political, economic, cultural, or scientific values which they feel they can satisfy only in the metropolises of the industrial world.[34]

While there is this movement from the top of the less-developed (PTM) nations to the more developed (TMN) ones, at the same time there is the movement from the bottom levels of the PTM nations, whereby cheap labour is shunted into the lower echelons of the TMN society (as unskilled labourers, domestic servants, etc.) left empty by the general upward mobility in these societies. In both these transactions the PTM nations may gain something, but they are clearly losing in terms of national cohesion, potential for future growth, and autonomy in relation to the TMN nations. The PTM nations may respond by trying to put collective pressure on the TMN nations: by selling their cheap labour at a higher price, requiring many and very cheap experts in return for brain drainage, etc. But clearly their success in pursuing this strategy will depend on how far the TMN nations need this type of resource from the less-developed world; and the indications are that they do not. As Herman Kahn has said of the brain-drain and foreign labour phenomenon in the US: 'This does not mean, as the Europeans think, that the United States is depending on this importation, but it does mean that we are benefiting; we are getting a subsidy from the rest of the world. This is a subsidy that is not too important to us.'[35]

The third main trend to note is the continuing low level of interaction between nations of the less-developed world. This follows directly from the feudal structure of the international system. All the indicators of international interaction, from plane flights to the volume or value of trade, confirm the feudal hypothesis, and point to the pattern whereby PTM nations are much more closely linked to particular TMN nations or groups of nations than to other PTM nations.[36] The factors creating this vertical system of dependency are obvious, stemming from the economic specialization first imposed during the colonial period; but recognizing them has proved much easier than changing them. It is indeed in this area that change seems most possible, as well as most desirable. Meanwhile, however, given the low level of solidarity between PTM nations, these nations are sitting ducks, to be taken 'one at a time' by the TMN nations. The more-developed nations are greatly helped here by their high level of both internal and external cohesion. This will lead to a rapid growth in the tendency to deal with the less-developed nations collectively, not necessarily through the UN, but typically through the EEC, the OECD, NATO, etc. Some of this dealing no doubt will have a benevolent purpose. But on current showing the developed nations will use aid and investment programmes primarily to tie individual PTM nations to themselves, in the form of clientage, often for military purposes, or for votes at the UN, etc. An alternative possibility, given the inward-turning tendencies in the developed world already noted, would be for the TMN nations to use their collective organizations to fend off the Third World, as dispensable and a nuisance. In either case the amount of leverage possessed by the Third World is very slight.

Finally we can turn to a consideration of the projections of overall economic growth in the Third World nations. Kahn and Wiener, using a five-fold typology of industrial development in terms of levels of *per capita* income (this overlaps heavily with Galtung's typology – see *Table 1*, above), present a forecast of the levels achieved by the various societies of the world in the year 2000 (see *Table 2* below). Summarizing their 'scenario' which they describe as 'on the whole, optimistic', they say:

'. . . the year 2000 will find a rather large island of wealth surrounded by 'misery', at least relative to the developed world and to 'rising expectations' . . . The post-industrial societies will contain about 40 per cent of the world's population: more than 90 per cent of the world's population will live in nations that have broken out of the historical \$50–\$200 *per capita* range. Yet at the same time the absolute gap in living standards, between countries or sectors of countries with developed (industrial, post-industrial, mass consumption) economies and those at pre-industrial level, will have widened abysmally (Kahn and Wiener 1967: 60–1).

Some selected items fill out this prediction of growing inequality between the more and the less-developed worlds. In 1965 the less-developed world (South America, Asia less Japan, Africa) contained about 68 per cent of the world's population but produced only 14·5 per cent of its output. By the year 2000 the less-developed world will contain three-quarters of the world's population and will account for about the same proportion of output as it did in 1965.[37]

Again, at the beginning of the period, 1965, the *per capita* product of the industrial world exceeded that of the less-developed nations by a factor of about twelve times. By the year 2000 this factor will approach a difference of eighteen times; this means that the gap between the two worlds will increase by 50 per cent in favour of the developed world by the year 2000 (Kahn and Wiener 1967: 142).

GNP, it is true, is only one indicator of a nation's health, and by no means necessarily the most important. But it is a good indicator of a nation's military-industrial power and, on that count, the projected trends[38] point to an overwhelming weakness of the less-developed as against the more-developed world for many decades to come. In this, they only confirm the general picture already sketched. On current trends, the future of the Third World seems to be this: internally, within each nation, a lack of cohesion due to the great 'internal development distance' between the more and the less-developed sectors, and between the nationalist elites and other groups, giving rise to internal conflicts of all kinds (revolutions, *coups d'état*, separatist movements);

TABLE 2

Six economic groupings in Year 2000 (millions of people)

(5) Visibly post-industrial		(3) Mature industrial	
US	320	Union of South Africa	50
Japan	120	Mexico, Uruguay, Chile,	
Canada	35	Cuba, Colombia, Peru,	
Scandinavia and Switzerland	30	Panama, Jamaica, etc.	250
France, W. Germany		N. Vietnam, S. Vietnam,	
Benelux	160	Thailand, the Philippines, etc.	250
	———	Turkey	75
	665	Lebanon, Iraq, Iran, etc.	75
			———
			700
(5) Early post-industrial			
United Kingdom	55	**(2) Large and partially industrialized**	
Soviet Union	350	Brazil	210
Italy, Austria	70	Pakistan	250
E. Germany, Czechoslovakia	35	China	1 300
Israel	5	India	950
Australia, New Zealand	25	Indonesia	240
	———	UAR	70
	540	Nigeria	160
			———
			3 180
(4) Mass consumption			
Spain, Portugal, Poland,		**(1) Pre-industrial or small and**	
Yugoslavia, Cyprus, Greece,		**partially industrialized**	
Bulgaria, Hungary, Ireland	180	Rest of Africa	350
Argentina, Venezuela	60	Rest of Arab World	100
Taiwan, N. Korea, S. Korea,		Rest of Asia	300
Hong Kong, Malaysia,		Rest of Latin America	100
Singapore	160		———
	———		850
	400		

Source: Kahn and Wiener 1967: 60.

externally, competition and conflict between Third World nations, because they all produce similar basic commodities, because they are placed in a parallel and competitive orientation towards the top ranks of the international system, and because they are mostly run by elites who are bourgeois nationalists. In relation to the developed world their bargaining power, always slight, seems to be declining further, due largely to developments within the industrial nations, who now seem increasingly to be in a position to turn their backs on the Third World.

As against these gloomy prognostications, some students (e.g.

Jenkins 1970: 148ff.) have discerned hopeful signs of a move towards Third World solidarity. Individual revolutions within particular countries are seen to be of limited effect so long as the international system is constituted as it is: Cuba simply substitutes Russia for the United States as the indispensable purchaser of her sugar. More significant, therefore, are considered the collective organizations of the underprivileged: such phenomena as the Bandung-, Beograd-, Cairo-Conferences; caucus groups of the Afro-Asians in the UN and its agencies; the more or less concerted initiatives by the less-developed nations in the United Nations Conference on Trade and Development (UNCTAD); and, most of all, the Tri-Continental Organization (OSPAAAL) which brings together most of the revolutionary movements of the Third World.

It is unnecessary here to go over the long list of obstacles to the achievement of Third World solidarity. But supposing some sort of real integration does take place, either at the bourgeois-national level or at the revolutionary party level, one can imagine two strategies. Following Galtung's suggestion (1969: 33) of the analogy of domestic trade-union history, we might expect Third World 'unions' to try 'collective bargaining' first. This means such things as putting higher prices on raw materials (but this assumes that the developed nations will not invent synthetic substitutes for most raw materials very quickly, nor indeed be prepared to exploit their own resources of raw materials, even though costly); and it means attempting to persuade or force the implementation of international welfare state policies (which assumes that the developed world will be willing or compelled to accept some form of heavily-progressive taxation, both direct and indirect, which may slow down their own development. At the moment none of the major political parties of the developed world seems prepared to put this to their electorates). Failing this, and given effective international organization on both sides, the scene is set for international class war. It is possible that the poorer nations would chance the likely disastrous consequences of a major war, or at any rate exploit the great social and technological vulnerability of the specialized and interdependent post-industrial nations: although direct appeals to the underprivileged of the developed societies seem likely to be unavailing. The developed nations, for their part, will try various strategies of conciliation and subterfuge to avoid all-out conflict. But to an important and perhaps increasing extent they will rely on preventive military and paramilitary operations to maintain their superiority. There will be many chances to intervene, given the predicted high amount of intra- and inter-state conflict within the less-developed world; and the developed nations will increasingly take the opportunity to install and maintain 'peace-keeping' forces in the Third World – in the long-term interests of the developed world.

The future remains always open, despite the attempts of some futurologists to close it. In projecting some of the important structural forces of today to look at the future, we are relying on persistencies from the past for our map of the future. Such persistencies would mark out a future existence so depressing for the Third World that we are almost justified in ignoring them and concentrating, however quixotically, on what we perceive as the agencies of change. But we need to remember Bacon's dictum, that nothing that has not yet been done, can be done, except by means that have not yet been tried. Certainly any fundamental change in the relations between the developed and the under-developed worlds will require, as a priority, equally basic changes in the structure of the societies of the developed world, and no one can say that that is a thing that has seriously been tried. If it is not, there are good grounds for thinking that, so far as the Third World is concerned, the future *will* be more rather than less like the present, and the past – only, again, writ large.

Notes

1 The number of institutes, organizations, and individuals currently engaged in systematic analysis of future trends runs into thousands; but the bulk of these are concerned with fairly short-term technological forecasting. Among the main bodies one would want to mention: the *Futuribles* project, under Bertrand de Jouvenal; the Commission on the Year 2000 of the American Academy of Arts and Sciences, chaired by Daniel Bell; The Institute for the Future (Middletown, Conn., USA), which publishes *Futures*; the Institut fuer Zukunftsfragen, directed by Robert Jungk; the Committee for the Next Thirty Years of the British Social Science Research Council, directed by Michael Young. Fairly comprehensive listings can be found in the PEP Survey of Future Studies (de Hoghton *et al.*, 1971); the annotated bibliography in Bell and Mau (1971); and Jantsch (1967).

2 For Bell, see note 17 below. References to the others mentioned are, in order: Etzioni (1969); Boulding (1964); Kahn and Wiener (1967); Drucker (1971); Brzezinski (1970); Dahrendorf (1964). This list is of course far from exhaustive. Bell has said that he has catalogued eighteen different versions of terms expressing 'transition'.

3 For a recent review of these influences on sociological theories of change, see Nisbet (1969).

4 The intellectual currents bringing about the re-orientation of social thought are well discussed in Hughes (1958).

5 For a summary of the various critiques of social evolutionism, see Gellner (1964: Ch. 1).

6 See, especially, Bock (1963).

7 See, for instance, Parsons (1966).

8 It is significant that, when Ossip Flechtheim coined the term 'futurology' in 1943, he had no immediate sociological tradition to which he could link his projected enterprise for large-scale social forecasting, and had to rely instead on discussions of Toynbee *et al.* See his essays of the 1940s and later, reprinted in Flechtheim (1966).

9 There now seems to be a number of good general critiques of mainstream sociology of development. I have found especially useful: Bendix (1966–7); Bernstein (1971); Gusfield (1967). I have also benefited greatly from an unpublished paper by Hilal (1970).

10 It seems, by now, conventional to cite the following warnings: Almond and Coleman (1960), esp. Almond's 'Introduction'; Lerner (1958); Rostow (1960).

11 For example, Raymond Aron's remark: 'In a sense it would not be wrong to define the advanced countries as those in which the Left and the Right are no longer opposed to each other on the question of development, because development can take place without any further fundamental changes' (Aron 1967: 45–6). A similar view, that the industrial society, once created, can 'manage' the stresses to which it gives rise, underlies the argument in Gellner (1964).

12 Surveys of those involved in 'future studies' have indicated a particular prominence of workers in engineering, economics, and the physical sciences. See the report in *Futures*, Vol. 2, No. 4 (Dec. 1970), 383–5.

13 See note 1, above. Especially noteworthy here are the attempts to set up international organizations of futurology, e.g. 'The First International Future Research Conference' held in Oslo, 1967, and whose proceedings are published in Jungk and Galtung (1969). For some idea of the co-ordinated study in the communist states, see Kumar (1972).

14 This work of popular synthesis seems to differ from that of the more sober futurologists only in its greater explicitness.

15 From a rather different point of view, John Goldthorpe has also argued that futurology has taken over much of the logical and conceptual apparatus of the nineteenth century. See Goldthorpe (1971).

16 For instance: in the whole of the massive report by Richta and his team (Richta, 1967) a mere six pages is given to the topic 'The

Scientific and Technological Revolution and the 'Third World' (vol. I, i–lxxi and i–lxxvii), and doom is written fairly clearly there. Daniel Bell has not, to my knowledge, discussed the matter seriously anywhere in his many writings on the post-industrial society.

17 Bell promises us a forthcoming book on the subject; meanwhile we have some sizeable articles to be going on with: Bell (1965 (a) and (b), 1967, 1968, 1971). Bell also provided the theoretical 'baseline' for the Commission on the Year 2000, and edited the volume of its papers (Bell 1968a).

18 See Dahrendorf (1964), where he claims (p. 262) that 'Europe is well under way toward a service class society'; also Richta *et al.* (1967) Vol. III: *Statistical Tables, tables 2–4*; and the comparison by continent and region in Bell (1968b: 153) *table I.* Japan shows the interesting and significant phenomenon of having supplanted the primary sector not first, as had been the rule, with the secondary sector, but with the tertiary sector: the secondary sector expanded fast with industrialization, but the tertiary sector expanded even faster *at the same time.* See Tominaga (1971), and for further speculation on the future of Japan's spectacular economic development, see Kahn (1970).

19 For US figures, with projections, see Bell (1968b: 155), *table II.* International comparisons are in Richta *et al.* (1967) Vol. III: *Statistical Tables 2–6 to 2–9.*

20 Cf. the comment of Kahn and Wiener: 'If the middle third of the twentieth century is known as the nuclear era, and if past times have been known as the age of steam, iron, power, or the automobile, then the next thirty-three years may well be known as the age of electronics, computers, automation, cybernation data processing, or some related idea' (Kahn and Wiener 1967: 86).

21 The idea of a 'knowledge society', focused on the society's intellectual institutions, as the central form of the future society, appears in various guises in most of the writings of the futurologists. See, for instance, Peter Drucker (1971: 9): 'Knowledge, during the last few decades, has become the central capital, the cost centre and the crucial resource of the economy.' And cf. the following echo of Bell: 'While the *Grosstadt* (the industrial city of 19th century industrial society) was founded on the industrial worker, the megalopolis (of post-industrial society) is founded on, and organized around, the knowledge worker, with information as its foremost output as well as its foremost need. The college campus rather than the factory chimney is likely to be the distinctive feature of the megalopolis, the college student rather than the "proletarian" its central political fact' (1967: 52). See also Robert Lane (1966) and – but drawing different inferences from the centrality of knowledge – Alain Touraine (1969).

22 For the full characterization of this basic long-term trend, see Kahn

and Wiener (1967: 7), *table I*. The specific expressions of this trend in the full picture of the post-industrial society is shown by them on p. 25, *table IX*. For another, fairly similar, summary characterization of what he prefers to call neo-modern society, see Galtung (1969: 37, n. 15).

23 Some forceful critical comments are made by Jean Floud (1971). I have tried to trace the ideological origins of the concept in Kumar (1971).

24 The phrase is Brzezinski's. See Brzezinski (1970: 33 ff.).

25 For some evidence, rather impressionistic, of the international life-style of the 'future people', see Toffler (1970: 36 ff).

26 For an account of some of these developments, see Druckner (1971: 118 ff).

27 For INGOs and IGOs, see Galtung (1969: 20–5).

28 Cf. the corroborative view of Robin Jenkins that, in the more-developed parts of the world 'there is every reason to believe that regional integration will become a more dominant political and economic force than the integration of nations' (Jenkins 1970: 53). Additional evidence comes from the pattern of integration of world regions: while 'regionalization' has been a global phenomenon, it is most marked in the industrial parts of the world. See Russett (1967).

29 Shonfield (1969: 23); see also Appendix I, 'The Industrial Countries as a Market for Capital Goods, pp. 428–9.

30 It was not altogether surprising to hear this last suggestion actually proposed by some Third World countries at the recent UN Conference on the Environment at Stockholm.

31 This view is presented, simply and powerfully, in Jenkins (1970).

32 Cf. the similar view of Galtung's, that 'East and West will rapidly disappear as meaningful contradictions, not because of any complete convergence in socio-economic systems, but because of the de-ideologization and technification of the economies and a relatively complete mutual interdependence' (Galtung 1969: 25).

33 For media development in the different countries, see Schramm (1964: 90–113), and especially the Tables in the Appendixes. Developments in education are summarized in Brzezinski (1970: 42–3).

34 It has been noted that the underdeveloped countries supplied almost exactly one half of the total number of engineers, scientists, and medical personnel who emigrated to the United States in the year ending June 1967: 10 254 out of 20 760. It is expected that this proportion will actually rise in the years to come. See Brzezinski (1970: 45).

35 Herman Kahn, commenting in discussion in 'Toward the Year 2000: Work in Progress', *Daedalus*, Summer 1967, p. 962.

36 For patterns of trade among Third World societies, see Tables in

Worsley (1964: 240). Other indicators of interaction are discussed by Jenkins (1970: 139 ff.).
37 Population assumptions are made as follows. For 1965, the population of the less-developed world was 2 267·9 millions, that of the developed world 1 080·9 millions (world total 3 348·9 millions); in 2000, the population of the less-developed world will be 4 777·0 millions, that of the developed world 1 612·0 millions (world total 6 389·0 millions). See Kahn and Wiener (1967: 142, table V).
38 On this there seems to be general agreement, however variously evaluated. See, for instance, the table (based on Kuznets) in the Club of Rome report (Meadows *et al.*, 1972: 40).

ACKNOWLEDGEMENTS

Table 1 is reprinted from *Mankind 2000* (p. 16) edited by R. Jungk and J. Galtung (1969) with the permission of the publishers, George Allen & Unwin Ltd (London).
Table 2 is reprinted from *The Year 2000* (p. 60) by Herman Kahn and Anthony Wiener, with the permission of the publishers, Macmillan Publishing Co. Inc. New York. © 1967 by the Hudson Institute, Inc.

References

ALMOND, G. and COLEMAN, J. S. (eds.) 1960. *The Politics of the Developing Areas*. Princeton: Princeton University Press.
ARON, R. 1967. *The Industrial Society*. London: Weidenfeld and Nicolson.
BELL, D. 1965. The Study of the Future. *The Public Interest*. (1) Fall.
—— 1967. Notes on the Post-Industrial Society, I & II. *The Public Interest* (6 & 7).
—— 1968a (ed.). *Toward the Year 2000*. Boston: Houghton Mifflin.
—— 1968b. The Measurement of Knowledge and Technology. In Sheldon and Moore, 1968. (eds.).
—— 1971a. The Post-Industrial Society: The Evolution of an Idea. *Survey* **17** (2).
—— 1971b. Technocracy and Politics. *Survey* **16** (1).
BELL, W. and MAU, J. A. (eds.) 1971. *The Sociology of the Future*. New York: Russell Sage Foundation.
BENDIX, R. 1966–7. Tradition and Modernity Reconsidered. *Comparative Studies in Society and History* **XI**.
BERNSTEIN, H. 1971. Modernization Theory and the Sociological Study of Development. *Journal of Development Studies* **7** (2).

BOCK, K. 1963. Evolution, Function, and Change. *American Sociological Review* **28** (2).

BOULDING, K. 1964. *The Meaning of the Twentieth Century: The Great Transition.* New York: Harper and Row.

BRZEZINSKI, Z. K. 1970. *Between Two Ages: America's Role in the Technetronic Era.* New York: The Viking Press.

CHOMSKY, N. 1969. The Welfare/Warfare Intellectuals. *New Society* 3 July.

DAHRENDORF, R. 1964. Recent Changes in the Class Structure of European Societies. *Daedalus* **93** (1).

DE HOGHTON, C. PAGE, W. and STREATFIELD, G. 1971. . . . *And Now the Future,* London: PEP.

DRUCKER, P. 1971. *The Age of Discontinuity.* London: Pan Books.

ETZIONI, A. 1969. *The Active Society.* New York: Free Press.

FLECHTHEIM, O. 1966. *History and Futurology.* Meisenheim am Glan: Verlag Anton Hain.

FLOUD, J. 1971. A Critique of Bell. *Survey* **16** (1).

FUCHS, V. 1966. The First Service Society. *The Public Interest* (2).

Futures **2** (4) December 1970: 383–5.

GALTUNG, J. 1966. East-West Interaction Patterns. *Journal of Peace Research* (2).

—— 1969. On the Future of the International System. In Jungk, R. and Galtung, J. (eds.) 1969.

GELLNER, E. 1964. *Thought and Change.* London: Weidenfeld and Nicolson.

GOLDTHORPE, J. 1971. Theories of Industrial Society: Reflections on the Recrudescence of Historicism and the Future of Futurology. *European Journal of Sociology* **XII** (2).

GUSFIELD, J. 1967. Tradition and Modernity: Misplaced Polarities in the Study of Social Change. *American Journal of Sociology* **72**.

HILAL, J. 1970. Sociology and Underdevelopment. Durham University. Unpublished.

HUGHES, H. STUART. 1958. *Consciousness and Society: The Reorientation of European Social Thought 1890–1930.* New York: Vintage Books.

JANTSCH, E. 1967. *Technological Forecasting in Perspective.* Paris: OECD.

JENKINS, R. 1970. *Exploitation: The World Power Structure and the Inequality of Nations.* London: Paladin Books.

JUNGK, R. and GALTUNG, J. (eds.) 1969. *Mankind 2000.* London: Allen and Unwin.

KAHN, H. 1967. Toward the Year 2000: Work in Progress. *Daedalus.* Summer 1967: 962.

KAHN, H. and WIENER, A. 1967. *The Year 2000.* New York: The Macmillan Co.

—— 1970. *The Emerging Japanese Superstate.* Englewood Cliffs: Prentice-Hall.

KUMAR, K. 1971. Futurology. *The Listener* 18 February.

—— 1972. Futurology – the View from Eastern Europe. *Futures* 4 (1).

LANE, R. 1966. The Decline of Politics and Ideology in a Knowledgeable Society. *American Sociological Review* 31 (5).

LERNER, D. 1958. *The Passing of Traditional Society.* New York: Free Press.

MEADOWS, H. D. *et al.* 1972. *The Limits to Growth.* London: Earth Island.

NISBET, R. 1967. *The Sociological Tradition.* London: Heinemann.

—— 1969. *Social Change and History: Aspects of the Western Theory of Development.* London: Oxford University Press.

PARSONS, T. 1966. *Societies: Evolutionary and Comparative Perspectives.* Englewood Cliffs: Prentice-Hall.

RADCLIFFE-BROWN, A. R., 1931. The Present Position of Anthropological Studies. *The Advancement of Science: 1931.* London.

RICHTA, R. *et al.* 1967. *Civilization at the Crossroads: Social and Human Implications of the Scientific and Technological Revolution* (3 Vols). Prague: Czechoslovak Institute of Arts and Sciences.

ROSTOW, W. W. 1960. *The Stages of Economic Growth.* Cambridge: Cambridge University Press.

RUSSETT, B. M. 1967. *International Regions and the International System.* Chicago: Rand McNally.

SCHRAMM, W. 1964. *Mass Media and National Development.* Stanford & Paris: UNESCO.

SEERS, D. 1971. Rich Countries and Poor. In Seers, D. & Joy, L. (eds.) 1971.

SEERS, D. and JOY, L. (eds.) 1971. *Development in a Divided World.* Harmondsworth: Penguin.

SHELDON, E. and MOORE, W. (eds.) 1968. *Indicators of Social Change.* New York: Russell Sage Foundation.

SHILS, E. 1970. Tradition, Ecology, and Institutions in the History of Sociology. *Daedalus* Fall.

SHONFIELD, A. 1969. *Modern Capitalism* (Revised edition). London: Oxford University Press.

TOFFLER, A. 1970. *Future Shock.* New York: Random House.

TOMINAGA, K. 1971. Post-Industrial Society and Cultural Diversity. *Survey* 16 (1).

TOURAINE, A. 1969. *La Société Post-Industrielle.* Paris: Éditions Denoël.

WORSLEY, P. 1964. *The Third World.* London: Weidenfeld and Nicolson.

Name Index

Adams, J. B., 237
Adegboye, R., 135n
Adelabu, A., 122, 125
Adlor, M., 92
Ainslie, R., 237
Akeredolu-Ale, E. O., 135n
Alavi, H., 89, 123
Alford, R., 304n
Almond, G., 355n
Amin, S., 84
Anderson, A., 263
Aquilar, 70
Aron, R., 355n
Arrighi, G., 83, 142
Avineri, S., 69

Bailey, F. G., 321
Balam, J., 175, 194n
Baldwin, S., 323
Banfield, E. C., 322
Baran, P. A., 2, 16, 27, 80
Barber, J., 35n
Barfield, R., 35n
Barratt Brown, M., 85, 93
Barth, F., 287
Beer, C. H., 129, 135n, 136n
Belaunde, F., 184
Bell, C., 35n
Bell, D., 2, 34n, 329, 335, 339-42, 354n, 356n
Belshaw, C., 304n
Bendix, R., 355n
Bernstein, H., 355n
Bernstein, T. P., 41
Berry, S. S., 123, 135n
Bettelheim, C., 69, 72
Bock, K., 355n
Bocke, 295
Booth, D., 95n
Bottomore, T., 1, 307n
Boulding, K., 329, 346-7
Bowles, W. D., 34n
Boyd, J., 302
Brett, S., 10, 171-94, 199
Brzezinski, Z. K., 329, 335, 347, 349
Buchanan, K., 235, 306
Buck, J. L., 44-5, 56
Budge, I., 304n
Burnett, C., 286
Burnett, G., 286

Burnham, J., 334
Busia, 243
Buxton, N., 307n

Cabral, A., 83, 86, 88-9, 90, 92
Caird, J., 300
Caldwell, M., 93-4
Campbell, R. H., 297-8, 306n
Carr, E. H., 35n
Carrere, D'Encausse H., 69
Carter, I., 6, 279-303
Casanova, P. G., 4, 12, 16n
Castro, F., 79
Chiang Kai-shek, 324, 326
Chinoy, E., 16n
Chomsky, N., 341
Chonchol, J., 294, 306n
Clark, C., 337
Cleaver, E., 92
Cnudde, C. F., 231
Cohen, R., 164n, 165n
Coker, I., 252n
Coleman, J. S., 252n, 355n
Collier, A., 280
Coltart, J. M., 236, 251n
Comte, A., 330, 334
Condon, J. C., 247
Coulbourne, R., 288
Craemer, W., 258, 261-2, 267-8, 270
Cregeen, E., 305n

Dahrendorf, R., 1, 319, 329, 356n
Darling, F., 280, 302
Davidson, B., 80
Davie, G., 304n
Davies, D. H., 258, 263
Davies, I. O., 165n
Davis, H. B., 72
Debray, R., 90-1
de Castro, J., 78
Diop, C. A., 80
Dore, R., 16n, 279
Douglas-Home, A., 240
Draper, T., 79, 242
Drucker, P., 329, 344, 365n, 357n
Dumont, R., 317
Dunayeskaya, R., 91
Durkheim, E., 319, 330

Eisenstadt, S. N., 317-9, 327n

Elizarov, V., 264, 272
Elliott, C., 14, 255
Elliott, K., 265
Elliott, P., 7, 229–51
Emmanuel, A., 73, 75, 85
Enahoro, Chief, 148
Engels, F., 315
Epstein, A. L., 165n
Erasmus, C., 322
Essang, S. M., 123
Etzioni, A., 329

Famoriyo, O. A., 135n
Fanon, F., 67, 68, 76, 86, 88, 92
Feith, H., 327n
Flechtheim, O., 355n
Floud, J., 341, 357n
Forsyth, F., 252n
Foster, G. M., 322
Foster-Carter, A., 2–3, 67–95
Fox, R. C., 258, 261–2, 267–8, 270
Frank, A. G., 2, 6, 8, 27, 69, 71, 80–2,
    84, 87–8, 91–2, 165n, 251n, 295–7,
    301–2, 306n, 318, 325
Frankenberg, R., 7–8, 255–76
Fried, M. H., 324
Friedman, J., 7
Frost, D., 345
Fuchs, V., 337
Furtado, C., 174, 295, 306n

Galetti, R., 123
Galtung, J., 238, 335–6, 342–5, 348,
    351, 353, 355, 357n
Gans, H., 251n
Gaskell, P., 292
de Gaulle, C., 345
Geertz, C., 317
Gellner, E., 355n
Germani, G., 175, 197
Gillanders, F., 293
Gish, O., 255–7, 273–4
Gluckman, M., 268
Golding, P., 7, 229–51
Goldrich, D., 194n
Goldthorpe, J., 355n
Gorky, M., 72
Gowon, General, 133
Gordon of Cluny, 300
Graham, H., 300
Gramsci, A., 76
Grant, I., 283, 286–7, 289, 305n
Gray, J., 2, 5, 39–65
Gray, M., 289, 291–2, 298–300, 307n
Griffin, K. B., 84
Grillo, R. D., 165n
Grunig, J. E., 251n
Guevara, E., 2, 68, 79–80
Gusfield, J., 355n

Hachten, W. A., 237–8, 245, 251n
Hagen, E., 233
Haldane, A., 298–9
Halloran, J. D., 251n
Hamilton, H., 298–9, 302
Hamilton, P. J. S., 263
Hansen, A. T., 177
Hauser, P., 197
Hawthorn, J., 307n
Hechter, M., 16n
Herrick, B., 194n
Herzen, A., 25, 349
Hilal, J., 92, 355n
Hilferding, R., 73
Hill, K. R., 267
Himmelstrand, U., 243, 252n
Hirschmann, A. O., 7, 14
Hobsbawm, E., 69, 91, 280–1, 305n,
    327n
Hobson, J. A., 73
Ho Chi-minh, 68
Hodgkin, T. L., 80
Horn, J., 274
Horowitz, I. L., 34n
Hughes, H. S., 355n
Huizer, G. J., 322

Illich, I., 9

Jackson, G., 92
Jalee, P., 69, 85
Jantsch, E., 354n
Jayaraman, R., 258, 262, 267–8, 270
Jenkins, G., 122, 125
Jenkins, R., 353, 357n, 358n
Jessop, W. J. E., 258, 267
Johns, F., 279
Johnson, C. A., 325
Johnson, S., 287
Johnson, T., 307n
Jouvenal, B. de, 354n
Jungk, R., 354n, 355n

Kahn, H., 329, 335, 338, 341, 348,
    350–2, 356n
Kanmi Isola Olobu, 131–2
Kautsky, J., 34n
Kautsky, K., 73
Kermack, W., 305n
Keynes, 77
Kidron, M., 85
Kiernan, V. G., 323
Kilby, P., 143, 165n
Kim Il Sung, 92
King, M., 255, 257, 259, 262–5, 270–1,
    276
Koll, M., 117, 135n
Kreysler, J., 262
Kriesel, H. C., 126

Kula, W., 316
Kumar, K., 15, 329–54, 355n
Kuusinen, 33

Laclau, E., 95n, 306n, 307n
Lambert, J., 294–7
Lane, D., 2, 9, 23–35
Lane, R., 356n
Lange, O., 92
Laufer, B., 315
Leeds, A., 178, 184, 187, 194n, 199
Leeson, J., 7–8, 255–76
Lehmann, D., 9
Le May, General, 80
Lenin, V. I., 23–35, 67, 75, 83, 90–1, 315, 347
Lerner, D., 24, 231–4, 251n, 315, 355n
Lewis, O., 193n, 194n
Lichtheim, G., 83
Lin Piao, 92
Lipton, M., 11
Lipset, S. M., 23
Li Ta Chao, 86
Liu Shao-ch'i, 63
Lloyd, B., 112
Lloyd, P. C., 111, 112, 134n, 141–2, 156, 164n
Lockwood, D., 1, 319
Lopes, J. R. B., 16n
Lukacs, F., 82–3
Luxemburg, R., 73, 91, 347

McClelland, D., 233
MacCormick, N., 304n
McCrone, D. J., 231
McCrone, G., 283, 293
MacEwan, A., 10–11, 192, 194n, 197–225
MacKay, D. I., 282
MacKenzie, A., 285
McNamara, R., 14
McGee, T. G., 92
Magdoff, H., 85
Mair, D., 307n
Malcolm X, 92
Malinowski, B., 332
Mandel, E., 85
Mangin, W., 174, 177, 193n, 197, 199
Mao Tse-tung, 39–65, 68, 83, 90, 260, 272
Marcuse, H., 23
Marek, F., 92
Marx, K., 69–71, 122, 141, 162, 330–3, 334–5, 341, 347
Mau, J. A., 354n
Mboya, T., 247
Melson, R., 146
Michels, R., 326
Miller, S. M., 85

Millikan, M. F., 229, 233
Mills, C. W., 1, 89
Mitchel, W. E., 261
Mitchison, R., 283
Mitrany, D., 71
Moisley, H., 300
Moore, B., 301
Moore, B. Jr., 133, 323–5
Moore, E., 81, 83
Morley, D., 264
Morner, M., 294
Moussa, P., 73
Mussolini, 73
Myrdal, G., 7, 79, 317, 321

Nadel, S. F., 111
Nairn, T., 306n
Nisbet, R., 330, 355n
Nkrumah, K., 243, 248
Nove, A., 6, 34n
Nurkse, R., 5, 43–4, 53–4, 64n

Obisesan, A., 125
Osoba, O., 110
Ostgaard, E., 240
Oxaal, I., 95n

Parkin, F., 6, 16n, 145
Parsons, T., 25, 355n
Patch, R., 193n
Peace, A., 4–5, 89, 134n, 135n
Peacock, J. L., 234
Pearse, A., 286
Pearson, L. B., 79
Peron, 214
Perroux, F., 6
Plekhanov, G., 26, 72
Pool, I. D., 233–4, 252n
Post, K. W. J., 88, 110, 122–3, 125
Potter, J., 280
Prebble, J., 300
Preobrazhensky, E., 72

Radcliffe-Brown, A. R., 319, 332
Reimer, E., 9
Rex, J. A., 319
Rhodes, R. I., 69
Ricardo, 26
Richta, R., 338–9, 355n, 356n
Riddell, D., 295
Rifkin, S., 274
Rogers, E., 232
Rostow, W. W., 23, 68–9, 316, 355n
Roy, M. N., 76, 88
Rubel, M., 307n
Ruge, M. H., 238
Ruggels, W. L., 251n
Ruopp, P., 316

Russett, B. M., 357n

Saint-Simon, 330, 334, 340–1
Salaman, R., 307n
Sartre, J.-P., 80, 92
Saul, J., 142
Schiller, H. J., 236
Schlesinger, A., 79
Schneider, L., 303n
Schramm, W., 233–4, 237, 251n, 357
Scott, R., 142, 165n
Seers, D., 13, 345
Segal, M., 16n
Shanin, T., 89
Shils, E., 334
Shonfield, A., 345
Sihanouk, Prince, 325
Singer, P., 9
Sjoberg, G., 177
Smith, A. D., 251n
Smith, Adam, 26, 290–2
Smith, T. B., 304n
Smout, T. C., 286–7, 291–3, 298, 301
Spencer, H., 330, 332
Stalin, J., 24–5, 32–3, 332
Stavenhagen, R., 174, 295
Stein, B., 306n
Stein, L., 263
Stein, S., 306n
Stokes, C., 193n
Strickon, A., 174
Sukarno, 325
Sulton Galiev, 76
Sun Yat-sen, 324
Suret-Canale, J., 87
Sweezy, P. M., 16n, 80, 91

Titchett, D., 64n
de Tocqueville, A., 330, 334

Toffler, A., 334, 357n
Tolstoy, L., 25
Tominaga, K., 356n
Touraine, A., 356n
Trotsky, L., 26, 67, 74
Tsuru, Shigeto, 16n
Tull, Jethro, 49
Turner, J., 10–11, 171–93, 194n, 199
Turnock, D., 293

Ulam, A., 31
Urwin, D., 304n

Valencia, E., 194n
Vaughan, J. P., 266, 269
Vine, J. M., 258, 267
Vitale, L., 295
Vysohlid, J., 273

Ward-Price, H., 135n
Warrand, D., 285
Watnick, M., 78
Weber, M., 16n, 31, 109, 112, 164,
  165n, 330, 334
Weeks, J., 17n, 135n, 141, 165n
Wertheim, W. F., 3, 14, 315–26
Whaton, C. R., 320
Wiener, A., 335, 338, 341, 348, 350–2,
  356n, 357n
Williams, G., 4–5, 94n, 109–34
Withrington, D., 304n
Wolf, E. R., 89, 133
Worsley, P., 89, 163, 347, 358n

Yakimova, T. A., 35n
Yesufu, T. M., 142
Young, M., 354n

Zollberg, A., 165n

Subject Index

'accelerators', 326
Africa, 80, 86–7, 235, 240, 244–8, 297, 317, 325
Agence France-Presse (AFP), 237
agrarian reform, 9–10
agricultural revolution, 280, 293
agricultural technology, 232
agriculture, maoist strategy, 39–65
aid, 347, 350
Albania, 91
'alternative futures', 339
American Broadcasting Company (ABC), 236
'applied economics', 1
'applied sociology', 1
Argentina, 10–11, 197–225, 294
arms spending, 85
'Asian Drama', 317
Associated Press, 237
Ayooya Report, 126

Bangla Desh, 324
Biafra, 243
Black Power, 87
'Bonanza', 236
Brazil, 82, 325
'breakdowns of modernization', 322
Britain, 70
  media, 229–41
  regional development, 281
British Broadcasting Corporation, 236, 239, 241
  World Service, 236
British industry, 240
British Labour Party, 29
Buenos Aires, 201
Burma, 325
Burmah Oil, 307n

Cambodia, 86, 325–6
capitalism, 347
Caracas, 185, 225
Cardiff, 236
'Celtic Fringe', 16n
Ceylon, 16n
changarin, 207–9, 214
Chekiang, 46
Chile, 9

China, 8–9, 39–65, 73, 79, 240, 316, 323–6
  Agricultural Producers' Co-opera-tives (APC), 40–65
    abstract statistical analysis, 56–61
    collectivization in practice, 61–4
    feasibility of model, 61
    Heilungchiang, 52–3
    Hojian *hsien* (Hopei), 51–2
    Huang Ning *hsien*, Kwangtung (Red Star), 49–51, 57
    input of capital, 43–4
    production plans, 49–55
    response to economic situation, 41
    size, 64n
    underemployment, 44–65
    use of surplus labour, 45–65
    Wang Kuo-fan, 46–8
    women in labour force, 59
  Communes, 43
  conservationism, 94
  co-operativization of agriculture, 40–65
    diversification of crops, 50, 52
    incentives, 54–62
    intensivization, 49–50, 52, 56–9
    irrigation, 50, 53, 59
    reclamation of land, 53, 59
  cultural revolution, 62–4, 79, 272, 274, 326
  exchange rate, 64n
  Great Leap Forward, 43, 62–4, 79
    poverty, 63
  grain deficiency, 46–8
  Health Ministry, 272, 274
  heavy industry, 61–2
  measurement of underemployment, 45
  mechanization of agriculture, 42
  medical practices, 256, 260, 262, 272, 274, 276
  Mutual Aid Team, 47
  participation, 63
  peasantry, 74–5
  revolution, 78
  Tanzam railway, 242
  technocratic elite, 62
  utilization of labour surplus, 46–65
Chinese Communist Party, 40, 42, 61
cinturon de miseria, 177

cinturon de seguridad, 177
class analysis, 3–6, 109–64
class consciousness, 8, 109–64
class solidarity, 322–3, 326
class structures, in San Pedro, 203–4
Cobdenism, 346
Cold War, 242, 247, 347
'collective bargaining', 15
collectivization, in China, 39–65
colonialism, 77, 234–5
Commission on the Year 2000, 354n
Committee for the Next Thirty Years, 354n
communicators, 233
    see also media
community development, 320
'conjectural histories', 331
consciousness
    political, 109–34
    workers', 141
conservative modernization, 301
Convenanting Wars, 290
'convergence' thesis, 331
Crieff, 298
crisis of non-development, 79
Cuba, 79, 91, 242, 353
cuenta propia, 207–8
Cuevas, 194n
'cultural imperialism', 273

Daily Express, 239
Daily Graphic, 244
Daily Mail, 239
Daily Mail (Nigeria), 244
Daily Mirror, 239–41
Daily Service, 133
Daily Sketch, 239
Daily Telegraph, 239
Daily Times, 128, 133, 241, 244
dependence, 6–8, 350
depth interviews, 202–3
development
    futurology, 329–54
    gradualist approach, 316
    index theory, 231–2
    as a Marxist concept, 69
    strategies, 335
'development aid', 322
development theory, and futurology, 334
differentiation, 197–225
division of labour, 141
'dual economies', 348

Economic Commission for Latin America, 197–8
economic growth
    conditions, 39
    as end in itself, 39
    obstacles, 39

economic imperialism, 234
Economist, 303
Edinburgh, 287
education, 9, 39, 231–2
EEC, 344, 350
El Augustino, 194n
'elective affinity', 31
elites, and revolution, 318, 321, 326
emancipation, 315–26
    liberation, 318
EMI, 235
empleados, 206–8
'end of ideology' thesis, 333
Engels, 'labour aristocracy', 75
England, 71, 81
    colonial traditions, 244
entrepreneurs, 39, 233–4, 318, 340
evolution
    biological, 331
    social, 331
evolutionism, 3, 315–16, 318–19, 325, 331–48
exploitation, 346–7

Falkirk, 297
feudal hypothesis, 350
Financial Times, 239
First World War, 315–16
Fleet Street, 245
folk tales, 319
foreign ownership, of media, 235
France, 70
    colonial traditions, 244
free enterprise, 232
free trade, 248
'frozen evolutionism', 332
functionalism, 1–2, 34, 332
Futures, 354n, 355n
Futuribles, 354n
futurology, 329–54

gay liberation, 87
gemeinschaft, 331
Germany, 70
gesellschaft, 331
Ghana, 242–3, 272, 325
ghetto, 175
Glasgow, 236, 287
'Great Chain of Being', 331
Greece, 325
Green Revolution, 320, 326
Gross National Product, 231, 343, 351

Guardian, 239
Hausa ram sellers, 120
health, 7–8
    developing countries, 255–76
        conservatism, 267
        delegation, 265
        health worker/educator, 262
        economy, 255, 257

in Zambia
attitudes to injections, 262
colonial hospital medicine, 272
communications, 269
Czech doctors, 272
demography, 256
District Hospitals, 263
doctors, 257–8, 263, 265–70, 272–3, 275
drain of postgraduates, 273, 276
elitism, 270–2
Flying Doctor Service, 264
Health Assistants, 259, 262
Health Centres, 262, 268
ideologies, 270–3
laboratory technicians, 259
Lusaka Central Hospital, 268
medical aid schemes, 271
Medical Assistants, 258–9, 266–70
medical auxiliary, 265–70
medical education, 264, 266
Mission Medic-Air, 264
population, 256
Provincial Medical Officer, 262
radiographers, 259
retraining, 266
rural health centres, 258–9, 262–3, 265, 268, 275–6
rural hospitals, 258
State Registered Nurses, 258–9, 268
status of medical staff, 267–70
Teaching Hospital, 263–4, 270–4
town hospitals, 263
traditional healers, 260–3, 275
Zambian Enrolled Nurses, 258, 267–8
High Tide of Socialism in the Chinese Countryside, 40–65
as myth, 40–1
Highlands and Islands Development Board, 281–3, 293, 302–3, 304n
Ho Chi-minh, and 5th Comintern Congress, 76
House of Commons, 240

Ibadan, 109–34
Adebo award, 132
Agbekoya rebellion, 126–34
Agodi jail, 127–8, 129
assessment, 129–34
Ayoola Commission, 127
causes, 126–7
Chief Awolowo, 128
demand for Yoruba Central State, 128, 133
events, 127–8
factionalism, 128–9
Folarin Idowu, 127

Governor Adebayu, 129, 132–3
hunters, 129–30
middle peasants, 130–1
Olorunda corner, 127
peasant consciousness, 131
scope, 133–4
Tafa Adeoye, 128–9, 132–4
tenants and 'overlords', 130
akoda (native administration officials), 125
alagbara, 109
Alhaji Busari Obisesan, 133
Chief Agbaje, 133
'cocoa pool', 125
colonial capitalism, 109–11
country and town, 123–4
contemporary values and aspirations, 111–14
attitudes to rich, 112–13
contradictions, 112
convergence of elites, 112
corruption, 113–14
education, 111–13
elites, 111
status and wealth, 111–12
craftsmen, 113–18
apprentices, 115–17
as a class, 122
competition from manufactured products, 115
consciousness, 122
craft organizations, 116–17
guilds, 115–17
hopes for the future, 118
individual resources, 117
market situation, 115
reinvestment of profits, 117–18
types, 115
economy, 109–10
employment, 114–15
entrepreneurs, 110
farmers, 123–34
education, 123
government intervention, 125–6
isakole (tribute), 124
lineages, 124–5
marketing-board system, 125
organization and dependence, 134
owe (communal labour), 124
peasant and 'overlord', 124–5
seasonal labour, 125
farmers and politicians, 133–4
Farmers Union, 126
hunter-warriors, 123
inflation, 131
landlords ('overlords'), 123
middle-men, 119–20, 125
mekunnu (ordinary person), 109, 122, 125, 134n, 135n
olola (nobles), 109

Ibadan – *cont.*
  olowo (wealthy), 109
    distinct from *olola* (man of
      honour), 111–12
  omowe (educated), 109
  opposition to colonial rule, 110
  peasants' political representation,
    132–3
  petty traders, 119–22
    beer retailers, 120–1
    controlled commodities, 120–1
    co-operation, 120
    licences, 119
    price control regulations, 120–1
  Prince Lamuye, 133
  rural stratification, 124–5
  size and function of city, 114–15
  social differentiation, 109–11
  traders and contractors, 118–22
    entrepreneurial skills, 119
    produce buying licences, 118
  urban drift, 123, 131
  see also Nigeria
Ibadan Bricklayers Association, 118
Ibadan Co-operative Produce Marketing Society, 125
Ijebu palm-oil sellers, 120
imperialism
  class struggles, 86
  health, 255
  neo-Marxism, 84–6
incentives, 39
India, 61, 70–1, 75, 79, 316, 320–1,
  323–5
  peasants' attitudes, 321–2
India–Pakistan war, 240, 243
Indo–China, 68
Indonesia, 320, 325–6
industrial protest, in Nigeria, 141–64
industrial societies, internal evolution,
  330
industrialization, 330
  and modernization, 317
Institute for the Future, 354n
integrationist model, 319
intermediate technology, and health,
  255–76
Intermediate Technology Development Group, 255, 260, 265, 267
International class war, 353
international government organizations, 344
International Labour Office, 11, 13–
  14, 17n
international non-governmental
  organizations, 344
internationalism, 344–5
IPC, 244
IPI, 247
Ireland, 71

Italian peasants, 322
Italy, 73, 76
ITN, 239, 241
Izvestiya, 35n

Jan Sangh, 324
Japan, 81, 301, 316–17, 320, 341, 356n
Java, 317, 325
Jehovah's Witnesses, 91
jornalero, 206–8
Journal of Development Studies, 13
journalists, ethos, 245–6, 248

kan-ch'ing, 324
Kano, 114
kinship, 324
'knowledge society', 329
Kuomintang, 325
Kuwait, 15
kwashiorkor, 261

Lagos, 114, 143–4
Laos, 86
latifundia, 9
  see also Latin America
Latin America, 6, 9, 12, 171, 189
  cities, 171–94
  development, 70
  dual economy, 295–7
  encomienda, 294
  feudalism, 294–6
  Harrod-Domar model, 84
  Iberian conquest, 295–7
  latifundia, 294–7, 301, 306n
  liberal economics, 294–5
  market economy, 297
  peasant unrest, 322
  town and country, 92
  urban explosion, 197
Lenin
  and anarchism, 29, 31
  and bureaucracy, 30
  and capitalism, 25–6
  'continuous' revolution, 26
  and investment outlets, 85
  and Leninism, 24
  and modernization, 24
  notion of 'trade union conscious-
    ness', 90
  and revolution, 73
  and Roy, M.N., 76, 88
  views about social change, 24–31
    benefits of industrial organization,
      25–6, 28
    contradictions, 25
    implementation, 31–4
    organization, 25, 29–31
    participation of masses, 25, 30–3
    pay, 30–1
    political elite, 31

in underdeveloped countries, 32
western capitalism and under-
    developed countries, 25–6, 29
work ethic, 28–9
Lewis, 280
Lima, 177, 224
    barriadas, 171, 185, 187
London, 237
los pobres, 204
Lusaka, 258, 260, 263, 268–9, 272

Malawi, 257
Malta, 241
'managed' societies, 333
marasmus, 261
marginality, 171, 176, 178, 190–2, 200
    theoretical problems, 197–8
Markpress Agency, 243
mass communications, and develop-
    ment, 231–2
Malthusiasm, 78
Maoism, 5, 39–65
    possibilities of organized farming,
        48
    and public opinion, 45
    see also China
marginados, 10–11
Marshall Aid, 77–8
Marxism, 23–94
    and colonialism, 69–70
    and imperialism, 73
    the national question, 71–2
    and peasantry, 71–2
    role of the third world, 74–6
    as theory of history, 68
    see also Soviet Union; neo-Marxism
mass media, 7
    see also media
means of production, 335
'measuring development', 13
media, 229–51
    academic research, 232–4, 250
    attitudes, 229, 233
    in Britain, 229–41
    and capitalism, 230, 235, 249
    commercial entertainment, 249
    corporations, 235–8
    correspondents, 238
    'cultural offensive', 235–6, 238
    deferred gratification, 233
    developments, 250–1
    differentiation, 251
    economic stories, 241–2
    education and training, 236
    ethnocentric identification, 233–4
    as external stimulation, 232, 234
    focus on social structures, 242–3
    foreign news, 238–44
    foreign news at home, definition,
        241

government involvement, 244–6
home news abroad, definition, 241
images, 238–44, 250
indigenous organizations, 236
integration, 229
international news, definition, 241
journalists, 236–7
national and international, 230,
    235–6, 238–48
and nationalism, 244–8
news agencies, 246–8
news role, definition, 241
in Nigeria, 229, 236, 241, 245–7
and political leaders, 242–3, 247
press freedom, 248–9
physical communications, 237–8
real foreign news, definition, 241
roles, 229–34
and social change, 229–51
and the social order, 249
story cycles, 243
'stringers', 236, 238
syndication of programming, 235–6
technology, 246
medical care services, 255
    see also health
'megalopolises', 341
Mexican peasants, 322
Mexico city, 186
Mezzogiorno, 283
mineral resources, 93
miracle rice, 320
mis-development, 2, 74
models, 11–12, 43–4, 56–61, 229–32
    'actors and observers', 202
    causal, 231–2
    Harrod-Domar, 84
    integrationalist, 319
    squatter settlements, 171–93
modernization, 1, 230–1, 315–22, 326
    ideology, 318
    non-participation, 322
    as process, 316
Mongolia, 91
multi-national business corporations,
    344
'mystification', 8

Napoleonic Wars, 297, 299–300
Narodny, 72
nation-state, 342–4
National Council of Nigeria and the
    Cameroons, 125
National Issues Society (Nigeria), 126
national liberation movements, 32
NATO, 350
Ndola, 258, 263
neo-colonialism, and health, 255
neo-evolutionism, 1
neo-Marxism, 2–5, 6–10, 67–95

neo-Marxism – *cont.*
the bourgeois background, 76–81
effect of Cold War, 78–80
rehabilitation of Africa, 80
'revisionist' historians, 80
classes, 83, 87–90
feudal groups, 87
the 'lumpen proletariat', 89
national bourgeoisie, 88
peasantry, 89–90
'petty bourgeoisie', 88–9
proletariat, 89
and communism, 91–2
definition, 67–8
ecology, 93–4
economy, 83–4
ideology, 81–2
entrepreneurialism, 82
nation building, 82
national bourgeoisie, 82
imperialism, 84–6
history, 82
morals and action, 92
nationalism, 86–7
paradoxes, 67–8
'redundantist' position, 85
revolution, 83, 90–1
totality, 82
town and country, 92–3
news, as commodity, 230
see also media
news agencies, 237–8
news capitals, 237
Nigeria, 5–7, 109–64, 229–47
Action Group Government, 125
Adebo, 157
managers and government, 161
Adebo Commission, 5–6, 146–9
the *cola* award, 147–55, 157,
159–60
contributions, 146–7
Enahoro's qualification, 148–9
establishment, 146
and Morgan Commission, 146
recommendations, 147
responses, 147–57
workers' hopes, 146
civil war, 126, 146, 242–3
class consciousness, 156
class relationships, 162–3
Commissioner for Labour, 151
Commissioner of Police in Lagos,
151
Decree, 53, 149, 151, 159
entrepreneurs, 145
Federal Government, and industrial
relations, 143
Federal Military Government, 146
general strike, 146
growth of class consciousness

inequality, 158
prices and incomes, 157–8
Ikeja industrial estate, 143–6
establishment, 143
house unions, 144
strike action and lockouts, 145–6
industrial action, as expression of
class consciousness, 142–3
industrial plants, 141
industrial protest, 141–64
balance of power, 149–53
case study: beer company, 153–6
case study: textile company,
149–53
civil war, 157
external influences, 153–6
management and government,
154–6
police intervention, 151, 154
union leaders and workers, 158–9
industrial relations
British model, 144
paternalism, 144
industrial workers,
class consciousness, 142
cognitive map, 144–5
colonial rule, 141–2
lack of organizational base, 141–2
as proletarian, 141–2
inflation, 146
lower-class solidarity, 161
Marketing Board, 119, 121, 125
media, 229, 236, 241, 245–7
Ministry of Labour, 152, 154
Morgan Commission, 146
Motor Transport Union, 121
National Provident Fund, 156
neo-colonialism, 161
Price Control Board, 118
Ports Authority, 144
power structure, 162
proletarian classes, existence of,
163–4
Railway Corporation, 144
Second Adebo Report, 159–62
recommendations, 159–60
workers' interpretations, 160
trade unions, workers' attachment,
145
tribal organizations, 142
union-management relations, 161
see also industrial protest
unions at Ikejo, 142
United Committee of Central
Labour Organizations, 146–7
United Labour Congress, 120
workers education, 144
see also Ibadan
Nigerian Broadcasting Corporation,
236, 246

NBC Radio (Nigeria), 241
NBC TV (Nigeria), 241
Nigerian Employers' Consultative
 Association, 148–9, 154–5
Nigerian National Democratic Party,
 127
Nigerian Tribune, 131
Nowell Report, 125

OECD, 350
organic metaphor, 331
'over-development', 349

Pacific War, 324
'palaeo-Marxism', 68
Pampa de Comas, 184
Pathet Lao, 94
Pearson Commission, 12–13
peasants
 and revolution, 321–6
 in England, 280
Peru, Junta Nacional de la Vivienda,
 171, 184
Poland, 42
political economy, 2
population control, 9
'post-civilization', 329
'post-industrial society', 329, 334–44
 economic sector, 337
 knowledge, 338–40
 scientists, 339–41
 service sector, 337–8
 technology, 338–9
'post-modern era', 329
propaganda, 40

radicalization, gradual, 325–6
railways, 70
'*rancho*, 211–12
reconvergence' thesis, 334
'Reed-IPC, 235
reform, agrarian, 9–10
Reformation, 290
resources, Ibadan, 109
Reuters, 237
revolution
 agricultural, 280, 293
 and evolution, 315
 peasant, 322–4
 social, 325–6
 socialist, 333
 working-class, 323
 world, 315, 326
'revolution of demands', 317
Rhodesia, 83, 240–1
Rio de Janeiro, 185

San Pedro, 201–25
Scapa Flow, 303
scarcity, 39, 93

scarification, 262
Scotland, 6, 279–94, 297–303
 Act of Union, 298
 attitudes, 286–7
 banking system, 298
 capitalist economy, 301
 cattle trade, 298
 Clanranald estates, 299–300
 crofters, 280–1, 283, 292–3, 300,
  302
 division of labour, 280–1
 Disarming Acts, 305n
 duine uaisle, 288
 education system, 280
 entrepreneurs, 300
 ethnic groups, 287
 feuferme land tenure, 289
 Gaelic culture, 287, 303
 Highland Clearances, 289, 292
 Invergordon Smelter (British Aluminium), 302–3
 Jacobitism, 290
 James VI, 286–7
 oil boom, 303
 potato famine, 293
 1745 Rebellion, 291–2
 religion, 280, 289–90
 rents, 288–9, 300
 runrig joint farms, 287–9, 292, 297,
  300
 tacksman, 288, 300
 Treaty of Edinburgh, 298
 Union of Crowns, 298
 Union Settlement, 1707, 280
 wardholding, 288, 291
Scots Law, 280, 304n
Scottish Highlands
 agriculture, 282
 black cattle trade, 298–9, 301
 clans, 283, 285–6, 288–9
 Clearances, 303, 307n
 commercialization of agriculture,
  292
 Crofters Holdings Act, 293
 definitions, 284
 'ecological devastation', 302
 emigration, 300
 feudalism, 288–91
 fishing, 282
 forestry, 282, 303
 Frank thesis, 297–303
 industry, 282–3
 kelp, 299–302
 kinship, 288–9, 307n
 marriages, 285–6
 mineral resources, 302
 Napier Commission, 293
 'pacification', 291
 peasant society, 292
 problems, 283

Scottish Highlands – *cont.*
 sheep-farming, 293, 301
 tourism, 293, 303
 trade, 291
Scottish Lowlands
 capitalism, 292
 consolidated farms, 292
 industrialists, 292
 manufacturing industry, 298
 marriages, 286
 parish schools, 290
Scottish Nationalism, 304n
Second World War, 315–6
'service class society', 329
Shanghai, 260
shanty-towns, *see* squatter settlements
social change
 classical conception, 332
 differentiation theories, 232
 directions, 331
 intrinsic mechanisms, 329, 331
 and media, 229–51
 psychological theories, 233
social security, 178
social status, housing, 173
social stratification, in Africa, 141
sociology
 of development, 329–54
 of health, 255–76
South Africa, 271
Soviet Union, 9, 23–35, 41, 71–2, 75,
 90, 189, 274, 315–16, 349, 353
 Bolshevik Party, 27–9, 31, 72
 convergence with capitalism, 33–4
 as a developing society, 23
 income differentials, 33
 medical experts in Zambia, 270, 273
 regional inequalities, 32
 revolution, 23, 72
Spain, 325
squatter settlements, 10–11, 171–94,
 197–225
 bridgeheaders, 176, 181–2, 185–7
 community services, 179
 consolidation, 199
 consolidators, 178, 185–7
 control of housing context, 188–90
 densities, 179
 differentiation, 198–225
  occupation and income, 206–11
 dynamism, 200–1
 ecological factors, 198–9
 ecological models, 186
 'encapsulation', 186–7, 193
 existential functions, 173
 feedbacks, 185
 feedback model, 188–90
 fragmentation, 209–25
 government intervention, 186
 growth potential, 185

housing needs, variables, 174–6
immigrants, 199
integration, 197–8
internal structure, 200–25
investment and growth, 180–1
input of resources, 182
kinship, 179–80
labour market, 174–5, 179, 184–5,
 187
land values, 175–6, 178–83, 185,
 189–90, 205
Las Canaletas, 194n, 201–25
 apprenticeships, 224
 associational patterns, 216–17
 bases for differentiation, 223
 class structures, 203–4
 classification of workers, 210
 differentiation, 205–17
 divisiveness, 224–5
 dockers, 210–11
 ecological distribution, 204–5
 education, 215–16, 219, 223
 household equipment, 212–14
 internal status hierarchy, 217–23
 kinship, 216–17, 224
 labour market, 224–5
 land values, 217
 migrants, 217
 mobility, 222–5
 neighbourhoods, 217, 219–23
 peer groups, 217, 224
 personal items, 214–15
 population, 201
 processes of differentiation, 222–3
 social prestige, 205–25
 status competition, 222–5
 subjective perception of status,
  220–3
 trades, 211
 types of dwelling, 211–12
legalistic criteria, 177, 199
location, 175
'marginalization' and 'integration',
 192
migrants, 175
motivation of squatters, 177, 185,
 188
movement, 200
myths, 199
needs and priorities, 172–81
participation, 197
pattern in differentiation, 200
'peripherality', 185
political factors, 188
political organization, 200
radial city expansion, 186
relational model, 192–3
residential mobility, 192
security of tenure, 173, 181–2
security-input model, 181–4

social factors, 198
socio-economic change, 205
socio-economic status, 179
stagnating settlements, 190, 200
status of squatters, 191
  subjective meaning, 202
stereotypes, 199
stratification, 190–1, 200
structural changes, 197
structural-functional relationships,
  199–200
sub-letting, 179, 186, 187
  threats, 178
  and towns, 205
  travel to work, 184
  Turner's model, 171–94
  scope of data, 184
  typology, 182–3
  unions, 208–11
  urban relocation, 189
strategy, 175
stratification, neo-Marxist approach,
  83
structural change, in industrial societies, 333
student power, 87
Stuttgart Congress of 1907, 75
Sun, 239
Sunday Mirror (Nigeria), 244
Sunday Times (Nigeria), 133
system maintenance, 1

Tanzania, 16n
  health care, 262
Tanzanian press, 247
Taylorism, 29
'technocratic era', 329
technological forecasting, 340
technology, agricultural, 232
Third World, 73, 78, 89, 171, 232,
  234, 236–7, 242, 246–7, 330, 325
  as actor in its own right, 85
  alienated elites, 349
  bargaining power, 352
  community development, 316
  competition, 352
  as concept, 69
  economic growth, 350–2
  future, 351–4
  'global ghetto-ization', 342
  medical exploitation, 273
  nationhood, 348
  'peace keeping' forces, 354
  political instability, 347
  relevance to industrial countries, 346
  solidarity, 353
  'subjective environment', 349
  trends in post industrialization,
    342–54
  world trade, 345

Thomson Organization, 236, 244
Times, 239–41, 243
trade, 235
Tri-Continental Organization
  (OSPAAAL), 353
Trotsky
  and peasants, 74–5
  and revolution, 73, 79

Uganda, health services, 263–4
UN, 344–5, 350, 353
  Conference on Trade and Develop-
    ment, 14, 79, 353
  Department of Economic and Social
    Affairs, 13
  Economic and Social Council, 347
  Economic Commission for Latin
    America, 12
  Reconstruction and Refugee
    Administration, 77–8
  Reports on the World Situation, 13
  Research Institute for Social
    Development, 13
underemployment, in China, 39–65
unemployment, 13–14
UNESCO, 231
uniformitarianism, 331
United Africa Co., 143
United Kingdom, National Health
    Service, 257, 274
United States, 23, 70, 235–6, 337–8,
    340–1, 350, 353
  and Cuba, 79
  and development, 81
  and Vietnam, 79–80
UPITN, 237

value-systems, 232
  counterpoint, 319, 326
Vietnam, 79–80, 86
Virgin Mary, 214
Visnews, 237, 246

Welsh nationalism, 307n
West Africa, 129
West Bengal, 324
women's liberation, 87
World Employment Programme, 14
World Health Organization, 258, 265,
    267
world trade, 345–6

Yorubaland, 144
Yugoslavia, 42

Zaire, medical practice, 261–2, 267,
    270

Zambia, 7–8, 15
  civil servants, 271
  First National Development Plan,
    258, 265
  GNP, 257
  health problems, 255–65, 267–76

  Manpower Report, 257, 260
  Red and Blue opinions, 270–3
  University Medical School,
    257
Zambia Mail, 268
Zambia Medical Council, 272

DATE DUE

DEMCO 38-297